Friends and Strangers

EARLY AMERICAN STUDIES

Series editors:
Daniel K. Richter
Kathleen M. Brown
David Waldstreicher

Exploring neglected aspects of our colonial, revolutionary, and early national history and culture, Early American Studies reinterprets familiar themes and events in fresh ways. Interdisciplinary in character, and with a special emphasis on the period from about 1600 to 1850, the series is published in partnership with the McNeil Center for Early American Studies.

A complete list of books in the series is available from the publisher.

Friends and Strangers

The Making of a Creole Culture
in Colonial Pennsylvania

John Smolenski

PENN

UNIVERSITY OF PENNSYLVANIA PRESS

PHILADELPHIA · OXFORD

Published by
University of Pennsylvania Press
Philadelphia, Pennsylvania 19104-4112

Printed in the United States of America on acid-free paper
10 9 8 7 6 5 4 3 2 1

Library of Congress Cataloging-in-Publication Data
Smolenski, John
    Friends and strangers : the making of a Creole culture in
colonial Pennsylvania/John Smolenski.
        p.   cm. — (Early American studies)
    Includes bibliographical references and index.
    ISBN 978-0-8122-4239-3 (hardcover : acid-free paper)
    1. Quakers—Pennsylvania—History. 2. Pennsylvania—
Ethnic relations. 3. Pennsylvania—History—Colonial
period, ca. 1600—1775. I. Title.
F160.F89S65   2010
974.8'02—dc22   2009044911

To Steph
My Sweetie

CONTENTS

PART III
Triumph

INTRODUCTION

The Origins of Quaker Pennsylvania

THE TERM "CREOLE" has a convoluted, even checkered, genealogy. It origi-
nated in sixteenth-century Latin America, where Portuguese and Spanish
writers used the terms *crioulo* and *criollo* respectively to refer to individuals
born in the Americas. Its meaning evolved over time. In Portuguese, the
term was overwhelmingly applied to individuals of African descent, while in
Spanish, it connoted European ancestry.[1] Nonetheless, it remained in constant use throughout the colonial period and beyond.[2] Its English language
history has taken a somewhat different path, having entered the vernacular
in the early seventeenth century to describe Americans of Spanish descent.
Later in the colonial period, it came to be used in reference to settlers of
English descent born in the Caribbean and peoples of African descent born
throughout the English colonies. In modern parlance, it has come to signify
the peoples, language, and culture native to French Louisiana (though there
has been considerable debate as to whether "creole" should refer to those of
purely French or Spanish ancestry or those of racially mixed descent).[3] Despite this complex etymology, one thing is clear: the word has, from the
colonial period to the present, carried exotic connotations, used to describe
cultural, linguistic, or racial migrants to the Americas, though never peoples
of European descent in mainland colonial British America.

But what of those people who migrated to North America from England? Did they not also create creole cultures in the New World? This book
examines the growth of a creole culture among one particular migrant group,
the Quakers, in one particular colony, Pennsylvania. My use of "creole" and
"creolization" to describe the cultural development of Quaker Pennsylvania
will likely seem unfamiliar to students of American history, as scholars have

used these terms extensively to describe changes in Latin American or African American communities but rarely if ever in reference to English American colonizers.[4] Eschewing the language and conceptual frameworks used to examine the experience of non-English "others," historians have reinforced the notion that "creole" implies foreign. In doing so, they have seemingly suggested that colonial Anglo-Americans were somehow different—exceptional, even—in their cultural origins.

This trend is especially noticeable when it comes to Pennsylvania. Both that colony and its founder William Penn have long held a special place in history. His contemporaries saw Penn as a man with an unmatched sense of justice. European philosophers David Hume and the Baron de Montesquieu described him as an American Confucius and modern-day Lycurgus, while Thomas Jefferson merely proclaimed him "the greatest law-giver the world has produced."[5] Voltaire celebrated Penn as the man who negotiated with Delaware Indians "the only treaty between those people and the Christians that was not ratified by an oath, and was never infringed."[6] Under the stewardship of Penn and his fellow Friends, Pennsylvania became a province hailed by American revolutionaries as a "peculiar land of freedom" in the years before independence, a place where men and women of all nationalities enjoyed unparalleled rights and individuals of all faiths had the liberty to practice their religion. The Quaker colony stood as a shining example to the rest of the world of what a society should be.[7] Modern scholars have tended to agree with these views, seeing Pennsylvania as the birthplace of modern tolerance, domesticity, and political liberalism.[8]

This narrative is a familiar one, memorialized not only in textbooks but also in paintings, tablecloths, china, playing cards, puzzles, advertisements, pageants, department store logos, and even video games.[9] But if this story is not entirely false, neither is it entirely accurate; those who have propagated it (including Quakers from colonial Pennsylvania) have committed, wittingly or unwittingly, errors of omission. Certainly, this celebratory tale represents how the province's early history was *supposed* to go. Penn definitely had utopian dreams for his American colony when he was awarded a proprietary charter in 1681. He wanted his colonists to enjoy unsurpassed liberties, he wanted to treat Indians as equals in a manner befitting the Quaker pacifist he was, and he wanted his people, "the tribe of Judah," to lead the way.

Things did not work according to Penn's plan, however. Problems of transmission and transplantation undermined his scheme from the start. The English liberties Penn cherished could not, as it happened, simply be moved

Figure 1. William Penn. William Penn's grandson Granville Penn presented this portrait of Pennsylvania's founder to the Historical Society of Pennsylvania in 1833. It shows Penn at age twenty-two, in 1666. Scholars believe that this is a late eighteenth-century copy of the original, now lost. Courtesy of The Atwater Kent Museum of Philadelphia, Historical Society of Pennsylvania Collection.

across the Atlantic and recreated in Pennsylvania; a colonial population that included significant numbers of Swedes, Finns, Dutch, and Germans needed to be educated on "their" rights as Englishmen. Similar problems beset the establishment of Quakerism in Pennsylvania, with a major theologian within the Society of Friends at one point accusing other Quakers of preaching "vomit, filth and error." Meanwhile, Native Americans in the region proved less tractable than the proprietor hoped they would be, bristling at some of Penn's "benevolent" diplomatic overtures. Finally, the provincial ruling elite Penn cultivated proved unable to "season" new immigrants as they arrived in the province; at times they seemed unable even to control themselves. Pennsylvania in its first decades was hardly the "peaceable kingdom" of myth and legend, which raises a critical question: what accounts for the difference between the reality and the myth?

The answer involves uncovering the often fraught process of identity formation hidden by those narratives that present the existence of "Quaker Pennsylvania" as an unquestioned fact. Penn's colony, despite his best hopes, was not born Quaker: it was made that way, through a series of contentious battles fought in various colonial institutions. The following chapters trace the challenges colonial Pennsylvanians overcame in creating stable political, legal, and religious institutions in the province. I argue that Pennsylvania's early struggles and eventual stabilization can best be understood as an ongoing process of cultural creolization, one in which European colonizers reshaped inherited cultural patterns in a new society. Making Pennsylvania Quaker, as it happened, involved a great deal of work, some of which included forgetting that any such cultural or political conflicts had ever taken place.

Throughout this book, I employ the terms *creolization*, *creole*, and *creolized* to analyze the evolution of early Pennsylvania. By *creolization*, I mean the creative process through which individuals and groups constructed new cultural habits and identities as they tried to make Old- World inheritances "fit" in a New-World environment.[10] The men and women who settled Pennsylvania did not achieve this goal by imposing English cultural patterns or Quaker religion on the colony's residents. Creating a provincial culture involved interaction, adaptation, and incorporation. I treat creolization as a multistage process.[11] It first involved efforts to create a kind of cultural lingua franca, a working (albeit limited) set of rules and habits through which colonial society could operate. Pennsylvanians, in fits and starts, elaborated this lingua franca into a more coherent, full-blown colonial culture. This elaboration involved not merely the cultivation of specific social practices but also the creation of particular narratives of identity that taught provincials about Pennsylvania's past and what made it distinct. These stories in turn spurred the development of a creole consciousness among colonial Pennsylvanians; they also facilitated the incorporation of more social groups into the province, encouraging new immigrants to accept the creolized culture as legitimate.

By *creole* or *creolized*, I mean the results of the historical process of creolization I trace. I use "creole" to describe people, institutions, or cultural forms born or created in America. As nearly all the Anglo-Pennsylvanians in this story were European born, I will primarily use the term to refer to institutions, cultural practices, or identities constructed in Pennsylvania. I use "creolized" primarily to refer to people, specifically groups or individuals who accepted the creole culture that emerged in Pennsylvania. Moreover, though provincial Friends, as the political and cultural elites in the colony, guided this process, it transformed them as well. Pennsylvania Friends most certainly practiced a creole Quakerism by the turn of the eighteenth century, no matter how much they denied it.

Crucially, not everyone in my story bought into Pennsylvania's creole culture, so to speak; many were not even invited in. Though Pennsylvania contained more naturalized, non-English residents than any other colony in English America, neither Penn nor other provincial politicians ever considered extending this legal status to Native Americans or individuals of African descent (the overwhelming majority of whom were enslaved). Meanwhile, provincial officials' efforts to create a stable creole diplomacy with Native American groups on the frontier foundered on the fact that while the various parties involved often relied on the same language in negotiations, they disagreed on the meaning of that language more often than not. The creation of a creole civic culture in early Pennsylvania involved exclusion as well as inclusion.

In many respects, this process of cultural development mirrored larger patterns in colonial American history, as colonizers and colonized peoples struggled to balance tradition and innovation as they formed new societies during a period of dramatic change. My study of identity formation in early Pennsylvania thus speaks to larger debates about the cultural origins of British North America. New World societies differed in ways great and small from the Old World societies from which their colonizers came. British North America certainly seemed like a ruder variant of the mother country to eighteenth-century observers. But where Scottish traveler Alexander Hamilton observed ordinary colonials living in a "primitive simplicity" that resembled the "state of our ancestors" in old Britain, Virginia gentleman William Byrd looked toward the frontier and saw them living in such a "dirty state of nature" that they had become something utterly alien.[12] Had Anglo-Americans completely lost their Englishness on the other side of the Atlantic? Tellingly, one of the very few times an Anglo-American described his fellow colonists as creoles occurred in 1690, when Puritan divine Cotton Mather warned New Englanders about "that sort of Criolian degeneracy observed to deprave the children of the most noble and worthy Europeans when transplanted to America." Similar questions surrounded colonial ventures to the south, with many Spaniards convinced that Iberian-American creoles were culturally or biologically inferior to their European brethren.[13] The presence of non-European communities within the colonies further complicated matters. Colonial America defied easy categorization by observers from both sides of the Atlantic.

This problem of cultural persistence and change has vexed scholars struggling to assess the relative importance of inheritance and environment in the formation of colonial Anglo-America. Many historians have seen a "Greater Britain" extending across the Atlantic, and have accordingly stressed continuities between the Old World and the New.[14] Other scholars, noting the radically different material and social environment colonists encountered, have emphasized the stark contrast between Britain and its American colonies: the latter was at best a simplified version of the former, recreated across the Atlantic. Some historians, most notably Frederick Jackson Turner, believed that this had a liberatory effect. The absence of custom and the weakness of European social institutions fostered a particular moral and psychological strength that encouraged individualistic and democratic tendencies among the colonists.[15] Other scholars, however, have followed Byrd's lead, seeing America as a backward offshoot of British society in which colonists, confronted with "bizarre" or "exotic" peoples living in a "wild, uncultivated land," fought to prevent themselves from slipping into savagery. British America was not merely different; it was abnormal.[16] Both interpretations led to the same conclusion, however: migration had, in some essential way, unmoored Anglo-American colonists from their cultural heritage.[17]

The difficulty mediating between these two analytic poles has led some historians to examine the importance of so-called "charter groups," defined alternately as "the first ethnic group to come into a previously unpopulated territory" or the first members of a particular ethnic group to settle within a society. This effort has involved assessing the cultural traditions these charter groups brought with them across the Atlantic and investigating how these groups shaped the experience of later immigrants. Historians have used this concept to analyze the origins of regional cultures in "Puritan New England" and the "Cavalier Chesapeake," as well as the formation of German and African identities in the British colonies.[18] These analyses, however, have not paid sufficient attention to how and why these charter groups developed the way they did. Moreover, scholars have often failed to interrogate the question of relative social power relations in the formation of charter groups in various social and geographic locations.

The experience of first generation Pennsylvania Quakers obviously differed from that of other charter groups, insofar as each group's evolution was shaped by its access to power on both sides of the Atlantic. For example, German Lutherans' political orientation—jealous of their liberties but uncertain about exercising power directly—reflected their experience as religious refugees in continental Europe and Great Britain. African charter generations' influence in crafting a syncretic black community in the seventeenth-century Chesapeake owed a great debt to their experience as go-betweens in the multicultural port cities along the Gold and Slave coasts. But their influence waned as Virginia's slave system developed; the hybrid slave culture that emerged was a product of necessity, as later generations of forced African immigrants from dissimilar backgrounds and unaccustomed to dealing with Europeans found themselves living and working together in brutal conditions. In the Delaware Valley, Quakers went from persecuted minority in England to colonial founders in America. The cultural strategies they employed in England to sustain a viable religious movement in the face of repression took on a very different valence across the Atlantic, as practices intended to maintain a coherent religious identity proved ineffective when used to build a common political one. At the same time, the fact that Friends exercised formal legal and political control gave them a greater ability to shape their own creolization. It also allowed them to shape the creolization of immigrants outside their tribal group in a way that an African or German charter group could not.

Pennsylvania offers an ideal opportunity to rethink the "charter group" approach to cultural development in colonial British America. Quakers would appear to be the archetypal charter group—settlers with a clearly identifiable cultural identity that they developed before migration who established a colony reflecting their cultural ethos.[19] Yet, as I demonstrate, the first generation of Friends to settle in the Delaware Valley exerted a powerful sway over the colony's development as a colonial charter group only after a decades-long struggle to create a stable Quaker identity in Pennsylvania; in other words, before they could creolize others, they first had to creolize themselves. This examination of early Pennsylvania also sheds important new light on the larger process of cultural creolization in colonial America. Historians and anthropologists have almost exclusively studied this phenomenon within African and African American communities, showing how enslaved peoples created new, hybrid cultures out of a wide variety of African and European influences. Some scholars have treated the syncretism that characterized Afro-Atlantic societies as creolization's defining feature, as if it necessarily involved the "interpenetration of civilizations" among a diverse population.[20] Other scholars, meanwhile, have suggested that this syncretism was an adaptive response to enslaved people's structural position within a brutally repressive social system rather than some inherent feature in the creolization process itself.[21]

The history of how Pennsylvania Friends made themselves into a provincial charter group demonstrates how creolization operated within an elite colonizing group. Their status as provincial founders and political leaders meant that Pennsylvania Quakers had a greater ability to reject cultural hybridity than either their Restoration-era English counterparts or creole African Americans in North America and the Caribbean. As a result, they created a Quaker identity through selective incorporation and rejection rather than a more general process of syncretism. Adaptation to an American social setting did not necessarily involve the adoption of hybrid cultural forms. Their social position also allowed Friends to exert greater influence on other groups within colonial society than others did on them. Though creolization in the case of colonial Quakers and enslaved African Americans involved conflict, differentiation, and cultural mixing, the actors involved did not play equal roles in shaping the outcome. Moreover, creolization in Pennsylvania involved conscious attempts to guide the colony's cultural development, not a slow drifting away from inherited norms in a new physical environment.[22] This book thus reveals how creolization varied in different geographic and social spaces. I focus on the history of Anglo-American Friends not to traffic in a kind of "Quaker exceptionalism" but because their history reveals the localized effects of a broader Atlantic phenomenon, the creolization process that created American cultures.[23]

In the early decades after settlement, the first generation of Quakers creolized principally through the development of a provincial civic culture. By "civic culture" I mean the habits, practices, symbols, and languages through which Pennsylvanians defined the meaning of established authority in their province. This approach analyzes culture as a construct not simply of language or behavior but of meanings shaped through the interplay of discourse and practice. This methodological approach relies on two primary assumptions. First, that civic discourse enabled people to explain the meaning of authority to themselves, thus serving to reflect and produce politico-cultural habits and feelings. Second, that civic practice, such as the manner in which ordinary people interacted with provincial magistrates in court, served as a crucial means through which people performed and reshaped their relationship to a larger political whole. This study of the creolization of civic culture in colonial Pennsylvania, then, traces both the often-tortured efforts of provincials to articulate a language of civic authority for a diverse populace and the struggle over which forms of civic performance best expressed a virtuous allegiance to the community.

The book is divided into three parts, organized chronologically and thematically. The first part explores Quakerism's English origins. Here I trace the rise of the Society of Friends as a dynamic and adaptable faith that drew its strength from its ability to incorporate elements from a variety of other dissenting faiths while establishing institutional mechanisms to maintain a coherent spiritual identity. This combination of qualities exerted a significant influence on William Penn in the years before he received his royal charter for an American colony; Penn's political philosophy, I argue, reflected both his theological commitments and his experience as one of the architects of the Quaker Meeting system.

The second part examines Penn's utopian hopes for Pennsylvania and the colony's inability to achieve them. Reflecting William Penn's unique political vision, the province was founded on a paradox. On the one hand, Penn intended the colony to be diverse, tolerant, and open. He supported religious liberty for all, a simplified and accessible legal system, and the willing incorporation of outsiders as participants in the province's political and legal order. At the same time, Penn intended the province to be orderly and, above all, ruled by Quakers—a diverse colony under the rule of a particular minority. To resolve the paradox at the heart of the "Holy Experiment," Penn and his fellow founding Friends drew heavily on schemes for cultivating community and discipline developed in the English Quaker Meeting. In effect, they hoped that a secular legal and political culture inflected by Quaker principles might both maintain order and legitimate Quaker rule. They likewise hoped to have peaceful relations with the region's native peoples, incorporating them into a system of equal justice for all, based on English principles of law.

Disorder in Pennsylvania's early years soon dashed Penn's hopes: colonists in Pennsylvania's first decade and a half both disagreed on the process of proper political interaction and rejected the legal rituals Penn had hoped would legitimate the province's courts. This tension culminated in the Keithian schism, an internal division among Pennsylvania Friends spurred by a fear among some that their religion had become bastardized in America. This conflict fractured the Quaker community, causing a major religious, political, and legal crisis in the early 1690s. Moreover, colonial and Native American diplomats faced difficulties in the "peaceable kingdom" in the years before 1710, as neither side could find common ground. Differences of culture and interest made the formation of a creole diplomatic culture impossible. These decades of instability represented a failure of creolization on two levels: unable to create a hybrid creole culture with other Pennsylvanians—European and Native American—or to solidify a stable creole identity of their own, Pennsylvania's founding Friends could not develop an authoritative civic lingua franca in a new society.

The final part tracks colonial Quakers' success at finally creating a creole civic culture that stabilized and legitimated their rule in the colony. In the aftermath of the Keithian schism, provincial Friends adopted a new strategy for stabilizing their authority. Borrowing from George Keith's strategy of building legitimacy through public debate, they cultivated Pennsylvania's growing print culture to define a provincial identity. They organized a Quaker ruling party that justified its authority through appeals to a mythical golden age of Quaker settlement. Drawing on their status as descendents of the province's founding "Ancient Settlers," they cast themselves as uniquely virtuous in civic affairs.

This new ruling party faced and overcame numerous opponents as they secured their control over the colony. Memorializing Pennsylvania's early history played a crucial role in solidifying a creolized Quaker identity and Quaker political rule. In diplomatic affairs, Indians and colonials each mobilized the myth of William Penn and his "antient friendship" with native groups in efforts to check or expand the expansion of colonial power on the frontier. Provincials' ability to make their narrative about the founder the dominant one reflected their victory over native interests. Politically, Friends consolidated their power in the face of a major internal challenge by making a specific appeal to the electorate that employed a political rhetoric that defined Pennsylvania as a uniquely free and harmonious society and cast Friends as the ideal civic stewards of these liberties. By the 1730s, then, the colony's civic culture possessed an increasingly elaborate set of political narratives, symbols, and practices that naturalized Quaker authority. Provincial civic life was dominated by a political fable, best captured in Caleb Pusey's 1725 history of the province that Pennsylvania should remain an essentially Quaker place because it had always been so. The defining characteristic of creole Quaker Pennsylvania was its refusal to acknowledge its creole-ness.

My concern throughout the book has been to emphasize that the identities, habits, symbols, and language surrounding civic life in early Pennsylvania were both products and drivers of a historical process of creolization. Every effort to define or control Pennsylvania's civic culture inevitably remade it.[24] Neither English tradition nor Quaker religion could simply be transplanted across the ocean, but colonial Pennsylvanians were not somehow deracinated by their trans-Atlantic voyage. Provincial culture evolved out of an interplay between tradition and novelty, even as colonists so frequently resisted the latter and proclaimed their love of the former. Our struggles to understand what made creole Pennsylvania Quaker in myth and reality reflect as much as anything else the difficulty provincial Friends had in making it so.

PART I

Beginnings

CHAPTER I

Quakerism's English Roots

THE POPULAR ACCOUNT of the origin of the Society of Friends is a familiar tale. This story centers on George Fox. A visionary prodigy, Fox had pursued a spiritual calling since childhood, searching out other religious "seekers" and mystical kindred spirits. After much spiritual travail, Fox underwent a particularly dramatic conversion that brought him into a state of perfection, as Adam and Eve had been before their expulsion from Eden. Upon receiving God, Fox wrote:

> Now I was come up in a spirit through the flaming sword, into the paradise of God. All things were new; and the creation gave unto me another smell than before, beyond what words can utter. I knew nothing but pureness, innocency, and righteousness; being renewed into the image of God by Christ Jesus.[1]

Almost singlehandedly, the story goes, Fox began the sect known alternately as the Friends of God (their preferred self-designation), or the Quakers, a pejorative title accorded it by critics. Sweeping through England and its Atlantic possessions, this spiritual movement challenged contemporary mores in several realms. Friends rejected worldly vices and vanities, they renounced war and violence, they attacked hierarchical forms of worship, and they recognized men and women as spiritual equals theologically and ecclesiastically; all of these positions emerged rather organically from the mystical theology Fox and his followers espoused. While respectable Quaker historians in the nineteenth and twentieth centuries said little about Fox's more extravagant acts—such as early claims to be a son of God or to have raised the dead—they were quick to credit him and his spiritual descendents with pioneering accomplishments in the women's rights, antislavery, and pacifist movements and in industrial and technological development.[2] Fox's dramatic spiritual journey epitomizes, from this perspective, the revolution underpinning many of these transformations. Driven by Fox's singlehanded efforts, the Quaker movement, in this familiar tale, has been a major force in the development of Anglo-American society. In this sense, traditional accounts of Quakerism's founding bear a marked resemblance to the ways in which historians have often memorialized Pennsylvania.

This narrative, however compelling to the Society's hagiographers, misses the mark on points that are critical to understanding the development of Quakerism prior to its arrival in North America. It elevates Fox's importance at the expense of other Quaker leaders.[3] This story also ignores the fact that Friends fought bitterly over questions of pacifism, spiritual individualism, and the role of women within the movement. Several major schisms rocked the Meeting during the movement's first three decades, belying the notion that Quakers always agreed on what we now see as the core elements of their faith and practice. Most of all, this hagiographic portrayal removes Quakerism from the cultural, religious, and political climate in which it emerged; its emphasis on the centrality of individual conscience within the Society of Friends, embodied by Fox's personal story, misses the fundamentally social dimensions of Quaker practices. The Society of Friends was only one of many dissenting groups formed in the 1640s and 1650s; early Quaker leaders knew well that the movement's success depended on its ability to develop a coherent religious identity among Friends, a project that required the creation of strict boundaries between those within and without the sect. Efforts to enforce spiritual conformity tempered spiritual individualism within the Society from its inception.

The process through which early Quakers instilled a sense of common purpose and identity within the movement would profoundly shape Friends' colonial efforts in Pennsylvania. Quakerism was founded in a tumultuous religious environment that bore more than a family resemblance to the New World Friends would face in America; Quakers in each instance faced the problem of creating a novel religious and cultural identity in a rapidly transforming social landscape. Fox and other leading Friends struggled to maintain a delicate balance as they guided a spiritual movement that incorporated elements from other groups while asserting its revolutionary character. The result was a hybrid faith that trumpeted its own uniqueness. The strategies

Fox and other leaders developed to manage the inherent tension between hybridity and uniqueness within their spiritual movement would later prove useful to American Friends struggling to create a creole religious identity across the Atlantic. In other words, English Friends had to become Quakers, and the manner in which they did so had a profound impact on the manner in which Quaker immigrants became Pennsylvania Friends. Understanding the influence of Quakerism's English origins on Friends' colonial project, however, requires analyzing the context in which the movement was born.

Swarms of Sectaries: The Explosion of Dissent in England

In May 1641, after years of contention between the established Church and their nonconformist opponents, parliamentarians in the House of Commons sympathetic to dissent secured passage of the "Protestation." This resolution warned of a conspiracy within the national Church, engineered by William Laud, archbishop of Canterbury, to reestablish the Roman Catholic Church in England, an action that would subvert not only the cause of true Protestantism but also the fundamental liberties all Englishmen possessed. The Protestation called upon loyal Englishmen to take a vow to reject "popery" and resist the extension of Rome's power. Initially directed at members of Parliament, it spread throughout the nation over the next year, as its supporters enjoined all Englishmen to fight Laudian subversion of church and state. Coming on the heels of a petition drive in 1640 to remove the national church's episcopacy "root and branch," the Protestation movement rendered any effort to enforce religious uniformity fruitless. As a result, "English religious culture was irreversibly fractured, and out of the cracks crawled swarms of sectaries," opening new worlds of spiritual possibilities.[4] A subsequent attempt to restore ecclesiastical authority at the Westminster Assembly in 1643 failed, as both moderates and radicals expressed displeasure at the Assembly's proposed reforms. Parliament failed to act on these recommendations until 1645 and made little effort to enforce them thereafter.[5]

In the absence of any effective governmental mechanism to tamp down nonconformity, radical religion flourished in England following the outbreak of war in 1642. The most popular sect, the Baptists, gained thousands of adherents during the 1640s. Demanding strict discipline and ascetic conduct from their members, Baptist congregations strove to create "primitive Christianity" in England, living as the apostles had done. Others, meanwhile, sensed the dawning of a new apostolic age after centuries of spiritual corruption and darkness; these "Seekers" waited patiently for new prophets to arrive and restore God's true church. Some religious radicals became ardent millenarians, anticipating a coming apocalyptic judgment. For these individuals, the fall of the Stuart monarchy prefigured a political as well as a religious revolution, leading to the establishment of Christ's kingdom on earth. Men like Samuel Fisher argued that the Bible was not the inerrant Word of God and could be subject to the same rational analysis as any other text.[6] Some Englishmen claimed prophetic gifts. John Reeve proclaimed himself a messenger of God and used his cousin Lodowick Muggleton as his "mouth" to spread the Lord's Word. John Robins claimed actually to be God, and announced that he would, with one of his female disciples, father a new Christ. So-called "Ranters" such as Jacob Bauthumley, Richard Coppin, and Laurence Clarkson asserted that having received God's grace through inward revelation they had become spiritually perfect, free from sin and free from the obligation to obey all earthly moral laws. Levellers encouraged their fellow Englishmen to follow a "practical Christianity" that emphasized "Feeding the Hungry, Clothing the naked, [and] visiting and comforting the sicke" as the best ways to please God.[7] After decades of underground existence, radical sectarianism flourished in England during the civil war.

This religious explosion alarmed many English men and women, including even those who had fought against the Laudian faction in the national church. The wild and unlettered radical preachers who claimed to have spoken to or to be speaking for God seemed intent on violating every religious precept sober Christians held dear. Thomas Edwards's three-volume tome *Gangraena* enumerated 270 theological errors propagated by the sectaries that flourished during the 1640s. Edwards argued that the religious ferment that followed the downfall of the national church threatened England's social fabric: "universall Toleration," he wrote, "tends to the laying of all waste, and dissolution of all Religion and good manners."[8] Members of Parliament agreed, enacting in 1648 a Blasphemy Act that prescribed the death penalty for those who denied God's existence, Christ's divinity, the Holy Trinity, or the Bible as the word of God.[9] Many Separatists' and Independents' support for the cause of dissent waned as they grew concerned about the Levellers' aggressive insistence on broad liberty of conscience as a fundamental right of the English people. The Levellers' defeat in 1649 effectively removed pressure on Parliament to extend religious toleration.[10] And the Blasphemy Act of 1650, passed by Parliament in response to public fear about the Ranter menace, resulted in the prosecution of preachers like Abiezer Coppe and Laurence Clarkson, whom many thought leaders of a Ranter movement.[11] A reactionary backlash had seemingly triumphed over religious radicalism as the 1650s began.

"Whirlwind come out of the north": The Beginnings of the Quaker Movement

This was the cultural milieu in which the Society of Friends was born. The Society coalesced in the early 1650s around the enthusiastic ministers of a number of individuals known by later Friends as the "First Publishers of Truth," under the leadership of George Fox.[12] Fox's own experience, as remembered and recorded in his *Journal*, offers insight into the earliest period of Quakerism, as well as a particularly dramatic account of his conversion. Born in 1624 to zealous Presbyterian parents in a region of England where radical Protestant groups such as the Lollards had thrived, Fox claimed to have exhibited a strong sense of spirituality and restlessness from childhood, showing a "gravity and stayedness of mind and spirit not usual in children." From then on, he made a point of finding other religious "Seekers" with whom he could discuss matters of faith. Believing "that to be bred at Oxford or Cambridge was not sufficient to be a minister of Christ," he shunned formal training and began at the age of nineteen to wander around England to find God "experimentally."[13]

By the mid-1640s, Fox had found some spiritual fellow travelers, later writing that "truth sprang up" in a handful of towns between 1644 and 1648. His fervor attracted Elizabeth Hooton, a preacher near Mansfield notorious for her public denunciations not only against the established church but also against the "deceits" of the Baptists.[14] Despite early success, however, Fox remained plagued by self-doubt until 1648. Then, "one day when I had been walking solitarily abroad and was come home, I was taken up in the love of God, so that I could not but admire the greatness of his love." This revelation did more than restore Fox's "living faith," as he called it; it also instilled in him a "pure fire," akin to "a refiner's fire." Opening Fox's powers of spiritual discernment, it made him see that his previous life had been guided by "the groans of the flesh," following his own, not God's, will. Seeing now that "the spiritual fire trieth all things," Fox learned "that which can live in his holy refining fire, and that [which] can live to God under his law." At this moment, he later wrote in his *Journal*, he understood for the first time how he might overcome "fleshy things and words" and become perfect: by following "the law of the Spirit of life," which superseded "the law of the Jews and the prophets," as given to Moses. The former led to perfection and salvation, while the latter led to "sin and death."[15]

Following this revelation, Fox continued his itinerant ministry with new-found vigor. He found the north of England, long a hotbed of Separatists, Baptists, and other nonconformists, and the Midlands particularly receptive to his message. By 1652, James Nayler, Francis Howgill, Margaret Fell, Edward Burrough, and William Dewsbury had joined Fox and Hooton as the leaders of a rapidly growing religious movement calling itself the "Children of Light."[16] Fell's convincement that year proved especially important. As the wife of Thomas Fell, a large landowner and prominent antiroyalist judge in Lancashire, she drew upon her wealth and family influence to support the movement. Swarthmoor Hall, the Fell family estate near Ulverston, quickly became the base from which Fox and Fell funded and coordinated missionary activity throughout England. Meanwhile, Judge Fell, although never "convinced" by Fox's message, used his position and influence to help shield his wife's coreligionists from prosecution and persecution. By 1654, the movement, now referring to itself as the "Society of Friends" but derisively dubbed the "Quakers" by their opponents, began missionary work to the south, including the first efforts to spread their message to London.[17] The English Revolution and its aftermath proved a fertile period for the sect's growth; the Society boasted as many as 35,000 adherents at the time of the Restoration.[18]

What accounted for the Society's rapid rise? Certainly, its message played a major role. At the center of Friends' theology lay the belief that all humanity possessed a fraction of Christ's essence within, a divine seed implanted by God after the expulsion from the Garden of Eden. This portion of Christ's body and blood allowed all men and women to communicate directly with God, without need for any spiritual intermediaries.[19] Christ had given to everyone, Fox wrote, a measure of his Light, through which a person might receive the Word through inward immediate revelation.[20] Friends assembling for worship thus required "no language, tongue, nor speech from any creature" to receive the Lord, as he would speak to them in silence in a heavenly, not earthly, tongue.[21] Rather than seeking guidance from an appointed minister, Friends meeting for worship waited in silence until one of the gathered felt moved by the Spirit to speak. Revelation, not liturgical formalities or prescribed roles, guided collective worship.

Friends' belief in direct revelation eliminated the need for an educated ministry within the sect. Training at Oxford or Cambridge may have given "professed ministers" in the established or Presbyterian churches mastery of "Natural Languages" such as Latin and Greek, but it could not grant true Christian power.[22] Indeed, detailed knowledge of Scripture itself was unnecessary for salvation. Fox himself repeatedly distinguished between the "Letter"—the Scriptures—and the "Word." The former, he argued, were but "types and figures," offering the "Form of Law," while the latter came directly from God, having existed "before Paper, and Ink, and Writings" and offering the "Law of Life." Thus, neither "the letter, nor the writing of the Scripture" could save souls, only "the ingrafted Word" within the faithful. Similarly, Barbara Siddall characterized the Bible as "not the word of God, but onely a dead letter," while Katherine Crook asserted that "Shee had Knowne the Lord if Shee had never scene [sic] nor read the Scriptures."[23] By arguing that the presence of a divine seed rendered all believers equally capable of receiving, interpreting, and preaching God's Word, Quakers undercut the very basis of ecclesiastical authority in more traditional English Protestant churches.

This belief in spiritual equality also eroded distinctions between men and women, a fact many Quaker critics found extremely disturbing. As all men and women possessed the same seed of Christ within, they could each testify on behalf of the Lord. As Fox wrote, "All the family of God, women as well as men, might know, possess, perform, and discharge" God's will.[24] Women played a far more active and integral role within Quakerism than within any other religious group in seventeenth-century England.[25] The Society of Friends afforded women opportunities to serve as the authors of religious tracts, as traveling ministers, and as elders within Quaker meetings— public roles that other English denominations reserved for men. Friends' belief in direct inward revelation fostered a sense of spiritual individualism and antiauthoritarianism that carried potentially radical implications.

The implanted seed did something else as well. Those who cultivated this measure of Christ's essence within by heeding the revelations they received found themselves transformed physically, freed of their earthly "body of sin and death" and regenerated in a perfect body. Transformed Friends wrote of the new senses of vision, hearing, and even smell conversion had granted them, as well as the new identities they assumed.[26] William Dewsbury informed readers of one tract that it came "From the Spirit of the Lord, written by one, whom the people of the world calls Quaker, whose name in the flesh is William Deusbery, but hath a New Name, the World knows not, written in the Book of Life." James Nayler, Edward Burrough, and George Fox referred to themselves in letters and in print in the same manner.[27]

Conversion manifested itself physically in a number of unusual, even extravagant, ways. Though Friends remained silent in meetings until called to preach, they did not hesitate to bear witness when moved. Their "quaking," crying, and even "singing" when possessed by the Spirit revealed its power. Opponents had first used "Quakers" as an epithet in 1652 in reference to the bodily convulsions many Friends experienced during worship. But Friends quickly seized upon the term as evidence of their divine inspiration. They published tracts offering copious scriptural examples of prophets and apostles trembling before God, effectively turning what others saw as an outward sign of their disorder into evidence of their piety. Some Friends even walked naked through town and city streets, their bare bodies offering evidence of their freedom from sin.[28] Conversion wrought a near total physical transformation: reborn Friends carried themselves with a distinctive gait and posture; one likened his attempt to master Quaker deportment after his convincement to learning to walk for the first time. This rebirth changed Friends spiritually as well, allowing them to achieve a state of sinless perfection on earth. Fox wrote that at the first gatherings of Friends in 1647 and 1648, he realized that God had turned him "to the State of Adam, which he was in before he fell." They had become, in Fox's words, perfect "babes of Christ," free from sin in a carnal world.[29]

Nor was the possibility of achieving this state of perfection limited to only some believers. God had not, Nayler wrote, saved the elect and condemned the damned before their birth, as Calvinist theologians believed. Doing so would have taken "the work of redemption and salvation" out of believers' hands "and thus encourage[ed] people to spend their days in folly," squandering the gifts God had blessed them with. Rather than distinguishing between an invisible church—composed of all those who had been or would be saved—and a visible church—its imperfect approximation on earth—Friends believed that they could construct a universal church "made up of living stones [and] living members" to which all could belong.[30] Salvation itself was not assured; God's grace may have been "Great, Universal, True, and Unfeined," Samuel Fisher wrote, but only those few who truly heeded God's voice would be reborn. Friends thus preached a faith that was inclusionary and exclusionary at the same time, where salvation was unlimited in theory but limited in practice. Nonetheless, their explicit belief in the possibility of universal redemption, coupled with their spiritual egalitarianism, undoubtedly explains much of Quakerism's rapid growth in the 1650s.[31]

One other factor helped drive the Society's rise as well. Quaker religious thought gave the movement a strongly propulsive character. Friends truly believed that they lived in a transformative historical moment; in one of Fox's earliest visions, he witnessed the breaking of the sixth seal as described in Revelations, signifying the imminent end of an old age and the beginning of a new one.[32] But this belief, combined with their belief in the possibility of universal salvation, gave their evangelical mission a sense of urgency. Quaker preachers felt obligated to "convince" as many souls as possible of the truth of God's Word before Christ's return, the event that would mark the culmination of the current era. Certain that only they could shepherd Christendom through the coming millennium, Fox, Nayler, and other leading Friends spread their message throughout the countryside with a fervor other Christian sects did not match. They persuaded tens of thousands of English men and women to abandon their old faiths for a new one. But Friends' growing public visibility increasingly convinced outsiders that the movement challenged the underpinnings of the English social order. If Fox and his compatriots were certain of their unique spiritual capabilities, their opponents seemed equally sure they posed a uniquely disturbing threat in an age of dramatic social, cultural, and political upheaval.

"Turners of the World Upside Down": Quaker Social and Political Thought

The maintenance of social power in seventeenth-century England was a delicate and multifaceted affair. Control of religious, political, and legal institutions played a significant role in this process, of course. But English elites also relied on a complex set of cultural practices to naturalize their authority. Civil society, as understood by contemporary English men and women, quite literally depended in no small degree on the enactment of particular codes of civility by supposed social superiors and inferiors.[33] Quakers thus threatened "the order of things" on nearly every count: their rejection of prevailing social mores and open disrespect for authority figures, combined with their denunciations of England's political and legal system, made their opponents fear that they were truly "turners of the world upside down."[34]

Their striking forms of worship notwithstanding, Friends developed an ascetic aesthetic in their daily lives. This project involved the creation of distinctive modes of dress, speech, and deportment that stood at odds with conventional manners. Quakers saw their so-called plain style as a way to take "up the cross" against "the language, fashions, customs, tithes, honour, and esteem in the world" that blinded men and women to their spiritual responsibilities.[35] Fox on his travels wore leather breeches and a doublet befitting the son of a tradesman and railed against those who sold ribbons, rings, or gaudy buttons. As the plain style developed, the Quaker Meeting urged Friends to wear gray and white dress bereft of other color, encouraged them to wear hooks instead of buttons, and forbade them from wearing ribbons, rings, or adornments of any kind.[36]

Quakers likewise had decidedly unconventional speech ways.[37] Most noticeably, they practiced a form of radical honesty. Following Fox's reminder that Friends should speak precisely and without superfluity, Friends insistently addressed individuals of all ranks with the archaic "thee" and "thou" form, reserving the "you" form of address for groups of people. Quaker authors enjoined Friends to avoid "idle communication, jesting and foolish talking" and remain sober at all times; they reminded merchants to avoid "defrauding, cozening . . . cheating" or even haggling at all, instead buying and selling goods at set prices.[38] They rejected the so-called "pagan" names of the months and days, referring, for example, to March and Sunday as "first month" and "first day" respectively. They refused even the most basic salutations for fear that they might lead Friends to utter untruth; was it not a lie to wish another "good day" if it was, in fact, an ill one?[39]

But Quaker speech practices frequently took on a decidedly more aggressive tone. They accorded established religious or political leaders little deference. Friends refused to remove their hats in church, in court, or in the presence of men and women of higher social rank, a major breach of contemporary etiquette. They removed their hats only during meetings of worship, when they stood before God. In their desire to speak truth to power against false faiths, Quakers had no compunction about interrupting the worship of other Christian sects and shouting down ministers or inviting them to impromptu debates, an obvious public attack on ministerial authority.[40] Their use of "thee" and "thou" in lieu of the more formal "you" in certain situations—Fox was even bold enough on one occasion to address Oliver Cromwell in this manner—presumed a social equality that elites found dangerous.[41]

They were defiant in the face of legal authority as well, refusing to swear oaths in any circumstances. Their religious faith prevented them from doing so. Christ had instructed his followers to "swear not at all." Thus, laws requiring English subjects to swear when they appeared in court or offer oaths of allegiance asked them to follow man's law instead of God's. Moreover, they saw oaths as an earthly means of compelling the fallen man who had strayed from God to tell the truth. Quakers, having been restored to a state of sinless perfection, needed no such compulsion to tell the truth. They extended this critique to other forms of compulsion English courts commonly used to encourage compliance. Imprisoned Friends, for example, would not post bond for good behavior to secure their release. This requirement, they argued, implied that they could not be trusted to keep the peace without the threat of external sanction. Bonds, like oaths, were for fallen men, not perfect ones.[42]

These repeated attacks on civility accompanied calls on the part of some Friends to reform the institutions that held English civil society together. Their rejection of ministerial authority, for example, went beyond mere questions about the necessity of formal training for preachers. Rather, leading Quakers attacked the mechanisms that kept the established church in power. They played the leading role in the fight against the tithing system that supported the ordained clergy. Fox and Burrough argued eloquently for the repeal of all laws punishing individuals for obeying dictates of conscience, such as those sanctioning individuals who declined to swear.[43]

Other Friends sounded more ominous notes. Some argued that Christ's impending return had made earthly laws moot. Anthony Pearson thus claimed that, having been justified by Christ, he and other Quakers were effectively "dead to the law" of England—or indeed, any nation. Dorothy White warned English politicians that "God will throw down and overturn, root up and consume both root and branch of all your Parliaments" until he had established Christ as king on earth.[44] The growing number of Quakers in arms—one scholar has argued that Crowmell's New Model Army served as a "major source of Quaker recruitment"—made it seem as if they might bring about the radical change they predicted violently.[45]

Accordingly, Friends became the subject of condemnation and, frequently, official and unofficial persecution. Quakers' belief that their immediate revelations represented a new dispensation from the Lord struck ministers from both established and dissenting churches as blasphemous, and their claim that all men and women might achieve a state of sinless perfection on earth sounded as if Friends had claimed a divinity reserved for God.[46]

Authorities, meanwhile, arrested Quakers in significant numbers for violating acts prohibiting blasphemy, disrupting Anglican Church services or failing to pay tithes. Itinerant ministers endured particularly severe punishments, including public floggings; many Friends were literally whipped out of town.[47] Friends' refusal to take a 1655 oath abjuring the authority of the Catholic Church crystallized fears inside and outside the government about their political radicalism. When governmental officials failed to act, local citizens frequently took matters into their own hands, violently breaking up Quaker meetings for worship and driving Friends out of town.[48]

Yet, despite some of their more radical writings, most Friends promoted political and legal reform rather than revolution. Though overrepresented among army rank and file, no Friends were convicted of bearing arms against the government during the Interregnum period.[49] Most sought political change to create a just government, not a perfect one, notwithstanding the aspirations of their more apocalyptic brethren. Governments, Isaac Penington wrote, owed their existence to "Civil Societies," not divine providence; rulers should thus focus on protecting the "Fundamental Right, Safety, and Liberty of the People," not establishing a godly kingdom on earth. Government by a representative body, chosen by the people and populated by wise men ready to stand as "Judges on behalf of the commonwealth," seemed the most appropriate way to achieve this goal. Rulers and ruled should be bound by a relationship of consent, not divine strictures.[50] Quaker authors offered some of the most insightful analyses of England's political system and most comprehensive calls for change but were not, in the main, political radicals in a meaningful sense.[51]

Friends similarly played a leading role in the seventeenth-century legal reform movement. The current legal system, they argued, failed on multiple counts. The common law erected too formidable barriers to those of middling means or education; the difficulty of navigating antiquated legal procedures that required plaintiffs and defendants to enter pleas in Latin or French rather than the vernacular and the assortment of expensive fees required even to file a case meant that the courts often offered a "remedy frequently worse than the disease."[52] English law, moreover, focused too much on doling out punishment, often in an arbitrary and excessive manner. Judges who meted out death sentences for those convicted of lesser offenses were no better than murderers, no matter their official capacity.[53]

Quaker reformers advocated several remedies for these defects. Fox demanded that "all Laws be drawn up in to a short Volume, that every one in the Nation may know them" and all laws be written exclusively in English.[54] Burrough, Paul Moon, and Edward Billing called for regular publication of laws, effectively ending lawyers' and judges' monopoly of legal knowledge. They similarly called for a dramatic expansion of juries' powers, convinced that the collective wisdom of laymen equaled or exceeded that of the appointed magistracy. Finally, they argued for changes in the criminal code to emphasize rehabilitation and restitution rather than punishment.[55] Such an approach was simultaneously more reasonable and more Christian.

At the heart of all Quaker calls for legal and political reform lay a conviction that the divine spark of truth within the hearts of all men granted them an understanding of earthly as well as divine law. Their understanding of the role that a secular conscience might play in law and politics paralleled their religious commitments: just as unlettered men and women attentive to the Light within surpassed university-trained ministers in their piety, so too might ordinary voters and jurymen possess a greater sense of justice in their hearts than more educated magistrates and assemblymen. Friends' belief that the power of "God's Witness in every man" enabled the meek and humble to assert their authority in law and politics as well as religion carried potentially far-reaching implications for the established English order.[56]

The Production of Quaker Identity

Despite Friends' self-presentation, their movement did not represent a radical break from the past. Other religious dissenters echoed Quaker critiques of England's social order. And though Penn described Fox as "an original, being no man's copy," the Quaker founder's teachings were hardly unique.[57] His theology contained traces of the hermetic teachings of Jacob Boehme in his belief in the possibility of perfectibility and of the continental Familists in his teaching that Christ dwelt within all, allowing the faithful to shed their carnal flesh and inhabit divine flesh once they had been saved.[58] Numerous other English sectarians and religious radicals had embraced religious beliefs similar to those Fox preached. William Walwyn and Gerrard Winstanley spoke out against the notion that the clergy possessed the sole authority to interpret Scripture, and even questioned the validity of Scripture itself. Meanwhile, William Erbury and John Saltmarsh argued vocally that spiritual knowledge came primarily from immediate revelation. The Particular and the General Baptists made each of these views central parts of their doctrine;

indeed, the latter sect's embrace of a theology of the possibility of universal salvation bore a marked resemblance to Quaker doctrine.[59] Saltmarsh and other so-called Ranter authors believed in the possibility of achieving a state of sinless perfection on earth, with the Ranters especially arguing that achieving this state eliminated the need to follow scriptural law at all, a radical antinomian position. And both the Seekers and the Fifth Monarchists sensed, as Friends did, that the world had entered a new age, one with a wide variety of spiritual and political possibilities.

Connections between these various groups appeared in more concrete terms as well. Many Baptists and Seekers became Quakers in the 1650s; Samuel Fisher, the most significant Quaker scriptural scholar, converted from Baptism to Quakerism. Dorcas Erbury, daughter of prominent Seeker William Erbury, became a minister after her convincement in 1654.[60] Leveller leader John Lilburne and Digger, or "True Leveller," leader Gerrard Winstanley became Quakers later in their lives. Friends shared more with these other sectarians than perhaps they were willing to admit. Indeed, the early Quaker movement may have resembled other Interregnum sects more than their spiritual heirs in the eighteenth century.[61]

But if Fox was not, to return to Penn's characterization, entirely original, neither was he anyone's copy. Fox, Nayler, and other leading Quakers had done something more than simply adopting the beliefs of England's other radical sects. In a period in which attacks on the established church called the very idea of a national religious identity into question, early Friends created, in essence, a truly syncretic religious movement. Rejecting their natal religious affiliations, they formed a new faith that drew its dynamism from its very hybridity. These characteristics made Quakerism ideally suited to incorporate people from a variety of different backgrounds into a common faith. They would also serve Friends well in America as they worked to create a creolized religious, political, and legal culture incorporating different peoples and cultures into a common civic society.[62]

The regulation and production of Quaker identity through a process of "gospel order" proved key. Despite the rhetorical and theatrical flourishes that so frequently marked Quaker worship, the movement was neither as anarchic nor as spiritually individualistic as it seemed. By the mid-1650s, Quaker leaders created a growing institutional structure through which they could keep order within the Society. They accomplished this in three primary ways: through an organized network of itinerants to spread the message, the creation of a Meeting structure to discipline or expel those whose conduct violated Quaker faith or unity, and the regulation of Friends' publishing output. All these developments were crucial in giving the Society a vitality that so many other Interregnum sects lacked.

At the center of Quakerism's rise lay the efforts of a relatively small core of itinerant preachers. Though hundreds of Friends in the seventeenth and eighteenth centuries would heed the call to travel all over the world to spread the truth, far fewer individuals participated in the Society's early missionary efforts. All told, about sixty to seventy ministers were responsible for Quakerism's initial growth in England, conducting missions through the countryside in twos and threes. After great success in the north and moderate success in the Midlands between 1652 and 1654, Quaker ministers headed south in 1655, most notably with the establishment of a London mission by Howgill, Burrough, and Nayler, three of the movement's most significant leaders.[63]

An even smaller group of Quaker leaders, most notably Margaret Fell, guided their efforts. Though Fox had founded and served as the unquestioned leader of the Society of Friends, Fell more than any other individual oversaw the growth of the Quakerism from a merely regional movement to a national one. She kept in regular correspondence with ministers, coordinated their travels, managed the Society's finances, interceded in theological and disciplinary disputes among Friends, and circulated the writings of leaders such as Fox and Nayler throughout the Society. Quaker ministers sent epistolary reports of their progress to Fox and Fell at Swarthmoor Hall. Fox's lengthy periods of incarceration, including a 1656 stay in a Launceston jail that lasted most of a year, meant that management of Friends' administrative affairs during this period of expansion fell squarely on Fell's shoulders.[64]

This network, run through Swarthmoor Hall, helped leading Friends not only spread their message but also strengthen nascent Quaker communities that had sprung up throughout the countryside. This practice began in the north of England in 1653, as Friends in various communities assembled in local meetings for worship. Each local meeting chose "one or two who are most grown in the Power and Life, in the pure discerning in the Truth" to guide them in their weekly worship.[65] These "elders" from each local meeting then gathered regularly for "general" meetings to discuss matters relating to the entire region. There they dealt with two major issues. First, they handled financial matters, allocating money to assist poor Friends, post bail for imprisoned Friends, and fund the travels of itinerants throughout England. Second, they addressed questions of "gospel order," a process that included clarifying particular points of Quaker theology and establishing a set of practices through which local meetings could promote piety and discipline way-ward Friends.[66]

Still, despite efforts to outline some general principles of church gover-nance, early Quakerism lacked any formal statement laying out the particu-lars of faith and practice. An Epistle written by elders gathered at a General Meeting held at Balby in Yorkshire in November 1656 represented the first effort to rectify that problem. The letter prescribed the proper method of Quaker preaching, enjoining the "Minister to speak the word of the Lord from the mouth of the Lord without adding or diminishing." Those who "spoke out of the Light," ceased to attend meetings, spoke evil of each other, or otherwise "walk[ed] disorderly" were to be dealt with "in private, then before two or three witnesses," and then, if still recalcitrant, reproved by the assembled meeting. The Balby Epistle also established the rules Friends should follow when marrying, stipulating that the prospective spouses appear before their local meeting for its approval before proceeding further.[67] Lead-ing Friends sent manuscript copies of the Balby Epistle to communities throughout England in an effort to regularize worship as the movement grew.

Finally, Quaker leaders built a church structure through the judicious use of print. Early Friends had an ambivalent relationship to print. On the one hand, they distrusted print as a means of evangelization, believing that books could easily deceive if not written and read in the Spirit. Print was often ill suited to convince audiences to avoid, in Fox's words, "corrupt communication" and heed only "pure communication." Martin Mason put the matter more simply: "Pen and Inck shall never make a sinner a saint."[68] On the other hand, printed materials could prove valuable when used to replicate rather than replace oral preaching. Many, if not most, early Quaker texts consisted of transcripts of extemporaneous preaching—oral communi-cation transposed into physical form. Effacing the line between these two genres of religious discourse made both more effective. Embracing the notion that, as William Tomlinson argued, "Preaching is publishing, or declaring abroad, or telling to one another openly, whether by conference or any other way" allowed ministers' sermons to go where they could not.[69]

Thus, the circulation of printed materials proved an effective means of developing a common Quaker identity in the movement's early years. And as the most prolific dissenting authors of the seventeenth century, Quakers published early and often. By 1656, nearly one hundred Friends had pub-lished tracts, authoring nearly three hundred titles. All told, nearly six hundred Friends saw print over the Society's first five decades, generating more than three thousand titles.[70]

Despite this abundance of authors, however, publishing served as a tool for the creation and centralization of institutional authority in the seventeenth century. A handful of leading Friends dominated the authorship of these tracts in the early years. More than four out of five Quaker authors before 1656 contributed to only a single publication; a group of eight leading Friends authored, individually or jointly, the large majority of works published. Most of these titles, moreover, issued from a single press, that of Giles Calvert. The rise of an alternative press in the mid-1650s did little to change this overall dynamic. Thomas Simmonds, Calvert's would-be competitor for Quaker business, was actually his rival's brother-in-law. As husband to Calvert's sister Martha Simmonds—one of James Nayler's most prominent supporters and the most prolific female Quaker author in the 1650s—he was firmly within Quakerism's inner circle. At the center stood Fell, who managed the fund that underwrote publication and more than anyone else coordinated the distribution of Quaker books from printer to preacher. A handful of individuals, then, produced the literature that defined Quaker doctrine and explained the movement to a wider world.[71] Friends created a more tightly integrated, more stringently disciplined network of publishers and distributers than any other sect during this period.[72]

These mechanisms for guiding Quakerism's growth worked in tandem. Itinerant ministers circulated printed and manuscript materials to the Friends they visited. They used manuscripts such as the Balby Epistle to bring a coherent set of practices to local meetings, which Quaker leaders saw as the entire purpose behind keeping written records.[73] They read extensively from these printed works when they addressed assembled Friends in these communities, transforming these textualized sermons back into oral form. And if these manuscript and printed texts helped shape Friends' devotional practices, the reverse was also true; the habits of "gospel order" developing in each local Quaker meeting provided a context through which these communities could interpret the writings of Fox, Nayler, Thomas Farnsworth, and others. Faith and practice reinforced each other.

This mode of transmission enabled itinerants to spread an increasingly standard body of Quaker thought, but it also enabled them to control, to some extent, the reception of this doctrine.[74] Early Quaker books had extremely small print runs, making missionaries the only source of this literature in the 1650s. Moreover, itinerants most often distributed books and manuscripts only to elders within local meetings. This meant that weighty Friends' ministrations offered general Friends' only exposure to these publications, lending particular power to the decisions that ministers and elders made as they chose which passages to read as they preached. Quakerism's rapid spread through England's spiritual hinterlands increased, not diminished, the authority the movement's leaders wielded.

These efforts to build an ecclesiastical structure facilitated the emergence of a particularly Quaker religious culture. Connected by a network of print and preaching, early Friends developed a shared symbolic world constructed through words and deeds. Various Quaker habits, such as their "plain" styles of speech and dress, took on a collective meaning—they symbolized not just each Friend's individual spiritual and physical transformation but the Society's rise as God's chosen people on earth. Bodily practices marked Quakers as participants in a grand eschatological narrative. Their disciplinary process, following the prescriptions laid out in the Balby Epistle, served a dual function as well. On a functional level, it allowed Friends to maintain the boundary between their sanctified community and the profane world. By "visiting" with disorderly Friends privately before taking any public action, Meeting elders gave sinners a chance to reform and thus put the onus of separation on the wayward. On a spiritual level, their ability to identify and admonish fallen brethren evidenced God's "mighty power [to] open the pure eternal Eye in you, to discern and separate between the Precious and Vile, the Holy and the Unholy," a sacred trust signifying their status.[75]

The denial of sinners became an essential part of Quaker identity. They frequently wrote about themselves in oppositional terms, informing their readers of who they were not. They were especially sensitive to accusations of Ranterism, publishing numerous works parrying the idea that their belief in sinless perfection represented Ranterish radical antinomianism in another guise. But Friends showed a strong desire to distinguish themselves from other, less controversial dissenting sects as well. Despite the fact that many of Fox's first converts came from "shattered Baptist" communities in the north, Friends seemed determined to deny that the Baptists had influenced Quakerism in any way. Similar in their theology, preaching style, universalist message, and ecclesiastical structure, the two sects took pains to distinguish themselves at every turn. Friends did so in particularly vehement terms, befitting their aggressive public style.

Friends' publications fostered a self-conscious movement identity in more positive ways as well, however. Authors took a term of opprobrium—

"Quaker"—and made it a sign of their faith, wearing the world's scorn as a badge. They made certain to identify themselves as Quakers in the title of nearly every printed tract, so that readers could identify the works as part of a cohesive whole. They even used the term to exaggerated effect, printing it in a different or often larger font on the title page.[76] Quaker authors also wrote about the Society's past almost from its inception, instilling a sense of history among Friends. Francis Howgill's 1655 *The Inheritance of Jacob*, which mixed spiritual autobiography with admonitions to sinful readers, was only the first attempt to craft a Quaker past. Published testimonies like Howgill's used personal history as a means of building a collective memory that helped Quaker culture endure through time and space.[77]

This cultural context made Friends' aggressive evangelical style not only logical but obligatory. Key actors in the last age of human history, Friends had a duty to try to bring others into the fold. Competing against false prophets such as the Baptists, Ranters, and Muggletonians, they required methods of differentiating themselves from others and holding on to converts. They hoped to do so by extending the disciplinary processes they used to maintain gospel order among themselves: hence, the publication of tracts such as Edward Burrough's *The Visitation of the Rebellious Nation of Ireland* in 1655.[78] These efforts went hand in hand with their open attacks on leaders of other faiths. Though obviously more aggressive than the sober warnings weighty Friends privately offered wayward brethren, these public challenges effectively functioned as personal visitations to ministers and their congregations.

The combination of propulsive and compulsive forces distinguished Quakerism from other nonconformist sects. Their active evangelical effort allowed Friends to become a national movement, while the Seekers, who shared similar theological beliefs but not the same missionary zeal, remained a regional one. And the hostility traveling Friends aroused among those Calvinists who favored a localist ecclesiastical structure went far beyond the antipathy toward itinerants Christian church fathers had traditionally displayed; Quaker ministers challenged the very essence of congregationalism.[79] Moreover, Friends' use of itinerancy to spread their message allowed Quakerism to penetrate the English countryside with a speed and scale that other dissenting groups could not match, particularly when used to transmit Quaker texts as well. Friends defined themselves by their overriding desire to spread their message and the development and embrace of specific—and effective—mechanisms for spreading it. Both these pathways for the dissemination of

Quaker culture and the impulse to use them were crucial parts of Quakerism itself.[80]

But this cultural network spread the faith by limiting it in some crucial ways. Fell's coordination of publications and ministry afforded Quaker leaders control over the movement's self-presentation through the countryside at large. Meanwhile, the nascent disciplinary system served a similar end by allowing local Quaker communities to define who could or could not call themselves a Friend of God. These forms of regulation acted as public "checks" on heterodoxy that gave the Quaker movement a coherency that groups such as the Seekers or Ranters, lacking any comparable institutional apparatus, could not attain.

This organizational structure allowed a religious movement deeply influenced by other dissenting groups to take on its own identity. The Meeting structure, in other words, served as the engine behind the creation of a hybridized Quaker culture created through the integration of new revelations and selectively appropriated elements of other faiths. It provided leading Friends an opportunity to reshape and refine the cultural "raw materials" of Quaker principles—beliefs and practices that were hardly uncommon in revolutionary England—into a stronger, more coherent whole. Fox and other early Friends may have developed the rudiments of the movement's faith and practice during Quakerism's earliest years, but it was the combination of print, itinerancy, and Meeting discipline that facilitated the elaboration of these early ideas and the flowering of a fully fledged Quaker way of apprehending and being in the world. Central to this Quaker identity, however, was a near total incapacity to acknowledge the debt owed to other dissenting sects.[81] At the heart of this nascent collective identity, in other words, lay an overriding cultural imperative to deny the very process by which it had come into being; it was a hybridized faith that needed to deny its hybrid origins.

Both the distinctive cultural identity early Friends developed and the mechanisms they used to maintain that identity would later shape Pennsylvania's formative years. But most crucially, they would enable the Society to weather the struggles it faced during the 1660s.

The Crises of Post-Restoration Quakerism

The Society of Friends faced internal and external threats during the early 1660s and 1670s. Politically, the sect came under siege after the Restoration of the Stuart monarchy in 1660, when waves of official and unofficial persecution threatened its existence as a national religious movement. Meanwhile, the Meeting endured a series of bitter schisms that threatened to unravel the organizational structure Quaker leaders had created. These crises led to significant innovations in Quaker theology and political philosophy as Friends reworked their conceptions of religious and political authority. By the 1670s, William Penn had combined these two projects, developing a philosophy of governance that translated Quaker understandings of religious order and power into the civic realm. Thus, English Quakerism's internal and external struggles during the 1660s and 1670s shaped both the creole Quakerism that evolved in Pennsylvania and also the creolized civic order Penn and his fellow founders constructed. Penn's American colony was a post-Restoration colony in more ways than one: a cultural as well as political product of its era.

The ascension of Charles II in 1660 and the years immediately following represented first disappointment and then devastation for the Society. Quaker disillusionment with Oliver Cromwell's government had grown throughout the 1650s as Friends believed the lord protector too often favored practicality over piety in his policies. But they believed the installation of Oliver's son Richard as protector provided an opportunity for change. Friends became increasingly politically vocal throughout 1659; that year saw the publication of many of the Society's most explicitly political tracts. It also saw their most impressive contribution to the campaign to abolish tithes, long the bane of English dissenters. One Quaker petition against the practice contained the signatures of over 7,000 Friends.[82] Others took more direct action. The Society had not yet articulated an unequivocal stance on war and violence, and a growing number of Friends seemed willing to take up arms for their cause. Some fought to suppress a royalist uprising in August of that year; other "foolish rash spirits" expressed a willingness to overthrow Richard Cromwell's Protectorate and establish a true "Reign of Christ" on earth.[83] Cooler heads advised caution, with Fox issuing an epistle reminding Friends that they should fight "the Lamb's War" on God's behalf with spiritual, not carnal, weapons, and other Meeting leaders penning a tract declaring the sect's neutrality in England's political struggles.[84]

Most, but not all, Friends greeted Charles II's return to power in spring 1660 with trepidation and cautious optimism, particularly after his declaration that he would not prohibit dissenters from peacefully practicing their religious beliefs.[85] Unfortunately, these hopes proved to be short lived.

Charles quickly backed down from his pledge of religious toleration in the face of parliamentary opposition. More significant in changing his religious policies was the January 1661 uprising led by Fifth Monarchist Thomas Venner. Hoping to establish a godly kingdom on earth, Venner and fifty followers took up arms against the Stuart monarchy, believing the time of Christ's restoration to be at hand. Their actions damaged the cause of toleration more than they did the government itself. Parliament responded with mass arrests, among them over 4,000 Friends. Fearing even harsher treatment, the Society issued its first definitive statement to the outside world declaring that Friends rejected armed warfare in all its forms.[86] But the damage to the Quaker cause was already done. In 1661, Parliament passed the first of the so-called Clarendon Code acts, laws aimed at eliminating religious nonconformity throughout the realm.

As the largest group of dissenters in England, Friends bore the brunt of the effort to impose orthodoxy. Sheriffs broke up meetings for worship with impunity, arresting some participants and threatening others with violence. Several thousand Friends were imprisoned in the first few years of Charles's reign for violating the Clarendon Code; hundreds died in prison.[87] Their testimony against swearing only compounded the difficulties the Penal Acts presented. Their inability to testify under oath left them unable to defend themselves in court, making them vulnerable to the worst abuses of the law. Their religious scruples likewise prevented them from taking the oath of allegiance to the Crown, heightening the suspicion with which outsiders viewed them. Many local meetings for worship struggled simply to survive during the 1660s.[88]

These laws posed an even greater threat to Quakerism as a national movement. Quaker authors found it increasingly difficult to publish and distribute their works as the Stuart monarchy took aggressive action against the sectarian printers that had proliferated during the Interregnum period.[89] Waves of persecution disrupted—indeed, nearly destroyed—the traveling ministry so central to the Society's earlier growth. Few itinerant Friends escaped jail.[90] With neither a reliable source of doctrinal and apologetic works nor a reliable means of distributing tracts that were written, the Society faced the possibility of fragmentation.

These external pressures exacerbated a growing crisis in authority in the Meeting itself. The 1660s saw a generational transition within the Society: early leaders such as James Nayler, Richard Hubberthorne, Francis Howgill, Edward Burrough, and John Audland passed away between 1660 and 1664;

second generation leaders George Keith, Robert Barclay, and William Penn joined the movement in 1663, 1666, and 1667 respectively.[91] The decade and a half after the Restoration also saw two major divisions, the Perrot affair and the Wilkinson-Story-Rogers "separation." These conflicts led to dramatic institutional and theological reformations; together they served as the crucible in which seventeenth- and eighteenth-century Anglo-American Quakerism was formed.

These controversies centered on the same fundamental issue: the nature of spiritual power in a sect championing direct individual revelation as one of its core principles. Who was authorized to speak on behalf of the Society in matters of faith and practice? On what grounds could they exercise such power? John Perrot's dispute with other leaders first revealed these problems. One of the Society's most charismatic evangelists, Perrot had spearheaded missionary efforts in the Mediterranean in the late 1650s. He unfortunately ran afoul of the Roman Inquisition, thwarting his ultimate goal of bringing Quakerism to Jerusalem. Returning to England in 1661 after three years in an Italian prison, he found himself uneasy with changes in Quaker worship that had occurred during his time away. In particular, he challenged Friends' practice of removing their hats during worship, arguing that Scripture did not require the faithful to remove their hats (or any other article of clothing, for that matter) while praying.[92] He similarly argued against holding regular "first day" (Sunday) meetings for worship at appointed places, asserting that Friends should only worship when and where they felt the Spirit move them.

Other Friends believed that Perrot's teachings went beyond simple explications of previous Quaker doctrine; they superseded, rather than elucidated, previous revelations and thus called into question the authority of Fox and his allies to establish and enforce a single set of rules governing Quaker doctrine. Hoping to avoid a serious confrontation, Perrot left for America in 1662. The dispute between his supporters and orthodox Quaker leaders continued through 1666, however, when Meeting leaders took steps to consolidate power in their own hands. That year, they issued a "Testimony of the Brethren" that tightened access to the ministry while making Meeting ministers and elders the sole arbiters on doctrinal issues among Friends.[93] Over the next three years, they established a permanent London Yearly Meeting with binding authority over all quarterly and monthly Meetings and issued epistles formalizing the rules governing marriage, operation of the Meeting system, dispute resolution among Friends, and the process by which Friends could be certified to evangelize. They also instituted a policy requiring Friends moving from one area to another to obtain a certificate from their former meeting attesting to their "clearness" in conduct before being allowed to join a new one.[94] All these, they hoped, would prevent future Perrots from causing trouble.

This ecclesiastical apparatus soon proved controversial, however, with a sizable minority of Friends rebelling against "Foxian" authority in the 1670s. Friends in the north, led by John Wilkinson and John Story, and in the southwest, led by William Rogers, began to reject the dictates of London Friends. They claimed that local meetings should have the authority to govern themselves in matters of worship and discipline; Quaker communities in Westmoreland went against Yearly Meeting prescriptions by holding private meetings for worship instead of public ones, while Bristol Quakers eliminated separate women's meetings in favor of a common "Meeting for Discipline" comprising weighty Friends of both sexes. Their actions earned Friends in each community a series of admonishments from leading orthodox ministers and finally official condemnation from the London Monthly Meeting in 1677. London leaders insinuated that the dissidents were "men of bad spirits" for criticizing Fox and his allies.[95] A final meeting between orthodox and dissenting leaders in 1678 led to a proclamation against would-be separatists. Some dissenters left the Meeting; Rogers became a rabid anti-Quaker polemicist. Others acquiesced to orthodox authority, despite their misgivings. Fox traveled extensively throughout the north and west visiting disgruntled communities, succeeding in bringing many back into the fold. Wilkinson and Story became silent but never publicly recanted their position.[96]

The triumph of a Quaker orthodoxy led by Fox, Fell, Barclay, Penn, and Keith represented only a tactical victory, not a strategic one, however. Leading Friends had succeeded in ridding the Society of dissenters without articulating a clear justification of what necessitated such action; their declaration that all religious opinions contrary to their own came from the same "dark, earthly Spirit" that drove the Ranters explained neither why competing revelations posed such a danger to "truth" nor the source of their authority to act as the sole arbiters of God's Word within the Society.[97] What explained the urgency to purge Perrot, Rogers, Wilkinson, Story, and their followers from their ranks?

This question had political and theological answers. Politically, Meeting leadership had a strong incentive during an era of intense persecution to prevent any form of religious expression that might inflame anti-Quaker sentiment. They hoped in particular to avoid a repeat of anything comparable to James Nayler's infamous 1656 journey to Bristol. Nayler's reenactment of Christ's triumphant return to Jerusalem—complete with acolytes singing "Holy, Holy, Lord God of Sabboth" as they led him into the city—confirmed the public's worst suspicions about Quaker blasphemy. In this light, Nayler's punishment under the Blasphemy Act, which included public whippings, having his tongue bored with an iron, and a "B" branded on his forehead, had seemed entirely justified.[98] Post-Restoration Friends simply could not afford any similarly extravagant prophetic displays.

Theological concerns weighed more heavily on the minds of leading Friends. The Restoration had, of course, dealt all those radical groups born during the Interregnum a grievous defeat. Unlike many other sects, however, Quakers experienced the return of the Stuart monarchy as an eschatological defeat as well as a political one.[99] Simply put, the apocalypse had not come, and Friends found themselves having to live in the world instead of at its end.

This fact called into question some of the basic tenets of Quakerism. Fox had preached that cultivating the seed of Christ within brought about a transformation through which Friends achieved physical and spiritual perfection on earth. This ability to reach the state in which Adam lived in the beginning supposedly marked the fulfillment of sacred time on earth. But Christ had not returned and the world had not ended, raising the possibility that Friends had not, in fact, been reborn in celestial flesh free from sin.

This dilemma led post-Restoration authors, such as by Penn, Keith, and especially Barclay, to revise their understanding of the natures of both the seed of God within and the conversion experience, two of the core elements of the Quaker faith. Each explicitly affirmed Fox's teachings while implicitly rejecting the founder's conceptions of these theological principles. On the surface, they subscribed to all the tenets Fox preached about inward divinity. All men, Barclay wrote, possessed a measure of "the *Seed of God*" within them; only by tending this seed could they escape their "*Natural Condition*" of sin and achieve salvation.[100] But where Fox and earlier Friends wrote of Christ within in material terms, second generation Friends wrote of it in spiritual ones. The Christ within each man and woman was not literally a portion of his body and blood but rather a *vehiculum dei*, the thing by which people came to know God; they could live in, but not as, Christ. Embracing this new, spiritualist understanding of God's seed led Quaker theologians to reconceptualize the conversion process and the state of perfection achieved therein. The flowering of the inward Christ raised the "*Spiritual Senses*" of reborn Friends but did not lead to a corporeal transformation.[101] Friends became "*dead* unto Sin" yet remained in mortal bodies.[102]

This understanding of conversion implied a certain amount of instability in the process, however. Here lay perhaps the most significant result of post-Restoration Quakers' spiritualization of the inner Christ. The notion that a bodily transformation signified the moment of conversion lent justification an air of finality: the possibility of a celestial body's becoming more perfect or a fallen saint's being "reborn" into a body of sin and death after having a celestial one seemed logically impossible. But nonmaterial conversion seemingly allowed for such change. Those who heeded Christ within, Barclay wrote, might reach "an even more perfect state" spiritually, while for those who resisted God, "there still remaineth the possibility of sinning," resulting in a fall from grace. Renewed commitment to the Light within could lead one back to the state one sought. The path to (or from) an inner Eden thus became cyclical, with perfection, followed by a fall, followed by a purging of sin and consequent rebirth. Returning to God might even, Barclay added, lead to an "*Increase and Stability in Truth*" as a result of such trials.[103] If Friends were made, not born, they could be unmade and remade as well. Thus, the essence of true piety lay not in the initial conversion experience but in a constant process of remaking one's faith.

This left Friends with the very real problem of avoiding Adam's fate, so that they might live in the state of ever-deepening perfection he had rejected. The Bible offered no sure answers. Though post-Restoration Friends treated it with less skepticism than their predecessors, they did not make it the center of their faith. As a representation of God's Word, Quaker theologians saw the Scriptures as "only a declaration of the *fountain*, and not the *fountain* itself, therefore they are not to be esteemed the principal ground of all truth and knowledge, nor yet the *adequate primary rule of faith and manners.*"[104] Revelation, Keith argued, provided a steadier base: "the inward Voice or Word of God immediately in the heart, can very well be understood to be more sure as to us, than any outward Voice of God from Heaven." It offered something that neither ear could hear nor tongue or pen express.[105] While Barclay insisted that Friends' inward revelations "neither do nor can ever contradict the outward testimony, of the scriptures, or tight and sound reason," Quaker authors left no doubt that the former guided their interpretations of the latter.[106]

In making these claims, second generation theologians clearly did not intend every Friend to follow the dictates of the inward Voice. After all, individuals might misinterpret the meaning of particular revelations. But where individual judgment might fail, collective wisdom would not. If God's Word as revealed outwardly in Scripture (when rightly understood) could never contradict his Word as revealed inwardly, neither could the revelations of Friends walking in the Light of Christ contradict each other. "The Light, Spirit, and Power in the Church, is never contrary to the Light, Spirit, and Power in any member," Penington wrote. "The greatest degree of Light owns and is at unity with the least: and the least degree of Light hath a sense of that which is in degree and measuring above it."[107] A true church contained no contrary opinions, never lacked certainty in matters of conscience, and was infallible when united under Christ.[108]

This formulation deftly provided a theological justification for the Meeting's institutional response to schismatics like Perrot, Rogers, Wilkinson, and Story and for any action taken against similar ministers in the future. If all spiritual truth flowed from the same source, then individuals who claimed knowledge of a new way to walk in the Light necessarily drew their inspiration from an impure source. Would-be members of the Society who offered contrary interpretations of God's message by challenging orthodox assertions of faith and practice revealed themselves as false Friends, lacking authentic divine knowledge. Spiritual authority came from God but could only be expressed legitimately through the Meeting. If the collective wisdom of the Meeting offered the only way of discerning the "Truth," then any dissent posed a grave threat. Spiritualizing the inner Christ only heightened the need to identify and purge those who strayed—and might lead others astray— from the path of righteousness. Meeting discipline thus assumed a spiritual as well as a sociological significance: Friends' desire to adhere to group conscience, expressed through an affirmation of the Meeting's authority, testified to the purity of their individual consciences.

Insisting that the Meeting play the primary role in interpreting the Word of God did not imply spiritual equality among those within the Society—far from it. As levels of perfection existed, so too did there exist levels of Light. The members of any church, Barclay wrote, possessed "*Diversities* of *Gifts*" among them. Naturally then, the spiritually "*strong*" church fathers should exercise loving authority over the "*weak, Babes,* and *Young Men*" among them. Behind every schism lay either an attempt by some to assume a higher spiritual position "than God will have them to be in" or church leaders shirking their responsibilities.[109] Only a group that embraced the variety of "different *Measures, Growths* and *Motions*" among its members could achieve the "pure *Unity* in the *Spirit*" and the "*Consenting* and *Oneness*" in faith and practice that marked a true church. And only when one had accepted one's place in and submitted wholly to this spiritual hierarchy could one exercise "true *Liberty* of the spirit."[110]

Thus, the "sense of the Meeting," as determined by Quaker ministers and elders, served the same purpose in the Society that Scripture did in more bibliocentric dissenting sects: it acted as a standard against which potentially outlying heterodox theological positions could be judged. Where those other sects relied on Scripture as an "infallible correlative to the self" during moments of spiritual uncertainty, Quakers relied on group conscience.[111] Though each Friend possessed a measure of God's Light within, knowledge of that Word was always partly someone else's; Quakers relied on each other to interpret it correctly.[112] This disciplinary system encouraged Friends to develop a reflective spiritual identity so that they might find greater harmony in a larger spiritual community. Individual spiritual identity, they believed, could only flourish in an intensely regulated communitarian setting like the Meeting. Quaker discipline acted as sign and process: commitment to Meeting prescriptions demonstrated commitment to the faith while helping individual Friends avoid straying from the righteous path. It produced and reflected Quaker religious identity.[113]

Post-Restoration Quakers had developed a religious culture in which individual experience took on meaning only in the context of group experience. Quaker piety existed not simply (or even primarily) as an inward construct but instead took shape in their ongoing interactions with each other and the outsiders in whose midst they lived.[114] Moreover, the centrality of immediate revelation in the Quaker worldview made religious conformity, produced by a thorough remaking of the self and regulated by local, regional, and national bodies, essential. Thus, Friends' intense cultural disposition toward spiritual individualism fostered an equally intense disposition toward ritual conformity. The Meeting system orthodox Friends created reenacted this process on a larger scale. In addition to adjudicating disputes, the London Yearly Meeting sent out annual epistles to its quarterly and monthly meetings laying out disciplinary prescriptions and celebrating the spirit of love and harmony within the Society. These regional and local meetings, for their part, sent letters in response, vocally assenting to the Yearly Meeting's decrees. This epistolary culture provided one more way for Friends to support God and each other simultaneously.

The rigid, hierarchical disciplinary and administrative structure Fox, Barclay, and Penn established thus served theological and practical ends. Indeed, its theological appeal stemmed from its practicality. Realizing that they did not live at the end of time and that Christ's return was not imminent, they understood that they could not depend on any further dispensation to guide their conduct but could only rely on each other. Post-Restoration Friends did not embrace a strict system of discipline out of need for respectability; rather, they embraced a new orthodoxy because it offered them a way of living together in the world as Friends.

Meeting leaders also felt the need to develop another tool in their efforts to strengthen a Quaker religious community: history. More specifically, they began to see the process of history making as a way of unifying Friends. In May 1676, the London Yearly Meeting sent a call to monthly and quarterly meetings to compile information that might be used to draft "a plain, true, & full Narrative or History" of the Society. They hoped in this regard to emulate the Israelites, whose chronicles of their tribulations and triumphs were central to their identity as a people. They also hoped to avoid the fate of the early Christian church, where a lack of authoritative histories prevented transmission of "one pure peece of Ancient Tradition" from Christ's time to the present. The letter requested information about when Quakerism first arrived in various communities and which ministers first brought God's message. The Meeting also wanted to know "Where bad spirits have risen, & false brethren appear'd" so that this, too, might become part of the Society's history.[115]

Written at the height of the Wilkinson-Story-Rogers controversy, the London Friends' letter revealed a remarkable self-awareness about the purposes and functions of history. They saw drafting a "true" account of the Quaker movement as an act of history making on multiple levels. It allowed Friends to cultivate their self-image as God's new chosen people, something very important for a persecuted community. It also allowed them an opportunity to write, quite literally, dissident Friends out of the official narrative of Quaker history. If the theological innovations articulated by second generation Friends justified elimination of dissent within the Meeting, the writing of a true history of Quakerism provided a vehicle through which Friends could explain these changes to themselves. Narrating the Quaker past had profound political implications for the Society's present and future.

These internal changes did not happen in a vacuum. The political climate of post-Restoration England forced Friends to rethink their place in the world while they reformulated their relationships to each other. Circumstance forced Quaker leaders to define and defend their civic rights and obligations as dissenters and as Englishmen. One individual stood at the nexus of these transitions: William Penn. A major figure in the internecine ecclesiastical battles of the 1670s, the young Quaker played by far the largest role in both advancing the political fortunes of Friends and creating a new Quaker political philosophy.

William Penn's Philosophy of Governance

William Penn's political philosophy defies easy characterization. An ardent proponent of legal reform, Penn justified his calls for change through appeals to natural reason, tradition, and pragmatism at a time when most jurists and reformers argued from one—and only one—of these schools of thought.[116] Active on behalf of Whig candidates for Parliament during the 1670s, he championed James II in his struggles against Whigs during the Exclusion Crisis and his brief reign as king.[117] Penn's political, constitutional, and legal writings were nothing if not eclectic; they show the influence of "commonwealth" writers such as James Harrington, common law jurists such as Sir William Coke, and radical reformers from the Interregnum period (including many fellow Quakers).[118] Penn's oeuvre, while extensive, lacks a magnum opus laying out his beliefs in systematic fashion; he wrote volumes advocating particular causes—primarily that of religious toleration—without producing a general political treatise, a fact that complicates attempts to pigeonhole him politically and intellectually.

Penn nonetheless developed over the 1670s a coherent philosophy of governance that reflected his intellectual influences, political commitments, and religious experiences. His work on behalf of fellow religious dissidents and his engagement with philosophical issues reinforced each other. His writings reveal a deep concern with the order and ordering of civil society—the rules on which a stable government should be based and the mechanisms by which the rulers and ruled might keep such a government properly operating.[119] Penn's early career as a political controversialist followed three tracks. First, he pleaded the Quaker cause in English courts as a criminal defendant, making the case in front of judge and jury against religious intolerance. Second, he lobbied friends and associates within England's political and social elite on behalf of imprisoned Quakers. Finally, he became an increasingly prolific author on the subject of religious liberty, as well as the topic of rights in general.

Though only twenty three years old at the time of his convincement in 1667, Penn involved himself with Quaker public life without hesitation. By 1670, he had already published a major work on Quaker theology, several works defending the Society against its critics, and multiple tracts challenging the legal prohibition of religious dissent under the Restoration government and the heavy sanctions levied on those who violated the laws.[120] These actions earned Penn a nine-month stay in Newgate prison in 1668–69, followed by an unofficial "exile" (at his father's, not the government's, behest) in Ireland. Penn continued to preach and write openly as a Quaker on his return to London in the summer of 1670. His participation at an outdoor meeting for worship in Gracechurch Street in London on August 15 led to a second arrest. The constable charged the participants with "Unlawfully and Tumultuously . . . Assembl[ing] and Congregat[ing] themselves together, to the Disturbance of the Peace" of the realm. Leading such meetings carried strict penalties under the Second Conventicle Act.[121]

Penn and his codefendant William Mead appeared before the court on 3 September. They made no attempt to deny or "vindicate the Assembling of our selves, to Preach, Pray, or Worship" God in Gracechurch Street, since Friends had an "indispensible Duty" to hold such meetings. Rather, Penn argued that a nonconformist meeting did not represent, in and of itself, a disturbance of the peace, meaning that he and Mead were being tried for a matter of conscience and not law. "The Question is not whether I am Guilty of this Indictment, but whether this Indictment be Legal," Penn believed. Moreover, he made this appeal not to the judge but to the jury, who ultimately concurred. When asked to report their verdict, the foreman responded that the jury had found the men "Guilty of Speaking in *Gracious-Street*." Incensed, the court ordered the jury imprisoned overnight "without Meat, Drink, Fire, or any other Accommodation," even "so much as a Chamber-Pot, though desired."[122] Penn, Mead, and the jury were ultimately vindicated, as the jury's verdict was upheld on appeal and all were freed.

The Penn-Mead trial made history in three ways, playing a crucial role in Anglo-American legal history, in constructing a Quaker hagiography, and in Penn's understanding of the historical foundations of constitutional law. Legally, the case represented a major milestone, securing the independence and authority of juries in Anglo-American law.[123] Beyond that, the published account of the trial, *The People's Ancient and Just Liberties*, became a crucial cultural touchstone for Anglo-American Friends. Appearing in three editions in 1670 and reprinted several times in England over the course of the seventeenth and eighteenth centuries, the trial transcript and the accompanying editorial gloss memorialized Friends' struggle against worldly persecution through its dramatization of Penn's conflict with and eventual triumph over the Newgate bench.[124] Through these repeated reprintings, this account of the most famous Quaker trial took its place alongside accounts of other imprisoned and martyred Friends as a foundational text in an increasingly voluminous and important canon of Quaker sufferings.

But the trial also represented Penn's first effort to articulate his views on the role of fundamental law in governance. Penn challenged the indictment on the grounds that it violated the rights laid out in the Magna Carta. This fundamental law, he claimed, secured the right of all Englishmen, regardless of religious persuasion, to their liberty and property. If the government had the power to violate this right arbitrarily—in this case, by claiming that men and women assembled to worship peacefully threatened the public order—dissenters would find themselves in a position where "our Liberties are openly to be invaded; our Wives to be Ravished; our Children Slaved; [and] our Families Ruined" at a magistrate's whim. Thus, any "Imprisonment or Amercement upon the people of England for any Act of Religious Worship . . . is destructive of the Great Charter" that guaranteed the English their "antient Rights and Privileges."[125]

Penn hardly believed in making this argument that the law allowed all forms of religious worship. The Second Conventicle Act, he averred, rightly prohibited seditious assemblies held under pretense of religion, a category that included Catholics whose political allegiance lay with Rome and not the Crown.[126] But the power to distinguish between peaceful and subversive forms of religious expression lay with the jury, not the judge. "Are [you] not," Penn asked the jurors in his case, "my proper Judges by the *Great Charter of England*?" The jury had the power "according to Fundamental Law" to determine not merely the facts—whether Penn and Mead led an outdoor meeting for worship—but also the relevant law—whether such a gathering represented a riot or tumult of the type prohibited by law. The court could not alienate a privilege granted by an authority higher than itself.[127]

Penn's arguments paralleled his religious convictions. By appealing directly to the jury, he made his legal defense not simply the "marshalling of evidence to support a point" but rather the description of an "overall conception" of the relationship between law and order that challenged established authority.[128] Just as Friends' emphasis on inward revelation undercut the authority of ecclesiastical intermediaries, so too did Penn's interpretation of fundamental law undercut the authority of legal intermediaries, namely, judges. Crucially, however, Penn placed his faith in the collective wisdom of the jury, not in the respective consciences of individual jurors, much as leading Quakers relied on the "sense of the Meeting" to check the worst extravagances of particular Friends. If, as Penn believed, all threats to "civill as well as religious society" stemmed from the same "short, brittle, hasty Disposition & Frame of Spirits," then remedies that worked in one domain would work in another.[129]

Thus, Penn envisioned legal conscience playing the same role in the civil realm that spiritual conscience did in the religious one. Moreover, his appeal to the fundamental law of the "Great Charter" and the people's "antient liberties" presumed the present immediacy of a mythic moral past and posited a declensionist narrative of England's legal and political history. In essence, he upheld the jury's ability to restore the moral order of the past in the present through the assertion of its own collective moral voice.

Penn refined his ideas about law and governance during his years as a political advocate. Drawing upon his legal training and connections at the Stuart royal court, he played the leading role in developing a legal defense strategy to help Friends withstand the heavy persecution they faced in Restoration England.[130] This involved public advocacy for liberty of conscience, which he defined as "*Liberty of the Mind*" and the ability to practice one's principles; he condemned the current English establishment and suggested alternatives.[131]

Penn's early letters and tracts focused on the problems associated with the establishment of religion. Governmental regulation of conscience represented, first of all, a clear usurpation of God's authority over matters spiritual by powers temporal. Mandating religious belief, he wrote, "*enthrones Man as King over Conscience, the lone just Claim and Priviledge of his Creator.*" Those "*Caesars* on Earth" who would compel their subjects to worship in a particular manner interfered with "*the invisible Operation of his Eternal Spirit*" within men. And as God's kingdom was spiritual, not carnal, only spiritual weapons "as heavenly as it's [sic] own Nature" could bring it about. Coercion could never, in Penn's opinion, promote spiritual fulfillment. It could only "subvert all *True Religion*; for where Men believe not because it is *True*, but because they are required to do so, there they will unbelieve, not because 'tis *False*, but so commanded by their *Superiours*," preventing faith from flourishing.[132]

Moreover, Penn believed that using a "Coercive Civil Power" to regulate faith went against not only "the express Letter of the Scripture" but also "the fundamental Laws of England."[133] These laws, "in Force & Use" since "time out of mind, that is, beyond record & History," represented England's "antient constitution," the basis of its entire legal system. They guaranteed the equality of all Englishmen before the law, protected their property and person from arbitrary power, and ensured that all legal penalties be in "*proportion . . . to the Crime committed.*" But instead of treating all English subjects as members of a common "Civil Body & Society of People," attempts to maintain religious unity effectively disenfranchised dissenters by drawing legal distinctions between those of different religious persuasions.[134] Crown and Parliament, Penn noted, had made heterodox religious practice punishable by imprisonment, heavy fines, or even banishment—sanctions too harsh "for faults purely intellectual."[135] Non-conformists, in other words, faced the loss of their person, property, and citizenship for their beliefs, denying them the legal protections that were "the proper *Birth-Right of Englishmen*." Penn even went as far as to suggest that this shared legal heritage defined the very meaning of "those two words, English men": their legal identity and cultural identity were inseparable.[136]

Neither Parliament nor the Church possessed the power to "disseize Englishmen of [their] Free-Customs." In defending the right of nonconformists to worship according to their conscience, Penn distinguished between different levels of law. Some laws were "Fundamental; & those are durable, and indissolveable," others "Circumstantial, & Superficial; & those be Alterable." The first category consisted of "all those Laws, that Constitute the Antient Civil Government of England," the second of those laws, "both Civil and Ecclesiastical," created to deal with specific issues or events. If these laws conflicted, the fundamental always took precedence over the temporary.[137] Moreover, as the "Civil Society" constituted by English custom "was in the world before the Protestant Profession"—indeed, before the time of William the Conqueror—it necessarily took precedence over the established Church's authority in all cases.[138] Even the king, though he be the "Head in Civils" in England, lacked the power to amend or annul the rights recognized in the "Great Charter" in any way.[139]

As Penn continued to agitate on behalf of religious toleration, however, his thinking evolved. He continued to argue that persecution represented Caesar's infringement on God's prerogative to judge matters of faith.[140] He also insisted that it violated dissenters' English liberties, inherited from their distant Saxon ancestors and ensconced in the country's fundamental law. He reminded his readers that "the Genius of this Nation is not inferiour to any in this World" in protecting its citizens' freedoms.[141] But he increasingly argued that regulating matters of conscience was not merely un-English but impractical and unreasonable as a general policy. Good governance entailed *"the right and proper disciplining of . . . Society"* through the application of kindness and justice in appropriate proportions. Human history, Penn argued, showed that individuals inevitably differed on matters of opinion, particularly on matters spiritual. Efforts to check this natural tendency toward diversity of religious sentiments would always backfire, increasing division in the end. Penn noted that "sad Experience" revealed "that the very Remedies applied to cure Dissension, increase it," rendering any such attempt futile. He continued, "the more Vigorously an *Uniformity* is Coercively Prosecuted, the wider Breaches grow, the more inflamed Persons are, and fix'd in their Resolutions to stand by their Principles," no matter the cost.[142]

Ultimately, he wrote, regulating opinion through force was impossible. Only someone ignorant of the history of civil government could "think it within the Reach of Humane Power to fetter Conscience, or to restrain it's [sic] Liberty *strictly taken*," especially when dealing with faithful Christians.[143] Governments thus wasted their energies seeking religious uniformity when they should instead concentrate on prosecuting crimes of action, not thought. Penn found it deeply troubling to see that magistrates allowed so many to "be *Drunk*, to *Whore*, to be *Voluptuous*, to *Game, Swear, Curse, Blaspheme*, and *Profane*," committing "Sins against Nature; and against *Government*, as well as against the *Written Laws* of God." Yet while these sinners "lay the Ax to the Root of *Human Society*," conscientious dissenters who did nothing to disturb the civil peace suffered for their faith.[144]

Above all, Penn argued that efforts to enforce religious unity through legal and political means subverted the very end of government. Civil government, he wrote, fulfilled a different function than ecclesiastical government. Christian churches existed to further the cause of Christ's spiritual kingdom on earth; they concerned themselves with maintaining spiritual uniformity among their members and exercised ecclesiastical authority appropriate to that end. Worldly authority, on the other hand, had its own purpose. "Civil

Interest," Penn wrote, "is the foundation and end of civil government."[145] Consequently, governments should seek to secure unity by protecting the liberty and prosperity of their citizens, regardless of religious faith. Secular authority even had, in Penn's eyes, its own form of blasphemy: "Disseizing *Freemen* of *England* of their *Freeholds, Liberties and Properties . . .* merely for the inoffensive Exercise of the Conscience to God in Matters of Religion, *is a Civil Sort of Sacrilege.*"[146]

Governments should rely on persuasion and not coercion to maintain the unity that was the "greatest End of Government," for in civil as well as ecclesiastical affairs, "*Force makes* Hypocites" while "*Perswuasion . . .* makes converts."[147] Civic allegiance was best secured through a consensual process of interaction between rulers and ruled where each side shared the same interest.[148] Any civil authority "which dare not rely solely upon the Power of Perswasion," he argued, oppressed its people and acted in a manner "inconsistent with Peace and Unity." A populace treated thus would inevitably become "Vindictive . . . in Maintenance of its Rights" and rise up in force against its government. While some rulers felt it essential to prevent the rise of new political or religious opinions through force, this approach toward governance was "inconsistent with the Safety of Government." Where governments meted out civil punishments solely for offenses against the state and secured the rights of the governed through persuasion and coercion, they could govern peacefully, regardless of their citizens' religious opinions.[149]

But such a political order required an established legal system that defined the terms by which the government ruled the people, keeping the will of leaders in check for the good of civil society as a whole. Law was the only basis of a truly stable civil society.[150] All governments, he wrote, must either stand upon "*Will and Power,* or *Condition and Contract*: The one Rules by Men, the other by Laws." In England, the terms of the ancient constitution, created by the consent of the people, served for the nation's "great Pilots" as their "*Stars* or *Compass* for them to Steer the Vessel of this Kingdom by," preventing tyranny.[151] But all peoples, not merely the English, possessed the natural reason necessary to grasp the fundamental laws that should guide rulers and limit, when necessary, the exercise of their power.[152] These laws would serve as the common civil language through which governors would persuade the governed of the justice of their actions. It was, moreover, a civic discourse the people had themselves generated, as fundamental law was the people's product, brought into being by their consent.

However, government based on persuasion could only exist if ultimate authority rested with the people, a sentiment that reflected the Whiggish character of Penn's thought.[153] Penn insisted that the authority of those who articulated and executed the laws derived their power from those they ruled, writing that "Every *Representative* may be call'd, the *Creature of the People*, because the People make them, and to them they owe their Being. Here is no Transessentiating or Transsubstantiation of Being, from People to Representative, no more than there is an absolute Transferring of a Title in a *Letter of Attorney*." The ruled literally created their rulers. Moreover, as the latter embodied the voice of the people and thus could not legitimately proclaim any law that might injure the people, "The Representative of the people is at best a true Copy, an Exemplification; the Free People are the Original, not cancellable by a transcript" that they themselves created.[154]

Thus, Penn understood the constitution of civic power in terms of discursive metaphor. The circulation of language between the people—the original—and their representatives—their copy—produced legitimate authority; the promulgation of laws from the latter to the former did not. The rule of law might create a common civic language essential for peace and unity, but it also relied on a prior, common discursive framework from which the rule of law might emerge. Penn's understanding of civil society, then, rested not only on a belief that all citizens were equal under the law but also on the assumption that citizens within this polity of equals were at some level identical or interchangeable: the process of representation implied a fundamental civic homogeneity. Diversity among the populace might render the process of representation through exemplification logically or practically impossible, while dissonance within the voice of the people would similarly imperil its transcription into a unifying civic language. In England, this common identity came from a shared civic inheritance—the fabled ancient constitution. Crucially, however, Penn did not speculate on the basis for a similar civic homogeneity in other polities, even as he argued that persuasion and the rule of law could and should be the basis of good governance in all societies.

In suggesting that authority be grounded in persuasion rather than force, Penn hardly intended to weaken government. Rather, he believed that instruments of state power, properly deployed, could transform society by remaking those that resided within its bounds. Governments concerned merely with suppressing vice—or worse, those that believed persecuting nonconformists suppressed vice—undermined themselves by weakening their subjects. Living under coercive rule rendered men "Drudges"[155] whose professed allegiance was not merely hypocritical but also chimerical, for no such individual could feel a true patriotic love for his country. And without sincerity, "the Foundation of all good Government, and only firm Bond of human Society," there could "be no Faith or Truth in Civil Society."[156] Those who believed they could rule by restraining their subjects' basest or unruliest instincts planted the seeds of their own defeat.

Such misguided governors erred, Penn argued, in their failure to grasp that government's greatest power lay not in its ability to repress vice but in its ability to encourage virtue. Instead of trying to enforce a particular creed or sect, governments should promote "general and practical religion," the basic precepts of virtue and charity that underlay all faiths. States could then manipulate "the very Natures of Men": the "*Lazy*" would become "conscientiously industrious," the "Industrious and Conscientious Man *chearful* at his Labour," and the "wild . . . cross and Jealous" man moderate, sober, and amicable.[157]

Making government a "Nursey of Virtue" would "render the Magistrates['] Province more facil," making governance "a Safe as well as Easy Thing." Eventually, Penn wrote, the promotion of general virtue would become self-perpetuating: cultivating habits of self-governance among the people at large would "increase the Number of Men fit to govern," who would then "sweeten [the] blood and Mollify" the passions of those they ruled. Governments had tremendous educative power over their citizens, analogous to that parents and teachers possessed over their children and students. Penn had, in fact, wrote his 1679 *Address to Protestants*—the longest political tract he ever published—to encourage both toleration for religious nonconformists and the proper education of youth, as these presented the most effectual means of promoting virtue within England. And just as children learned well when encouraged to emulate their teachers and poorly when living in fear of the rod, so too would subjects best adopt habits of self-governance (collectively and individually) when ruled mildly.[158]

These beliefs on governance distinguished Penn from other earlier Quaker reformers. Authors such as Edward Billing, Edward Burrough, and Isaac Penington argued for reforms intended to check the influence of legal and political institutions on English subjects' rights, particularly with respect to religion; when Penington distinguished spiritual and civil modes of authority, he did so to limit the latter's reach. Penn, on the other hand, argued for government's productive power, blurring the line between spiritual and civil modes of authority as a means of expanding the power of the latter. He hoped to construct a government that would shape its subjects' civil conscience in much the same way that the Quaker Meeting shaped Friends' religious conscience. An ongoing dialogue between rulers and ruled—who were, after all, essentially one and the same—would serve to secure the allegiance of the governed, while virtuous civil officials could encourage right forms of conduct. Penn's experience in the Meeting accounted for the differences between his political views and those of other Friends; of all of the Quakers who wrote on politics, he played the greatest role in creating a Meeting structure in which elites spoke to and for the people.

Ruling according to the precepts Penn had outlined posed a major challenge, namely the problem of crafting a civic idiom that would effect the love and unity in the worldly realm that Christ's "unworldly way of speaking" had in the spiritual realm.[159] After all, Penn's notion that governments might produce virtue by crafting a collective civic discourse bore more than a slight resemblance to disciplinary processes within the Quaker Meeting—but his firm belief in religious toleration precluded the simple adoption of Quaker modes of ordering authority as a tool of governance. England's American colonies, however, might give Penn a chance to develop a novel civic culture. The establishment of a "New Planted Colony" always allowed those "Free People" who settled there to "supply what was defective in their own Government, or add some New Freedom to themselves."[160] Penn and his fellow Friends would get their opportunity to establish such a society in West Jersey, on the banks of the Delaware River in North America.

West Jersey: A Quaker Colonial Experiment

The founding of West Jersey is a history of titles rapidly changing hands, whether by force, grant, or purchase. On 29 August, 1664, Peter Stuyvesant, governor of New Netherlands, surrendered Fort New Amsterdam to a contingent of English warships under the command of Colonel John Nicolls. The colony fell into English hands without a shot being fired. The territory then came under the control of James Duke of York, brother of Charles II and heir to the English throne, by virtue of royal grant.[161] Concerned with ruling a province of such immense size and eager to reward his political allies, James then granted land south of the mouth of the Hudson River and east of the Delaware River to Sir John Berkeley and Sir George Carteret, forming the colony of Nova Caesaria, or New Jersey. The colony attracted little immigration before the Dutch reconquered and then returned it (in 1673 and 1674 respectively). The colony's slow growth convinced Berkeley to sell his portion of New Jersey to Friends John Fenwick and Edward Billing in March 1674, leading to the establishment of West Jersey later that year.[162]

Wrangling between Billing and Fenwick over title to the colony prevented the establishment of any formal colonial institutions, hindered settlement, and eventually necessitated the appointment of a group of trustees—one of whom was William Penn—to oversee West Jersey's management.[163] Their appointment brought a measure of stability; by 1676, over one hundred investors had purchased lands in West Jersey. Having thus secured (temporarily) the colony's financial basis, Billing, Fenwick, and the trustees then set about establishing its political foundations, drafting a provincial constitution. On 3 March 1677, the colony's rulers and shareholders signed the West Jersey Concessions and Agreements.

The Concessions and Agreements has earned a justified reputation among scholars as one of the most, if not *the* most, radical colonial constitutions ever enacted.[164] It embodied the legal and political reforms Quakers had championed since the Interregnum period. Though the exact authorship of the Concessions is unknown, its most radical elements addressed the main problems that had preoccupied Billing, Penn, and other Quaker authors in the 1650s.[165] It guaranteed a wide range of privileges and liberties, most significantly, the broadest protections for liberty of conscience in the Anglo-American world. Believing "That no men, nor number of men upon earth, hath power or authority to rule over men's consciences in religious matters," the authors decreed "that all and every such person and persons, may from time to time, and at all times, freely and fully have and enjoy his and their judgments, and the exercise of their consciences, in matters of religious worship throughout all the said province."[166] Nowhere else could Christians (of any type) and non-Christians (including atheists) live unmolested by the government.

The West Jersey constitution also protected colonists' political, economic, and legal privileges. It established a unicameral legislature composed of one hundred freeholders elected annually by the province's residents; this legislature was empowered to enact all laws "agreeable to the primitive antient and Fundamentall Laws of the nation of England" that did not violate the Concessions themselves. Moreover, to encourage broad participation in provincial governance, the Concessions established minimal property requirements for voting and office holding. It contained a variety of other provisions designed to check abuse of political authority, including limits on plural office holding, mandatory term rotation after each year in the assembly, and secret balloting in all provincial elections.[167]

The Concessions secured colonists' property rights by establishing strict terms by which the provincial government could survey settlers' lands, including a provision prohibiting the resurveying of any land after seven year's possession. It also stipulated that taxes on real or personal property could be levied only by the authority of the General Assembly and "only in [the] manner and for the good ends and uses" to which the Assembly had given its assent.[168] Here, too, the Concessions' authors placed sovereign authority in the hands of a popularly elected branch of government while nonetheless checking its powers.

Finally, the Concessions and Agreements enacted a wide range of reforms designed to mitigate the English legal system's worst abuses. It stipulated that all punishments (including fines) be commensurate with the severity of the crime committed, simultaneously reducing greatly the number of crimes punishable by corporal and capital punishment. It also eliminated debtor's prison, one of the banes of seventeenth-century Quakers' existence. The Concessions also facilitated broad legal participation. Court fees were eliminated and clients encouraged to plead their own cases. Juries possessed not only the authority to decide fact and law but also the power to override any action or ruling by the presiding judge they deemed inappropriate. The Concessions and Agreements, in essence, put every principle earlier Quaker reformers had advocated into practice.

British Friends, then, had understandably high hopes about the West Jersey settlement. Its founding offered Friends a safe haven at a moment when their sufferings at the hands of the English government seemed intolerable. The colony offered challenges as well as opportunities. In an epistle issued on 4 March 1677, George Fox warned, "My Dear Friends, in New Jersey, and you that go to New Jersey, My desire is, that you may all be kept in the Fear of God, . . . For many Eyes of other Governments or Colonies will be upon you; yea [even] the *Indians*, to see how you order your Lives and Conversations."[169]

This first Quaker colonial venture did not, unfortunately, proceed as planned. No sooner had the province's proprietors signed their constitution than they learned that their title to the western portion of New Jersey did not necessarily include the right to rule that territory, as New York governor Sir Edmund Andros steadfastly insisted that it remain under his jurisdiction. The issue was not settled conclusively until 1680, when the duke of York conceded the right of government. As a result, the radical system of self-rule outlined in the Concessions failed to materialize. With the validity of the Concessions in limbo, no elections were held before 1681; provincial governance during this interim period fell to nine commissioners, first appointed by the West Jersey trustees and later elected by its inhabitants.[170] By 1683, the unicameral assembly with sole power to draft and pass laws had been replaced by a bicameral system in which an appointed upper council proposed laws that the general assembly then approved.[171] Meanwhile, affairs between West Jersey settlers and Edward Billing (in whom the duke of York vested sole proprietorship in 1680) quickly degenerated as the latter sought ever-expanding powers as provincial governor—a post the 1677 Concessions did not provide for.[172] It was clear to any observer that West Jersey could never meet its founders' high expectations.

But William Penn soon found a chance to try again. On 1 June 1680, Penn petitioned Charles II "for a grant of a tract of land in America lying north of Maryland, on the east bounded with Delaware River, on the west limited as Maryland is, and northward to extend as far as plantable, which is altogether Indian."[173] Concerned with more pressing political matters, the Crown ignored the petition until October, when Penn's request was sent to the Lords of Trade and several other influential members of the government.[174] After approximately four months of deliberation, Charles approved Penn's request, granting him on 4 March 1681 a charter for an American colony across the Delaware Valley from West Jersey; the charter also gave him possession of the counties of Sussex, New Castle and Kent, established at the mouth of the Delaware river under the Duke of York's stewardship. The reasons for Charles's acquiescence are unclear—he may have been inclined to look favorably at Penn's request because granting it offered an opportunity to erase a £16,000 debt he owed the Quaker gentleman, to encourage emigration of England's most numerous and controversial dissenting sect, to ease the costs his brother James incurred administering the royal colony of New York, or to curry favor with London merchants sympathetic to Penn's commercial interests. Most likely he considered all these factors. In the end, Penn got his charter.

The colony on the Delaware River gave Penn an opportunity to create a society along the lines he had envisioned. It seems clear that, from its inception, Penn viewed his new province as different from other American settlements—even West Jersey. Writing to James Harrison on August 25, 1681, Penn described his hopes for the colony, discounting his own role in securing a charter from the Crown and attributing his success to God: "[I] owe it [more] to His hand and power than to any other way." Nor, Penn continued, had he obtained the colony for his own profit or glory: it existed as a testament to the glory of God. Penn expressed his ardent desire to "do that which may answer his Kind providence and serve his truth and people," so that the proprietor "may not be unworthy" of God's love. The New World offered an opportunity for more than personal fame. Penn hoped that, in Pennsylvania, "an example may be set up to the nations[;] there may be room there, though not here, for such an holy experiment."[175]

Pennsylvania, then, was intended to be the ultimate expression of Quaker values: a community of the "people of God," as Friends referred to themselves, living in his Light. Created through the Lord's "Kind providence," the colony existed for God's truth. If the example of Pennsylvania could convince those outside the Society to open themselves to the Light within, even better. Penn intended the colony to be a holy experiment in the truest seventeenth-century meaning of the word.[176] He saw it not as a trial to see whether such a community would succeed or fail (as in the modern sense of the word), for surely it would succeed. No, Penn meant for Pennsylvania to be a truly holy *experience*, a living, vibrant expression of Quaker principles—and, perhaps, something more. In writing to Thomas Janney four days before the letter to Harrison, Penn had expressed his belief that "God will plan[t] Americha & it shall have its day: the 5th kingdom or Gloryous day of [Jesus] Christ in us Reserved to the last dayes, may have the last parte of the world, the setting of the son or western world to shine in."[177] Perhaps Pennsylvania might become the seat of Christ's millennial reign.

Penn's expectations ran high as he planned the venture, hoping that Pennsylvania might indeed be the "Fifth Kingdom" of revelation. Pennsylvania afforded the opportunity to create in present time the visions of alternate futures Friends had dreamed of, to create their own orderly society. It was left to William Penn to envision what that society would look like.

PART II

Disorder

CHAPTER 2

William Penn Settles His Colony

The Problem of Legitimacy in Early Pennsylvania

THOUGH WILLIAM PENN may have been, as one of his biographers has asserted, a reckless and negligent businessman, he was, nonetheless, a businessman.[1] One of his chief concerns as he prepared to set sail across the Atlantic
in late 1681 was the advertising and promotion of Pennsylvania. Penn meant
to turn a profit on his colonial endeavor, hoping that the sale of choice
lands along the Delaware River would underwrite his financial support of the
Quaker movement in England and Ireland and his somewhat extravagant
lifestyle (though not necessarily in that order). To that end, he published in
1681 *Some Account of the Province of Pennsylvania*, a tract that described the
province, Penn's sense of who should emigrate to North America, and a list
of suggested supplies necessary for life in America.[2]

    Some Account offered a window onto the hopes, anxieties, and assump-
tions behind the founding of Pennsylvania. Penn acknowledged that some
English authors, fearing that emigration to America might weaken the nation, argued against overseas colonization. But he countered that the founding of Pennsylvania marked instead a moment of great historical import,
equal to the spread of Greek and Roman civilizations or the arrival of the
ancient Israelites in the Promised Land after forty years in the wilderness. Its
settlement would reverse the inevitable *"luxury and corruption of manners"*
and the addiction to *"pleasure* and *effeminacy"* that all nations suffered,
thereby strengthening England. It would also, he hoped, be a lodestone for
particularly virtuous men and women, serving as an example for reform in
England.[3]

For this, though, Penn needed a special type of settler. While the colony
needed tradesmen and mechanics, it also required

> *men of universal spirits* that have an eye to the good of posterity, and that
> both understand and delight to promote good discipline and just govern-
> ment among a plain and well intending people. Such persons may find
> *room in colonies for their good counsel and contrivance*, who are shut out
> from being of much use or service to great nations under settled cus-
> toms.[4]

Previous proponents of English colonization such as the famed Richard
Hakluyt thought America needed "stronge and lusty men" who could bear
arms against European or native invaders.[5] Penn, however, sought as settlers
the same kinds of men he believed responsible for the glory of the ancient
world: people worthy of esteem, leaders whom other colonists would emulate, individuals who embodied the spread of civilization to regions where
new customs and traditions could take root. Pennsylvania could become a
"nurser[y] of people" where virtue flowered, the model society he had described two years previous in his *Address to Protestants of all Perswasions*.[6]
While Penn stressed the difficulty of planting an American colony, even in
such a lustrous landscape, he framed its moral and spiritual rise as inevitable.
After all, as Penn had noted before, the settlers of any "New Planted Colony," as the "First and Corner Stones" of that society, determined the level
of harmony, liberty, and prosperity "their Posterity" would experience. In
England, the Saxons had left behind a set of customs and freedoms that
would later be inscribed in that country's Great Charter—the Magna Carta.[7]
Pennsylvania's "men of universal spirits" could surely do the same for their
progeny.

Some Account did more than simply reflect the proprietor's high hopes
for this enterprise. It also revealed the tensions and ambiguities inherent in
this particular utopian project. Penn knew that his colony would attract a
particular kind of public man who would act out of deference to a larger good
rather than his own self-interest. The responsibility for cultivating public life
in Pennsylvania would lie with a small group of "universal spirits," not with
the "plain" citizenry. But while he felt such men would "delight" in fostering
collective discipline, he did not specify how this process might operate in
practice, leaving unanswered such questions as how colonial leaders might be
identified, how the kinds of universal values he hoped to inculcate among

the citizenry might be defined, or how such values might be communicated to ordinary people.

The tract also hinted at potential conflicts between Penn's grand project and his immediate political reality. He told readers that Pennsylvania would be a new place, free of the "Debauchery in this Kingdom," while assuring them that the province would be firmly English. Pennsylvanians would enjoy "the rights and freedoms of *England* (*the best and largest in* Europe)" and their virtuous leaders would never act against their allegiance to England or deviate from its laws at any point.[8] But while he hoped that *Some Account* would convince those of "other Nations" to move to Pennsylvania where they might join English settlers and "many thousand *blacks* and *Indians*," he failed to specify how such a diverse group might be brought into the provincial "just government" he envisioned. He was, in other words, vague on both the nature of the creole colony he aimed to create in America—like the "mother country" but different, English but more than English—and the creolization process through which he would bring that colonial society into being.

Some Account revealed the cultural dimensions of the law Penn hoped to establish in America. It affords a view into what would be, in Penn's mind, law's time, law's space, and law's subject in Pennsylvania.[9] Penn's colony would become a new space outside Europe—geographically and culturally—where a different kind of citizen, "shut out" of the old, "great nations" across the Atlantic, could prosper. This colony, on the edges of England's Atlantic empire, would offer room within its boundaries for this type of citizen. The tract hinted at the central role religious toleration would play in Pennsylvania's development. Penn hoped that many of his fellow dissenters, disenfranchised and persecuted in Europe, might see themselves as the well-intentioned individuals shut out of political life that he wrote of. But it also illustrated the problems facing settlers as they embarked on this colonial endeavor, especially the tensions between tradition and innovation in the creation of a virtuous creole government and the difficulty of finding a universal language by which provincial leaders might communicate their authority to such a diverse population. In each case, the proprietor emphasized Pennsylvania's promise but not the very significant cultural work necessary to achieve it. He did not recognize the contradictions within his narrative. Indeed, admitting the promotion of discipline among Pennsylvanians as a potential problem would have sapped much of *Some Account*'s rhetorical power as a promotional document.

In this respect, the tract reflected the ambiguities and paradoxes in Penn's plans. Without any historical model to draw upon and unable to assume a cultural homogeneity among the citizenry, Penn and his fellow Quaker founders had to create the collective sense of the common good essential for the cultivation of provincial virtue and order. They found this task challenging from the province's inception. Moreover, their stated goals of protecting religious toleration and maintaining civic order frequently came into conflict, further complicating their attempts to legitimate provincial authority. Ultimately, provincial founders focused their efforts less on crafting a perfect legal code than on specifying the relationship between legal officers and citizens and the effects they hoped the administration of justice would produce. In essence, their efforts to legitimate their rule relied less on law than on legality, what Christopher L. Tomlins has described as the social, administrative, and disciplinary mechanisms through which governing bodies effect the law's authority. Not the body of timeless or universal principles the law is often purported to be, "legality, in contrast, is a condition with social and cultural existence; it has specificity, its effects can be measured, its incarnations investigated."[10] Penn and his fellow Quaker leaders did not believe process mattered more than product when it came to creating a creole society; they saw the creolization process as an integral part of the product.

Colonial leaders worked diligently during the early years of settlement to establish the foundations of Pennsylvania's civic order. This required delineating the modes through which certain legal principles would be enacted while defining the broader cultural significance these practices held. This colonial project spanned institutional boundaries and literary genres.[11] It involved multiple strands of rule making as colonizers crafted the constitutional and statutory laws that would govern the province and worked out the diplomatic accords that structured their relationship with the region's Indians. Pennsylvania's civic order was also, to some extent, a literary production. Provincial authors published various tracts to encourage settlement and investment in the colony, inspire spiritual development, educate residents on their civic liberties and obligations, or describe the cultural habits and practices of local Native Americans. These promotional, didactic, and ethnographic accounts described nascent structures of authority as part of a larger story about the colony's orderly development. Provincial elites intended all these various texts to work in tandem to buttress an institutional system that could effectively creolize new colonists. Aware of the novelty of their "Holy Experiment" and the problems cultural diversity posed, Pennsylvania's founders hoped that a carefully constructed, interactive culture of legality might create a virtuous civic homogeneity.

These plans rested on two unspoken and ultimately ill-founded assumptions. First, Penn hoped that a well-crafted constitution administered by a virtuous civic elite would successfully assimilate immigrants to his new American colony. Provincial leaders, in other words, would make the people they ruled more like themselves. But neither Penn nor his fellow founding Friends anticipated that the members of this Quaker ruling class might themselves change in their interactions with others. The former were supposed to creolize the latter, not vice versa. The collective failure to consider this possibility represented a crucial flaw in Pennsylvania's design.

Colonists' approach toward diplomacy proved similarly well-intentioned and flawed. In their dealings with Indians, Quakers focused on the relationship between discourse and power, both within Native American society and in colonial-Indian diplomacy. Friends believed they had found a people whose conceptions of piety and polity mirrored their own and that this similarity would allow them to incorporate Indians into the colonial legal order they sought to create. They failed to consider, however, that constructing a truly creole diplomatic discourse that Indians and colonziers each found legitimate would necessarily involve transformation and adaptation on both sides. Here, too, provincial founders based their colonial hopes on the notion that the settlement process would leave them untouched. The belief that they could creolize without being creolized represented a major crack in the foundation of Pennsylvania's civic order.

To "Preserve True Christian and Civill Liberty": Constituting Provincial Authority

William Penn's constitutions, drafted before he left England, did more than simply establish the province's governing institutions: they also outlined a general theory of governance that showed how specific applications of the law might create civic order out of colonial chaos, producing a common civic culture.[12] In many respects, they represented a concretization of the political philosophy he had developed throughout the 1670s.[13] Two texts, the "Fundamentall Constitutions of Pennsylvania" and the proposed provincial Frame of Government, both written in 1682, discussed the origins, necessity, and purpose of government itself. The concept of governance Penn articulated in these documents was notable in three respects.

First, Penn saw government as fundamentally a social institution, not a divine one. It consisted at its heart of "a Constitution of J[u]st laws, wisely Sett together for the well ordering of men in Society, to prevent Corruption or justly to Correct it." To be sure, he believed that government and religion served parallel ends. Government provided of a set of "external precepts" to discipline those who chose not to obey the "righteous law within" the hearts of all men and women.[14] But while religion "directly remove[d] the cause" of evil through its "free and mental" operations, government could merely "crush the effects of evil" through its "corporal and compulsive" operations.[15] It furthered "the virtue, peace, and prosperity of the people, to which all form and customs ought to yield" but could not express divine authority.[16] It existed by mutual consent of the governed, not by divine compact; government answered to divine authority only in the extent to which the people ruled wished that it would.

Penn believed that good government was contextual. He rejected contemporary notions that either history and custom on the one hand or reason on the other served as the only legitimate grounds on which fundamental law rested.[17] He admitted as much when he noted the difficulties in "fram[ing] a civil government that shall serve all places alike" and claimed that he steadfastly "refuse[d] the assistance that may be yielded from the wisdom of other governments, whether ancient or modern."[18] Penn even argued that the structure of a government mattered little when considering how best to balance freedom and order in a society: "any government is free where the laws rule, and people are a party to those laws," as such a people would never allow tyranny or oligarchy to take root. Moreover, the laws themselves mattered less than the characteristics of the magistrates and citizens who ruled and lived under them: "though good laws do well, good men do better; for good laws may want good men . . . but good men never want good laws nor suffer ill ones."[19]

Reflecting the more theoretical treatises he had written in England, Penn's constitutional writings emphasized the law's productive possibilities. Nearly all previous legislators and magistrates, he argued, had underestimated the relationship between law and order. Most commentators framed the law merely in terms of the repression of social corruption or disorder, a view he found thoroughly misguided. True, the law often operated through punishment and correction, "but that is only to evildoers; government in itself being otherwise as capable of kindness, goodness, and charity as a private society. They weakly err that think that there is no other use of government than correction, which is the coarsest part of it."[20] This illuminating passage showed the proprietor's belief in law's power. Essentially, he hoped that the law might ultimately be so powerful in its operations as to render itself unnecessary: it would transform its subjects into a citizenry whose moral discipline came from within. The limits of legal authority lay in the imagination of those who devised and executed it, with possibilities far greater than those errant thinkers who conceived of legal power merely as force had envisioned. Penn recognized, well ahead of other European jurists like Britain's famed William Blackstone, that the law's vast disciplinary potential law came not from its "coarsest," corrective applications but from its subtlest, productive ones.[21] Its power rested in its ability to produce good citizens who did not need correction.

Penn's faith in the power of law revealed the utopian dimensions of his colonial project. His belief that law might operate differently in America than it had in Europe, that it might reach its ultimate potential to cultivate civic virtue, reflected his belief that Pennsylvania *was* unprecedented in human history, a break from all "settled customs." Its novelty would allow those mechanisms for civic and moral progress to produce a new kind of citizen. The ratification of the Frame of Government of Pennsylvania in April 1683 allowed Penn to articulate this vision of colonial civic culture to prospective settlers.

Upon arrival in Pennsylvania in October 1682, Penn quickly went about founding his government and establishing peaceful diplomatic relations with the region's indigenous peoples.[22] The proprietor clashed with colonial settlers almost immediately, as they rejected the Frame he had drafted. Despite this initial conflict between Penn and the colonial settlers, however, the provincial government they agreed upon in 1683 hewed rather closely to the ideological vision he had expressed in his early constitutional drafts.[23] The 1683 Frame of Government reflected the tensions and contradictions in the Quaker colonial enterprise, establishing a government that facilitated broad political participation by giving the franchise to most white men while placing substantive political power in the hands of a few. The Frame reflected the English philosopher James Harrington's influence on Penn's political thought; it created two popularly elected branches of legislature, an Assembly and a smaller Provincial Council, composed of "persons of most note for their *Wisdom*, *Virtue*, and *Ability*," exactly the structure Harrington outlined in his treatise *Oceana*.[24] It gave the Council the sole power to initiate legislation, reducing the Assembly to the role of a plebiscite that voted the Council's proposals up or down. This meant that while provincial representatives may have embodied the voice of the people, Penn and his fellow legislators intended them to express this voice by assenting to the role of a notable few, not in initiating debate on their own.

Penn's critics at the time—and some historians since—have seen the concentration of legislative power in the hands of an elected upper house as an attempt to limit the people's ability to govern themselves. Fellow Quaker Benjamin Furly, for example, criticized Penn's decision to bar the Assembly from initiating legislation. Furly urged Penn to keep the legislative structure laid out in the "Fundamentall Constitutions," which gave the Assembly the sole power of drafting legislation and afforded the Provincial Council a merely advisory role.[25] Historian Gary B. Nash has concurred with Furly, finding that the revisions between the "Constitutions" and the 1682 and 1683 Frames were a concession to Penn's wealthy investors, who would not be pleased to settle in a province where the people had an appreciable amount of power: "Men of substance, upon whom [Penn] relied for leadership and financial backing, would not exchange carefully cultivated estates in England for the uncertainties of a proprietary wilderness unless they were promised far-reaching power."[26] The elevation of the Provincial Council's authority, then, might be seen as an effort to remove popular will significantly from the lawmaking process. But reducing Penn's political interests to his financial ones misses the similarity between the lines of authority prescribed in the 1683 Frame and Penn's larger political notion that good government produced civic virtue among rulers and ruled by binding them in a common legal culture.

The legislative structure delineated in the Frame reflected Penn's understanding of the function of colonial leadership and his conception of the role that popular will should play in government. Penn certainly shared the contemporary view that political leaders needed to embody an example for the governed to emulate. Civic order would collapse without leaders modeling virtuous behavior. As Penn reminded his provincial commissioners shortly after the colony's founding, "there can be no union, no comfortable society" without godly rulers.[27] Moreover, provincial government depended on its leaders' self-governance, so that the people might learn from their moral example.[28] A handful of wise men, exercising their authority judiciously, could help secure the credit, reputation, and prosperity of a province.[29] In many respects, Penn's vision of Provincial Councilors as exemplars and cultivators of civic virtue corresponded with the role that "weighty" Friends played in modeling and maintaining "Gospel Order" through Meeting discipline. In attempting to define the councilors' role, he applied Quaker modes of producing religious virtue to the political realm. He thought it important that provincial leaders see themselves not as distinct from the rest of the people but as part of the people; they could thus better guide the process through which provincial society could police itself. In the Meeting, Quaker ministers and elders uttered the Word to and for Friends at large. In Pennsylvania's government, the "good men" would ideally do the same.

Provincial political leaders would play an especially important function in Pennsylvania, where settlers found themselves in unfamiliar surroundings with unfamiliar people. Disorders, Penn noted, were common in "new and mix't colonies."[30] Aware, then, of the difficulties that diversity and dislocation might cause, Penn felt that provincial magistrates played the crucial role in helping immigrants acculturate to colonial society. Where his contemporaries spoke of the "seasoning" process as that period where immigrants adapted to an American natural environment, Penn used the same language to describe settlers' adaption to provincial culture. Here, leadership mattered: colonial elites, he informed the Provincial Council, were obliged "to be the lights & Salt of the Province; to direct & season thos[e] that are under you, by your good example." His fears of moral degeneracy among settlers made the Councilors' job even more important. Being "less under notice & so more left to themselves in the wilderness of America, than in thes[e] more planted & crowded parts of the world," the people "have more need to watch over themselves & become a law to themselves," requiring moral leaders to emulate.[31] Provincial officials thus became a critical part of the mechanism through which the colonial polity incorporated new settlers: civic leaders creolized new immigrants.

At the same time, Penn regarded the role of the Assembly as limited but not insignificant. The Assembly represented the voice of the people, the ordinary freeholders of Pennsylvania, but it possessed, in Penn's mind, a "Negative voice," not a "debateing, mending, or altering" one.[32] It served a juridical function, passing verdicts on the legislation initiated and debated by the Provincial Council. In describing its relation to the Council, he was adamant that the Assembly might not choose a speaker to address the Council but allowed that assemblymen "may as Juries Chuse a foreman to Speak for them" to the Council.[33] The Assembly was to function, in effect, as the

people's jury, passing verdicts on Council's efforts. Moreover, its pronouncements—unlike the Council's deliberations—were public events. At the end
of the colony's second legislative session, Penn moved to invite the people to
attend the first and last days of the Assembly's tenure so that they might
"come in and hear what shall be spoken unto them."[34] The proprietor saw
the Assembly's performative role as crucial to building a civic culture that
bound the people and their rulers together through public ritual. By splitting
the legislature into two elective houses, each with distinct roles, Penn mediated the voice of the people through multiple channels in the belief that
dispersing the people's authority throughout the legislative process might
increase, rather than decrease, its legitimating power. Here, too, Penn drew
upon Quaker models of church governance, expecting the people and their
Assembly to assent to the Council's wisdom just as monthly and quarterly
meetings wrote regular epistles affirming their support for the Yearly Meeting's leadership.

    This vision of colonial governance made several assumptions, notably
that Pennsylvanians could agree on which characteristics marked one as a
potential political leader and identify who among them best exemplified these
properties. Penn's vision also presumed that the people, having elected their
representative, would then deferentially consent to the Council's actions.[35] It
reflected Penn's and his fellow legislators' shared belief that orderly governance relied upon a common civic language even as it fostered discursive
unity.[36] It failed, however, to explain how that civic language might build
unity in a colonial settlement.

Legislating Community

If the Frame of Government failed to address this problem, Pennsylvania's
early legislation did. Law-makers spent most of their time crafting laws designed to create a legal speech community they hoped would produce common standards of socially appropriate speech.[37] Pressed to define the terms of
the civic speech community they hoped would stabilize provincial order,
legislators drew on a familiar example: the discursive practices that structured
discipline within the Quaker Meeting. In essence, they designed a system of
legal proscriptions and prescriptions they hoped would create a provincial
political speech economy modeled on Quaker culture. Meeting practices
would define the unofficial rules that determined who was allowed to speak

on civic topics and which speech patterns were considered legitimate or appropriate for provincial public discourse.[38] An examination of Pennsylvania's early statutory history shows legislators' efforts to construct authority and legitimacy through the regulation of interpersonal interactions between magistrates and citizens, particularly by granting magistrates broad powers to regulate their subjects' behavior, similar to those weighty Friends exercised within the Meeting against wayward Friends.[39] Believing that a carefully regulated system of legality could produce provincial civic unity, Pennsylvania's founders applied Quaker disciplinary practices to create an early legal culture distinctive within colonial British America.

Most of Pennsylvania's early legislative activity was concentrated in the first two years, before Penn's return to England in 1684.[40] In consultation with Governor Penn, the predominantly Quaker legislature passed over 150 laws in this time, a number that surpassed the government's legislative output between 1684 and 1699, when Penn returned to America.[41] The laws passed during the province's first years fell into several categories, including laws regulating and reforming legal proceedings, vice laws, and laws regulating public speech, all emphasizing the inclusiveness and authority of the legal system. They also reveal the ways in which Friends hoped to use colonial legalities to define the nature of citizenship in early Pennsylvania.

First, Penn and his legislators constructed a legal system that incorporated the reforms that many Friends in seventeenth-century England had championed.[42] Chief among these were the protection of liberty of conscience and a revamped penal code. Committed to creating a society in which God and Caesar might have their respective dues, the very first law the predominantly Quaker legislature passed in Pennsylvania was an act protecting liberty of conscience. It guaranteed that all "Who shall Confess and acknowledge one Almighty God, to be the Creator Upholder & Ruler of the World, And that professeth him or her self Obliged in Conscience to Live peaceably & justly, under the Civil government" should "freely & fully enjoy his or her Christian Liberty in that respect without any Interruption or reflection."[43]

Quaker legislators also established a penal code that emphasized reformation and restitution over punishment. A more humane penal code, they argued, could better achieve civil peace, conformity, and prosperity. They eliminated capital punishment, except for willful and premeditated murder; dramatically reduced the number of crimes for which corporal punishment could be used; and eliminated branding altogether. This emphasis distinguished them from efforts at legal reform in colonies like Massachusetts and

Connecticut, which actually increased the number of crimes punishable by death.[44] Pennsylvania's prisons became workhouses, so that laboring criminals could both repay their victims, and cultivate a sense of morality and industry through hard work. Provincial authorities disciplined criminal offenders differently from those in England. Rather than punishing individuals through confining or inflicting pain on criminal bodies, Pennsylvania's penal code forced the convicted to change their behavior. In essence, it attempted to shape criminals' interior "selves" through the forced embodiment of appropriate civic and social behaviors.

Quaker legislators also worked to facilitate legal participation among citizens, both by making the courts more accessible and extending the legal system's reach outside the court. Legislators mandated that all legal proceedings be in English "and in an ordinary and plain Character, that they may be easily read, and understood, and justice speedily administered." They also required the regular printing of provincial laws, so that everyone might have equal knowledge of them.[45] Both provisions mitigated the authority of specialized legal practitioners like judges and lawyers and thereby made the courts more amendable and responsive to ordinary litigants. Similarly, Quaker legislators took steps to make the law negotiable outside the courts, blurring the line between public authority and private life. Befitting a sect that emphasized plain and honest speaking and proscribed haggling, Pennsylvania's early laws mandated that all oral agreements be considered as binding as written contracts, under pain of twofold compensation to the aggrieved party if one side should break the deal. And in what many scholars have seen as Friends' most celebrated contribution to legal reform, provincial legislators passed laws to make the Quaker method of settling disputes legally, as well as religiously, authoritative. They empowered justices of the peace to settle out of court debt cases under forty shillings and decreed that three "peacemakers" be chosen in every county who would be empowered to pass legally valid judgments on all disputes they heard. This latter provision did more than give Quaker practices a legal sanction: it also broadened the ability of authorized individuals chosen by the government to act and speak with full legal legitimacy outside court, thus establishing a precedent for extending provincial legal authority into different social spaces and a variety of cultural domains.

Pennsylvania's simplified legal order reflected the conscious intent of its Quaker framers far more than it did the necessities of founding a new American society. Colonial courts exhibited a somewhat rude quality; the colonists' relative legal ignorance meant that legal systems throughout seventeenth-century North America were less formal and sophisticated than in England.[46] But as with their Puritan brethren in New England, the stripped-down nature of Quaker jurisprudence grew out of Friends' religious commitments. They picked and chose which English precedents they wished to import.[47]

Pennsylvania's founders also passed a series of vice laws designed to prohibit moral offenses so "That Loosness, irreligion & Atheism may not Creep in under pretense of Conscience." The first provincial legislature outlawed drunkenness under pain of fine or hard labor. In an attempt to curb sexual licentiousness, they also made it a crime to allow guests to become inebriated in one's house, under similar pain of fine or labor. The vice laws of Pennsylvania's first two legislatures showed a typically Quaker abstemiousness toward public amusements, proscribing the frequenting of "rude and riotous sports and practices as Prizes, Stage-plays, masques, Revels, Bull-Baitings, Cock-fightings, and such Like." Culprits were to be declared publicly by the court as "Breakers of the Peace" and fined twenty shillings or sentenced to ten days' hard labor—the same penalty as for assault and battery. Card playing, lotteries, dice, or, for that matter, any sports or games were outlawed as well.[48] Through their restriction of alternative public cultures and their use of exemplary punishments—such as public hard labor—in sanctioning offenders, these early vice laws maintained provincial morality by granting virtuous magistrates strict control over public discourse and behavior, albeit in a more humane, particularly Quaker way.

This flurry of legislative activity represented a rejection of English precedent. Judged by the number of statutes passed, early Quaker legislators focused most of their energy not on protecting liberty of conscience, legal reform, or regulating public morality—all topics close to Friends' hearts—but on regulating public and private discourse. Nearly half of the legislative output of Pennsylvania's first two sessions directly touched upon either prescription or proscription of speech acts. Similarly, legislators designed a number of other statutes to regulate different aspects of Pennsylvania's speech economy, such as those acts regarding the reputation of magistrates. Through these laws, as well as the adoption of broad powers for peacemakers and justices of the peace, Penn and his fellow Quaker legislators articulated a positive vision for Pennsylvania's legal order. They designed these laws to inculcate a system of Quaker morality without forcing Quaker worship upon the colony's residents.

Some of these laws dealt with simple restrictions on speech governing both the pragmatics and semantics of acceptable discourse. The penal code proscribed forms of speech in geographic space, governing where or when certain things could be uttered. It also regulated speech in social space, determining who could say certain things to whom, depending on the social status of the discussants. And it controlled speech in cultural space, exercising authority over what could be said. Various laws prohibited swearing, using the Lord's name in vain, or obscenity, whereas others forbade verbally menacing authority figures such as parents, masters, or magistrates. On a mundane level, the legislature mandated that the days of the week be called "first day," "second day," and so on in the Quaker style, although this law carried no fines. On a more serious level—at least in terms of the sanctions it commanded—the law commanded magistrates to fine "any person [who] shall speak, write, or act anything tending to Sedition or Disturbance of the Peace" at least twenty shillings, leaving open to magistrates exactly what this meant.[49]

These restrictions helped construct social hierarchies. In what may have been an attempt to protect the public reputation of the province's patriarchs, the legislature also proscribed spreading false news and scandalous reports and acting "Clamorous, Scolding, & Railing with [the] tongue," under pain of hard labor. Apparently concerned that this law did not sufficiently regulate unruly speech and protect masculine prerogative, the Assembly in 1683 strengthened it: "To the end that the Exorbitancy of the tongue may be bridled and Rebuked . . . every person Convicted before any Court or Magistrate for Rayling or Scolding; Shall Stand one whole hour in the most public place . . . with a Gagg in their mouth or pay five shillings." The province's regulation of public speech even threatened to infringe on Penn's most sacred principle: liberty of conscience. Although the Assembly allowed for "Conscientious persuasion or practice" of the Christian faith, "abusing or deriding" other faiths was considered slander and accordingly outlawed.[50]

Legislators also protected Pennsylvania's public institutions from derogation. They restricted civic participation to individuals of good character, by limiting officeholding and the franchise to adult Christians of good reputation.[51] During its first two sessions, the legislature passed laws to protect the authority (and public perceptions of authority) of legal and political institutions. It outlawed speaking against government officials for any reasons, under penalty of a twenty-shilling fine or ten days hard labor. This act meant that, in monetary terms at least, the good names of Pennsylvania's magistrates were four times as valuable as that of Jesus Christ.[52] Another statute protected the legal system itself by prohibiting "speak[ing] in Derogation of the Sentence or Judgment of any Court," with the penalty left solely to the judge's discretion."[53]

Pennsylvania's Quaker legislators did more than simply proscribe certain forms of speech. They also prescribed that a broad variety of actions be witnessed and made public by citizens. This included mandating witnesses to wills, gifts, and deeds, as well as the creation of a county registry to record these events. It also included injunctions to expose false witness. Two statutes required that perjurers "be publicly exposed as a false witness, never to be Credited again in any Court, or before any Magistrate in the said Province &c"and that those who lied outside court be fined.[54] The legislature likewise mandated that those found guilty of fraud have their names published as such and that disorderly people be publicly termed "Breakers of the Peace."[55] It repeatedly enacted laws requiring honest citizens to give public testimony exposing lawbreakers, checking illegality through publicity.

Even these speech prescriptions fell short of Penn's initial plans. The proprietor had hoped to include in the statutory code a provision that would prohibit all travelers from leaving the province "without publication being made thereof in the marketplace three weeks before, and certificate from some justice of the peace of his clearness with his neighbors," as if the world were a Quaker meeting. He had also tried to require that inn- and tavern keepers report the movement of outsiders into the province, requiring them to "give an account to the next justice of the peace in the place, of the name of every stranger and traveler that comes to the house from time to time after daylight."[56] Although these attempts to police the province's boundaries through the productive regulation of speech did not become law, they reveal how Penn thought that this colonial legal culture might offer inducements to virtuous citizenship as well as disincentives to bad civic action. Quaker rulers saw the regulation of interpersonal interactions, so that they might more closely resemble Quaker modes of conduct, as the key to maintaining provincial order.

These legal rules, then, were both creole and creolizing. A novel legal apparatus reflecting the influence of the English legal reform tradition and Quaker principles and practice, they worked to incorporate individuals of different national and religious backgrounds into a common civic community. Reflecting Quaker conceptions of the self, they encouraged the production of a particular form of civic personhood, granting individuals authority within the legal system while also placing obligations on them. Furthermore, the emphasis on labor as punishment emphasized moral reform and the development of an interior subjectivity—a disciplined self—rather than correction through punishment of the body. The vice laws, similarly, encouraged a care of the body, so that a particular type of pious, plain, public self might be deployed. Just as the disciplinary process within the Friends' Meeting structure provided a ritualized mechanism in which a social actor could learn and perform the role of a pious Quaker, so too the legal process provided a structure for learning and performing public, pious citizenship in America. Fusing legal procedures with Quaker disciplinary practices, Pennsylvania's early laws established a means by which provincial public authorities could cultivate a secularized, civic self within all Pennsylvania citizens, not just its Friends. Colonial civic practices worked in a Quaker idiom, with accents from other legal discourses.

But as the proposed provisions for reporting on the activities of traveling strangers reveals, Penn and his fellow Quaker founders recognized that they needed to do more than create a civic order among themselves. They also needed to find a way to deal with the outsiders in their midst, those of different civic persuasions living within and along their borders. The proprietor knew he had to address the status of the native peoples in the region and the several hundred Europeans—some English but mostly non-English— who had already colonized the Delaware Valley.[57] He affirmed his determination "not [to] usurp the right of any, or oppress his person." Indeed, Penn felt that he had been divinely ordained to end religious oppression in his colony: "God has furnished me with a better resolution, and has given me His grace to keep it."[58] Pennsylvania officials, following Penn's lead, worked more assiduously than any other Anglo-Americans to incorporate non-English residents.

Under William Penn's guidance, provincial authorities made active efforts to incorporate Swedes, Dutch, and Germans living within the colony into Pennsylvania's legal and political structure. Here, Pennsylvania stood at the forefront of efforts to assimilate foreigners into the English empire.[59] English law in the seventeenth century drew sharp distinctions between native-born English and "strangers" (as those born under a foreign government were called). The former were legally classified as subjects by virtue of their birth. They were assumed to have a perpetual, inalienable allegiance to the Crown of England and, in return, were protected by the fabled "rights of Englishmen," including the right to own property and pass it on to their heirs.

The legal condition of foreigners on English territory was much different, however. Aliens suffered several legal disabilities: they were unable to own property, hold any office, or bring any actions to law. Ultimately, aliens resided on English soil at the pleasure of the Crown and could be expelled from the realm at any time. Aliens might be incorporated into the English polity in two ways. First, they could be granted patents of denization by the Crown. Denizens occupied a civic middle ground between native-born subjects and aliens; they could legally own property and possessed other, selected, rights. But denizens could only pass their property on to their heirs in limited cases. Likewise, the children of denizens could, in some circumstances, be considered natural-born English subjects, but this was by no means universal. Denizens, too, ultimately resided in England at the Crown's pleasure. Subjectship was logically assumed to be inalienable and unconditional; denizen status, on the other hand, was conditional and could be revoked at any time. This possibility remained more theoretical than actual, as English jurists disagreed on what, exactly, were just grounds for revocation of a patent of denization. But it was clear to jurists, governmental officials, and "strangers" in seventeenth-century England that denization represented only a partial integration into English society.

Second, Parliament might pass acts of naturalization, which unconditionally and irrevocably incorporated foreign-born citizens into the English polity as subjects with rights equal to those of native-born Englishmen, but these were relatively rare and were private acts, covering only the persons specified in the individual act. The English government in the seventeenth century thus had no legal mechanism for the general or open-ended incorporation of foreigners into the English body politic. The process of naturalization was costly and time-consuming, further reducing its frequency. Foreign birth and English subjectship were, in nearly all cases, mutually exclusive; the "rights of Englishmen" were literally restricted.[60]

Penn vowed to break with this traditional approach toward alien residents in English territory for practical and idealistic reasons. On the practical side, he recognized the need to engender good will on the part of the Dutch, Finnish, and especially Swedish colonists who had lived in the Delaware Valley since 1638. To that end, he appointed the Swede Lasse Cock as his first Indian agent and also appointed several Swedes to official positions in Chester County, where most resided. Moreover, Penn had promoted Pennsylvania as a haven for religious dissenters of all nationalities and advertised the province in several languages. As a businessman, he could hardly afford the negative publicity that reports of English aggression against non-English settlers would bring. Penn similarly believed that his own private interests coincided with the greater good; anticipating the arguments of John Locke and later proponents of overseas expansion, he saw the naturalization of foreign subjects as a critical means of increasing the population of England's colonies—and thus critical to the expansion of England's power.[61]

On a more ideological level, Penn was committed to equal treatment toward settlers of all nationalities. Their behavior mattered; their ancestry did not. Writing to the European inhabitants of Pennsylvania, the proprietor promised that they would "live [as] a free and, if you will, a sober and industrious people."[62] Seeing civic virtue as an achieved, rather than in-born, attribute, he believed his colony could readily accommodate the incorporation of "strangers" through naturalization. Participation within a common legal structure might just as easily produce civic personhood among naturalized citizens as among native-born ones. Thus, while some English authors feared that overseas colonial ventures would weaken the nation by encouraging the naturalization of foreigners, Penn argued that the English incorporation of foreigners in their overseas colonies would civilize immigrants and strengthen the empire. The English, he wrote, would in their colonial efforts emulate the Romans who "moraliz'd the Manners of the Nations they subjected; so that they may have been rather said to conquer their Barbarity than Them."[63] It was simply a matter of finding the particular mechanisms of legality through which "strangers" might be transformed into civic participants.

The legislature passed an Act of Naturalization in its very first session, in December 1682. The Act showed Penn's understanding and concern over the issue of civic status and radically simplified naturalization procedures. It noted that that many current residents were not "free-men according to the acceptation of the Law of England," a fact that might be "injurious to the prosperity of this Province & territories thereof." The Act then declared that all foreigners or strangers residing in Pennsylvania who declared in open court their fidelity to the king of England and the proprietor William Penn "shall be held and reputed free-men of the province & Counties aforesaid, in as ample & full a Manner as any person residing therin." It also allowed any future foreigner residing in Pennsylvania to naturalize upon making a similar declaration in a county court and paying a twenty-shilling fee.[64] These efforts quickly bore fruit: Swedish residents immediately applied for naturalization, and their eager participation in provincial courts revealed that they found the legal system legitimate from the start.[65]

This process of naturalization was a radical departure from precedent both in England and its colonies. It greatly lowered the bar for entry into the polity as a naturalized subject. Even those colonies that had experimented with liberalizing naturalization procedures—both to encourage settlement and to deal with the presence of foreign residents in lands conquered from other European powers—had imposed more stringent requirements. In Jamaica, for example, conquered by England in 1655 and possessed of a small population of Spanish settlers, naturalized subjects were required to put up a £10 bond security and take an oath of allegiance, presumably as a hedge against the possibility that their declaration of allegiance was less than genuine.[66] Pennsylvania's Act, by contrast, relied upon the assumption that the declaration of faith and allegiance was genuine.

Pennsylvania alone created an open-ended process for naturalizing foreign settlers, instead of merely relying on case-by-case, private declarations or acts. In essence, this Act of Naturalization articulated a fungible conception of civic identity in which performative declarations of allegiance constructed subjectship. Penn, then, had laid out a bold vision for incorporating foreigners into Pennsylvania, one followed by other provincial leaders. His American colony had provided him the perfect opportunity to enact the theories about law, language, and civic unity he had developed over the previous decade. It seemed in its early years that he had succeed in creating a civic lingua franca that might form the basis for a later, more fully elaborated, creole civic culture that rejected the notion that civic authority belongs to any single group.

Indeed, some Friends expressed their concern that Pennsylvania would quickly be overrun by non-Quakers, ruining the colony as a safe haven for persecuted Friends. Mindful of these fears, Penn wrote to fellow Friend Jasper Batt in 1683 of his wish "that the entailment of the government of this province may be to David's stock, the tribe of Judah."[67] Penn intended that Quakers serve as Pennsylvania's ruling tribe, governing with special care over a province to which they had a collective proprietary right. Mindful of the persecution Friends had suffered in England and elsewhere, however, Penn did not intend Quakers to rule by force or exclusion. This criticism, he wrote Batt, "has been often flung at us, viz., if you Quakers had the power, none should have a part in the government but those of your own way."

No, the decision as to who would rule would be left to the freemen. But if Penn was not certain of Friends' power enduring after his death, he was clear that their divine authority to rule would endure, assuring Batt that "if these freemen and their heirs fear God, the entailment will be to David's stock."[68] An appropriately God-fearing populace, in Penn's view, would allow his tribe to rule in perpetuity. What he did not say was exactly how Pennsylvanians would maintain a balance between the civic openness he had designed and Quaker hegemony, an omission that mirrored his silence as to how the ruling elite he believed would "season" the colonists would resist being creolized themselves.

Promoting "Good Order": The Publication of Early Pennsylvania

The development of colonial society would rest on more than a complex system of legality, a fact that William Penn, his investors, and provincial leaders recognized. They knew that Pennsylvania's prosperity depended on continued settlement, which, in turn, required the heavy promotion of its reputation. It also required a unified civic purpose. To that end, Penn and various other authors published dozens of tracts during the province's first decade to advertise the benefits of migration to Pennsylvania and to cultivate collective order and identity within the province itself.

These two genres of writing aimed at multiple audiences and served multiple ends, but efforts at projecting an outward colonial image and at consolidating an internal civic culture were deeply intertwined. Those tracts extolling Pennsylvania's virtues and those exhorting order and discipline among the colonists frequently used the same language, described the same events, and focused on the same themes. At the same time, contrasting these two literatures reveals tensions, ambiguities, and anxieties within the larger project of the discursive construction of Pennsylvania. This fact should hardly be surprising in and of itself. Numerous scholars have analyzed with great precision the ways in which colonial authors in America struggled with anxieties over identity and authority, especially creole ones. Sensitive over having an inferior or secondary place in the empire, these writers feared that their spatial distance from the metropole signified a marked cultural difference as well.[69] The process took a different turn in Pennsylvania, however. There, provincial authors in the 1680s and early 1690s wrote not as a creole generation looking backward to understand their place in the provinces of an Atlantic empire but as a creolizing generation striving to establish a new society. Thus, the disjuncture between the commercial promotion of the colony abroad and the promotion of provincial unity at home stemmed less from general tensions all colonial or creole authors confronted than from the specific complications of the colonization process in Pennsylvania.

Promoters emphasized the order, stability, and productivity the province had achieved so quickly. They described Pennsylvania as a thriving province thanks to both natural fecundity and to good social order. Penn stressed "that the Earth is very fertile, and the Lord has done his part, if Man use but a moderate Dilligence."[70] He gave detailed instructions to prospective settlers to show that, with proper planning and management, they might turn a profit quickly in America.[71] Thomas Budd offered similar assessments of the province's agricultural prospects, predicting that Pennsylvania would soon produce wines superior to those made in France.[72] Promotional authors also praised Pennsylvania's rapidly growing population. "Philadelphia," one wrote, "daily increases in houses and inhabitants," while another wrote of the steady stream of ships arriving from England with eager settlers.[73] Many signs, then, pointed to Pennsylvania's productive and fruitful character and the possibilities it offered.

Promotional authors also stressed the province's orderly character. The establishment of good government in Pennsylvania, they argued, had produced unity and harmony among the peoples of the region. Penn celebrated the "Concord and Dispatch" with which early elected Assemblies conducted their business, informing his readers that over the first two years, "at least seventy Laws were past without one Dissent in any material thing."[74] By 1685, the government had, according to Penn, already achieved its principal aims, namely, "Duty to the King, the Preservation of Right to all, the suppression of Vice, and encouragement of Vertue and Arts; with Liberty to all People to worship Almighty God, according to their Faith and Perswasion."[75] Authors praised the province's laws to encourage their readers to settle there. Budd noted that certain fundamental laws protected property and religious conscience from government interference.[76] German Friend Francis Daniel Pastorius argued that the proprietor "ha[d] laid a good foundation for a righteous government" and that prospective immigrants should see the colony's "useful laws" as an inducement to settle.[77] Apparently, these efforts to publicize Pennsylvania's legal order had their desired effect. One of the proprietor's correspondents in Barbados informed him that the copies of the province's fundamental laws circulating in that colony delighted Friends and others sympathetic to Penn's colonial goals.[78]

Provincial governance also achieved an unprecedented unity among Pennsylvania's diverse settler population. Promotional reports noted both the political and cultural bonds that had formed in Pennsylvania. Pastorius, Penn, and Philip Ford (Penn's business secretary) wrote about the variety

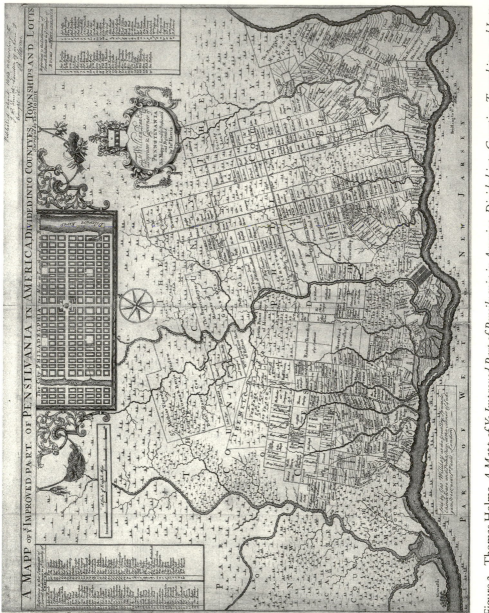

Figure 2. Thomas Holme, *A Mapp of Ye Improved Part of Pensilvania in America, Divided into Counties, Townships, and Lotts* (London: 1685). This is the earliest map of Pennsylvania. Courtesy of The Library Company of Philadelphia.

of settlers of different nationalities who had become naturalized subjects in Pennsylvania.[79] But the civil union they described seemed to show not simply a common legal status but the creation of a colonial people united behind Penn's government. They emphasized that the colony's previous residents welcomed Penn's rule from the start. One newspaper reported that the settlers greeted William Markham, Penn's lieutenant, with "a troop of horse and a company of foot, with drums beating and colors flying, having silk ensigns." The account pointedly noted that the companies were composed of "English, Dutch, and Swedes."[80]

Penn received a similar welcome. Ford informed his English audience that the province's non-English inhabitants were ecstatic when the proprietor arrived, greeting "him with great expressions of joy" as they watched his ship sail up the Delaware. Local Swedes informed Penn that they would "*Serve, Love and Obey him with all they had.*"[81] Within three years, Penn wrote, all ethnic and national differences had fallen away: the province's "French, Dutch, Germans, Swedes, Danes, Finns, Scotch, Irish, and English" lived as "one kind, and in once Place and under One Allegiance . . . like People of One Country, which Civil Union has had a considerable influence towards the prosperity of that place."[82]

Thus, the literature promoting Pennsylvania to investors and potential immigrants presented the province's productivity, civil unity, and harmony as of a piece. It described a colony that had experienced no growing pains, no economic dislocation, no conflict with Indians, and no political or cultural anxieties as an English colony in which non-English residents comprised, according to Penn's estimates, at least half the population.[83] Nor did these authors dwell on the colony's Quaker character, despite repeated mentions of the province's protections for freedom of conscience or Penn's status as the most visible Quaker politician in England. Only one tract narrated the establishment of Pennsylvania in overtly spiritual terms, casting the colony's settlement as a sign of God's favor toward Friends and the coming judgment against the "Emperours and Kings, Popes and Bishops" who would "vex the People of the Lord."[84] Through their focus on the province's laws and governance, these accounts both admitted and obscured the fact that civil union in Pennsylvania was a consciously constructed artifact. Certainly, the emphasis on the province's legal edifice as a selling point for prospective immigrants highlighted the novelty in Penn's colonial project, suggesting the very real possibility that the proprietor had managed to forge a civil union where one did not naturally exist. Pennsylvania's burgeoning growth was testament to Penn's success on this score.

At the same time, by presenting this transformation as a fait accompli, these tracts omitted any discussion of the process through which the creation of a single polity out of such diversity occurred. They left answered the question of how, exactly, the provincial government might achieve the unity it sought in the absence of the spontaneous celebrations that greeted Penn and Markham; indeed, they left the question unasked. Even the tantalizing account of the naturalization of Pennsylvania's "Foreigners" in Ford's *Vindication* was ambiguous on this score. By describing the end product but not the ritual itself, it left the performative meaning of these acts unclear. Did these naturalizations—which required affirming loyalty to proprietor and Crown—reflect or effect a transfer of civic allegiance? Could these declarations, which did not require an oath, be taken at face value?

Only one promotional publication, Budd's *Good Order Established in Pennsilvania & New-Jersey in America*, addressed these questions, thus casting the silences of the other tracts in greater relief. Budd outlined in detail a program for the construction of schools in the Delaware Valley to teach any "useful Art or Mystery" to children. He wanted to help all boys and girls, "the Children of poor People and the Children of *Indians*" included, receive a practical education that included reading, writing, arithmetic, and gender-specific trades.[85] This kind of instruction, he hoped, would facilitate the region's general economic development; it would also keep Pennsylvania's children from "running into that Excess of Riot and Wickedness" to which youth often succumbed.[86] Budd's *Good Order Established*, then, elaborated ways of establishing order in far greater detail than it described order already established.

Budd's *Good Order* was notable not merely because it was the only promotional tract to offer a plan for inculcating virtue and order among Pennsylvania's citizenry: it was also the only one of these tracts published in America—and the only one to admit the very real possibility of cultural and moral degeneration in the New World. (This was a major concern of Budd's that would lead to his joining a dissident faction of Quakers in the early 1690s.)[87] *Good Order* thus revealed the tensions between the literature directed at encouraging colonial settlement and investment "at home" in England and the literature directed at promoting spiritual, political, and moral order "at home" in Pennsylvania. Although both were interested in fostering colonial unity, promoters took for granted what American authors worked to achieve. When writing for a provincial audience, colonial authors concerned themselves with the coherence of colonial culture, but their interest lay in consolidating collective identities within a diverse population. During Pennsylvania's first decade, they wrote predominantly didactic literature, designed to educate settlers on basic spiritual and civic matters and thereby ease their incorporation into a common culture. Some writers based in Pennsylvania, of course, published for audiences on both sides of the Atlantic, but they addressed different concerns when writing for an American audience than when writing for an English one.

Some provincial authors used print to foster a Quaker identity among colonists. Quaker religious writings comprised the single largest genre of works published in the colony's first decade, accounting for nearly 40 percent of all titles issued on Pennsylvania's presses. Some of these were controversialist tracts, written in response to anti-Quaker authors elsewhere. Most, however, addressed local Friends, laying out the Society's basic principles and practices. Scottish Friend George Keith, who moved to Philadelphia in 1689, played the leading role, writing *A Plain Short Catechism for Children & Youth*, explaining to children that God's seed was present in every person and enjoining them to cultivate that seed through prayer and "holy conversation."[88] The Philadelphia Yearly Meeting printed a brief tract affirming belief in Christ and the Holy Trinity as well as their belief that salvation could only be achieved through grace, not works.[89] Another printed message from the Meeting laid out disciplinary procedures whereby Friends might "in Brotherly and Sisterly regard" help wayward Quakers back on the path of righteousness. It offered these restatements of Quaker faith and practice "in the Gospel-fellowship and Unity of the Ancient Truth,"[90] intending to strengthen Quaker identity through public instruction. Colonial Friends, the Meeting reminded its audience, had a special mission in America. Quakers had to watch "how we Live, how we rule, and how we Obey," as the eyes of the world were upon them. By building "*Zion*" in America, Pennsylvania Quakers could, through their example, inspire the peoples of the earth.[91]

But these early Quaker religious works took as their primary theme the immense danger that Pennsylvania presented for pious Friends. While Penn may have celebrated the union of diverse nationalities into a single political community, Pennsylvania Quakers worried about the possibility of mixing with non-Friends; though God had distributed his seed among the peoples of "all Nations," not all men and women cultivated it. Ultimately, individuals' behavior marked them as possessing either (in Keith's words) the "good seed" or the Evil seed." Those possessed of the good, or cultivated, seed, he intoned, must ensure they did not join with those with the evil, or uncultivated, seed. If they had done so unwittingly, they must cast out the bad seeds before it was too late.[92] Satan himself, the Meeting warned, had singled the Friends out for special scorn by convincing scandalous individuals to identify themselves falsely as Friends, thereby sullying the Society's name and reputation. Each Quaker must, therefore, "own none to be of our fellowship" who had not endured the "inward Circumcision" of conversion. The fact that conversion itself left no "outward Signs, Shadows, or Figur[e]s" greatly complicated but did not lessen the need to expel the unconverted from their midst.[93] Marriage posed a particular dilemma; John Willsford warned his audience that consorting with outsiders made as much sense as Christ associating with Belial. Moreover, Pennsylvania's tolerant religious atmosphere meant that Friends had "rather more need here than we had in our Native Land" to guard against comingling with "Canaanites," since "many come to our Meeting, and will get a Friend by the hand, that know little of Truth in our hearts." They otherwise ran the risk of becoming a "mixt People" and incurring the Lord's wrath. Thus, Pennsylvania's opportunities were at the same times its snares, with toleration and diversity increasing the chances that impurity would be introduced into Friends' "Sion on Earth."[94]

In this context, one of these early Quaker devotional texts seems particularly curious. Published by the Philadelphia Yearly Meeting under the title *A Loving Exhortation to Friends*, this tract was nominally a call maintain "that good Order established among us in our Native Land" during the movement's early years. As such, it offered both a description of disciplinary practices and an exhortation to parents to "frequently and faithfully mind one another of the Virtuous and Christian Education of your Youth and Children."[95] But though its authors claimed that they intended the tract merely to facilitate the transplantation of Quaker faith and practice overseas, it had a more ambivalent meaning. In fact, *A Loving Exhortation* offered more innovation than tradition, laying out the mechanics of church discipline in greater detail than English Friends ever had. Moreover, its invocation of gospel order in "our Native Land" conflated the practices of English, Irish, and Scottish Quakers when in fact they differed significantly. Scottish Friends, Barclay and Keith included, had been the first theoreticians of Quaker gospel order. Similarly, Irish Friends, contemporaries agreed, had achieved the greatest success in building local disciplinary networks to surveil and punish their unruly brethren and sistren and in their commitment to an ascetic code of conduct.[96] The "Native" lands that supposedly inspired the tract stood on the fringes of British Quakerism, away from the center of movement authority.

The authors of *A Loving Exhortation* thus posited a fictional unity among British Friends in the service of building a coherent provincial Quaker order, one whose existence Friends' other devotional literature belied. Their innovation lay in their creation of an imagined Old World tradition that could then be mobilized to develop new American practices.[97] The tract was a creole and creolizing artifact, something that only needed to be written—that could only be written—in a place where a stable Quaker community had not yet taken root.

Nor did early provincial print culture deal only with the construction of religious identities. Although only one political tract comparable to the Quaker Meeting's devotional literature appeared during the province's first decade, its subject matter, tone, and internal contradictions also highlighted the tensions between the cultural work done by Pennsylvania's promotional literature and its provincial literature. In 1687, William Penn wrote *The Excellent Priviledge of Liberty and Property*. This book reprinted the Magna Carta—the first copy published in North America—accompanied by Penn's commentary and other documents such as the Charter of Liberties, Penn's colonial charter, and the 1683 Frame of Government. The proprietor knew that many "in this part of the world" were "strangers . . . to the true understanding of that inestimable Inheritance that every Free-born Subject of England is Heir unto by Birth-Right" since the colony contained many non-English inhabitants. And as "this Country is not furnished with Law-Books," those non-English who naturalized needed a means of learning about their rights as newly minted subjects. Thus, Penn published *The Excellent Priviledge* to further civic education and political creolization in Pennsylvania. He hoped that reprinting and glossing these crucial texts in the English legal tradition might help Pennsylvanians "take up the good Example of our Ancestors" and further English ways in America.[98]

Penn's introduction to the book reiterated many of the central elements of his philosophy of governance. England, he wrote, differed from other European nations in that it was governed through the rule of law, with each subject possessing rights the monarch could not violate.[99] English subjects, he noted, lodged executive power with the monarch. The election of representatives to Parliament allowed the people a role, albeit an indirect one, in the creation of the law, while the right to trial by jury allowed them direct power over its enforcement. Thus, power could only be exercised through the consent of the freemen. The Magna Carta cataloged but did not grant these liberties. These rights were inherent and inalienable, unless an English subject were to be outlawed or exiled "according to the law of the land."[100]

Penn's celebration of English liberties raised the same types of questions regarding tradition and authority that the Quaker Meeting's publications did. The contradictions and silences in *The Excellent Priviledge* revealed the difficulties Pennsylvanians faced in constituting colonial authority. Penn's stated goal of educating his readers about the customs of "our Ancestors" seemed curious, especially given his ostensible audience: the province's large foreign-born population. This formulation suggested that the proprietor believed that naturalization had anglicized the colony's Swedes, Dutch, and German residents culturally as well as politically—an unlikely proposition in 1687. But the very fact that Penn felt the need to explain "our" constitutional heritage hinted at the worrisome possibility that Pennsylvania's English needed anglicization as well. He was correct in one important sense, for the colony lacked not only "Law Books" but a significant number of legal literates in general, defined as individuals trained in or having knowledge about the law.[101] To the extent to which the law played a crucial role in the transplantation of English culture overseas, then, Pennsylvanians' relative ignorance of these traditions seemingly made them poor agents of cultural transmission.[102]

The "curriculum" the proprietor included in *The Excellent Priviledge* evinced some very curious qualities as well. Penn cited numerous jurists for his explication of his ancestral legal traditions, most notably Sir Edward Coke, the foremost seventeenth-century scholar on common law. But Penn failed to note that the idea of "the law" in England was something of a fiction, as England possessed not a single legal system but a variety of overlapping legal systems, each of which claimed jurisdiction over different areas of life. This polyphonous quality was one of the most salient characteristics of English legal culture. Coke authored in the early seventeenth century extensive commentaries on the common law in an attempt to create a single, national legal order in England.[103] The legal past Penn wanted his readers to learn, then, never truly existed, in the sense he implied. Trained in the law and a defender of Quaker rights, Penn knew this.

The proprietor's extensive reliance on Coke's works was curious in another respect as well. That he cited Coke as an authority to claim that the English liberties he described were the inalienable birthright of free-born

English subjects was hardly surprising, given Coke's prominence. Penn remained silent, however, on the ways in which Coke's opinions on American colonists' legal status differed from his own. The famed jurist held that Englishmen born in the North American colonies were natural subjects of the Crown entitled to English rights while in England. But neither Parliament nor Crown accepted the validity of naturalizations granted outside England as valid within the realm; aliens could only obtain the same rights as the monarch's native-born subjects by Parliamentary act within England itself. The suggestion that there existed multiple classes of subjects throughout England's empire and that the Swedes, Finns, and Dutch under Penn's authority could become second-class subjects at best complicated the proprietor's visions of civic harmony and unity.[104]

Moreover, the proprietor's argument that the seminal constitutional documents included in *The Excellent Priviledge* merely made explicit traditional liberties that the English had always enjoyed *"per legem terre"*—by the law of the land—ignored the logical impossibility of claiming English rights on such customary grounds in a colony that had been in existence for less than a decade. Did these rights exist in a new land, in America? Penn's belief that they did agreed with the efforts of other colonial founders who wanted their settlers to enjoy "all [the] Liberties, Franchises, and Immunities" Englishmen at home possessed, but it stood at odds with leading English scholars who, following Coke, believed that while the common law and the rights guaranteed therein existed time out of mind, they "meddle with nothing that is done beyond the seas." Legislators and jurists, including Coke, had no qualms about protesting the arbitrary power of the Stuart monarchy while endorsing the imposition of martial law and the institution of chattel slavery in the seventeenth-century Chesapeake.[105] Common law rights did not, except in limited cases, travel with Englishmen overseas

Finally, Penn's efforts to legitimate provincial government by folding it into a grand tradition of English constitutionalism rested uneasily with the legal-reform project at the heart of Pennsylvania's legal structure. He may have wanted to convince his readers that the Frame of 1683 was the logical successor to the Magna Carta, but the reality was more complicated. After all, the proprietor's efforts to simplify legal codes and make the courts more accessible to all citizens represented a move away from common law traditions, not toward them. By basing his defense of English rights on such traditional authorities, he actually underscored the novelty and innovation of Pennsylvania's constitutional structure. Penn met his goal of creating a distinctive Quaker form of jurisprudence in Pennsylvania but offered a public explanation of Pennsylvania's legal heritage that denied this fact.

In Pennsylvania's first years, William Penn and other founding Friends created a remarkably coherent constitutional and legislative structure to promote colonial order. Reflecting Penn's belief in the positive power of government to produce civic virtue, he and his fellow legislators created a legal apparatus that sought to regulate the provincial speech economy as a means of producing order and unity. They established a set of rules to govern civic practice, which bore more than a family resemblance to Quaker disciplinary practices, intended to bind a diverse citizenry together. But while provincial founders had prescribed certain practices through which virtuous citizenship could be performed, they had not articulated a civic discourse that might give these practices an authoritative meaning. The tension between their efforts to solidify a Quaker identity and their efforts to create a colonial political identity that included non-Friends meant contradictions in their final product. Put more bluntly, when Quaker religious and political tracts spoke of defending "our" liberties or honoring "our" spiritual ancestors, what "we" were they writing about? Early promotional tracts written in England assumed a civic unity that had not been achieved. Penn and his fellow Quaker leaders had created a relatively brittle civic lingua franca: a set of creole civic practices and institutions well suited to incorporating outsiders into the colony but less well suited to respond to change from below. The process of creolization they envisioned went in one direction only. (After all, no one intended the "good men" enforcing Pennsylvania's "good laws" to follow the leadership of ordinary provincials or the province's leaders to be "seasoned" by those they led.) Political tensions over the next two decades would reveal the gap between the founders' hopes and Pennsylvania's reality, as colonists struggled not only over civic practices but the very meaning of provincial citizenship and authority itself.

Relations between colonists and Indians suffered from similar strains. Penn and other provincial leaders sought to establish peaceful relations with the indigenous inhabitants of the Delaware Valley. But these efforts foundered on their inability to decide whether they desired to incorporate Native Americans into the new polity they had formed. Did provincials hope to treat Indians as equal partners in a creole diplomacy or to creolize them so that they might become coparticipants in Pennsylvania's civic culture? This question hung over the misperceptions and miscommunications that characterized early negotiations.

"Unsavage Savages": Early Quaker Ethnology

Perhaps alone of all the founders of the British American colonies, William Penn resolved to treat the native peoples of North America with fairness and justice. He did his best to give Pennsylvania's Indians equality under the law, to purchase lands fairly from them, and to treat them peacefully. He found these actions rewarded at the province's inception and quickly "settled a firm & advantageous Correspondency" with the Lenape Indians who lived in what by mid-1683 had become southeastern Pennsylvania.[106] But Penn did not differ from his countrymen simply in his approach to purchasing land from the natives: he also showed a greater interest in indigenous culture. Penn praised the Lenape style of government, noting that Indian "Great Men" were singularly impressive for their "Wisdom, Truth, and Justice." This seemed an implicit comparison to Pennsylvania's "Great Men" in the Provincial Council and Assembly, who so frequently lacked such qualities.[107] Penn even learned what he believed to be the Lenape language, including a lengthy ethnographic description of Lenape words, grammar, and speech ways in his 1683 *Letter from William Penn to the Committee of the Free Society of Traders*. Penn found the Lenape "Language lofty, yet narrow, . . . in Signification full, like Short hand in writing; one word serveth in the place of three," suggesting a marvelous economy. It is difficult to imagine another colonial founder, Roger Williams excepted, taking such an interest in native culture and making such an effort to create a colonial relationship that was truly more dialogue than monologue.[108]

But this description oversimplifies reality. The key to this complication lay in Penn's description of the Lenape language itself: the reason it so resembled shorthand was that it *was* shorthand, of a sort. In his efforts to learn the Lenape language, Penn had learned instead "Pidgin Delaware," a simplified version of Lenape proper used by traders and diplomats.[109] Like all pidgins, this language had no native speakers and, although useful for trade and conducting some rudimentary land sales, was not adequate to the kind of cross-cultural exchange Penn hoped to foster, nor even the "Correspondency" he thought he had already achieved.

Penn's ability to mistake a pidgin dialect for a fully developed language ironically epitomized colonial-Indian relations during the province's first years. Established as the only Anglo-American colony with a truly pacifist Indian policy, Pennsylvania seemingly had a unique opportunity to build a truly "creole" civic culture. Quaker ethnographic writings and early diplomatic encounters provided ample testimony of provincial leaders' hopes in this respect. But these desires obscured the very real difficulties creating such a common culture entailed. Efforts to create a political unity between colonizers and Indians foundered in much the same way that Quaker plans for fostering civic homogeneity among Euro-Americans did. The realities of imperial politics and policy proved more durable than anticipated.

Befitting a people who made speech a central part of their own collective self-identity, Quaker ethnographers placed a great deal of emphasis on speech in their accounts of Delaware Valley Native Americans.[110] Indeed, speech ways provided the dominant lens through which Friends understood Indian culture. Pennsylvania Friends resembled other authors in this respect; nearly all Euro-American commentators on the New World discussed—often at great length—Indian languages and speech ways.[111] Colonial ethnographers and ethnologists collected and analyzed words and phrases from Indian languages, constructed dictionaries to make them comprehensible to European audiences, and used philological techniques to place these languages historically against European languages, ancient and modern.[112] The results of these studies led many, if not most, early modern European anthropologists to find Indian cultures temporally and spatially inferior to European cultures. To these writers, not only were American cultures completely different from European ones, but they also represented an earlier stage of historical development from which Europeans had long since emerged. Indians became, in this interpretation, both irrevocably "other" *and* a reflection of the "wild man" that dwelled in the past of European civilization.[113]

In the context of these developments in Euro-American concepts of history and anthropology, however, Quaker ethnographers stood apart from a colonial mainstream.[114] Describing the Lenape people as "unsavage savages," they wrote that they knew "not a Language spoken in Europe, that hath words of more sweetness or greatness, in Accent and Emphasis, than" the Lenape one.[115] Rather than constructing the Indians as antitheses of themselves, Quaker authors sought a kinship, even a partial identity, with them; they emphasized similarities between Quaker culture and the native cultures they encountered.[116] This effort focused most seriously on analyzing Indian speech ways, understanding patterns of negotiation in native political discussions, and assessing how styles of discourse and of political speech combined to define community and authority among native peoples. In other words, Quaker ethnographers studied in native cultures the same nexus of discourse and authority that the Friends in Pennsylvania employed in building their own nascent creolizing political speech community.

Quaker ethnography of Pennsylvania's native peoples focused on four major areas of Indian culture: language and discourse, government and political structure, customs and social life (including religion), and origins.[117] Like many other English ethnographers, Quaker writers included vocabularies with translations of common Lenape words. Readers of Penn's *Letter from William Penn to the Committee of the Society of Free Traders* (1683) would have learned to call their Lenape friends *Netap* and ask for *metse* (bread) to eat, while correspondents of Francis Daniel Pastorius would have been able to use such handy phrases as "Hittuck nipa" (There is a tree-full) and "Chingo metschi" (When do you journey again from this place?).[118] Penn and Pastorius also included comparisons of the Lenape language to European languages, ancient and modern. Penn noted that Lenape was "like the Hebrew," while Pastorius found it a "little inferior to the Italian in gravity" but nonetheless similar.[119] Evidently, both authors entertained notions of situating Lenape in a European cultural geography as well as a European conjectural history.

Yet these attempts at analyzing the Lenape language paled in comparison to similar attempts at linguistic analysis made by other English ethnographers. The energy expended by New Englanders John Eliot and Roger Williams in constructing Indian grammars and dictionaries, for example, far outstripped the haphazard discussions offered by Penn and Pastorius. Even William Wood and Thomas Hariot, who dealt with the same range of topics as Penn and Pastorius, gave the subject of Indian language and culture more attention than did their Quaker counterparts.[120] In comparison to the work of other English ethnographers—let alone those of French and Spanish authors in other parts of the Americas[121]—these early Quaker discussions look perfunctory indeed.

While Quaker ethnographers showed relatively little interest in Indian languages, though, they showed great interest in Indian discourse—the ways in which Indians actually spoke. In other words, Quaker ethnographers dealt far less with that they said than how they said it. Penn's, Pastorius's, and Thomas Budd's discussions of Delaware Valley Indians all included extensive descriptions of native speech acts. Penn noted that the Lenape "do speak little, but fervently, and with Elegancy: I have never seen more natural Sagacity." Conversation among the Lenape, he argued, relied less on the words themselves than on the performance of and the relationship between speaker and hearer. The meaning of their "lofty, yet narrow" language derived not from the spoken words themselves but was largely "supplied by the Under-standing of the Hearer."[122] Pastorius argued that the Lenape "neither curse nor swear" and were a people "serious and of few words, and are amazed when they perceive so much unnecessary chatter, as well as other foolish behavior, on the part of Christians."[123] Recording the words of Ockanichon, a dying Lenape from Burlington in West Jersey, Thomas Budd noted the sachem's plea to his family "to be plain and fair with all, Indians and Chris-tians."[124] Emphasizing either the plainness and simplicity or the sincerity of Lenape speech, Quaker authors saw in Pennsylvania's Indians a people whose speech ways bore a remarkable resemblance to their own.

Pennsylvania Quakers paid particular interest in the relationship between speech ways and order in Indian life. Penn noted the importance of silence in Lenape society. Budd similarly transcribed Ockanichon's reminder that "when Speeches are made, do not thou speak first, but let all speak before thee." Moreover, "in their publick meetings of Business, they have excellent Order, one speaking after another, and while one is speaking all the rest keep silent, and do not so much as whisper one to the other."[125] Writing of one of his initial diplomatic meetings with the Lenape, Penn described the great council, "consist[ing] of all the Old and wise men of [the] Nation," which was convened to determine the community's position on political issues and authorize sachems and diplomats to act on the community's behalf. Political action did not reflect the will of any one leader. "'Tis admirable to consider," Penn continued, "how Powerful the Kings are, and yet how they move by the Breath of their People." This consensus came only slowly, as "it was the Indian custom to deliberate, and take up much time in council, before they resolve."[126] In their ethnographers' eyes, Lenape patterns of negotiation and consensus building resembled the ideal to which Quaker religious meetings and gatherings of the Quaker-led Assembly should aspire.

Quakers' appreciation for Lenape culture extended beyond their praise for its political style. Friends interpreted many aspects of Lenape culture as indicative of the Indians' humility and natural spirituality. Penn, meanwhile, found the Lenape Indians exemplars of the material frugality that he and other Friends had championed in their attacks on worldly vanity and con-sumption in England: "They care for little, because they want but little; . . . if they are ignorant of our Pleasures, they are also free from our Pains."[127] Pastorius, likewise, thought that the Lenape Indians knew "nothing of the pride of life, and of the fashions in clothes to which we cling so closely" and were "temperate in their food and drink." He also found local Indians "much averse to war and the shedding of human blood, and would far rather be at peace with all men. . . . In my ten years of residence here I have never heard that they have attempted to do violence to anyone, far less murdered anyone, although they have had frequent opportunity to do so."[128]

These Quaker authors saw Indian humility, simplicity, frugality, and pacifism as not merely analogous but homologous to these same behaviors in Friends. In each case, these actions manifested inward piety outwardly. Penn emphasized that while "these poor People are under a dark Night in things relating to Religion . . . yet they believe in a God and Immortality, without the help of Metaphysicks." Just as his earliest entreaties to the Lenape had emphasized that Quaker and Indian worshipped the same "great God," so too did his discussion of their religion stress its Quaker-like aspects.[129] Even Friends' discussions of the Lenapes' origins seemed to highlight the affinities between themselves and Indians. While Pennsylvania's Quakers were hardly alone in theorizing that local Indians were the lost Tribe of Israel,[130] this claim took on a different valence when delivered by a Christian sect that presented itself as ancient Israelites returned to create a New Jerusalem on earth.[131] Hence, rather than appearing as a savage antecedent to European civility, Pennsylvania's Native Americans seemed to their ethnographers the embodiment of the primitive state these Quakers hoped to achieve.[132]

Early Quaker ethnography, then, revealed quite a bit about the relationship Friends perceived between language and cultures and about the importance of that relationship in constructing a moral, ordered community. In the Lenape Indians, Friends saw not only a society notable for its level of consensus; they also saw a society in which plain and orderly discourse offered proof of the inner piety of individual Lenapes while the self-regulation of speech and conduct provided the means through which Lenape self and character were shaped. Lenape discourse, like Quaker discourse, both constituted and reflected proper order. These Quaker authors drew no definitive religious, cultural, moral, political, or discursive boundaries between their society and Indian society. Thus, rather than locating themselves within a core of European civilization confronting natives relegated to a savage periphery, these writers positioned both newcomer and native within a common discursive and cultural space. They saw in their neighbors a people with similar methods of constructing public order, which in their minds explained the harmonious nature of Quaker-Indian relations. These Friends felt that shared conceptions and performances of discourse, self, and community would provide the basis for stable public discussions between colonizers and natives, much as they believed that the creation of an orderly provincial speech economy would breed civic comity among Euro-Pennsylvanians.[133] The major work involved maintaining these shared perceptions between those on the colonial frontier and those at home.

But this Quaker interpretation of Indian culture through speech ways was as problematic as it was well intentioned. The fact that Quaker musings on the relationship between Lenape language and culture relied on an analysis of the Lenape pidgin rendered them substantively flawed. More seriously, in mistaking a pidgin for a fully developed language, Quaker authors proved themselves unable to distinguish a simplified form of Lenape produced to deal with outsiders from the real thing, revealing limitations in their ability to build real and long-lasting bridges between English and Indian cultures. How could they create a creole culture that incorporated English and Lenape elements if they could not distinguish the Lenape language from the Lenape pidgin? Finally, their exclusive focus on a single Indian group blinded them to the reality of the region's changing demographics, something that would greatly complicate Quaker efforts to build political and cultural alliances with indigenous peoples in the region over the coming years.[134]

In many respects, these authors' efforts acted merely as an ethnographic analogue to their early attempts to publicize Pennsylvania: most of the same men had written promotional accounts of the colony, oftentimes in the same publications. By making a simplified but celebrated form of Lenape society stand in for the diverse but contentious reality of native life on Pennsylvania's borders during this period, they had envisioned the same "order," imaginary though it may have been, on Pennsylvania's frontier that they presumed existed in the colony's core. Penn had desperately wanted to enter into a cultural dialogue with Pennsylvania's native peoples, using words rather than arms to settle the colony. To that end, he and his fellow Quakers had anthropologically created Indians they could talk to.

To "Make No Differences":
Incorporating Indians into Colonial Rule

Penn had been determined from the start to break with previous English practice toward indigenous peoples and pursue what he felt was a more tolerant and Christian policy. Before his departure from England, he sent a letter to local Indians stating that with the law "written in his heart," he fervently hoped to end the "unkindness and injustice that has been too much exercised towards [Indians] by the people of these parts of the world."[135] Penn's insistent stance that his province have a just policy toward Native Americans represented as radical a break with English colonial traditions as his attitudes on the naturalization of European foreigners. He wanted all government officials to "Be tender of offending the Indians" and hoped that this respectful treatment might help native peoples "see that we have their good in our eye, equal with our own interest."[136]

Moreover, Penn saw the Indian governments in the Delaware Valley as the sovereign entities in the region and believed that his colony could only be legitimately planted if he purchased its land from the original owners. As he explained to William Markham, his cousin and agent in Pennsylvania, "the law of all nations" held that "whosoever buys anything of the true owners becomes rightful owner of that which he bought." Indian claims to ownership, Penn argued, could hardly be dismissed as somehow inferior to European claims, as they were the "natural Lords of the Soil," with claims to nationhood that equaled those of any European country. Pennsylvanians were thus obligated to secure legal title from them before settlement. Contrasting the Dutch approach to colonization in the region to that of English proprietors such as Maryland's Lord Baltimore, Penn noted that while the Dutch had proceeded appropriately by securing "the Natives Right, of whom they fairly purchased it," Baltimore had done little to demonstrate his ownership of the land according to either civil law or the law of nations.[137] Penn made clear in his instructions to Markham and his other deputies to determine which Indian nations owned the land around the Delaware River and "to buy [the] land of the true owners."[138]

Most English authors, however, justified overseas colonization in very different terms. Through the sixteenth and beginning of the seventeenth centuries, English colonizers followed the legal formula, contained in papal bulls of donation that legitimated Spanish colonization as the just conquest of infidel peoples. Patents to John Cabot in 1496, Sir Humphrey Gilbert in 1578, and Walter Raleigh in 1584, for example, authorized their respective enterprises to "conquer and possess" any territory unsettled by Christians, repeating the language of Alexander VI's grant to Spain almost exactly.[139] English colonial promoters and apologists ultimately found this legitimation of colonization unsatisfying for two reasons. First, given the imperial rivalry between Protestant England and Catholic Spain, justifications for colonization grounded in papal declarations seemed inappropriate. Second, most jurists subscribed to the constitutional doctrine that a conquered people retained their legal and political traditions after conquest, a position consistent with the traditional view that English common law extended back before the Norman Conquest of the Saxons; Penn himself drew on this argument at length in his attacks on the established church.[140] Justifying colonial settlement and the extension of English authority into America through conquest would have meant adopting a legal doctrine that, if applied to England itself, would have invalidated the common law in 1066.[141]

Thus, by the middle of the seventeenth century, some English authors had begun to legitimate their overseas expansion in different terms. Beginning in the 1620s, they justified settlement in North America by the doctrine of *res nullius*, the legal concept that "empty things," including unoccupied land, possessed no owner until affirmatively claimed. North America, they argued, had no owners because the Indians native to the region had failed to develop or improve the land, thereby taking possession of it. Since the Indians had not claimed ownership of the land, English settlement could not be logically considered "dispossession." Indeed, English colonization was, from this perspective, a positive good since the colonists intended to develop the land agriculturally, rather than allowing it to lay fallow as "waste."[142]

John Locke expressed this view most fully in his *Second Treatise on Government*. Writing that "thus in the beginning, all the World was *America*," Locke used Indian societies in North America as the prototypical example of peoples in a state of nature without a concept of private property.[143] Moreover, since Locke viewed the protection of property as one of the primary reasons to form a government, his characterization of Indian society as lacking property meant that Native Americans were unable to form governments as well. When Locke wrote of "vacant places of *America*,"[144] he referred both to its unsettled character and to the lack of any sovereign authority over the land. Describing the implications of these theories on actual colonial efforts, Richard Tuck has written that colonizers' "practice of buying land in order to indemnify themselves against the claims of the native rulers was thus, on Locke's account, illogical and unnecessary."[145]

Through both statutes and treaties, however, colonial leaders in Pennsylvania pursued an alternate path in their relations with Indians. Under Penn's guidance, provincial legislators passed three laws in 1682 and 1683 designed specifically to protect Indians from colonial encroachment. First, they banned the sale of liquor to Indians. Second, they prohibited private individuals from purchasing Indian land without the proprietor's assent. Most interestingly, they also established—at Penn's behest—a mixed-jury system to deal with crimes of "international law." Having earlier insisted to his First Purchasers that Indians would be protected by English law, Penn initiated a law to secure this in 1683. Intended to deal with situations where an Englishman committed a crime against an Indian (or vice versa), this law decreed that if any Indian committed a crime against an Englishman, "Notice shall be given to the king of the Indians, that he relates to, that the offender be brought to triall, And shall be tried by six of the freedman of the same county where the Abuse was Committed, and six of the Indians that are Nearest to the place." And if a European settler harmed an Indian, colonial officers would assemble a similarly mixed jury to try him or her in an English court, with a provision that "the kind to whom such Indians doth belong shall have notice thereof, That he may be present and see justice done on both sides." Juries, of course, would draw upon English law as they dealt out appropriate punishments.[146]

More critical in defining the legal relationship between Penn's colonial project and indigenous peoples were the treaties negotiated between provincial officials and local Indians. Though these hardly amounted to the "Great Treaty" that later artists would commemorate, Penn and his agents secured land claims for Pennsylvania through a series of negotiations from 1681 to 1683. These negotiations set the colony's geographic boundaries, marking off territory in what would become Philadelphia, Bucks, and Chester counties.[147] They also defined the social boundaries between natives and colonists, although only in a cursory way. In contrast with the legislature in its efforts to restrict sailors' abilities to taint, tempt, or trick Pennsylvania's citizens, treaty negotiators showed no concern with Indians' traveling freely throughout the colony. A treaty at Lasse Cock's house signed on August 1, 1682, for example, affirmed natives' rights to pass "without molestation . . . quietly among us" as they had done. The Lenape who agreed to the treaty also affirmed "That they [would] make no differences between the Quakers and English" and themselves.[148] The provincial government, then, established semipermeable boundaries between Indian and colonial society, regulating movement in one direction but not the other. In making provisions for a mixed-jury system, provincial legislators failed to establish clear legal boundaries between Pennsylvania and Indian country. Thus, the outer limits of colonial sovereignty were—at least in this initial conception—to be marked not by fences, boundary lines, or fixed borders but by legal dialogues between colonists and Indians.[149]

Penn's Indian policies, then, aimed in many respects to treat Indians as

Figure 3. Great Belt of Wampum, Photograph, Society Photograph Collection (Box.FF §8.1). This belt commemorates William Penn's treaties with the Lenape Indians. Though scholars believe that the belt dates to the seventeenth century, the precise date of its production is unknown. Courtesy of the Historical Society of Pennsylvania.

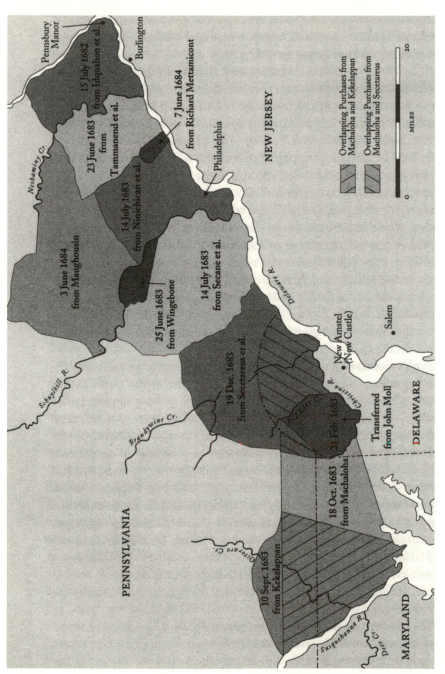

Figure 4. Map of William Penn's Land Purchases, 1682–84. Reproduced from *The Papers of William Penn* by Dunn and Dunn (1981–86), 2: 491, with revisions by Louis Waddell. Reprinted with permission of the University of Pennsylvania Press.

equals. Having adopted the stance that local Indian polities were sovereign nations, Penn endeavored to treat them with justice according to the established law of nations. He rejected *res nullius* arguments used to deny Indian ownership or authority over their own lands and set up mechanisms—such as the mixed-jury system—through which a cross-cultural system of justice could be established, if necessary. Given Penn's own advocacy of jurors' authority, his willingness to empower Indians as potential jurors over English defendants made a strong statement about his belief in their capacity as civic actors within a colonial setting. At the same time, however, his approach to treating Indians as equals implicitly incorporated them into an English system of legality rather than creating a truly creole one. Penn also assumed a unified Indian sovereignty that, in fact, did not exist. Lenape tribal governance was far more decentralized than Penn assumed: there were no "Kings of the Indians" who had authority over all the villages in the region and with whom one could negotiate as such.[150] Nor did Lenape sachems wield authority over the non-Lenape peoples in eastern Pennsylvania, whose numbers began to grow in the 1690s.

Thus, Penn's policies toward the Indians contained the potential for profound misunderstandings, largely because the cultural dialogues Penn envisioned leading to justice for both sides ran the risk of becoming merely monologues. To use another linguistic metaphor, the legal "pidgin" Penn envisioned would most certainly be organized around English grammatical rules, not Indian ones. Finally, his presumption of a single "Indian" cultural, political, and legal authority revealed that he did, on some level, see the Indians as outsiders within his multiethnic colony. This stance, while well intentioned, made it easy to envision Natives as a potentially dangerous "other" who could not be assimilated into colonial society.

Early colonial promoters praised the peaceful relationship between colonists and Indians. Nicholas More noted that the colonists' purchasing legal title to the land from Indian leaders went smoothly and affirmed the great affection the natives had for Penn.[151] Penn claimed that local sachems had pledged to "Love the Christians, and particularly live in Peace with me, and the People under my Government."[152] Previous European settlers, they argued, had earned Indian enmity by treating them with disdain. Associating with these "so-called Christians" had corrupted the Indians, rendering them "crafty and deceitful."[153] But, Thomas Paschall wrote, the Indians "live much better since the English came . . . many of them begin to speake English, I have heard one say *Swead no good, Dutch man no good,* but *Englishman good.*[154] Colonists' efforts to treat Indians with "justice gains and aws them," so much that, according to the proprietor, the Natives agreed to live by colonial laws and "submit to be punished by them" should they break them.[155]

But the harmony between colonizers and Indians provincial ethnographers trumpeted was as ephemeral as the unity celebrated in the self-promotional tracts. To be sure, they reflected colonial realities, at least to a point; Penn had laid a solid foundation for a peaceful relationship between his colony and local Native Americans, just as he and his fellow legislators had created a workable legislative framework capable of bringing Swedish, Finnish, and German "strangers" into provincial civic society. But they did so only to a point. Subsequent negotiations between provincial and Indian diplomats would demonstrate how frequently political interest trumped intention when ideals and reality came into conflict.

William Penn, in conjunction with other Quaker leaders, accomplished an astonishing amount during Pennsylvania's first years. Most notably, he constructed a series of procedures for incorporating newcomers into the colonial system he had established. Furthermore, Penn was prescient enough to realize that this process would require more than just the creation of rules to govern the colony. Settlers needed to buy into the colonial order he had created. The range of didactic literature provincial leaders produced sought to accept the colonial order as legitimate. Penn desired his people to follow the legal and cultural prescriptions Pennsylvania's leaders established. But more than that, he wanted them to want to follow the rules. He also hoped that his good intensions and good behavior toward the colony's Native Americans would convince them to welcome the Europeans who settled among them.

But Penn had created guiding rules, not fitting ones. He well understood the productive role governance played in creolizing settlers. Neither he nor his fellow provincial founders, however, stressed the need to create social rules adapted to the particular colonial situation in which they found themselves. This approach bespoke a certain inflexibility. Optimistic about their utopia on the Delaware, Quaker leaders seemed unwilling to acknowledge a crucial fact. Despite their best efforts to explain the meaning of the civic order they had created, they could not control how ordinary colonists performed the roles they prescribed. Much to Penn's chagrin, provincial settlers constantly made and remade their civic identities during the province's next dozen years. With each performance, they redefined what it meant to be an Englishman and to be a Quaker in America.

CHAPTER 3

Words and Things

Contesting Civic Identity in Early Pennsylvania

FROM MAY TO August 1685, William Penn sent a series of letters to Pennsylvania conveying his increasing frustration at the course of events in his American colony. They addressed three major themes. First, he worried about the growing reputation of lawlessness in the colony, noting the "great complaints" he had heard against the "Court of Philadelphia" regarding the adjudication of some controversial cases. "Such rumors," he wrote, "doe mightily disserve the province" and damage its reputation in England among potential investors.[1] Penn also expressed concern about reports emerging of scandalous behavior among leading Friends, including an unnamed "business" involving John Songhurst that was garnering public attention. Here, too, he feared his correspondents insufficiently cognizant of the dangers of allowing such news to spread, writing, "Dear Friends, no good is got by such publick righteousness, unless the evil be so too."[2] The airing of Quaker dirty laundry in public—especially when so many leaders within the Quaker Meeting also served as leading political figures—benefited no one; "publick righteousness" thus potentially threatened the legitimacy of Pennsylvania's political leadership. The proprietor worried most of all about conflict in the colony's governing institutions. Though "I am sorry at heart for yr Anemositys," he implored his correspondents "for the love of god, me & the poor Country, be not so Governmentish, so Noisy & open in yr dissatisfactions."[3]

Penn's laments in summer 1685 comprised only part of a longer litany of complaints about his colonists' unruliness. Nor were these reports inaccurate. Provincial politicians spent a seemingly inordinate amount of time arguing over procedural details great and small: questioning whether legislation had been enacted properly, debating who had the authority to dissolve the legislature at the end of each session, and challenging the authenticity of official commissions. Nor was it strange that these reports reached Penn in England, for Pennsylvanians seldom felt shy about airing their grievances with the legislature, the courts, or any other provincial institutions. They wrote letters, loudly threatened in taverns to overthrow the proprietary government, or used a position on the county bench to denounce enemies. Indeed, given the regularity with which Pennsylvanians turned opportunities to speak publicly into opportunities for public slander, it would have been surprising had news of this behavior *not* reached Penn. Provincials, especially Quakers, seemed petty, almost jealous, of any attempt on Penn's part to exert his proprietary authority. When Penn's appointed deputy governor John Blackwell arrived in Philadelphia in December 1688, for example, not a single member of the Provincial Council came out to greet him, refusing the highest official in the land even the most elementary civility. A session of the Council ground to a halt two months later when some "members declared themselves offended with [Blackwell's] words and Carriage," accusing him of inflating his own authority.[4]

To modern eyes, this behavior appears strange. These Friends seem consumed with procedure at the expense of results, with gossip at the expense of actual governance. From one angle, early Pennsylvania's governing Quakers look almost like a cliché—a dissenting group so long denied power that they became intoxicated with even a whiff of it. Having lost sight of the goal of governance, they had have become, in Penn's words, "governmentish" instead. In the words of early Pennsylvania's most eminent historian, Gary B. Nash, early provincials created "a make-believe world" in which "words became more important than actions and points of ceremonial propriety took precedent over legislative proposals."[5] Surely—a modern observer might think—something else must have lain behind this provincial obstinacy, this excessive attention to political ritual and language: perhaps tension over Penn's rent policies, or perhaps a deeply ingrained antiauthoritarianism within Quaker culture.[6] How else to explain why Friends wasted so much time on trivial matters?

Penn's complaints suggest that this question misses the point, though. His litany reveals that he knew words themselves could be actions. Some verbal utterances were performative, effecting real social change. He knew, then, that, in some cases, words could become things, objects of power in and of themselves.[7] Moreover, he realized that while the province's constitution and statutes defined the rules for a provincial civic speech economy—the exchange of language or civic speech between rulers and ruled—its ongoing regulation remained crucial to the maintenance of civic authority. Penn believed, in other words, that a relationship existed between the Provincial Councilors' manners toward Blackwell and the construction of political order. The Councilors should have deferred to his representative as they would have to him; this personal recognition of the deputy governor's authority could then model the orderly, political speech economy Penn hoped would develop between the government and the people.[8]

Penn wanted, in other words, a deferential political society in which ordinary citizens easily recognized the superior leadership capabilities of the ruling class, one in which the former took the latter's leadership in matters of governance to be natural. In this sense, as in his efforts to structure the government, Penn drew upon the ideas of James Harrington, who believed that in an ideal commonwealth, the many would defer to the few in matters political.[9] The very goal of manipulating the civic speech economy, writ large and small, was to bring this society into being. For in aspiring to create this exchange between rulers and ruled, the proprietor had intuited what Walter Bagehot, the nineteenth-century English historian and theorist of deference, would later state explicitly: that rulers "must first gain authority, and then use authority"; only then could they expect the loyalty of the people.[10] In Penn's case, he realized that one could not simply transplant political authority from England: before it could be exercised in America, it had to be made in America. For the people to recognize instinctively the leadership capabilities of the governing class, the signs and symbols that marked the governing class as such needed to be created, a process that had taken decades in other English American settlements. The governing class needed to be built from the bottom up.[11] Likewise, the form these rituals of power would take in a nascent society had to be defined. Penn could not assume that what worked in England would work in Pennsylvania.

Thus, neither Penn nor any other Quaker rulers during the founding period saw deference as an end in itself. They aimed, always, to create not just an orderly society but orderly citizens. As the Pennsylvania legal code reflected, Penn and his fellow Quaker magistrates believed that the administration of the law might prove a powerful tool to create civic-minded colonists. They intended by crafting a deferential political speech economy to define a particular type of civic identity—virtuous, loyal to the proprietary government, and reflecting the kind of Quakerized (but not Quaker) values embodied in the colony's legal code.

Thus, Penn's frustration with his provincial correspondents stemmed not from their excessive attention to political ritual but rather from their inept attention to it. They had failed to create a viable leadership class, failed to establish the orderly colony he had envisioned, and failed to enact his vision of cultivating virtuous civic behavior among the inhabitants. Although they faced substantive issues other than political ritual and procedure, the difficulty of creating a working politico-legal culture within which such problems could be debated effectively precluded the possibility of resolving these issues. Their inability to agree on such basic questions as how allegiance should be performed and authority displayed rendered consensus on other issues impossible. Litigants and legislators turned colonial courtrooms and assemblies into contested sites as colonists struggled to define the parameters of provincial civic culture. What emerged was a collective product. If colonists rejected Penn as the benevolent political father he believed himself to be, they nonetheless accepted his notion that civic legitimacy drew its greatest power when it came from an ongoing dialogue between the rulers and the ruled.

Oddly enough, Pennsylvania's early relations with Native Americans revealed the logic and limitations of this strategy. Determined to rule fairly and peacefully, colonial diplomats endeavored to secure their sovereignty over Indian lands and peoples through a system of voluntary compliance in which Native Americans deferred to colonial rule in exchange for certain governmental protections. But Indians proved less amenable to the transformation of native land into colonial territory than their initial encounters with provincial negotiators suggested. Struggles over the form of diplomatic engagements mirrored struggles over their meaning. Indians and colonists could agree neither on the appropriate language they should use to talk about their relationship to each other nor the obligations they owed each other as allies. Creating a diplomatic discourse that Indians and colonists found legitimate proved far more difficult in practice than it appeared in theory.

Beneath these persistent conflicts about the management of political, diplomatic, and legal discourse lay unresolved questions about the nature of colonial authority and identity in early Pennsylvania. The mechanisms by which Penn hoped to tighten civic bonds instead revealed fractures within them.

Signs and Seals: Failures of Leadership in Early Pennsylvania

Penn saw his hopes for order in Pennsylvania realized, at least during the first two years of his "Holy Experiment." Writing to fellow Friend John Alloway in November 1683, he expressed his pleasure at the prospect of harvesting the region's two resources, grain and souls, describing the latter as a "great Harvast in America." Penn likewise noted that he had during his time in America "held two Generall Assemblies with precious Harmony, Scarce one Law that did not pass with a Nemine Contradicente, and as our opening of them was deepe and wth heavenly Authority, So our Conclusions were with the word and prayer." This kind of order did not surprise him, since "men fearing god in power are both loved and feared"—exactly what he wanted. Penn was "deeply affected" by Alloway's concern for "my Christian reputation in the Governmt and affairs of this province" but nonetheless felt satisfied that "Our Wilderness flourishes as a Garden, and our desert springs like as a Greene field" due to the efforts of the first settlers and the blessings of God. Penn looked during the colony's first few months for particular evidence of Pennsylvania's success. Bountiful harvests—of grain and souls—signified neither luck nor skill but their "righteousness" in "plant[ing] the Lords earth."[12] Penn assessed the government's progress differently, thinking that the Assembly's functioning as a Quaker Meeting—a body of godly men, speaking in one voice—augured its power, effectiveness, and righteousness. Penn addressed the Assemblymen in this kind of spiritual-political language, and he expected them to speak that language as well.[13] He believed this form of address signified the government's legitimacy, and took comfort in its appearance; his correspondent Alloway surely agreed.

Over the next decade, this auspicious beginning proved to be a mirage. Penn's dispute with Lord Baltimore over the boundary between Pennsylvania and Maryland forced him to return to England in 1684 to press his claim against his southern rival. Disharmony reigned in Pennsylvania politics over the next decade and a half, as legislators quarreled over issues great and small. Even worse—from Penn's perspective—a governing class in Pennsylvania failed to coalesce. The "godly" men, those of "virtue, worth, and ability" he had hoped might lead the province, proved to be those who instigated the disputes. They exemplified not unity but backbiting, criticizing each other in public and levying charges and countercharges of sedition against each other. They even squabbled over the possession and use of one of the colony's major symbols of political power, the provincial Great Seal.

These disputes had real consequences. A fight between the Assembly and Provincial Council over the relative privileges of each body prevented the passage of legislation from 1685 to 1687. Pennsylvania's political leaders simply could not create a stable polity in the years following Penn's letter to Alloway, creating instead a government that was contentious at best, ineffectual at worst.[14] The disastrously brief tenure of John Blackwell as deputy governor from 1688–89 epitomized the depths of this dilemma.

Penn saw the relative ease with which legislators established Pennsylvania's initial legal code as evidence of the power of "The Living Word" among the province's ruling class.[15] Politicians soon began grumbling against each other and the proprietor, however. The Pennsylvania government suffered its first accusation of treason in 1683, even before Penn's departure. The Provincial Council learned in March that Nicholas More, a justice in New Castle and president of the Free Society of Traders, had declared that the governor, Council, and Assembly had "this day broken the Charter, & therefore all that you do will come to Nothing," in a Philadelphia tavern. He added that "hundreds in England will curse you for what you have done, & their children after them," predicting "that you may hereafter be impeacht for Treason for" violating the Free Society's charter.[16] Under questioning from the governor and Council, More said he intended his words as "Query rather than assertion" and that he "spake not with such an Intent" as to brand his fellow civic leaders traitors. Releasing him, Penn and the Council informed him "his Discourse being unreasonable and imprudent, he was exhorted to prevent the like for the future."[17]

The warning obviously did not take, as the Provincial Council impeached More for his conduct as a judge two years later. The action was merited. Any provincial government in Anglo-America would have found his decision to try a civil case of "trover and conversion" as a criminal felony case and sentence "the Defendant to be Publickly Whipt & . . . to be fined to pay three fould" a gross miscarriage of justice. But the Provincial Council also included in More's articles of impeachment charges that he had expressed contempt for his fellow justices' authority. One article detailed More's public criticism of the judgment of other justices, a second his habit of "publickly affronting" members of other courts while serving as a visiting justice, and a third his refusal to acknowledge the Provincial Council's authority over him.[18] Indeed, the Council found itself four days into More's trial for impeachment debating the "Contemptuous and Derogatory Expressions" in which he "call[ed] the Memb[ers] thereof fooles & Logerheads, and said it were well if all the Laws had Drapt, and that it would never be good Times as Long as the Quakers had the Administration."[19] More's insistence on criticizing the government in the harshest language possible had caused his removal from his position as much as his shoddy behavior behind the bench.

More's situation proved extreme but not unique: other members of Pennsylvania's leadership seemed either ready to utter seditious words against the government or to lend themselves readily to slandering. The Provincial Council in 1686 dealt with the Philadelphia County Court's complaint against Patrick Robinson, the court clerk, for his "Great abuse offered . . . to [the] Judges then sitting on [the] bench, to [the] great hazard of [the] good, quiet, and peaceable Constitution of the Government, and Great disturbance of [the] Government, and Great Disturbance and hindrance of Justice in [the] highest Court of this Province." The Council thereupon summoned Robinson and dismissed him from his office.[20] It debated in 1687 the suitability of one John Curtis to serve as a member; although rightfully elected from Kent County, Curtis had two years past lain "under Suspicion of Speaking treasonable words," necessitating investigation by a special commission. Although a grand jury had found no cause of action, the Council still thought "it our Duty to Dismiss him," unable to suffer a man accused of treason to sit as one of its members.[21] That same year the Council spent time investigating "Scurrilous Invective Libel against Rob[er]t Turner, a worthy member of this board" and working to find the "forgers, or first Contrivers, as well as [the] Publishers of [the] same, that they may be brought to Condigne punishment."[22] In 1688, Council adjudicated, as the final court of appeal in the province, a case in which a county court had convicted an Assemblyman of criminally defaming a Councilman, sentencing him to twenty-one lashes; the Council let the conviction stand but suspended the sentence, presumably to send the message that one could not defame elected leaders with impunity while avoiding the spectacle of one elected leader having another whipped half naked at the public whipping post.[23] Members of the government seemed concerned enough about their own—and the government's—reputations that they made protecting them a significant part of their official business.

Provincial officials had reason for concern, as they themselves continued to spread scandalizing rumors. Penn lamented that "quarrels among the Magistrates whereby the[y] make selves cheap to the people they should be awfull to" merely spread gossip about the province. These internecine conflicts prevented officials from "giv[ing] the lye to those vile & repeated slanders cast on the Province" in England, Penn complained. These attacks cast the magistracy as overly ambitious and "partial to offenders that profess [the] truth" of Quakerism—charges that may have, in the wake of More's impeachment, struck too close to home.[24]

Penn felt colonial officials had invited such talk by arguing among themselves instead of speaking to the public with a single voice. He later complained that his appointed representatives in Pennsylvania refused to send him a single public letter detailing affairs but instead sent several private letters "tho from publick persons," each contradicting the other and telling unflattering stories about colleagues. Such "Contradiction as well as diversity" in this correspondence among his leadership led Penn to declare "I am one of the unhappiest Proprietarys with one of the best People."[25] Within months this rush of rumors led Penn's surveyor general, Thomas Holme, to complain of "secret enemies who Indian like stand behind a tree to shoot at one," leaving him under siege. He professed that he would rather deal with a "heathen" than those who would lie instead of speaking with him "according to the order of truth, & christs words"—implying that those slandering him were Friends.[26] Considering that Lenape Indians had previously threatened to drive Holme from his land a few years previous and to murder his deputy, Israel Taylor, he must have believed that his fellow colonists' behavior had grown quite bad indeed.[27]

Penn's disappointment spoke directly to the failure of Pennsylvania's leaders to develop an authoritative political language during the province's early years. He had helped in part to create this problem with the governmental structure he had set up. Penn had in his letters suggested that he hoped the legislature would function like a Quaker Meeting, embodying the harmonious voice of the people. The Frame of Government created a structure that could only approximate the Quaker Meeting, however. Within a bicameral legislature that empowered the Council to initiate legislation and reduced the Assembly to the role of a plebiscite, neither body could ever represent the voice of the people; each only spoke for the people, at different times. Thus, neither could claim an authority analogous to the Meeting's. Penn's desire to enshrine a leadership class within the Provincial Council while asking the councilors to function as one with the Assembly made a conflict between the legislature's two bodies over prerogative inevitable.

The Assembly strove to gain more power throughout the 1680s and early 1690s, pushing for the authority to debate and initiate legislation and to choose their own speaker without consulting the Provincial Council. Assemblymen even resented the indignity of having to stand in conference while the Council sat.[28] Penn's publication of *The Excellent Priviledge of Liberty and Property* in 1687 likely did nothing to smooth over these problems.[29] Educating the colonists about their English liberties only reminded Assemblymen of the vastly different powers the House of Commons possessed, stiffening their resolve to fight for greater privileges in America. Provincial politicians had no true English model to emulate as they struggled over political power. Penn and the legislators who ratified the Frame had created a truly hybrid, creole set of political institutions without an effective way of convincing people to accept it as legitimate.

In the absence of an English model to emulate, Pennsylvanians clashed over questions of institutional procedure and protocol. The two-year standoff between the Assembly and the Provincial Council began in 1685 after the former complained that the latter had submitted laws for Penn's assent by the authority of "President [of the Provincial Council] and the Council," ignoring the Assembly's constitutional role. Feeling slighted, the Assembly refused to approve any legislation until the Council amended this language and gave the lower house its proper due.[30] Beyond that, the Assembly began to insist upon their right to choose its own speaker and to debate legislation, maintaining that it should function as a mirror of both the Provincial Council and the House of Commons; the assemblymen persisted in their efforts even as Penn and his deputies repeatedly stated that theirs should only be a "negative voice . . . not a debateing, mending, [or] altering" power."[31] Seizing upon English precedent to defend their liberty and power, they rejected the very practices the 1683 Frame had established for creating law.

Colonial courtrooms experienced similar disruptions. Grand juries halted presentments to debate whether they acted in the name of Crown and country or in the name of the proprietor.[32] Juries and judges disagreed over whether they could grant official legal documents "sufitient power without further proofe," dragging cases on for months.[33] A conflict in a Sussex court between Thomas Lloyd, one of Penn's five commissioners of state and the keeper of the provincial Great Seal, and erstwhile traitor Nicolas More demonstrated some of the chaos that often reined in legal proceedings. What began as a civil case regarding the finances of the Free Society of Traders degenerated into a larger conflict involving civility and the rules of the court. After More, as the presiding judge, attempted to prevent Lloyd from speaking without his leave, Lloyd announced, "I tell thee I may speak here or in any Court of this Government, as I am the Cheiff Justice in it by being Keeper of the Seal." More found this invocation of Lloyd's status as "Keeper of the Seal" decidedly unimpressive, countering the latter's declaration by responding that "I never saw that power yet . . . but if you are . . . then pray sitt upon the Bench that I may know where to Direct my Speech."[34]

Both the Great Seal and the Lesser Seal remained significant status objects, however. Colonial officials fought over a half dozen times over who should hold the Seals, who might use them, and the relative legal status of "sealed" versus "unsealed" documents. Officials fought, in other words, not just over the Seals themselves but over the legal and cultural power they conveyed.[35] These arguments epitomized colonial officials' difficulties in creating clear governmental structures that commanded cultural and political authority.

The tenure of the Puritan deputy governor John Blackwell in 1688–89 marked the culmination—or nadir—of the struggle.[36] Sent by Penn to restore order and shore up his proprietary power, Blackwell quickly ran afoul of Lloyd. Lloyd made his disrespect for Penn's deputy evident when he failed to greet Blackwell upon the deputy governor's arrival and pronounced the latter's commission invalid because it lacked the stamp of the Great Seal—a mark only Lloyd could have given it.[37] This rocky beginning convinced Blackwell that he needed to check Quaker power in Pennsylvania. But Blackwell's fights with Quaker leaders centered on many of the same issues that had defined internecine Friends' early conflicts. The deputy governor fought Lloyd over possession of the Great Seal, which Lloyd refused to surrender despite Penn's explicit instructions to do so.[38] Other Friends rallied to Lloyd's defense; when Blackwell asked the Council to force Lloyd to hand over the Seal and censure him, one councilor suggested that this was equivalent to asking a man to surrender his sword and using it to murder him.[39]

Blackwell similarly clashed with Friends over the pomp and pageantry of governmental offices. A politician of his era, the deputy governor was accustomed to the parades, bonfires, and festive events through which Restoration officials in England and colonial governors in America displayed royal power and authority.[40] Writing that "There is some thing of Reverence payd to the Emblems of Grandeur in Governmt," he suggested that the colonial government's ineffectiveness stemmed from its meager efforts to display its authority publicly. He complained to Penn that "'tis an old saying in London, That the city is not so much Governd by the Wisdome of the Maior, as the Capparisens of his Horse, the Cap of maintenance & sword carried by him that bears it."[41] Blackwell continued to face challenges from Councilors such as Arthur Cook and Samuel Richardson, who questioned the legitimacy of his commission; after Richardson declared in council that "he did not owne [the] Goverr to be Goverr," Blackwell ejected him from the Council. (Cook stayed, offering that he merely insisted that Penn, as governor, could appoint a deputy governor and that Blackwell should properly refer to himself as such.)[42]

Finally, Blackwell attacked political enemies who he felt had started factions by spreading political discourse illegitimately. In April 1689, he attacked Joseph Growden for circulating a published copy of the Frame of Government, despite the fact that provincial statue mandated the regular publication of the Frame and all other colonial laws.[43] Blackwell argued that "he looked upon it as being of a dangerous nature (in the present Condition of our affayrs, and distractions the Country was in)" and that these actions left Growden "liable to Censure." Only the deputy governor's growing unpopularity—and the councilors' sense that more pressing business awaited—saved the latter from more serious sanction.[44] The next month he took similar action against a "Caball" held at Assemblyman Benjamin Chambers's house, a so-called "Charter Club," where members of the Assembly had gathered to plan their political strategies.[45]

Each of these conflicts began with disputes over the form as well as the function of political power. The "governmentish" nature of Pennsylvania's early political system reflected the fact that its early leadership class had failed to develop the cultural markers that legitimated Pennsylvania's political structures—and they knew it. Penn found this failure especially galling given his hope that provincial leaders would "season" those new to America. He expected them to play a major part in creating a virtuous creolized citizenry: "much depends on thos[e] in pow[e]r; for I never heard of a Country undone nor made without them."[46]

These struggles over political ritual also raised a much deeper political problem regarding the relationship between religion and power. They sparked debates over Pennsylvania's status as a particularly Quaker colony and if Friends could speak and act on behalf of the entire polity when they served in political and judicial offices. Many Anglicans questioned this, and more than a few suggested that Friends held certain offices not because they best represented the colonists' interests but because Penn insured that "none are put in places of power but friends."[47] Religious factionalism caused at least some of the conflict between Blackwell and Quakers in the Provincial Council and Assembly. Governing Friends were aghast that Penn had sent "one thus foreigne & strange to us" to rule over them. Unhappy that the Puritan deputy governor had referred to "the best of the People" in the Provincial Council "as Factious, Mutionous, Seditious, turbulent & the like," they resolved "as men & Christians" to stand against him in the hope that Penn would "lett us have one from amongst our Brethren[.]"[48] Blackwell, for his part, attributed his difficulties to Quaker "principles un-suitable to civill Governm[e]nt & polity," implying that it was impossible for Friends ever to govern effectively, let alone represent the diverse interests of a heterogeneous population. His assessment only confirmed fears outsiders had about the dangers of giving members of the Society political power.[49] Blackwell clearly saw Pennsylvania's Quakers as a faction sowing dissent within the province, with all of the negative associations that the term implied for seventeenth-century Englishmen.[50] Governing Friends, meanwhile, just as clearly saw themselves as leading members of a Quaker colony, eminently capable of embodying the province as a whole. These unresolved tensions revealed the true failure of Pennsylvania's early ruling Friends—their inability to cultivate a coherent civic identity among the colony's population.

Discourse and Allegiance: Struggling to Define a Creole Civic Identity

Even as Pennsylvania's leadership class failed in its attempts to convey its authority in the colony's early years, it faced a larger problem: the need to define the relationship between the provincial residents and their government. What kind of bonds tied ordinary colonials to the government? What rights did Penn the proprietor—and by extension, the government—owe the people? What obligations did provincials owe the government? Pennsylvania's leaders struggled mightily to cultivate the allegiance of many of the province's residents during the province's first decade—and wavered themselves in their allegiance to Penn—because the answers to these questions remained unresolved. Born primarily English, Scots, or ethnically German, nearly all Pennsylvania residents had been accustomed to a world where civic identities and their associated web of privileges and obligations were inalienable and defined by birth.[51] But living now in a world where all European setters were immigrants, provincials found themselves forced to create a creole colonial civic culture.

Theoretically, of course, the question of subjectship should have been easy to determine. Pennsylvania's early legal code provided a ready mechanism for non-English colonists to become naturalized subjects of the realm, and Penn encouraged them to take advantage of this opportunity; many did. Indeed, the provincial government naturalized so many individuals in Pennsylvania's first decade that some accused the government of currying favor with non-English residents with an overly liberal naturalization policy.[52] In practice, however, the process of defining civic identity involved more than simply establishing the legal parameters of subjectship. It also invited debates over the meaning of such practices as serving in the militia or going to court, raising for the first time the potential irreconcilability of Penn's dreams of civic inclusiveness and of founding a Quaker utopia. Residents in early Pennsylvania saw civic identity less as a community membership fixed by "official" rules and boundaries than as a set of practices, obligations, and privileges that they struggled over.[53] Colonists knew that citizenship was not something they possessed but something they did as members of a political community. Civic identity became a "contested truth."[54] Events quickly made clear that Penn and his fellow legislators had not foreseen all the problems that would arise.

As colonists increasingly clashed with Penn over other matters of governance, provincials realized that the colony's proprietary status complicated questions of civic status and allegiance. They wondered, in effect, how their rights and obligations vis-à-vis Penn impacted their status as English subjects. Joseph Growden, a member of the Provincial Council, first broached this question in 1691, following a letter from Penn. The Council's treatment of Blackwell had driven the deputy governor from office after less than a year, infuriating the proprietor and prompting him to send a blistering letter suggesting the councilors had broken their obligations to him. Growden's response revealed a provincial understanding of subjectship that stood at odds with Penn's understanding of the relationship between proprietor and colonists.

Growden began by reminding the proprietor that the colonists were "borne subjects unto the King of England and goe where we will we cannot be quit of our allegiance to him but must continue it still," reflecting prevailing English law. The allegiance they owed Penn, though, differed in one significant way: it resulted not from their birth but from their migration to Pennsylvania. They thus owed Penn conditional, not inalienable, allegiance. Growden asserted that "our own act hath made us thy Homagess condicionall, and thee our Governor, and soe consequently doe wee owe thee fidelity wch continues noe longer then wee hold our interest and habitation here," emphasizing the contingency of the "homage" they paid Penn. Growden concluded, "quitting that, wee owe unto thee No more fidelity than thou unto us, but are fellow Subjects wth thee."[55] Their allegiance to the Crown was not mediated by Penn or indeed any other of their fellow subjects. More-over, Growden's sharp distinction between inalienable and conditional alle-giance reminded Penn of his precarious situation as proprietor. He commanded the allegiance of his settlers only as long as their interests re-mained materially tied to America.

Growden's emphasis on residence suggested that Penn held a more tenu-ous claim to his colonists' allegiance than he suspected. Growden's definition of proprietary allegiance as provisional, volitional, and linked to residence evoked reciprocity; he offered more than a hint that Penn's sustained absence since 1684 had weakened the ties between the proprietor and his "homagess condicionall." Growden closed his letter by appealing to Penn's Quaker spirit, suggesting that colonial Friends saw Penn as a father figure. Noting that Friends comprised a large majority of the government, Growden felt certain that "what ever misunderstandings there may be . . . between thee and us, they can noe more cease to love thee nor forsake thee when thor-oughly tried then good and obedient Children forsake their parents."[56]

Unfortunately for Penn, other colonials agreed with Growden. Less than a month after Growden's letter, the Provincial Council and Assembly to-gether drafted a letter responding to Penn's complaints and asking for re-forms in the Frame of Government, specifically a desire to allow the Assembly to propose legislation. This jointly drafted letter also focused on questions of loyalty, allegiance, and the transfer of English subjecthood to America in making its case against Penn. Their anger with Penn, the Councilors and Assemblymen argued, stemmed from his assumption that they owed him unconditional loyalty, regardless of the rights he provided or obligations he performed. "Surely Governr our fidelity to thee is not native but Dative, not Universall but Locall," given at pleasure and not in perpetuity, in the par-lance of the times.[57] The Council saw their political commitments to Penn as decidedly creole, a product of American settlement: "it will not be thought unreasonable if we insist on those privileges which thou has Declared to be the undouted rights of the free borne English." These privileges "are not Cancelled by Coming hither, nor Can be Lawfully Denyed by thee, or abdi-cated and Dissolved by Us" in any case; they merely saw the ability to elect assemblies empowered to draft legislation as one of these rights.[58]

Certain that the king did not intend his subject's rights to be abridged but instead wished them "Corroborated and Enlarged by [the] Settling of a New Colony," the authors of the letter insisted that they asked for no major innovations. They merely desired the restoration of English traditions. "Let us at Least Revert to the Good old English ways of Government," they wrote, "without any way of Alteracions of English usages if possible, Excepting Regular and yearly Assemblys," even though they would not have had those rights in England. They wanted, in other words, to maintain traditional rights, except in those cases in which Pennsylvania's innovative constitution granted them more expansive ones.

The contradictions in the joint letter, like those in Growden's, represented more than self-serving rhetoric. They highlighted the problems inherent in defining a creole citizenship in Pennsylvania. This missive also emphasized the provisional nature of the authors' allegiance to Penn. They offer a "dative" loyalty, subject to constant renegotiation, precisely because no "native" civic ties existed in Pennsylvania. All ties of loyalty, fidelity, and allegiance, except to the king, were born in America and thus prototypically creole. And while the authors offered a spirited defense of their right to all English liberties—perhaps making Penn regret his publication of *The Excellent Priviledge*—they never explained why or how settlement had enlarged their rights at a moment when jurists disagreed about the transmission of English rights to America.[59] By couching their request for old and new political privileges in an appeal to traditional rights, these authors showed an awareness, less than a decade into Pennsylvania's settlement, that their migration to America had made them both English and American.

Moreover, Growden's appeal to the religious bond provincial politicians shared with Penn revealed a major problem governing Quakers faced, namely, the difficulty of balancing Quaker pacifism with their duties as provincial leaders. A minor issue at the time of Pennsylvania's settlement, it became a major issue in the aftermath of the Glorious Revolution and the outbreak of King William's War (1689–97) in Europe and the Americas. Forced to address provincial defense in 1689, Friends on the Provincial Council temporized, which non-Quaker councilors saw as a violation of an Englishman's duty in a time of war. Even after receiving orders from England for each colony to arm itself and a report from Blackwell about the attacks visited upon New England colonists, Griffith Jones suggested that "he saw no cause of danger if we can but Keepe quiet among ourselves." John Simcock added that "I see no danger but from the Bears & Wolves. We are well, & in peace & quiet: Let us Keep ourselves so." More cautious—and realistic—Friends worried about Indian diplomacy, suggesting that arming the colony would damage the peaceful relations they had worked so hard to build.[60]

Only after Luke Watson, a non-Quaker, noted that the king had given an express order "to settle a Militia to defend his Ma[jes]ties Subjects" and that the people of Pennsylvania believed that they had a right to defend themselves did Friends on the Council begin to relent. They could not agree with Blackwell's argument that the clause in Penn's charter requiring the government to "at all times have the care of peace and safety of the Province" necessitated raising a defensive force. But Friends on the Council decided that if they could not in good conscience assist a militia, they could not as good English subjects prevent the raising of one either. Griffith Jones summarized the view of his fellow Quakers when he declared that "The case is hard. I desire to be passive & not to concern my self in it, either to give a negative or affirmative."[61]

This Quaker indecision—especially in the face of Watson's indignation—revealed how little common ground existed among the provincial leaders regarding the meaning of civic obligation. They split over the significance of military service to civic duty, despite the centrality of this duty to European and especially English conceptions of citizenship; loyalty necessitated a willingness to serve in defense of one's country. Even Penn's intellectual role model Harrington saw the capacity and willingness to bear arms as a necessary precondition for political rights.[62] In the face of this tradition, the Provincial Council offered a "publique instrument" declaring their loyalty to the Crown, which they instructed all county sheriffs to proclaim. They performed their civic obligations through words rather than through any form of physical sacrifice or call to arms.

The councilors' insistence on linking their Quaker faith and their duties as provincial rulers ensured the creation of two types of citizens in Pennsylvania: Quakers whose religious commitments took precedence over their duty to obey the king's orders and protect the common good in times of war and the rest of the polity, who presumably bore the brunt of those civic obligations. They transformed civic performance into something that divided, rather than united, those who shared the same legal status. A 1690 petition signed by several non-Quakers and presented to the Provincial Council drove the point home. The petitioners implored Blackwell to assist them in defending the province "by force of arms" because they felt "duty bound" to defend their corner of the King's dominions.[63] By emphasizing religious faith as a crucial part of their civic identity, ruling Friends solidified the bonds holding the majority of the colony together while fracturing their ties to a vocal minority. More worrisome, they left the colony vulnerable to Indian attack.

Continuing warfare divided the colony even further. As King William's War persisted, governors in New York and Maryland warned imperial officials at home that Pennsylvania's pacifism "will be fatal to most of these Colonies" unless checked.[64] The Crown responded to these concerns in October 1692 by transferring control of the colony from Penn to Benjamin Fletcher, the governor of New York.[65] Imperial officials appointed Fletcher primarily to secure assistance for military efforts on New York's frontier. While Fletcher understood that Quaker principles prevented them from actively waging war, he expected them at the very least to show their loyalty by "feed[ing] the Hungrie and Cloath[ing] the Naked" among the soldiers—providing money instead of men.[66] But Friends proved no more willing to assist Fletcher than Blackwell. During his roughly two years as deputy governor, Fletcher could only coax the legislature to raise a small amount of money to fund the war effort, far less than what he had asked for.[67]

Fletcher's demands only exacerbated tensions between residents of Quaker-dominated Bucks, Chester, and Philadelphia counties and the primarily non-Quaker "Lower Counties" of Sussex, New Castle, and Kent in what would become Delaware. Quaker pacifists comprised a majority of the population in the former but a small minority in the latter. Tired of the government's inaction, residents of the Lower Counties organized a private militia to defend themselves from attack by sea and welcomed the new governor's efforts to defend the colony. The local militia greeted Fletcher's arrival in New Castle to publish his commission with a "fireing of guns, great shouting, and joy."[68]

Conflict between the Upper and Lower Counties in Pennsylvania certainly preceded Fletcher. Quakers in the north worried that the already settled Lower Counties would outvote them in the Assembly and Provincial Council, while Lutherans and especially Anglicans to the south disliked having a dissenter as their proprietor.[69] Representatives from the different counties also argued about the administration of the courts and the appointment of judges, leading members from the Lower Counties to walk out of a meeting of the Provincial Council and establish their own council.[70] The question of provincial defense lent this conflict a sharper edge. The difference between the reception Fletcher received in Pennsylvania's northern and southern counties revealed just how large a gap existed between the province's Quaker and non-Quaker residents over questions of civic duty.

Penn had predicted these problems, knowing that Friends' efforts at merging their religious and civic identities had contributed to disunity in the colony. Writing in response to Growden's and the joint letters, Penn had lamented that "Though you are not of one Judgment in Religion, you are of one Family in Civills and should Aime at the publick good, and your owne private Interests only in that"—defining the Quaker religion as solely private in matters of governance.[71] Though determined to keep government in the hands of the "tribe of Judah," he nonetheless realized that too strong an emphasis on their tribal identity had prevented ruling Friends from becoming the truly authoritative provincial fathers they needed to be to govern a diverse colony. Nothing happened during Fletcher's tenure to change Penn's essential point. Penn grasped what the councilors missed—that Quakerism, while a powerful agent for cultural cohesion, could not in itself serve as a powerful agent for *civil* cohesion in a diverse colony. Building governmental authority and bringing Pennsylvanians together required other forms of cultural power.

Clearly, politics had failed in unifying Pennsylvania's citizenry or in defining a common civic identity. Pennsylvania politicians found themselves bogged down in questions of procedure, ritual, and detail. Meanwhile, substantive issues—regarding Penn's land policy, the institutional relationship between the Assembly and the Provincial Council, and the status of the Lower Counties—all cried out for attention and went relatively unaddressed. So too did crucial questions about land, jurisdiction, and war in the backcountry. Civic discord among Pennsylvanians paralleled diplomatic conflicts between colonists and indigenous peoples living on the frontier.

Settling with the Indians: Early Negotiations with Pennsylvania's Indigenous Peoples

At first, Pennsylvania's diplomatic negotiations with its indigenous neighbors followed Penn's vision. Before his return to England, Penn secured large tracts of land along the Delaware, Schuylkill, and southern Susquehanna Rivers from Lenape and Susquehannock sachems through nine major purchases from July 1682 through June 1684.[72] He also began negotiations to extend the colony even further west, asking his agents James Graham and

William Haige to "treat with the sachems of the Mohawk and Seneca Indians and their allies for the purchasing of the lands lying on both sides of Susquehanna River," a move which, if successful, would have greatly increased Pennsylvania's size.[73] Although these negotiations failed, they revealed Penn's seriousness about ensuring that he acquired title to all land in his colony legally, through treaties amenable to all parties.[74] More significantly, Penn achieved one of his major diplomatic reforms by securing the consent of Lenape and other local Indians in May 1684 "to be punished as the English were" when they violated provincial law, provided the province continue to allow the sale of rum. In effect, the Indians who made this agreement had submitted to colonial law in exchange for the continuation of a commodity trade. Penn had seemingly found the same civic voluntarism on the colonial periphery that he sought at its core. Awed by the offer of protection under the aegis of colonial justice, the Lenape sachems had willingly assented to colonial power, a dialogic exchange that cemented political bonds between the two peoples.[75] Through their legal institutions, benevolent Quaker fathers would creolize local Indians, after a fashion, teaching them valuable lessons about colonial authority.

These apparent successes masked larger problems, however. Contradictory logic drove Penn's negotiations with the Iroquois. He instructed Graham and Haige to insist concerning the Valley that "nobody lives upon it, and consequently [it is] open to the next pretender," suggesting that Penn subscribed to the doctrine of *res nullius* that he seemingly rejected by negotiating with the Iroquois in the first place. But he also instructed his agents to inform the Mohawk and Seneca that he was negotiating with them because he had "hear[d] they had some claim by conquest, or at least that the remainder of the Susquehannocks, who are the right owners thereof, are amongst them," two mutually exclusive reasons for treating the Iroquois as owners of the land.[76] Penn's efforts to extinguish alternative claims to the land only confused the issue of who held possession of the Susquehanna Valley. By treating the Iroquois as its rightful owners, he had unwittingly validated their ambiguous claims to have gained the valley by "conquest."[77] Indeed, his attempts to make himself sovereign over the region practically required this maneuver. In order to extinguish alternative claims to the valley, he first needed to find some imperial entity willing to cede its sovereignty. If this meant accepting the contested Iroquois claims of conquest, so be it. That Penn needed to play the "deed game" merely underscored the contrast between the confident optimism of his Indian policy and the messy reality of diplomatic life on the late seventeenth-century frontier between natives and colonizers.[78]

Similar problems riddled the Lenape sachems' supposed submission to English law. What might have seemed the triumph of Penn's diplomacy turned out to be unworkable and even undesirable. The proprietor soon broke the spirit (if not the letter) of his promise regarding the rum trade, urging provincials to cease its sale to Indians. Though it still remained legal, he hoped to apply pressure, personally and through the Quaker Meeting, to end the trade.[79] Nor did Indian leaders prove very willing to submit to colonial authority when conflict arose. Less than a year after the proprietor's departure for England, the Lenape sachem Tammanend angrily threatened to drive off colonists who had settled in Bucks County, believing he had not been paid for the land. Penn responded to this news by insisting to his agent that "If the Indians will not punish [Tammanend], we will and must, for they must never see you afraid of executing the Justice they ought to do."[80] But this ignored the fact that Indians lacked the desire to accede to provincial demands and colonists lacked the means to force them to do so; neither side could force its interpretation of the May 1684 agreement on the other.[81]

Over the next fifteen years, similar disagreements, miscommunications, and missed opportunities marked colonial-native relations. Some diplomatic meetings were devoted to clearing up rumors of violence between colonists and Indians on the frontier. In July 1685, some Indians lodged a complaint about a recent visit paid to Jasper Farmer, a Philadelphia County settler. They accused Farmer's servants of getting them drunk, "then Lying with their Wives." They also questioned whether the government had fully paid for the land Farmer occupied.[82] A little over a year later, Zachariah Whitpaine arrived in the capital reporting that angry Indians had attacked and murdered Nicholas Scull—a tenant of Farmer's and one of the province's deputy surveyors—and Scull's entire family.[83] Although it turned out that Scull and his family had not been harmed, the Provincial Council felt obliged to send three negotiators out to the frontier to determine the cause of the attack and bring the Indians "to punishment according to Law" if they were guilty of breaking and entering and theft as charged by Scull. Despite traveling throughout the region, the negotiators "Found none of The Indians . . . that belonged to those Indians that did the Fact." They did, however, encounter disgruntled natives who "thretned to Kill Israell Taylor," another of the province's deputy surveyors, "if he surveyed any more Land before it be bought"—a warning that the Scull incident might not be last of its kind.[84] Another rumored attack by 500 Indian warriors in 1688 proved to be a false alarm but still showed the fragility of the peace between colonists and Indians. This episode too centered on an Indian charge that colonials had not properly paid for land they had now settled on.[85] These continued debates over ownership and sovereignty—the right to possess land and to sanction those who lived on it— revealed miscommunications and presaged future debates.

Circumstance accounted for much of the difficulty that colonists and Indians faced in crafting a diplomatic language that was "native" to both sides, namely, the outbreak of war in 1689. Delaware Valley Native Americans and Quaker provincials had different views on the matter. Once the conflict began, rumors of war and questions of allegiance became the most frequent topic of negotiation. Fearful of reports of Catholics and French-allied Indians from the Chesapeake region trying to incite Pennsylvania's Indians to attack the colony, the Provincial Council in 1690 asked Lenape leaders to provide news of the designs of the French and "their Indians" should the war reach the colony. The Council also resolved to assure them that any defensive posture the colony might take was done with a "good Intention towards them and their people," not as a threat."[86] Both Native Americans and colonists had an interest in alleviating war fears and making their allegiances clear, as a 1694 conference instigated by the Lenape Indians showed; the assembled sachems restated firmly their "continuous friendship with all the Christians and old Inhabitants of this river" and assured the Provincial Council that rumors to the contrary were false. The Council thanked the assembled sachems, exchanged gifts with them, and rebuked one colonist guilty of spreading such tales.[87]

However, just as often it seemed in these early years as if various Indians and colonists spoke different languages rather than forming a common one. Divergent interests on both sides prevented any such diplomatic discourse from emerging. Pacifist Quakers refused military assistance, while various factions of the Lenape Indians disagreed on whether to intervene on the English side during the war or push for peace. Ironically, the most successful attempt to craft a diplomatic discourse amenable to both English and Indian interests occurred during Governor Benjamin Fletcher's brief tenure, when both Fletcher and the natives he treated with used a gendered, militaristic language to define themselves and their relationship to each other.[88] When some Lenape Indians from the northern branch of the Delaware River visited Fletcher in 1693, they expressed disdain for the Quaker style of negotiation and of governance in general. They complained that the chronic instability in Quaker politics, where "sometimes one man & sometimes another pretended to be Governor," made real alliances difficult. Even worse, they felt, "when wee were in feare of the French and their Indians, and inclined to make warr with them, they would not encourage us, nor make anie preparations themselves, nor give us assistance"—the very problem Blackwell and Fletcher had had with Pennsylvania's Quaker government. The Lenape likewise insisted to Fletcher that they could aid the English war effort as "wee are men & know fighting."[89]

Fletcher's response demonstrated how much common ground he shared with these northern Lenape. He emphasized that "he was a man of armes and not of the Quakers principle" and asked for "proofe of their Manhood and valor by sending some of their best men up to Albany, to assist our people ag[ains]t the enemy." In the end, the Indians "profess[ed] wee will be one Heart and true to the English," finding Fletcher's words convincing.[90] But while this discourse, based on a shared martial masculinity, worked in this case for Fletcher and the northern Lenape Indians, it held no appeal for either provincial Friends or the Contestoga and southern Lenape Indians who stayed neutral during the war (and found themselves castigated as "women" by the Iroquois for their inaction).[91]

Thus, the reality of circumstance and competing interests thwarted Penn's hopes that he and his successors might unite all the region's natives under a single, benevolent authority. Most notably, the negotiators within the government continued to face difficulties as they attempted to extend colonial sovereignty over frontier space (in the face of Indian resistance) and to find a set of legitimating themes or symbols out of which a creole diplomatic language—one that seemed "native" to both sides—might emerge.

In many respects, then, Pennsylvania's leaders failed in their educative functions. They provided ample proof of their inability to convince their fellow colonists or Native Americans within the region of their legitimacy. The Provincial Council, the Assembly, and the office of Lieutenant Governor all operated with varying degrees of ineffectiveness on this score. One civic institution, however, served, in its own way, to educate the population as Penn hoped it would: the colony's legal system, inflected with Quaker values but not in itself sectarian. While it did not produce one "Family in Civills" in exactly the manner its authors intended, the legal system during Pennsylvania's first decade and a half gradually produced, through its rituals and punishments, its disciplines and sanctions, a definition of a civic subject.

Subjects and Objects: Narratives of Legal Life

In June 1686, the Philadelphia Court of Quarter Sessions and Common Pleas promulgated its "Rules of Court" to prevent disorders that might "bring [the] Magistracie (wch is God's ordinance) & Courts of Justice into Scorne and Contempte." Penn would have agreed with the Court's prescriptions. They decreed that no one not immediately concerned with the business under consideration "presume to speake wtout Leave under peine of a fine." They likewise announced that all litigants and witnesses "speake directly to the pointe in question" and "that they forbeare reflections & recriminations on the Court, Juries, or on one another under penalty of a fine."[92] With these rules, the court hoped to control both the content and the manner of legal speech in court. It expected participants in the legal system to show due deference to magistrates, each other, and the institution itself, both by holding their tongues at inappropriate times and by refraining from derogatory language. The court reserved the power to determine appropriate or derogatory language.

The Court of Quarter Session's insistence on defining the rules regulating speech within the courtroom did not mean that the justices intended conversation to flow in only one direction, though. Creating the legal system's legitimacy necessitated the active participation of the litigants. In the court's eyes—or, perhaps, to the court's ears—the authority of the legal performances within the courthouse depended on the fact that they emerged from legal dialogues between rulers and ruled, not simply from monological pronouncements from the magistrates to the people. Vocal affirmation, not silent assent, legitimated the court's authority and provincial authority in general. The judges issuing the rules knew that their fellow colonists' most meaningful interactions with the provincial government took place in the courthouse, not in the statehouse or at the ballot box. Thus, they strove to secure the deference of those they ruled at this most basic level of government.[93]

George Stroud's presentment by the Chester County grand jury in 1693 for "speaking some words" against a county justice epitomized the Philadelphia Court's ideal. Originally brought before a single justice, Stroud requested an audience before all the county justices, whereupon he acknowledged his crime and submitted himself to the bench. The court then ordered that "If he [Stroud] behave himselfe well towards the majestrates and All other of the kings liege Peopell for A year and A Day and pay the Charges

Figure 5. The Rules of Court of the Philadelphia Court of Quarter Sessions and Common Pleas, June 2, 1686. Record of the Philadelphia Courts, 1685–86, Call #AM 3902, Historical Society of Pennsylvania, 24. Courtesy of the Historical Society of Pennsylvania.

he be for this time Discharged."[94] This represented the proper functioning of the provincial legal speech economy, the appropriate performative exchange to secure the sociolegal order. Willingly and publicly penitent, Stroud, on his part, focused on reforming his behavior in the future; magnanimous and lenient, the judges, on their part, focused on reincorporating Stroud into the community. This verbal exchange bound Stroud and the judges in a web of mutual civic obligation. Modeled on the rituals of public atonement and forgiveness central to the disciplinary process in the Quaker Meeting, this exchange epitomized Penn's vision of civic governance, writ small.

If Stroud's presentment represented the ideal, then the trial and sentencing of Thomas Tunneclift revealed the realities colonial courts so often faced. On October 14, 1687, Tunneclift appeared in the Bucks County courthouse on a charge of abuse.[95] Hannah Overton, another resident of Bucks, attested to Justice William Yardley that "Tunneclif was abusive to her [and] that she was afraid of her Life & of her Chdrns lifes." Yardley, convinced that Tunneclift's threats posed a real danger to the Overton family, ordered the defendant to post a recognizance or "peace bond" of £20 mandating his appearance at the next meeting of the Quarter Sessions. Moreover, the terms of this recognizance required more than simply the convicted's appearance before the bench three months hence; it also obliged Tunneclift to "acknowledge him self to stand Indebted to the govrnrs use in £20 to be leviyed on his lands good & Chattles" should he break the peace in any manner in the interim. Tunneclift not having £20, two other Bucks residents, Joseph Miller and Francis Rossill, each pledged £10 as sureties to cover the bond if Tunneclift's behavior forfeited it.

Their investment quickly proved ill advised, however. As soon as Miller and Rossill made their pledges, "Tho: Tunneclf Imediately as he was bond abused the bench & Said I care not A pin for none of you you have abused me & wronged me & bid them do their worst." Accordingly, "the Court adjudge[d] that the abovesaid sum be pticularly levied on the lands goods and Chattels of" Miller and Rossill. Having forfeited his sureties' bonds with his abusive outburst against the judge's integrity, Tunneclift was free to go on his way.[96]

In general, legal performances in Pennsylvania's early courts were neither as orderly as the Philadelphia Court's prescriptions nor as disorderly as Tunneclift's outburst. Nor did participants in provincial courts, for that matter, spend much time reaffirming or resisting that institution's power. Indeed, these two examples stood out precisely because the ruling authority (in the former instance) and the object of that authority (in the latter instance) made defining the relationship between the court and those whom it would rule the explicit subject of their legal performance. Colonists' experiences in court more commonly resembled that of Jacob Farbrushes. Farbrushes sued Peter Erickson in 1682 for defamation after Erickson told Chester County Sheriff John Test that "This old Rogue [Farbrushes] will * mee."[97] Upon hearing the sheriff attest to Erickson's words, the jury ruled in the plaintiff's favor. Farbrushes's desire to use the courts to clear his name provides a means of examining the subjects and objects of legal discourse in early Pennsylvania's courts, encompassing the topics of legal discussion, the grievances for which litigants sought legal remedies, the people embedded within this web of legal truth and consequences, and those agents who used the courts for those ends.

Ordinary colonists like Jacob Farbrushes used the courts not as sites in which to stage displays of deference or defiance but for decidedly more routine activities. The legal culture that the colonists—both ordinary litigants and magistrates—created emerged not from scripted rituals but from legal dialogues much like the ones in Farbrushes' case.[98] These narratives of everyday legal life, if not always dramatic, reveal the ways in which colonists used the legal system to help define their relationship to each other. They also show how legal performance defined the contours of civic identity and authority in early Pennsylvania.

Pennsylvanians went to court for a variety of reasons in the colony's early years: to exchange lands, recover debts, defend themselves against criminal accusations, or guard their reputation.[99] They used the courts, for example, to transfer, secure, or contest title to property. The courts served as the sites where participants could "declare in Open Cort" their desire to exchange gifts and deeds, making the exchange official through its inscription into the Court of Common Pleas minute book.[100] Indeed, within any given session of early provincial courts, most cases involved neither criminal nor civil suits but declarations of this kind, making Pennsylvania's courts typical for colonial English America.

At times, litigants called upon the courts to adjudicate between conflicting stories about property, as in Arnoldus Delgrande's suit against Otto Ernest Cock for possession of Tinicum Island. This case forced jurors to weigh not only the trustworthiness of the evidence each side offered but also the relative merits of different genres of evidence: oral testimony given in court on Cock's behalf versus written testimony given on Delgrande's behalf. After two witnesses testified about an alleged deal made between Delgrande's father and Cock for Tinicum Island, Delgrande submitted as evidence "the Testimony of Nicolas More," secretary of the Society of Free Traders, "in writing under his own hand." More's testimony offered a detailed conversation he had had with Cock in which the latter appeared to have admitted that "I have wronged Lagranges Children from their Rights." Swayed either by More's significantly more detailed account or by his social status as a wealthy merchant and Philadelphia county judge, the jury found for Delgrande and awarded him the land, plus 40 shillings damage.[101] The courts even served as sites for the dissemination of nonlinguistic, but still extremely important, forms of communication, as farmers routinely announced the pattern of their brands so that others could easily identify their animals.[102] Judges and juries, then, created property out of the legal narratives that circulated in court, turning stories of land and brands into farms and livestock.[103]

Beyond matters of property, litigants brought a wide variety of cases to trial, most often dealing with debt, "case," or trespass and less often with assault or sexual offenses. Pennsylvanians differed little in this respect from colonists elsewhere in British America.[104] The stories from the outside world that circulated in court ranged from the sensational to the mundane. Jurors in Sussex County listened to justices debate whether Thomas Morton was a bastard, to reports that witnesses overheard Edward Harrison "saying that hee Lay with Sarah Willshire all night after She was marryed unto John Dyer," and to Timothy Dowgan's recounting Joseph Ayliff's "Dogging, Pursuing, and Following the Complainant in sundry places on the Highways and Assulting him with Some Blows to the Complaintants Great Terror."[105] A Bucks County marital dispute led to Joseph Smalwood's prosecution for abusing his wife and a subsequent appearance before the court on a report that "he had since threatened to do her further mischiefe." Bucks jurors also heard Isaac Partington and William Fower testify to Randolph Smalwood's "abusing and endeavouring to force Elizabeth Wilson."[106] In all Pennsylvania county courts, witnesses and litigants recounted tales of abuse, theft, and fornication on the part of some of the province's most humble—and occasionally most notable—citizens, in varying degrees of detail.

But very often, chroniclers of the legal narratives presented in colonial courts told tales about words, especially during Pennsylvania's early years. Or rather, they told stories about the problem of unruly or disruptive words, as many Pennsylvanians dragged other provincials into court simply for opening their mouths. County courts saw numerous cases every year involving some infractions of the provincial speech economy, including accusations of slander, swearing oaths, spreading false news, or speaking out against provincial authorities, whether magistrates, the government, or the courts themselves. Judging by the cases that made it to trial, the speech economy of Pennsylvania in its first decade was at least as disorderly, and social and civic authority at least as tenuous, as in other English colonies in their early days.[107] The prevalence of these speech cases in provincial courts resulted from colonists' sensitivity to inflammatory language (as in the case involving Farbrushes and Erickson); like provincials elsewhere in British America, Pennsylvanians showed a remarkable willingness to take their neighbors to court for slander or defamation during the province's early years.[108] These slander cases dealt primarily with three types of accusations: commercial chicanery, sexual impropriety, and official misbehavior on the part of magistrates or other public servants.

Some colonists filed charges of slander and defamation in response to accusations of commercial malfeasance. Such insults could have a potentially disastrous effect in an economic world where an individual's livelihood depended on trust. Men and women worried about this possibility. Anne Milcome, a Bucks County widow, took a neighboring husband and wife to court on charges of defamation, worried that their aspersions against her business practices would imperil her credit.[109] John Beachem sued George Robeson for calling Beachem and his father "West Country Rogue[s]" and "Sharp Stealing Beggers and Dogs." Beachem argued that these "False feigned Scandalous & malitious words" damaged his business as a butcher.[110] In other instances, men sued to defend themselves against gossip that they had defaulted on loans, written fraudulent contracts, or, in one case, burned another man's brands out of horses and cattle to steal them.[111] In comparison to other colonies, though, Pennsylvanians felt either less offended by their neighbors' making these types of accusations or less inclined to turn these insults into a legal matter.[112]

At other times, colonists used the court as a forum to repair their civic reputation or ease civic tension. On September 13, 1681, at the very first meeting of the Chester County Court following the granting of Penn's colonial charter, Lasse Cock, who had recently become Penn's Indian agent in America, arrived in court with a proclamation. He demanded "That if any had anything against him, They should declare it." As "Daniel Brenson & Charles Brigham upon oath," he continued, "together with Walter Pumphrey upon his Solemne Attestation, declared what they heard certain Indians speake again[st] him [Cock] and Capt Edmond Cantwell." Although the court failed to record the Indians' alleged claim, the charges clearly moved Cock: "upon oath," he "declared his Innocence, And hee had never spoken those words to the Indians, or any of that nature." The court thereupon cleared Cock, despite the fact that no one had apparently even filed formal charges against him.[113] That Cock clearly felt the need to rebut publicly rumors spread by local Native Americans, by proclamation in court and for posterity, revealed just how closely he, a Swedish man serving as mediator between the proprietor of an English colony and a variety of Indian polities, guarded his public reputation.

Cock's willingness to go to court reflected his sensitivity not merely to Indian opinion but also to English opinion. His fears had merit, as more than one Anglo-Pennsylvanian shared the belief that the colony's Swedes had, through their close association over the decades with the region's natives, degenerated into a cruder, more barbarous state than their European counterparts.[114] Richard Crosby's 1687 appearance in court testified to this fact. While the Chester County grand jury initially indicted Crosby on charges of drunken disorder and verbal abuse of a constable, the trial itself turned on an ethnic slur, suggesting ulterior motives behind the prosecution. Both William Goford and Johannes Friend repeated in court Crosby's (alleged) loud proclamation that "the Sweades were rogues and did take part with the Indians."[115] This charge must have given special offense given the (false) rumor that had swept the colony the previous year about the murder of Nicholas Scull and his family. In electing to prosecute Crosby, county officials may have hoped to avoid any possible divisions among the county's Euro-American settlers. Both the jury's decision to convict Crosby and the severity of his punishment—a £7 fine—reflected the fact that they too recognized the threat his words and deeds posed to the colony's nascent civic bonds.

Pennsylvanians more frequently sued those circulating rumors about domestic indiscretions, whether the gossip dealt with husbands abusing or abandoning wives, wives cuckolding husbands, or women's low public reputation (especially concerning illicit sexual encounters). Both the men bringing these cases and the grand juries prosecuting them aimed at restoring a husband's good name through the restoration of his wife's reputation, thus (it was hoped) restoring a measure of social order. Henry Stretcher of Sussex County, for example, brought a civil suit against Adam Johnson for spreading the story that Stretcher's wife Sarah had borne a "Bastard Child by a Negro." A jury ruled in Stretcher's favor after six local women and a local man, called upon to examine the infant, attested that the child "looked swarthy, but grew whiter and whiter."[116] Similarly, Sussex justice Luke Watson persisted in his defamation case against Henry Bowman even after the latter's death. Watson insisted on reading aloud in court the depositions of three English matrons attesting that his wife Mary had not borne a child out of wedlock in England before coming to America. In so doggedly defending both his wife's and, by extension, his own honor, the judge had managed to give the rumor its most public airing yet, even after the dead slanderer had stopped spreading the tale.[117]

Criminal prosecutions for slander or defamation followed similar patterns. In 1688, a Bucks grand jury presented Israel Taylor for the defamation of "ffrancis, wife of John Swift." The petit jury during the trial heard three witnesses testify that "Israel Taylor Sayd he verily believed that nick meaneing Nicholas Randolph the Servant of John Swift did lye with John Swifts Wife and that he believed in his Conscience he did god service in Telling of it" to his neighbors. Taylor presented in his defense a witness who attributed that particular rumor to one Gabriel Shallow. Taylor's witness failed to persuade the jury, however, who found Taylor guilty of criminal defamation and ordered him and a surety to bond themselves in the sum of £5 each for Taylor's good behavior until the next court of quarter sessions.[118] As with Stretcher's suit, this nexus of rumor and scandal called Swift's masculine authority over his wife into public question. But Swift may have felt more ambiguous about the verdict in this case than Stretcher had, as binding Taylor to good behavior offered the court a means to assert its authority over the defendant while offering no restitution to the aggrieved party in the defamation itself.

These legal narratives about speech most commonly entered the courtroom because of colonial officials' aggressive efforts to regulate the provincial speech economy. Criminal prosecutions for speech offenses comprised nearly three of every four speech-related cases that made it to court.[119] Concerned about disorderly speech in general and challenges to their own authority in particular, provincial officials enforced criminal sanctions against a wide range of verbal offenses. Their concern here mirrored their concern for their reputation elsewhere. They prosecuted their fellow colonists not only for offenses like lying, swearing, or blasphemy but also for challenging their authority or refusing to answer questions; they likewise regularly fined individuals present at court for swearing, talking back, or refusing to submit to the court's authority. Colonists faced charges of contempt in Pennsylvania more frequently than anywhere else in British North America.[120] If such sanctions did not always succeed in garnering the respect of those who had spoken inappropriately to the court—one man responded to the bench's fine by "saucilie anser[ing] Let the Court gett it how they can"[121]—they showed how central magistrates saw the legal speech economy to the development of authority in a young colony.

But at times it seemed that provincial judges, sheriffs, and constables concerned themselves not simply with punishing disorderly behavior in court or with protecting the legal system's reputation but with protecting their own reputations. The massive fines meted out for verbal abuse of magistrates illustrated the officers' of the court sensitivity to attacks on their character. Although the law called for a minimum fine of twenty shillings "according to the quality of the magistrate and the nature of the offence," in practice the fines ranged from a minimum of £5 to a maximum of £40. In some cases, the magistrates valued their names even higher; when James Claypoole felt that William Guest had slandered him and damaged his credit and status as a justice, he asked for £100 in damages. (The jury disagreed with Claypoole and ruled for Guest.)[122]

Indeed, prosecutions for speaking out against provincial authority often resulted from personal attacks on colonial officials. When John Maddock disagreed with the result of his case, he chose not to complain about the court's failures in general but instead proclaimed "in Open Cort . . . that the said prtyes" John Simcock and John Bristow, two county judges, were "two of the greatest Rogues that ever came into America." Maddock's pronouncement earned him a £5 fine.[123] And nearly a decade after casting aspersions on the loyalty of the province's Swedish residents, Crosby appeared before the court for calling a justice of the peace a "Pittyful sorrowfull fellow" who had "sold" his office. Only after submitting to the bench and apologizing for his offense was Crosby released with no fine.[124]

Maddock's and Crosby's prosecutions represented extreme, but not unique, examples of these types of cases. Pennsylvania's provincial officials were as sensitive to challenges to their authority as their counterparts in New England or Virginia. Compared with early Puritan Massachusetts, for example—a colony that one historian has argued afforded disorderly speech a "particular weight" compared to other English colonial settlements—court officials prosecuted defendants for verbally abusing colonial authority figures at least as often as did magistrates in the Bay colony.[125] Moreover, Pennsylvania differed from Massachusetts in one crucial respect: while the latter prosecuted those who spoke out improperly against a wide variety of colonial authority figures—including fathers, masters, ministers, magistrates, or other provincial officials—Pennsylvania afforded special protection only to the reputations of those holding governmental offices.[126] In cases where witnesses specifically denounced clergy, Pennsylvania courts allowed such heated words without comment or sanction. In Justa Anderson's property suit against the minister Lawrentius Carolus, for example, multiple witnesses referred to the defendant as a cheat—and Carolus lost the case.[127] Though masters and ministers may have hoped for some of the protection from public abuse the legal system afforded their counterparts to the north, they did not get it.

A close look at the subjects and objects of these legal narratives of everyday life in Pennsylvania's first years suggests some of the contradictions inherent in legal officials' efforts to build their legitimacy through regulating the legal speech economy. The Philadelphia Court of Quarter Sessions hoped that it could prescribe certain modes of interaction between magistrates and ordinary provincials. Prosecuting deviants for infractions such as contempt of court or verbal abuse of constables and justices might have seemed like an effective mechanism to produce such relationships: sanctioning offenders might either silence the dissent and serve as an object lesson to others or might elicit—as in Crosby's case—the willing submission of the offender and an acknowledgment of the court's authority.

Attempting to produce these outcomes, though, ran the risk that the object of such discipline would not acknowledge the court's authority, turning a display of power into one of weakness. The case of Thomas Tunneclift served as evidence of that. Moreover, prosecuting those who had slandered justices or sheriffs outside the courthouse necessitated recirculating the slander to a broader audience in order to combat it, precisely the same problem that wounded patriarchs faced when they initiated civil suits against men supposedly damaging their reputation. It proved impossible to unsay the slurs that they feared had weakened their legitimacy.[128] Colonial leaders learned their efforts to curb abusive or slanderous speech toward men in positions of authority through prosecution yielded limited results.

If provincial officials failed to achieve the goals they initially sought, their efforts had pervasive, if subtler, effects on colonial civic identity, however. Through cases involving both civil and criminal speech offenses, particularly those involving slander and defamation, the courts reshaped the relationship between gender, speech, and authority; their interrelationship became both a subject and an object of colonial legal narratives. Gender loomed large in these types of cases for two reasons. First, colonial men viewed sexual insults, especially those lodged against their wives, as particularly damaging to their reputations; they believed their sense of masculine authority was tightly linked to the reputations of their female dependants. Second, women appeared disproportionately often as litigants in these cases.[129]

Male and female colonial litigants initiated slander and defamation for similar reasons, such as repairing their reputations as honest traders or good householders. They experienced these cases differently, though. This distinction lay not in the fact that women were publicly held to strict sexual standards while juries held men to strict financial ones; the public at large held men to strict sexual standards as well, as those plaintiffs eager to quash rumors of cuckoldry could attest.[130] It came instead from the relationships to civic culture that the regulation of public discourse ensconced for men and women. For while women in Pennsylvania, like women elsewhere in the Anglo-American world, acted as plaintiffs or defendants in slander and defamation cases more frequently than they did other cases, they were still the overwhelming minority in each category: men brought six of every seven slander suits to court and comprised nearly three of every four defendants in such suits.[131] So while many of these civil speech cases were *about* women—or more particularly, about gender relations between men and women—women's participation was often limited. When Luke Watson sued Henry Bowman and Henry Stretcher sued Adam Johnson, each acted to protect his wife's reputation. The husbands initiated and settled these disputes against other men about their wives. Thus, even those cases in which women most frequently participated exemplified how women became *objects* of legal discourse and action in early Pennsylvania more than *subjects* speaking and acting in court.

This gender disparity in slander and defamation cases mirrored women's experiences in other court cases as well. Women's words and actions were reported by men far more than by the women themselves. Women seldom acted alone in either criminal or civil cases. Most female plaintiffs were married, and thus brought suit with their husbands.[132] Although women participated more frequently in legal proceedings as witnesses than as plaintiffs or defendants, here too they found their authority somewhat circumscribed. With the exception of a handful of cases dealing with fornication, pregnancy, rape, or other sexual matters—cases in which juries of women were appointed to examine women's bodies as evidence and return with a report—women never served as the sole witness(es) in either a civil or criminal case.[133] Moreover, Quaker legal reforms intended to encourage dispute settlements outside the court probably reduced women's participation in court further, as they were disproportionately likely to be involved in smaller commercial disputes. Efforts at simplification had an unintended consequence for women. Women's words could be powerful but only when circumscribed within a certain sphere.[134]

Thus, female speech almost never stood alone in early Pennsylvania courts but was heard almost always alongside other (male) voices. Women's words were granted neither the legitimacy nor the legitimating effects of men's in court. Legal stories about gender relations repeatedly emphasized the importance of gender in shaping social power but in ways that belied the active role women's speech played in shaping social power in everyday life. Not all men participated in this legal discursive culture as subjects. Free adult males with property predominated, while boys, unfree men, nonwhites, and the propertyless appeared as speaking legal subjects less often or not at all.[135] Nor were women categorically excluded, as the suit brought by Anne Milcome illustrates. In practice, however, the process of subjectification and objectification through legal participation privileged male voices. Public legal identity, as defined by speaking in court, spoke in a masculine tone.

And if the relationship between speaking and being spoken of in court revealed and created gender hierarchies at the same time, so too did it affect the racial and cultural hierarchies central to the English colonial project in the Delaware Valley. Indigenous peoples only rarely appeared in colonial courts and then nearly exclusively to sell their land; in only one instance did an Indian appear in a Pennsylvania court to press a civil claim, as a provincial might. African Americans, meanwhile, appeared infrequently and then only as objects of the court's disciplinary power.[136] Lasse Cock's ironic proclamation, standing as it did at the beginning of Penn's "Holy Experiment" on the Delaware, foretold the future of European expansion as it reflected the current balance of power. Cock may have worried about the effect of Indian words on his reputation and his income as a go-between, but he expressed these concerns in a Pennsylvanian court. Indian words in Cock's present held strong consequences; in the decades to come, only European words in Anglo-American courts would become law.[137]

In the end, Pennsylvania's magistrates failed to control the provincial legal speech economy in the colony's early years as they had intended. The high rate of prosecution for lying, swearing, or speech against authority may have reflected their desire to maintain orderly or "Quakerized" speech ways in Pennsylvania, but it also reflected the impossibility of maintaining those ideals in practice. Though their efforts to secure their legitimacy through the careful management of discourse inside and outside the courtroom could not foster appropriate respect for governmental authority, they nonetheless shaped provincial civic identity. Through their attempts to ground their legitimacy in a verbal exchange between rulers and ruled, provincial officials encouraged and achieved a remarkably broad-based participation in the legal system.[138] But given the exclusions from these legal dialogues, civic participation, intentionally or not, took on racial and gendered overtones. The magistracy thus worked toward a unified civic identity that defined the idealized citizen through his acknowledged respect for provincial institutions but constructed an imagined civic subject defined by gender and race.

Bonds and Bodies

In March 1690, the grand jury of Bucks County indicted Richard Thatcher, Jr., on suspicion of stealing one of his neighbor's hogs. After hearing from the neighbor who reported a missing hog, a man who noticed that Thatcher had suddenly acquired a new hog, and a third man who had purchased said hog from Thatcher even as he suspected it stolen, the petit jury took little time to deliberate. It found Thatcher guilty of theft, ordering him to make threefold satisfaction to the pig's owner and to receive twenty-one stripes on his bare back in public. Following this judgment, however, Thatcher again appeared before the court, this time to enter into a bond worth £20 to appear at the next meeting of the Court of Quarter Sessions "and to be of good abearing in the meane time." In exchange for this submission to its authority, the court deferred, but not remitted, Thatcher's punishment: it replaced a severe and spectacular punishment on his body with a threatened punishment against his property. Thatcher showed his gratitude for the court's leniency; though he would later run afoul of the law, he kept his word—and the peace—after his conviction for theft and did not forfeit his bond.[139]

Thatcher's experience reflected the ameliorative effects of Quaker legal reform on those convicted or even accused of serious crimes. In the years before Penn received his charter, criminals in what became Pennsylvania faced severe sanctions. The "Duke's Laws," the criminal code in force between 1676 and 1682, placed a heavy emphasis on corporal punishments such as whippings and branding as deterrents to crime, much like the English criminal code. (The Duke's Laws, for example, called for hog thieves such as Thatcher to lose their ears.)[140] When a 1680 Kent County jury convicted John Cannaway of theft, shortly before Penn took control of the Lower Counties, county justices sentenced him to twenty-one lashes for the crime, as prescribed by law. They did not have the option of deferring punishment through a mechanism like the peace bond.[141] Quaker legislators, though, eschewed these practices when they crafted a criminal code, emphasizing reform over corporal punishment. The resolution of the Thatcher and Cannaway cases epitomized the difference between these approaches. The latter case ended in the punishment of the convicted's body, the former with the threat of sanction against the convicted's property: one with the public ritual of a whipping and the other with the public ritual of a promise.

Not everyone experienced Quaker legal reform equally, though. In 1687, the grand jury for the Chester Court of Quarter Sessions presented Anne Neales for keeping dogs that killed her neighbors' livestock and for "Deteining in her Service an Indian Boy named Cato" who regularly hunted neighbors' livestock as well. Neales immediately acknowledged her crime and put herself on the mercy of the court, and the county justices responded with leniency for the damage caused by her unruly canines; she received only a ten-shilling fine, plus a charge of court costs. After Neales's sentencing, the court turned its attention to Cato, who appeared to have been responsible for the illicit hunting in the case. The court did not call upon Cato to testify, ask for a confession, sentence him to a flogging, or even—as the Bucks justices would with Richard Thatcher over two years later—bind him to the peace. Instead, the Bucks Court bound Andrew Friend in the amount of £20 that Cato would keep the peace for the foreseeable future.[142] While Thatcher had bound himself to the peace to avoid a whipping, the Chester Court showed no interest in a promise of good behavior from either the Indian servant Cato or even the propertied Neales. Only Friend's word (and bond) mattered.

The differences between Thatcher's, Neales's, and Cato's experiences illustrate the unintended consequences of Quaker legal reforms. Although magistrates attempted earnestly to avoid corporal punishment whenever possible through the extensive use of peace bonds, they did so selectively. They proved increasingly willing to employ peace bonds to control the behavior of property-owning adult white males, while subjecting the unpropertied— especially white women and African Americans—to a different range of punishments. Colonists increasingly thought some bodies good to whip.[143] At the same time, they thought only certain individuals capable of publicly professing their intentions to reform their behavior. The law sanctioned the conduct of most white men differently than it did the conduct of others: it permitted the former to escape corporal punishment by offering word and bond while prohibiting the latter this same opportunity.[144]

This unequal distribution of punishments shaped the meaning of race, gender, and property in early Pennsylvania. Although Penn and his fellow reformers hoped that making the legal system more accessible might erode social distinctions, the sanctioning process worked to create new distinctions among Pennsylvania's settler population. It helped map the social topology of colonial Pennsylvania, solidifying the meaning of race and gender by ensuring that different groups interacted with the government in different ways.[145] A central element of Quaker jurisprudence—recognizances, or peace bonds—proved particularly important in shaping hierarchical civic identities in early Pennsylvania.

The use of recognizances hardly rendered provincial magistrates unique. Their counterparts elsewhere in the Anglo-Atlantic world found them a helpful tool for maintaining social order in the seventeenth century.[146] Anglo-American courts employed recognizances in two different ways.[147] Sheriffs and justices routinely forced suspected criminals, plaintiffs, defendants, or even sometimes witnesses to enter into a recognizance of a certain amount requiring their presence at court; failure to appear meant forfeiting the bond. Used this way, bonds played a crucial role in the pretrial process. But magistrates also used recognizances to prevent disorder; Anglo-American judges frequently required both suspect and convicted criminals to enter into a recognizance, or peace bond, to keep the peace or remain "of good behavior" for a particular period of time. In most cases, they merely required the guilty to keep the peace until the next meeting of the Quarter Sessions. At other times, they extended the length of these bonds. The value of these types of recognizances varied, ranging in England and in Pennsylvania from £5 to £40; if an individual did not own the property necessary to pay the bond, he or she needed to find sureties who could put up the money in his or her stead.

Thus, magistrates used peace bonds as a means of preventing crime by peremptorily bonding prospective criminals outside the courtroom to keep the peace or by making the peace bond part of a criminal sentence—as in the cases of Richard Thatcher or Thomas Tunneclift, for example. Pennsylvania's governing class found peace bonds, which acted on the will instead of the body, well suited to accomplish its goal of encouraging the development of a disciplined self among the populace and made the peace bond its primary instrument in achieving this goal.[148] The peace bond differed from other instruments of punishment in several ways. First, it displaced punishment temporally. Most other forms of sanction punished past deviant behavior in present time. New England magistrates may have insisted that slanders offer public apologies to the slandered, but these performances could not unsay words already said, nor could they influence future conduct. Fines and corporal punishments such as lashing, branding, or mutilations likewise visited immediate punishment on person and property for crimes already committed. They offered a brief sanction; even the effects of these punishments lasted longer.

Peace bonds, on the other hand, regulated future behavior: the bond itself represented a pledge for ordered conduct from that point forward.[149] Threatening to sanction property instead of person, it required the bonded individual to exercise self-discipline in lieu of corporal discipline, under pain of forfeiting the bond. Given the size of the bonds—larger than those given out by magistrates in England[150]—those bonded found the financial incentives to exercise self-discipline and honor the bond quite strong. Bonds also served a social purpose as well, for offenders who found themselves forced to rely on sureties to help cover the bond if they lacked the capital; the bonds deepened the social ties between the convicted and their sureties. Nor did justices limit themselves to using peace bonds to sanction individuals for crimes they had already committed; they frequently bound individuals for the mere suspicion of criminal activity, disciplining citizens, in effect, for crimes they might commit in the future.[151] Moreover, the bonds had a potentially unlimited duration. While justices most often bound criminals for a short period, such as the next meeting of the Quarter Sessions, their ability to renew the length of the bonds gave them enormous discretionary power.

Second, peace bonds displaced the subject of punishment. Sanctions such as whipping, placing offenders in stocks, and even forcing convicted offenders to wear visible signs of their offense—such as the "Roman T" courts sometimes ordered convicted thieves to wear[152]—targeted the surface of the body as the locus of punishment. Peace bonds, however, emphasized embodied behavior; they provided a means of translating speech—the pledge to keep the peace—into embodiment, through the threat of future sanction. The operation of peace bonds as an effective social sanction both assumed the existence of an interior social self capable of exercising self-discipline and provided a means of producing that self. The bond operated as a secularized form of the disciplinary rituals of gospel order by which Quaker meetings produced and regulated pious Quaker selves. Much like Friends' disciplinary practice of the visitation, magistrates used the ritual of bonding and releasing accused and suspected criminals as a coerced performance whose goal was to lead deviants to a performance of self that displayed a unity with institutional authority.

Finally, the use of the peace bond helped produce the speech economy Penn desired, especially when applied as part of a criminal sentence. The bond required its subject to affirm, ritually and publicly, his submission to the government, "oblidg[ing]" to the "governor his heirs & successors" or pledging to "behave himselfe towards all his Magisties Leedge Subjects & well & trewly keepe the kings peace."[153] They offered this pledge publicly, before their community. Moreover, the bonds' requirement that bonded individuals appear subsequently in court ensured the repetition of this initial performance, further modeling the subject's submission. The use of peace bonds as a form of deferred punishment produced the ritual performances of deference to provincial institutions that Pennsylvania's leaders sought.

For all these reasons, peace bonds proved extremely popular among Quaker jurists. Pennsylvania's magistrates bonded criminals to the peace during the colony's first decade and a half at a rate significantly higher than their counterparts in other Anglo-American colonies, issuing nearly five bonds per year during this period.[154] Moreover, the courts' use of peace bonds as a tool of punishment and prevention revealed a marked preference for disciplining the penitent self of convicted criminals rather than punishing their bodies: Pennsylvania courts sentenced only thirty-two criminals to public lashings during colony's first fifteen years. Convicted criminals thus received sentences deferring punishment more than twice as often than they received sentences mandating corporal punishment. Through the use of peace bonds, Quaker leaders had seemingly achieved their twin goals of a more humane, orderly legal system and incorporating a broad range of colonists into their civic order—albeit through compulsory civic rituals.

This success came at a significant cost, however. It sacrificed Quaker tradition. English Friends had refused to offer bonds for good behavior, believing that posting a bond implied a form of untrustworthiness. Those who had been saved needed no external compulsion to obey the law. Pennsylvania's Quaker magistrates, however, had no compunctions about placing this form of compulsion against alleged or convicted lawbreakers. Moreover, they bound Quakers, such as Thomas Tunneclift and Richard Thatcher, and non-Quakers alike. Friends' use of recognizances was profoundly ironic. They embraced it because they believed, and not without reason, that this mechanism of legal control would encourage settlers to embody Quaker habits of self-discipline as they adapted to life in an American settlement. Peace bonds would "Quakerize" colonists as well as creolizing them. But Friends could only achieve this goal by departing from the religious practices of their "ancestors." Their most effective tool for civic creolization was itself creole.

Their use of peace bonds failed to achieve another crucial Quaker reform goal: the creation of a more egalitarian legal system. Indeed, peace bonds, perhaps unintentionally, helped inscribe inequalities of property, race, and gender within Pennsylvania's early legal order. The peace bond proved both a reformist and an exclusionary legal tool. Based on a threat against property, it obviously favored the propertied. Even presuming that unpropertied individuals might secure sureties to help put up the sums necessary to pay the peace bond—and many did—the system put Pennsylvanians of limited means at a great disadvantage.

Even beyond the distinction they drew between the propertied and the unpropertied, peace bonds in their ordinary application helped solidify racial and gender differences among participants in Pennsylvania's legal system as well.[155] Overall, the courts used peace bonds as a mechanism against white men, who accounted for more than eleven of every twelve individuals bonded between 1681 and 1695. Courts rarely bonded white women alone, sometimes preferring, as in the case of Sarah Smith, to bond a male relative as well that she keep the peace.[156] Moreover, the only instance in which a court issued a peace bond on behalf of a nonwhite individual occurred in Anne Neale's case, in which Andrew Friend obligated himself to monitor Cato's behavior. The near-total absence of white women and total absence of nonwhites from the bonding process signified their exclusion from a crucial civic dialogue through which provincial magistrates affirmed their authority and tied citizens more tightly to the government. In rendering these racialized and gendered "others" spectators to this civic ritual, the process of peace bonding reinforced the notion that only white men had civic selves that needed discipline and that only white men deserved to participate in legal dialogues with provincial magistrates.

The unequal distribution of peace bonds had one other crucial implication. Peace bonds appealed to Quaker leaders because of their humane character, furthering their goal of limiting corporal punishment. But while white men nearly exclusively received the peace bond as a form of punishment, the courts used corporal punishments such as whippings against a much wider range of the convicted. Though they made up an extremely small number of those bonded, white women and African American men and women comprised two of every five individuals whipped. White women and African Americans may have made inappropriate subjects to pledge themselves ritually and publicly to keep the peace and affirm their loyalty to proprietor and king, but their bodies made appropriate sites for public punishment.

Two cases—one in a Sussex County court, one initiated by a Philadelphia County court—epitomize the strange alchemy that occurred in which the prerogatives of property ensconced in the peace-bond process became the prerogatives of race and gender. In one instance, William Kaning of Sussex reported widely that George Young and Henry Pullin "stole hogs." Young and Pullin then sued Kaning for slander, each claiming damage to his reputation. The jury found for the plaintiffs, determining that the "deft deserv[ed] Corporall punishment according to the law." Kaning then petitioned the "Worshipfull Court and Humbly b[e]g[ged] and submit[ed] myselfe to you upon my bare knees to forgive me this once more and not to bring me more publick shame to me and mine for ever, and for the future time to come I shall take more care for doeing the like again and y[ou]r peitioner in duty bound shall pray[.]" Young and Pullin accepted Kaning's apology, and after his "declaration [was] reapeated publickly in open Court word for word and the Court Accepted his soe doeing as corporall punishment, after which the Court passed Judgment for Costs of suite."[157] Thus, Kaning required neither personal property nor that pledged by sureties to avoid whipping: words could substitute for punishment on his person.

African Americans did not have the same range of options to speak in court, of course. In March 1693, the Philadelphia Court of Quarter Sessions, concerned about disorder on the Sabbath, "Ordered that a Warr[an]t be drawn for the keeping the Watch, And that Negroes & loose people be taken up that are playing about the Streets on the First day."[158] Spurred by the county court's warrant, the Provincial Council took matters even further, empowering not only the constables but indeed

> anie person whatsoever to have power to take up Negroes, male or female, whom they should find gadding abroad on the said first dayes of the week, without a ticket from their Mr. or Mris., or not in their Compa[ny], or to carry them to goale, there to remaine that night, & that without meat or drink, & to Cause them to be publickly whipt the next morning with 39 Lashes, well laid on, on their bare backs, for which their sd Mr. or Mris. should pay 15d to the whipper at his deliverie of them.[159]

The Council had authorized all whites—and only whites—to mete out punishment and had singled out (potentially) all blacks as fit subjects for one of the harshest penalties reserved under the law.

Thus, colonists' civic identities in Pennsylvania emerged from two different legal economies of punishment. White men found their civic identities defined largely through a legal economy of speech provincial magistrates worked hard to construct. White women and all African Americans found their experiences in court shaped by a legal economy of violence—the range of permissible violent punishments that defined who could inflict violence against whom as well as who was an appropriate object of such violence.[160] While white men's legal identities were shaped through their participation in a broad range of legal speech performances—including an overrepresentation in peace bonding, the legal tool central to Quaker civic reform efforts—they were underrepresented in the legal economy of violence that corporal punishment represented.[161]

On the other hand, the courts excluded white women and African Americans and Native Americans of both sexes from a wide range of speech performances in court, including the peace-bond process, while these groups were overrepresented in the infliction of whippings. Through selective enforcement of peace bonds and corporal punishment, provincial magistrates had begun to define some bodies as appropriate for civic participation and some as appropriate for punishment, thereby sustaining crucial status hierarchies. Through their efforts to police provincial speech codes, through their efforts to define the rules by which people spoke in court, and through the deference they tried to inculcate, provincial magistrates tried to effect a certain type of civic authority. Ironically, perhaps, they had more success sharpening lines of race and gender in early Pennsylvania than building the ideal civic subject.

On February 16, 1684, Anthony Weston presented a petition containing a list of proposals to the Provincial Council criticizing Penn's plans for Philadelphia and suggesting possible alternatives. Two of the men who had met in Thomas Hooton's tavern to discuss and subscribe to Weston's petition appeared with him before the Council and informed the assembled officials that they "would stand to his [Weston's] paper."

The "great presumption" these men had shown displeased Governor Penn and the Council. Penn immediately asked the councilors what punishment Weston, as the ringleader, deserved; they thought it best to "have him Whypt." They thereupon sentenced Weston to three public whippings of ten lashes each in the "Market place on Market daye," starting immediately, "this being [the] first day." They bound the others who had subscribed to the petition in recognizances of £50 each for varying terms. They bound the freemen until the next sitting of the Assembly. Both the servants who signed Weston's petition and their masters found themselves punished more severely, however; the Council bound each in the sum of £50 to keep the peace for the respective servant's remaining time. Satisfied with this outcome, the Council adjourned for the day.[162]

This interaction encapsulated the relationship between the economies of speech and violence that shaped punishment in early Pennsylvania. In the ruling elite's calculus of who could say what to whom, they clearly did not feel that ordinary freemen and servants had the right to petition and criticize the government. Much like the Assembly, Penn presumed that the role of freemen was, like the role of the Assembly, analogous to that of a plebiscite—able certainly to express their views through voting but certainly not qualified to have a "debateing" voice, particularly with their betters in the Provincial Council or with the proprietor himself. And it revealed how the use of a particular form of Quaker sanction—the peace bond—created identities for those it incorporated into the legal order. Both free and unfree men had access to this gendered form of sanction, giving their word, under pain of £50, as a form of deferred punishment. For violating the rules of the political speech economy, Anthony Weston's compatriots offered legal speech acts that reincorporated them into the civic whole.

That Weston himself was not so lucky—no words could save his thirty lashes on market day—revealed early on the limits of Penn's plans to create a unified citizenry solely through the creation of a deferential speech economy. Penn's legal code reflected his belief in the ability of state power to produce virtuous citizens in a manner that largely eschewed corporal punishment. The fact that Penn felt the need to sanction Weston's words by punishing his body so harshly, however, illustrates that even Penn saw the limits of deference in maintaining social order. Words alone could neither produce virtuous citizens nor construct a unified civic identity among the populace. Penn lamented to Thomas Lloyd that he hoped "thos[e] that once feared I had to[o] much pow[e]r will now see I have not enough," only two years after the Weston affair. He could only hope that his colonists would see, as he had, "that excess of pow[e]r does not the misceif [sic] that Licentiousness does to a state" and the danger liberty posed. Given the choice between prosperity and too much liberty and an order enforced by strong state power, Penn wrote, "order & peace with poverty is certainly better."[163]

Nor could the regulation of civic speech resolve differences between the Upper and Lower Counties or between Quakers and non-Quakers in Pennsylvania. Real differences in interest and outlook separated these two regions. Resolving the conflict between Quakers and non-Quakers throughout the province proved difficult as well. They disagreed vehemently over the question of civic obligation, particularly with respect to military service during time of war. The fact that Fletcher and other provincial Anglicans shared more common ground with Native Americans than their Quaker compatriots in this respect demonstrated the fragility of Pennsylvania's civic culture. Words could hardly solve these problems. But if Penn's notion of politics failed at constructing civic unity, the Quaker legal system was somewhat successful, slowly shaping its own forms of civic identity through ordinary citizens' interactions with magistrates and each other.

These early efforts at forming a civic identity through structures of politics and legality succeeded only partially. They failed to resolve some of the vexing paradoxes that Penn himself had created in founding his "Holy Experiment" or, indeed, that the very notion of creating a creole civic identity posed. Nor did these paradoxes and contradictions face early Pennsylvanians only in the civic realm. The Keithian controversy that wracked the colony throughout the mid-1690s revealed the fractures in Quaker identity, showing the problems that creolization posed for the creation of any stable cultural forms during the founding years.

CHAPTER 4

"Bastard Quakers" in America

The Keithian Schism and the Creation of Creole Quakerism in Early Pennsylvania, 1691–1693

The Proclamation

BY 25 AUGUST 1692, Philadelphia's justices had had enough of George Keith. What had begun as a conflict among ministers within the Quaker Meeting over the nature of Christ's incarnate and resurrected body had escalated, leading Keith to public criticism not just of the Meeting but of prominent Friends in government as well. Upset at these attacks on their character in conversation and print, city magistrates drafted a "Publick Writing" warning Keith of the consequences of continuing the political and religious dispute that had begun last year. Their paper was then "proclaimed by the Common Crier in the Market place against *G.K.*"[1] The crier opened by announcing the justices' opinion "that George Keith . . . did, contrary to his Duty, publickly revile" Thomas Lloyd, the province's deputy governor. He then proceeded to list the insults Keith had levied against Lloyd. Keith, the crier shouted, had "call[ed] him [Lloyd] an impudent Man, telling him he was not fit to be Governour, and that his Name would stink, with many other slighting and abusive expressions." Nor was that the last of Keith's offenses; the crier also reported that Keith had questioned some of the magistrates' recent actions "*with an unusual insolency*" and that by publishing these disagreements he and William Bradford, the colony's only printer, had "laboured to possess the Readers of their Pamphlet That it is inconsistent for those who are Ministers of the Gospel to act as Magistrates."

The crier stressed that this public condemnation of Keith and his follow-ers resulted from neither personal nor sectarian partisanship. The county's Quaker justices could endure the Keithians' "many personal Reflections against us, and their gross Reveilings of our Religious Society." But to "pass by or connive at such part of the said Pamphlet and Speeches, that have a tendency to Sedition or Disturbance of the Peace" would violate "our Trust to the King and Governour, as also to the Inhabitants of this Government," making them poor civic stewards. "Therefore, for the undeceiving of all Peo-ple," the justices "have thought fit by this Publick Writing . . . to Caution such who are well affected to the Security, Peace, and Legal Administration of Justice in this place, that they give no Countenance to any Revilers and Contemners of Authority, Magistrates, or Magistracy." He added as warning "to all other persons, that they forbear the future publishing and spreading of the Pamphlet, as they will answer the contrary at their Peril." The recent arrest of Bradford and his assistant John McComb for printing and distribut-ing Keithian pamphlets attested to the seriousness of this warning. Finally the justices, for good measure, took efforts to ensure that this proclamation would be posted in "Town and Country" throughout the province.[2]

On the face of it, this public proclamation seems an odd choice of action for the aggrieved Philadelphia justices. By ordering a declaration written in "Private Sessions" among the judges to be read in the city marketplace, they had made public the very insults against Lloyd and themselves that they had desired, through prohibiting them, to keep private.[3] Moreover, their use of a town crier to promulgate their message would appear to be the wrong me-dium given their stated goal of the "undeceiving of all People." Why counter Keith's print with speech? If they hoped to reach "all People," why rely on speech, a medium of communication they believed more local—and there-fore less likely to reach a wider audience—than print?[4] In lieu of fighting fire with fire and engaging the Keithians in a public dialogue through print, Keith's opponents had attempted to seize political legitimacy by staging a public reading of their own authority.[5] Rather than win the public over through persuasion, they sought compliance through assertion.[6] The Phila-delphia County justices who issued the August 1692 proclamation—all of whom were Quaker ministers—had intended it to be the end of public dis-cussion of the Keithian schism, not the beginning. They had sent the town crier to the public marketplace not to exchange words but to pronounce them authoritatively, as if from on high.[7] They had spoken to and for the colony, just as Quaker ministers spoke to and for the entire Meeting.

In the short term, their efforts failed. Keith continued to harangue his enemies within the Society publicly, and in September the Philadelphia Yearly Meeting disowned him and his followers. His continued agitation finally led the justices to carry out the threat in their August proclamation: Keith was arrested, tried, and convicted—along with four of his associates—at the Philadelphia Court of Quarter Sessions in December 1692.[8] Prosecution and disownment failed to end the schism; in February 1693 Keith traveled to England to plead his case before the London Yearly Meeting, which finally disowned him for his continued attacks on his provincial brethren. In Pennsylvania, meanwhile, the Keithian movement continued, through a variety of twists and turns, until its last congregation disbanded in 1703. After plaguing the colony's ruling establishment for around a decade, the Keithian movement ultimately, in the words of its foremost chronicler, "went nowhere."[9]

The schism has long puzzled historians. They have offered several explanations for the rift. Some have analyzed it in terms of social or class conflict, alternately emphasizing its roots in economic discontent and political factionalism, describing it as part of a battle by social "superiors" to police their "inferiors'" speech, or a revolt by rank-and-file Friends against ministerial authority.[10] Others point to Quaker attitudes toward family and education or the contradictory nature of Quaker theology itself.[11] Keith himself has been portrayed as a psychologically disturbed individual, a stubborn mystic who was never "really" a Quaker, or a valued early leader of the Society of Friends who simply fell victim to one of the many schisms that wracked the Quaker movement in the seventeenth century.[12]

Conflicts over religious authority, the niceties of Quaker theology, ideas of family and community, and political factionalism all played a role. Yet these explanations do not account for the vehemence and timing of the schism. Its impact seems outsized; though the controversy at its height dramatically ground Pennsylvania's religious, legal, and political institutions to a halt, the Keithians may have comprised as few as one in twelve of the colony's Friends.[13] How did a theological dispute about the nature of Christ's body in heaven lead ruling Friends to violate some of their most sacred principles regarding liberty of conscience and the administration of justice? Nor does the schism's timing seem obvious. Keith himself appeared satisfied with the state of official Quaker doctrine in Britain, having written numerous volumes on the topic and having supported efforts by Robert Barclay and others to create something of a theological orthodoxy in the Society. Why then, after three decades as a member of the Society, did he feel a pressing need to enforce doctrinal conformity in America? Most significantly, what did the controversy reveal about early Pennsylvania?

The Keithian schism can best be understood as a crisis in creolization. The conflict erupted as Friends like Keith discovered that identities that seemed stable in England, Ireland, and Scotland now appeared to have shifted. Quaker leaders could no longer take for granted the boundaries of spiritual community established following the development of the Meeting system, prompting new efforts to define these limits. The conflict escalated as Friends discovered the ineffectiveness of the signs and symbols through which they hoped to communicate authority. Lacking a common language of power, they could not resolve their disputes through "gospel order." Nor could Pennsylvania's nascent legal and political institutions handle the task. Understanding the conflict as a crisis of creolization requires, at least in part, grasping the nature of the proclamation read in the market in August 1692. Within that speech—in its rhetoric, its manner of presentation, and its intended effects—lie clues to the relationships among religion, communication, and power in creole Pennsylvania. The proclamation helps explain why a dispute over the nature of Christ's body so thoroughly disrupted the social body of the Quaker Meeting and the province's body politic. Appreciating why six Philadelphia County justices hoped to silence public dissent through the verbal "Undeceiving of all People" sheds crucial light on the difficulty colonial rulers had in developing creolized habits of power and authority in Pennsylvania's first decades.

The Controversy

The Keithian schism began in earnest in the summer of 1691 with a dispute between Keith and William Stockdale, a minister in the Philadelphia Monthly Meeting, over the nature of the Light within. Stockdale took offense at Keith's contention that Friends needed to cultivate that measure of Christ within their hearts while developing a faith in Christ as he had died and been resurrected for the good of all God's people. Stockdale accused the Scottish preacher of denying the sufficiency of the Light within for salvation; he then accused Keith of preaching two Christs, one of body and one of spirit. Keith, in turn, felt that Stockdale's charges represented an unacceptable ignorance about Christ's nature. Each demanded satisfaction from the Monthly Meeting for their respective heresies.[14]

The Philadelphia Yearly Meeting's attempts to resolve the dispute at its September 1691 meeting failed. If anything, the six sessions the Philadelphia Monthly, Yearly, and Ministers' Meetings devoted to resolving Keith's and Stockdale's charges and countercharges of heresy made the situation worse. By the 29 January 1692 Philadelphia Monthly Meeting, Keith had extended his attack, pronouncing as heretical as well Philadelphia minister Thomas Fitzwater's assertions that Christ was "onely a Spirit in Heaven" who had not been resurrected on earth. Fitzwater, meanwhile, repeated Stockdale's claim that Keith had denied the sufficiency of the Light within for salvation.[15] With these attacks on Stockdale's and Fitzwater's conceptions of Christ and the Light within, Keith had broken into open disagreement with two prominent Quaker ministers over theological issues that the Meeting had supposedly settled in the aftermath of the Wilkinson-Story-Rogers separation in the 1670s.[16]

Of course, the fact that Keith had embroiled himself in a religious conflict may not have been entirely surprising. Perhaps the Society of Friends' most tireless controversialist in the post-Restoration period, Keith had published dozens of tracts refuting attacks on Quakerism while traveling through England, Scotland, Ireland, and Germany.[17] After crossing the Atlantic in 1685, Keith quickly began an itinerant ministry to Friends in Maryland and Massachusetts. His trips north saw him engage in heated debates with numerous New England ministers. In person, he exhibited a "litigious" style, alternately launching sharp attacks on his Puritan opponents and offering long-winded metaphors explaining the finer points of Quaker doctrine to his audience. In print, he adopted an even harsher tone. In one notable instance, he took Increase Mather to task for holding up a community of "singing Quakers" on Long Island as an example of the iniquities of the Quaker faith. Denying this collection of ecstatic "*Ranters* and *Libertines*" to be true Friends, Keith denounced Mather as a peddler of "gross Abuses, Lyes, and Slanders." Noting that Puritan ministers denied the sufficiency of the Light within for salvation, Keith derided their doctrine as "poyson." In "Doctrine and Life," New England's supposed saints had "degenerated" more than a little since their migration across the Atlantic. He continued to publish on New England's evils after his return to Pennsylvania, while Cotton Mather continued to publish screeds combating Keith's arguments in Massachusetts.[18]

Nor did the faults of his fellow Friends escape his notice. Keith grew anxious about heresies in American Quakerism long before September 1691. In a May 1688 letter from East Jersey to George Fox and George Whitehead, he lamented that Delaware Valley Friends "are but little acquainted and known in the Holy Scriptures."[19] This concern explained his eagerness to serve in 1689 on a ministerial committee that authored the first Quaker instructive literature issued in the colony and his publication of *A Plain Short Catechism for Children & Youth* the following year.[20]

Keith's most serious attempt at reform within the Philadelphia Meeting before the schism was his proposal for "Gospel Order Improved" that he circulated within the Philadelphia Ministers' Meeting in 1690.[21] Concerned that "many are crept into the form and profession of Friends' way, who are not really Friends of Truth and have taken up the outward profession not from any true convincement by the Spirit of God," Keith hoped to introduce "some note or manner of distinction" into the Meeting to tell true Friends from false ones. To that end, he recommended that individuals be required to offer a confession of faith before full admission into the Society; he hoped that American Friends, like the early Christian apostles, might be joined together "not only by feeling an inward knitting and uniting of their hearts and soules together by the power and Spirit of Christ inwardly revealed . . . but by some open declaration and profession of faith." Keith even advocated ending the practice of automatically accepting the children of Friends into the Meeting, arguing that they should be required to offer public confessions as well. These confessions, he believed, need only consist of "a few words" affirming belief in "the most principall and necessary Doctrines of the Truth" accepted by Friends.[22] This radical step—a departure from earlier Quaker attitudes regarding membership[23]—was necessary, he argued, because Friends in Pennsylvania had mixed too much with worldly outsiders and fallen from an earlier purity. "Did we not separate from other Societyee" he asked, looking back at the origins of the Quaker movement, "because of the vicious life and evill conversation and practices which were to be found among many" English people? "Ought we not," he wondered, "do our utmost diligence to be a separate people still, and purge out all the old leaven that we may be a whole new lump?"[24]

In suggesting that confessions be required for membership in the Meeting, Keith did not intend to change Quakerism's reliance on the Light within as the central aspect of its spiritual cosmology. Acknowledging the embodiment of the plain style in one's speech and behavior as "good things," he insisted that "yet the only full Test and Touchstone" for true Christianity was to receive the Holy Spirit. That Keith felt no need to enumerate the specific principles he believed prospective members should affirm in their "confession of faith" suggests that he saw this as secondary to cultivation of the inner Christ in preparing individuals to join the Meeting.[25] He hoped instead that, through these reforms, "the faithful among us" would be blessed "with a spirit of discerning" that would enable them to ensure that the outward tests of membership reflected inner fellowship with God.[26] Keith concluded "Gospel Order and Discipline" with several other suggested reforms he thought might achieve these goals, including renewed efforts at children's education, stronger efforts to discipline (and even disown) wayward Friends, a more accurate membership registry, mandatory attendance at monthly, quarterly, and yearly meetings, and appointment of elders and deacons to help catechize members.[27] Thus, in the same year that his theological sparring mate Cotton Mather warned his fellow New Englanders about the dangers of "Criolian degeneracy," Keith took steps to address the same problem in Pennsylvania.[28] Philadelphia's ministers considered "Gospel Order Improved" at three different meetings but ultimately elected not to enact Keith's suggestions.[29]

Keith also found himself involved in one other seemingly minor internecine conflict before his open feud with Stockdale. Rumors spread in the spring of 1691 about Keith's involvement in the editing and publication of a 1684 volume by the esoteric philosopher Francis Mercury van Helmont titled *Two Hundred Queries Moderately Propounded Concerning the Doctrine of the Revolution of Humane Souls*.[30] Drawing on Kabbalist thought, van Helmont argued that the soul did not stay dormant upon the body's death; instead, it transmigrated to another body, to live another life. Each soul went through twelve lifetimes, or "revolutions," between its spiritual birth and its final judgment.[31] An avid Hebrew scholar himself, Keith quickly became friends with van Helmont after meeting him in 1675. Each proved a major influence on the other: van Helmont introduced Keith to the Kabbalah, while the latter helped convince the former to convert to Quakerism in 1677. This close association, however, lent the rumors about Keith's role in the publication of *Two Hundred Queries* significant credence. Concerned that unnamed individuals ascribed to him such unorthodox views, Keith published in early summer 1691 a brief tract defending himself against these accusations and denying any belief in the doctrine of the revolution or transmigration of souls.[32] By the time Keith's defense saw print, however, his conflict with Stockdale had become public. Both he and his critics had more pressing concerns.

The Condemnation

Hearing Stockdale's and Fitzwater's pronouncements on Christ's body and the irrelevance of scripture to salvation confirmed Keith's worst suspicions: Quaker religion had, indeed, degenerated in America. He quickly took steps to restore spiritual order. At the Philadelphia Monthly Meeting at the end of February 1692, Keith quizzed Fitzwater on Christ and scripture and found him wanting, "At which many were greatly offended to find him so ignorant, having been so long a Preacher." Keith also produced several witnesses to clear himself of Fitzwater's and Stockdale's accusations.[33] A cohort of Philadelphia Friends reconvened the next day "in the Schoolhouse, where the Meeting used to be kept at times In the Winter Season."[34] Here Keith, the colony's school master, managed to procure a "unanimous judgement" against Stockdale declaring that Stockdale "had abused G. K." and insisting he publicly repent for doing so. The schoolhouse Meeting also asked "*that he* [Stockdale] *desist offering his Gift by way of Testimony, till he hath done so.*" A condemnation against Fitzwater, with similar sanctions, was likewise issued.[35]

Instead of resolving the controversy, however, these condemnations only made things worse. Keith's opponents in the Philadelphia Quarterly Meeting rejected the papers, denying that "them that gave the Judgment [were] a true Monthly Meeting."[36] They further declared that many of those at the schoolhouse meeting "were not in the *Profession of Truth*," impugning the Quakerism of Keith's followers.[37] They also denied the validity of the condemnations on the grounds that only meetings of elders and ministers, and not those of rank-and-file Quakers, had the authority to judge questions of doctrine, echoing a position for which Keith had fought during the leadership struggles of the 1670s. Keith responded by calling the Philadelphia Quarterly Meeting's actions "*Rank Popery*" and arguing "that there was not more Damnable Errors, and Doctrine of Divels amongst any of the Protestant Professions, than was amongst the Quakers."[38] For these charges, the Philadelphia Meeting of Ministers appointed three of their members to admonish him "for Several great Abuses, and unchristian reflections by him cast upon Friends both in Publique and Private."[39]

The ministers quickly found face-to-face discussions fruitless. Their visitation with Keith to "tenderly admonish" him of his errors ended after he announced to his former brethren that "he denied our Authority, he denied our judgment, he did not value it a pin, he would trample it as dirt under his feet." When Griffith Owen, a member of the ministerial visitation committee, warned Keith about his unruly behavior, he told Owen to "see what Excessive passion thou art in, look [at] thy face in a glass see what a face thou hast."[40] He rebuffed further attempts to make peace by two visiting ministers from London, Thomas Wilson and James Dickenson, by informing them that their travelling ministry in North America "had done more hurt than good in this Country."[41] Keith had now managed to alienate English as well as American Friends.

In late spring, Keith and his followers issued two statements fanning the controversy further, *Some Reasons and Causes of the Late Separation* and "Some Propositions in Order to Heale the Breache."[42] In these two documents, they accused their orthodox opponents in the Meeting of having fallen away from God's grace and argued that this degeneracy made the Keithians' extreme actions against the Meeting necessary. The ministers leading the Pennsylvania's Quaker Meeting, the Keithians argued, preached "dreadful and astonishing . . . Vomit and Filth" to their brethren, spreading "Ignorance and Error."[43] These ministers, they continued, were either fallen Quakers "highly pretending to Truth" or, worse yet, had never been Friends, merely interlopers within the Quaker movement. Either way, Keith believed that the Meeting's actions against him to be the result of machinations by "*Bastard Quakers in America*."[44] Quaker ministers had become, in the Keithians' eyes, the literal embodiment of disorder in Pennsylvania, having succumbed to the same degeneration that plagued all those living in the New World. Moreover, the Keithians' suspicions about their opponents' spiritual decay easily slipped into fears of racial decay; they argued that the "*Anger and Passion*" in the ministers' attacks on the Keithians had revealed their enemies as "worse than Either Turk[,] Jew[,] or Indian" in their piety."[45] A religious difference signified, in their eyes, a creolian degeneracy or racial decay.

Interpreting the controversy as a sign that "the approaching Glory of Gods blessed Day" had arrived, the Keithians called for their brethren in Pennsylvania to remove the poisonous weeds from their spiritual garden—that is, Philadelphia's Quaker ministers.[46] The Keithians strove to revive the practices of "Ancient *Christians*" and "the most sound Antient and Present Friends of Truth" by instituting the rigorous discipline Robert Barclay called for in his *Anarchy of the Ranters*.[47] In doing so, they hoped to restore the Meeting from its present fallen state—in which it was "more like Babylon than a Church of Christ"—to its former glory.[48] Coming as they did on the

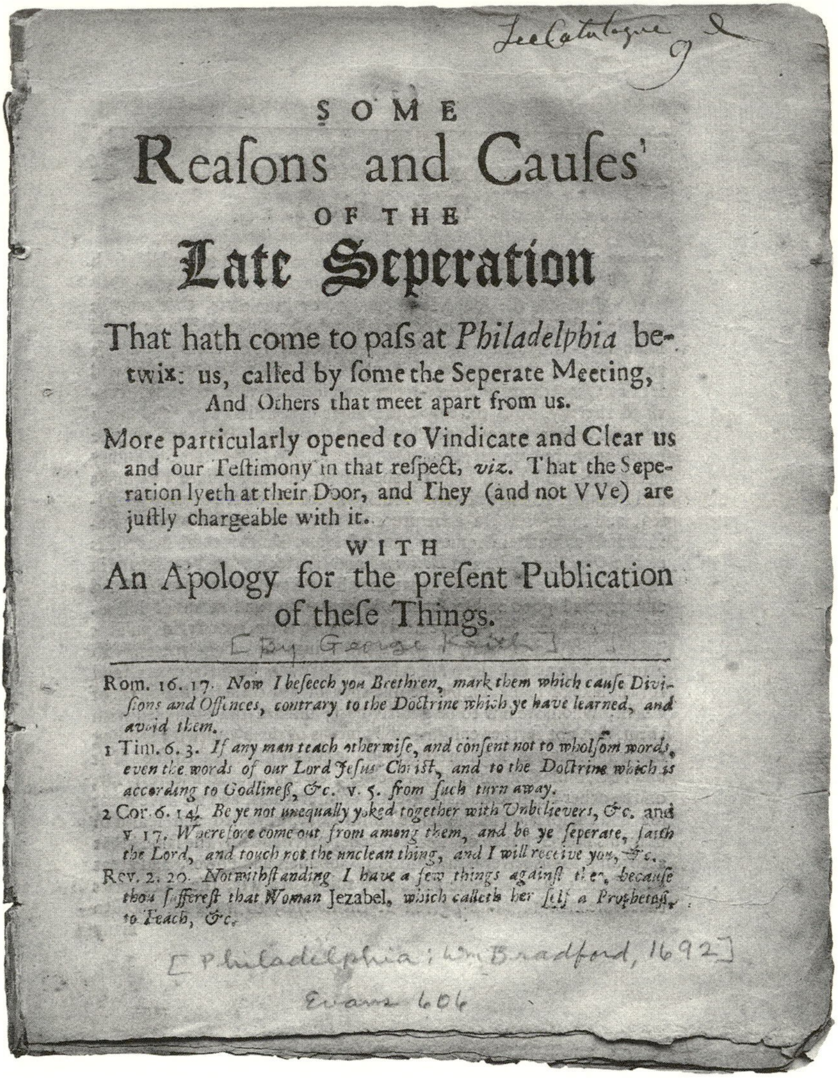

SOME

Reaſons and Cauſes

OF THE

Late Seperation

That hath come to paſs at *Philadelphia* betwixt us, called by ſome the Seperate Meeting, And Others that meet apart from us.

More particularly opened to Vindicate and Clear us and our Teſtimony in that reſpect, *viz.* That the Seperation lyeth at their Door, and They (and not VVe) are juſtly chargeable with it.

WITH

An Apology for the preſent Publication of theſe Things.

[By George Keith]

Rom. 16. 17. *Now I beſeech you Brethren, mark them which cauſe Diviſions and Offences, contrary to the Doctrine which ye have learned, and avoid them.*

1 Tim. 6. 3. *If any man teach otherwiſe, and conſent not to wholſom words, even the words of our Lord Jeſus Christ, and to the Doctrine which is according to Godlineſs, &c.* v. 5. *from ſuch turn away.*

2 Cor. 6. 14. *Be ye not unequally yoked together with Unbelievers, &c.* and v. 17. *Wherefore come out from among them, and be ye ſeperate, ſaith the Lord, and touch not the unclean thing, and I will receive you, &c.*

Rev. 2. 20. *Notwithſtanding I have a few things againſt thee, becauſe thou ſuffereſt that Woman* Jezabel, *which calleth her ſelf a Propheteſs, to Teach, &c.*

[Philadelphia: Wm Bradford, 1692]

Evans 606

Figure 6. *Some reasons and causes of the late seperation that hath come to pass at Philadelphia betwixt us . . .* Title page of George Keith's 1692 account of the schism. Courtesy of the American Antiquarian Society.

heels of Keith's insults toward the visiting English Friends, these two tracts caused the tide of ill-will toward the Keithians to well up even further.

On 17 June 1692, the dam broke. During its summer session, the Philadelphia Meeting of Ministers issued a condemnation of Keith, formally beginning the process of disowning him and his followers.[49] Drafted in the form of a conventional Quaker epistle and addressed to Friends in London, this letter opened with exhortations to their "ancient Love of Eternal Truth" and assured their audience of their faithfulness to their "first love and habitations in the Truth." Keith's "rude and abusive Carriage," however, had brought an end to the brief golden age that had reigned in the six years before his arrival: "for before he became an Inhabitant, and troubler of the place, its union gave it its greatest fame and Beauty." Without Keith, they continued, Pennsylvanians "would soon remember the good times we have had together, and Come and Sit down with us in their former Simplicity." The ministers placed the "evil Burden of Separation" on Keith for his continued insistence on enforcing a new catechism; while they acknowledged that they "would Subscribe to any Confession of faith put out by Antient approved Friends," they thought it "Safer and Modester to own . . . what was already publique" than draft anything new. Likewise, they harshly criticized Bradford and Keith for "printing anything without the knowledge and Consent of Friends." For these reasons, then, the ministers urged all Friends to cast the Keithians out as one might pluck out a sinful eye.

Three days later, they issued a second letter of condemnation.[50] This second letter denounced Keith in even stronger terms for the ways in which he had argued his case. The ministers noted "With mourning and lamentation" how Keith had "degenerated from the lowly[,] meek[,] and peaceable Spirit of Christ Jesus." Moreover, if Keith had condemned his opponents degeneration in racial language, the latter condemned the former in gendered terms, writing that while Keith once "knew the Government of Truth over his own Spirit, and witnessed the same to be a Bridle to his Tongue," he was now given to "*ungodly speeches.*" Using invectives most commonly leveled against women in early Anglo-American culture, the ministers condemned Keith for his "railing Accusatories" and "*extravagant Tongue.*" Caleb Pusey spoke more directly, characterizing Keith's behavior during the schism as "very Unmanly . . . as well as Unchristianly."[51] Keith's spiritual degeneration had also caused him to lose control of his emotions, acting alternately "cool in Charity" or with "Heat and Passion." Keith's inability to master his own will made him the embodiment of disorder. Finally, the ministers assailed

Keith for involving non-Quakers in his dispute. Many of his public speeches against his opponents had occurred in "mixt Auditories of some Hundreds" where he "endeavour[ed] . . . by the Press and other ways" to spread his grievances as widely as possible. The epistle ended by reiterating Keith's disunity and urging his disownment by the Yearly Meeting.

The charges and countercharges the ministers and Keith hurled at each other encapsulated the challenges inherent in transplanting Quaker culture and institutions in America. Each side drew upon British Quaker precedents as they denounced their opponents. In Keith's case, the Scotsman appealed to the writings of his countryman Robert Barclay on faith and church governance; his calls for the standardization of church authority drew explicitly on Barclay's *Anarchy of the Ranters*, while his campaign against Stockdale's and Fitzwater's supposedly heterodox ideas showed the influence of Barclay's *Apology for the True Christian Divinity* and *Catechism and Confession of Faith*.[52] Pennsylvania's ministers, meanwhile, had learned a different lesson from the Society's post-Restoration struggles. They found spiritual truth not in a particular set of theological principles but in the unity of the Meeting. Both groups had the same motivation: their desire to maintain a sense of Quakerness across the Atlantic. They desperately wanted to avoid creole degeneracy in a situation that necessitated religious creolization.

The ambiguity of the Society's traditions and the contradictory nature of the colonial project in Pennsylvania each magnified the scope of the problem. Looking back at the twists and turns in Quaker faith and practice, both Keith and his opponents had ample reason to think their respective approaches legitimate responses to spiritual disorder. And spiritual disorder was inevitable in Penn's colony. The proprietor had founded a "mix't colony" with power firmly in the hands of the "tribe of Judah." He hoped that a careful regulation of the province's speech economy would help leading Friends creolize new settlers, especially non-Quakers who might be skeptical of Friends' authority. But this task had led to an open dispute between Friends before "mixt Auditories," something that Quakers, fearful of becoming a "mixt People," found profoundly threatening. Ultimately, the rightness of these contending approaches mattered less than their utility. Which could best facilitate the creation of a creole Quaker community while obscuring the differences between British and American Quakerism? And which could protect this creole Quaker community from the dangers it faced in a "mix't colony"?

After the Ministers' Meeting's response, Keith took the steps that ultimately led to the "Publick Writing" read against him that 25 August. Dissatisfied with the ministers' decision, Keith again appealed to a wider public in print. Hoping to influence those attending the September 1692 Yearly Meeting, Keith and his followers published *An Appeal from the Twenty Eight Judges* and *The Plea of the Innocent* during the summer. These tracts, written by Keith in conjunction with his supporters, criticized both the ministers' doctrine and their handling of Keith's disputes with Stockdale and Fitzwater. The authors reiterated Keith's earlier claim that his ministerial opponents were "*guilty of cloaking more damnable Heresies and Errors, than any Protestant Society in Christendom*" and called for a "Publick Hearing" to settle these issues. They adopted a different rhetorical pose than they had in their earlier writings. Indeed, by inviting responses from readers and other authors, the *Appeal* and the *Plea* represented a decided break from all other works published in Pennsylvania's first years. While the authors of the didactic literature that comprised so much of printer Bradford's early output spoke to their audience to convey information and their own authority, the Keithians who wrote the *Appeal* and the *Plea* invited their provincial audience to speak back.[53]

These two publications broadened the conflict substantively as well as rhetorically, raising serious questions about the conflicts between politics and piety Quaker magistrates faced. The Keithians asked their readers to consider whether their opponents, several of whom held positions of authority in the government as well as in the Meeting, had strayed from the Quaker testimony against "all use of the carnal Sword." Leading Friends, they noted, had "provid[ed] the *Indians* with Powder and Lead, to fight against other *Indians*," allowed Friends to use force against privateers, and countenanced capital punishment for some offenses.[54] With these last charges, the Keithians had subtly changed the terms of this struggle; where Keith had earlier attacked the legitimacy of his opponents' theology and the legitimacy of various Philadelphia meetings to discipline him, he now openly questioned the legitimacy of Pennsylvania's political structure itself. Moreover, the *Appeal* called attention to the dangers of conflating Pennsylvania politics with Meeting discipline. Mixture corrupted each.

Nor did the Keithians stop at merely printing their disagreements. As the Yearly Meeting approached, they took to placing copies of the *Appeal* "upon the Posts of [the] Town of *Philadelphia* and elsewhere."[55] John McComb, a tavern keeper associated with the Keithian movement and an associate of Bradford's, distributed copies of the *Appeal* to patrons in his ordinary.[56]

Presumably, he also made the schism a prominent topic of conversation at the tavern—or, at least, the Keithans' version of the controversy. Given that McComb ran one of the few taverns in the city, such an act would have generated considerable publicity for the Keithians' cause, circulating news of the conflict throughout the region.[57] Meanwhile, some Keithians "with diverse others of the Rabble" began following the ministers in public and "did rail and snarl intolerably" at them in earshot of other Philadelphians.[58] Keith himself kept in touch with the Philadelphia ministers through an epistle in late summer, although this, too, proved to be disruptive when the messenger attempting to deliver the letter to an orthodox meeting for worship "climb[ed] into our Meeting house Window (tho the door was open) stood in the said Window with his Hat on, and read part of it while our ancient Friend *Tho. Janney* was at Prayer."[59] The Keithians actively propagated their message through several channels, attempting to engage the public in an open debate over the schism, reaching out to Quakers and non-Quakers alike.

Provincial magistrates found this attempt to encourage religious and political debate in public no more appealing than Penn found the Assembly's desire to exercise a "debateing voice" in government. On 24 August 1692, they issued a mittimus mandating that Bradford and McComb be brought before them by John White, the county sheriff, for "Publishing, Uttering, and Spreading a Malicious and Seditious Paper" that "tend[ed] to the Disturbance of the Peace, and Subversion of the present Government."[60] Ordering the pair to appear at the next Court of Quarter Sessions, the magistrates offered Bradford and McComb the option of going free until their trial, provided that they found sureties who posted bond for their behavior.[61] Faced with this quintessentially American Quaker form of sanction, the printer and his assistant turned instead to English Quaker precedent. Echoing Quaker founders such as William Dewsbury who denounced peace bonds as sinful, McComb and Bradford saw the magistrates' offer as a statement about the defendants' lack of trustworthiness and refused to find sureties. They were both jailed.[62] In violation of both Pennsylvania's laws and a well-established Quaker antipathy to such punitive police practices, White also seized Bradford's press, leaving his wife and children without a means to support themselves while he was in prison.[63]

By the time the town crier arrived at the city market that August 25, then, the orthodox Quakers serving in both the ministry and the magistracy had already drawn the line against the Keithians. Having reaffirmed to themselves and their brethren in London and the New World the legitimacy of their efforts to communicate with Keith and reincorporate him into the fold through acceptable channels such as visitations, epistles, and the like, they now rendered the Keithians' attempts to continue the dispute through other communicative channels not only un-Quaker but illegal. They hoped by outlawing the "publishing, uttering, or spreading" of words they disapproved of to prevent the proliferation of unruly discourse that might disrupt what fragile order the province's religious and political leaders had constructed. Thus, the curious performance of the town crier—repeating proscribed insults in the city's most crowded public arena, uttering lies for the purpose of "undeception," and circulating "official" speech at one of the city's centers of "unofficial" speech—represented an attempt to monopolize political discourse in the colony. Their "Publick Writing" substituted the performance of authority through a single communication for the varied attempts at public persuasion (as raucous as they were) employed by the Keithians. They answered Keith's calls for a public dialogue with a monologue.[64]

The August warning also met failure, and Friends at the September Philadelphia Yearly Meeting formally disowned Keith and his followers.[65] Not satisfied with ejecting the Keithians from the Quaker Meeting, Philadelphia's Quaker magistrates pressed legal action as well. Some time in the fall, after the September Yearly Meeting, they arrested Keith and Budd for committing sedition in their publication of *Plea of the Innocent* and *Some Reasons and Causes*. Peter Boss, another Keithian, was arrested for slandering Samuel Jennings in private letters he sent to the judge during the summer. Keith, Budd, Bradford, Boss, and McComb came to trial in December. Both the Keithians and their opponents were acutely aware of the courtroom's theatrical potential. The trial provided each side a stage on which to perform its own vision of authority.

The Trial

The trials of the Keithian five began on 9 December and lasted through 12 December 1692.[66] The trials differed sharply from the quotidian operations of Pennsylvania's courts, marked as they were by discussions of debt, trespass, and thievery. The Keithian trials, by contrast, upheld the tradition of legal spectacle established by English Friends in the Restoration period and proved a fitting climax to the Keithian controversy. The courtroom debate centered on the relationship between religious authority and legal authority in Penn-

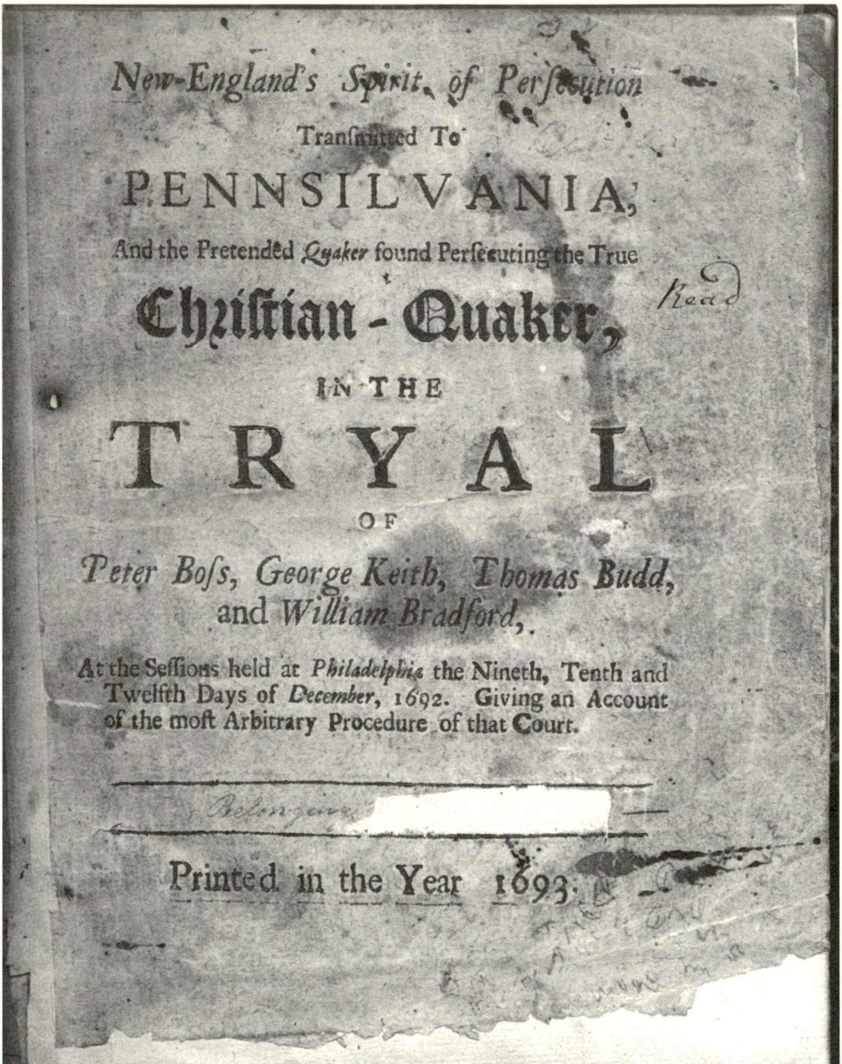

New-England's Spirit of Perſecution
Tranſmitted To
PENNSILVANIA,
And the Pretended *Quaker* found Perſecuting the True
Chriſtian-Quaker,
IN THE
TRYAL
OF
Peter Boſs, George Keith, Thomas Budd, and *William Bradford,*
At the Seſſions held at *Philadelphia* the Nineth, Tenth and Twelfth Days of *December*, 1692. Giving an Account of the moſt Arbitrary Procedure of that Court.

Printed in the Year 1693.

Figure 7. *New-England's spirit of persecution transmitted to Pennsilvania, and the pretended Quaker found persecuting the true Christian-Quaker, in the tryal of Peter Boss, George Keith, Thomas Budd, and William Bradford, at the sessions held at Philadelphia the nineth, tenth and twelfth days of December, 1692 . . .* Title page of Keithians' account of their trial. Courtesy of the Historical Society of Pennsylvania.

sylvania, with each side cloaking itself in the mythology of early Quakerism to justify its own legitimacy.

The first trial dealt with accusations by Boss, Keith, and Budd against Samuel Jennings's character. Boss was charged with spreading rumors about the Quaker justice, while Keith and Budd were charged for slandering him in print in *A Plea of the Innocent*. It opened with attempts by the former two defendants to declare the court's authority over the controversy void and to have all charges dismissed. Charged with slandering Jennings as an unfit judge, a gambler, and a drunkard, Boss argued that his comments failed to violate the law because he had offered them as one Friend reproaching a fellow traveler; he told the bench that "if a Man speak slightly of a Magistrate, if he be when he is not in the exercise of his Office, it is no defaming of him as a Magistrate, and so no trespass against the Law alleged." He supported his argument by referencing to William Sheppard's *Faithful Councellor*, a popular legal treatise in England and an invaluable resource in a colony with few trained lawyers or legal texts.[67] Boss's arguments raised implicit concerns about the transfer of English customs to America. Questions regarding the relationship between Jennings's status as a magistrate and his status as a Quaker would have been moot in England, where the law barred Friends from holding governmental office. Nor would the contending parties have debated the applicability of English precedent.

Keith followed with a further attempt to dismiss the charges. Citing the Philadelphia Yearly Meeting's insistence that Friends "go to law" with each other only after exhausting the meeting's disciplinary procedures, Keith argued that this conflict, "belong[ing] to a Spiritual Court, and not to this," should be settled by "Gospel Order." David Lloyd, acting as Penn's attorney general, denied Keith's and Boss's claims, asserting provincial judges' power over matters spiritual as well as temporal. He intoned to Keith that "This is a spiritual Court; for in England they can try Atheism in this Court." Lloyd's assertions that these laws protecting public officials from injurious speech rendered even ministers from the established Church of England immune from rebuke did more than present a particular interpretation of provincial law; they also elicited an outcry from Friends in the gallery attending the trial, many of whom had spoken out, at great coast, against the established church in England. Ralph Ward, a Keithian, was forcibly removed from the courtroom when he asserted Quakers' God-given right to reprove the Church of England.[68]

Boss's and Keith's respective trial strategies reflected their initial pleadings. Boss enumerated the sins of the colony's magistrates in exquisite detail. Jurors and onlookers heard about Jennings's and John Simcock's inebriated exploits, including the former's fondness for drunken horse racing and the latter's propensity for becoming so intoxicated that he needed to be carried to bed. Boss also produced multiple accounts of Jennings's miserable character as a master. The Quaker magistrate, witnesses noted, had been seen choking one servant, forcing another to "go almost naked" in wintertime as punishment for questioning his master's authority, and meting out an "Inhumane Whipping of his Servant Maid naked in her bed."[69] Though the jury found Boss guilty and levied a £6 fine, Jennings had won something of a pyrrhic victory. Like those husbands who sued for slander to restore their own reputation or that of their wives, he found that this attempt to defend his honor had given these accusations a wider public circulation than they would have otherwise received.[70]

Keith struck a different note. His testimony revealed the ways in which he and his followers saw themselves as the spiritual heirs to Quakerism's persecuted founders and their struggle against their orthodox opponents as one of mythic proportions. Asked by the judges for a plea, Keith instead requested that the judges and the gallery "consider, that both ye and we are as a Beacon set on a Hill, and the Eye of God, Angels, and Men are upon us."[71] Keith's subsequent testimony reflected the panache of his introductory flourish. Repeatedly invoking Quaker lore to discredit the government's authority, he even challenged the legality and legitimacy of Pennsylvania's laws. Told by David Lloyd that "publish[ing] anything in derogation of the Sentence of Court" was prohibited, Keith reminded them that English Friends such as Penn and Whitehead had repeatedly used the press as a weapon against oppression.[72] He then proceeded to dispute every aspect of the court's authority in the case, engaging in debates with Lloyd over matters as arcane as the distinction between actionable and presentable in English law and whether a jury could decide law as well as fact in criminal cases—a precedent established in Penn's famous trial at the Old Bailey. Frustrated by Keith's petulant behavior, Lloyd cut off the debate, proclaiming Keith's offenses "Tho' not Actionable, yet Presentable." Displaying exquisite absurdist logic, Lloyd had declared, in essence, that although the court had no legal authority to punish Keith, it had an indisputable right to try him. Lloyd concluded his verbal dance with Keith by ordering the court reporter to strike the latter's testimony and record merely *Nihil Dicit*," marking perhaps the only time during the schism when the anti-Keithians failed to give their antagonist credit for his long-winded pomposity.[73]

Neither Keith nor Budd denied writing *Plea of the Innocent*. Following their admission of that fact, Lloyd ordered the jury, which included four self-proclaimed anti-Keithians, to return a verdict. Echoing the jury at Penn's trial at the Old Bailey, the Philadelphia jurors asserted their authority to decide law as well as fact, in defiance of Lloyd and the rest of the province's ruling elite. They found Keith and Budd guilty in fact of calling Jennings imperious and haughty, but they held that these accusations had broken no law. Ignoring both the power afforded juries in Pennsylvania's Frame of Government and Penn's own writings on the matter, the justices then ordered the jury's verdict disregarded and slapped the defendants with a £5 fine for defamation.[74] The justices' actions notwithstanding, the jury's verdict revealed the power of the mythology of Quaker suffering Keith had invoked. Through both their invocations of Quaker legal principles and their questions about the status of English precedents in North America, Keith and Budd had eroded the magistrates' self-proclaimed bases for legitimacy; through their verdict, the jury had shown their support for the Keithians' actions.

By the time Bradford came to trial, it seemed clear that the authority that the Quaker justices had so assiduously cultivated had begun to slip away. Bradford's trial opened with his request that the justices show him specifically which law he had broken, in keeping with the commitment to legal transparency and simplicity that characterized Quaker legal reformism.[75] Lloyd dismissed Bradford's request, claiming that, as the defendant had violated common law, the magistrates were under no obligation to disclose what law he had broken.[76] During the trial, Bradford adopted the same strategy that Keith and Budd had: he appealed to Penn's plea in his trial in 1670. Bradford admitted that he had printed the tracts in question but claimed that this action was not seditious and, therefore, not unlawful.

The jury's verdict and the six justices' reaction to it brought the spectacle of the Keithians' trial to an end. Hearing Bradford's appeal to Penn's precedent, the jurors—who counted among their number one Quaker man, Joseph Kirke, who had asked to be removed from the jury because of his strong bias against Bradford—pronounced that the printer was free to go. This verdict so enraged the justices that they ordered the court bailiff to confine the jury "without Meat, Drink, Fire, or Tobacco" until they returned the "proper" verdict, echoing almost exactly the punishment meted out to the jury that set Penn free nearly a quarter century before.[77]

With this order, history had indeed repeated itself, as farce rather than as tragedy.[78] Unwittingly or not, Lloyd, Jennings, Simcock, Arthur Cook, Anthony Morris, and Robert Ewer had reenacted Penn's 1670 trial at the Old Bailey exactly, playing the role of the established church rather than the part of the persecuted Quakers.[79] Their attempt to enact the government's authority had instead revealed its institutional and cultural weaknesses, as evidenced by questions over the transfer of English law to America and the lack of deference accorded to leaders like Samuel Jennings inside and outside the courtroom. Moreover, it provided a theater within which the Keithians and the jury could stage a performance of their own moral authority. Drawing on the collective memory of suffering so integral to the creation and maintenance of Quaker identity, they improvised a display of their solidarity against those Friends who controlled the magistracy and the Meeting. They turned the trial into a history-making event, in two senses: by inserting themselves into an established Quaker narrative of persecution and triumph, they hoped to change the course of Pennsylvania's development and thereby redeem its future.

In the end, the justices' attempts to coerce the jury were in vain. The hefty fines leveled against Keith, Budd, McComb, and Boss went uncollected, and Bradford's press was eventually returned. After the public proclamation in the city streets and the spectacular trial, Keith's Quaker enemies were in the end unable to punish him legally for his insolence.

Endgame

The trial may have marked the dramatic high point of the schism, but its conclusion did not mark the end of the schism itself. Keith and his allies continued their public attacks on Pennsylvania's ruling Friends, hammering home charges that these provincial leaders had compromised too much with the world in their quest for earthly power. Having previously questioned particular policies embraced by Quaker magistrates, they now warned all Friends to protect their souls by staying clear of the comprises and capitulations governance involved.[80] Affirming their belief "that Negroes, Blacks and Taunies are a real part of Mankind . . . and are capable of Salvation as well as White Men," Keithian Quakers issued a statement cautioning Friends against the sin of slaveholding, an exhortation that implicated many of the wealthy and powerful men who headed Pennsylvania's Quaker community.[81] Provincial Friends found their authority undermined at every turn.

Keith next turned his attention eastward. Indeed, the intended audience for his publications now was British more than Pennsylvanian, as his arrangements to have his works sold in London by Quaker booksellers made clear.[82] Unsatisfied with his treatment in Philadelphia, the preacher headed to London in late 1693 with his family in tow; Robert Hannay, one of his major supporters in Pennsylvania, also made the trip. Samuel Jennings, David Lloyd, Arthur Cook, John Delavall, and Griffith Owen followed soon after.[83] Keith moved aggressively against his provincial antagonists, pushing the London Yearly Meeting to condemn colonial ministers who preached supposedly heretical doctrine and others in the ministry who enabled the preaching of such heresy. London Friends disappointed him, however. Acknowledging at its May session that "some few persons" in Pennsylvania had "given offence either through erroneous Doctrines, [and] Unsound Expressions," the Yearly Meeting nonetheless reproved Keith for his vehemence and laid the burden of fault on him.[84] Though the Meeting declined to disown him for his actions, it clearly expected him to cease his attacks on his brethren.

This time it was Keith's turn to disappoint. Hannay's publication of the Yearly Meeting's remonstrance—accompanied, of course, with a gloss on the proceedings—made it clear that the Keithian contingent would not forebear. By fall 1694, the Scottish preacher had begun to canvass the countryside for support, convinced that local meetings might support him where the Yearly Meeting did not. He took special care to cultivate support in those areas where Quaker dissidents John Wilkinson, John Story, and William Rogers had received the most encouragement in the 1670s. This behavior led to a particularly harsh indignity: disownment by the Aberdeen Monthly Meeting, his former home Meeting. In May 1695, London Friends followed suit, formally cutting ties with Keith.[85] Though Keith continued to spar with British and American Friends in public and in print for more than a decade, the schism had, in a literal sense, drawn to a close.

Some Reasons and Causes

This account of the Keithians' circus-like trial and "acquittal" only begins to explain the controversy, however. Certainly, English Friends found the matter perplexing, unsure why a theological schism had so aroused the ire of orthodox Friends. George Whitehead pointedly informed the minister-magistrates who had tried Keith "that King David Patiently bore a greater affront from Shimel than some Justices had from G. K."[86] They also seemed uncertain about how such a dispute happened in the first place. After all, the theological conundrums at the center of the center of the controversy had been settled in Britain for some time. Barclay, Penn, Whitehead, and Keith himself had defined the Society's official position on Christology in the 1660s, seemingly obviating the need for further debate. English Friends' confusion stemmed from the fact that they were, well, English. They failed to appreciate the schism's fundamentally creole nature. They found the Keithian controversy bewildering because such an event could have happened only in America.

Pennsylvania, of course, had something Britain lacked: Indians. The cultural encounter between native peoples and Europeans and the establishment of colonial society in Pennsylvania heightened particular cultural anxieties among the settlers, just as it had in other regions of British America. Unlike cultural contact in the seventeenth-century Chesapeake, which generated ethnological questions about the differences between European and Indian bodies, manners, and genders, encounters with Indians in Pennsylvania caused settlers to revisit with renewed vigor old questions about souls, salvation, and resurrection, while at the same time asking new questions about the Indians' place in this unfolding biblical history.[87] Life on the western margins of Britain's empire led Keith to reconsider such foundational questions as the sufficiency of the Light within and Scripture for salvation and ultimately to reembrace a hermetic doctrine that orthodox Friends on both sides of the Atlantic had abandoned.

Keith argued before coming to America that Indians proved that only the "Divine Law" written in the hearts of all people was necessary for salvation. Native Americans, he wrote, may "want the Scripture," but on the last day they would be judged by "the Law of God, writ in their Hearts."[88] This statement echoed views expressed by William Penn and Francis Daniel Pastorius, among others, about Native Americans having the same "Light" in their hearts that Friends did. But his interactions with Indians during his time in New Jersey and Pennsylvania had convinced Keith that the "natural religion" they possessed would not suffice. Though God's mercy had allowed them knowledge of this inner Christ, their ignorance of the outer Christ kept them from being saved. Avoiding damnation required acceptance of Christ's incarnation, crucifixion, and resurrection as described in the Gospels.[89] Keith attacked his Puritan opponents in print for denying the sufficiency of the Light within when it came to English souls even as he deemed it insufficient to save Indian ones.

This contradiction posed a major spiritual conundrum for Keith, however. He as much as any Friend embraced the notion that all men and women had the possibility of salvation, but an insistence on the importance of the outer Christ placed Native Americans in an impossible situation. Though their ignorance of Scripture stemmed from historical circumstance rather than any concerted effort to shun the Christian faith, it damned them nonetheless. To solve this problem, Keith turned to an esoteric doctrine with which he had once been enamored but had seemingly abandoned: the notion of the transmigration of souls. If each soul went through twelve revolutions before the millennium, then pious and sober Indians who, lacking exposure to Christianity, died in a state of "Gentilism" would nonetheless have an opportunity to embrace God's Word in a future lifetime and be saved. If one accepted the possibility of universal salvation while also insisting on a saving faith in the outward Christ, then logic demanded a belief in some form of transmigration.[90]

The doctrine of transmigration held one further appeal. Those Kabbalist authors who influenced van Helmont subscribed to the view that behavior in one lifetime influenced outcomes in the next; individuals who lived godly lives would find their status raised in the next "revolution," while evildoers would find their status lowered. The vicissitudes of fortune souls experienced in their various lives reflected their movement toward or away from the divine.[91] Viewed in this light, the Kabbalist notion of redemption bore a striking resemblance to the Quaker notion of salvation as an ongoing process in which Friends strove to achieve ever higher levels of perfection without backsliding and descending into sin. This esoteric Jewish doctrine allowed Keith to assimilate the religious questions Native Americans raised into a Quaker religious idiom. It made it easier for the Scottish minister to fit Friends and Indians into a common spiritual universe.

This conflation of long- and short-term processes of spiritual perfection had another, more ominous implication. If Indians possessed of "natural religion" but lacking a true knowledge of the Gospel represented what Friends might have been in a previous life, they also exemplified what Friends might become if they neglected their faith in America. In Keith's eyes, overemphasis on the sufficiency of the Light within for salvation posed a tremendous danger. Friends who failed to preach the necessity of Christ without imperiled more than their own souls, however; they also ran the risk of dooming their "Posterity to be *Indians*."[92] Keith feared a particular form of creole degeneracy, one in which a collective fall from grace in the present generation would visit a bodily transformation upon future ones. A failure to nurture children properly would lead to a change of their bodily nature.[93]

Keith's theories profoundly disturbed many in the Meeting. Some of their disapproval, to be sure, stemmed from a discomfort with the esoteric tradition Keith drew from so approvingly. The Philadelphia Monthly Meeting had reproved future Keithian Daniel Leeds for his extensive discussions of astrology in the 1687 edition of his almanac and ultimately disowned him for publishing a collection of the works of Jacob Boehme and George Wither, two German and English mystics respectively.[94] But this explanation hardly suffices. English Friends, including George Fox, had expressed interested in esoteric doctrine in the 1670s. So too did prominent anti-Keithians in Pennsylvania. Pastorius, for example, owned works by continental philosopher Paracelsus and Boehme's English acolyte Jane Lead as well as a volume critiquing Wither's writings. Pastorius would later cite Hermes Trismegistus (the ancient founder of the hermetic tradition) approvingly in an "onamastical" analysis of John Penn's name on the occasion of his birth to William and Hannah Penn.[95] Phineas Pemberton drew upon Kabalist thought in a refutation of Keith's writings in a letter sent to London Friends in 1694.[96] Moreover, numerous Friends disagreed with his beliefs about the sufficiency of the inner Christ for salvation. Despite repeated efforts on the part of Barclay, Penn, Whitehead, and Keith to reform the Society's Christology, leading Quaker ministers in Pennsylvania such as Caleb Pusey insisted that knowledge of the historical Christ was not essential for redemption. Thus, Stockdale and Fitzwater were not, in this sense, unique.[97]

At the same time, provincial Friends found that Keith's musings on salvation and resurrection seemed to posit an alarming equivalence between Indians and Quakers. Indeed, the implications of Keith's theories for their relationship to Native Americans caused perhaps greater unease among anti-Keithians than any other part of his doctrine. As the most child-centered Protestant group in the Anglo-American world, Friends understandably worried about the suggestion that a "poor Infant" who died without an outward knowledge of Christ would suffer the same spiritual fate as "an honest *Indian*." Neither could be "perfectly saved" without knowledge of Scripture.[98]

The doctrine of the revolution of souls held even less appeal. Disturbed at the thought that they might be reincarnations of people from places or sects around the globe, provincial Friends grew even more distraught at the idea that their souls and the souls of their children might be reincarnated in Indian bodies before their eventual spiritual resurrection in heaven.[99] Keith had broken no new ground in comparing Native Americans to children; many other authors, Protestant and Catholic, had long characterized Indians as spiritual children.[100] Pennsylvania's Quakers, however, objected strongly to this analogy, but not because of their concern for indigenous peoples. They objected because saying Indians were like children meant that Indians were like *their* children. More than simply a spiritual leveling that placed Friends on the same religious plane as honest Indians, transmigration represented a kind of spiritual miscegenation that most Quakers found clearly unacceptable.[101]

Their anxiety on this score came through in one particular document from the schism. Sensitive to the charges of heterodoxy Keith had leveled against them, provincial ministers published in 1695 an account of their Christology. The "Antient Testimony" represented a curious mixture. On the one hand, it affirmed their commitment to faith in the outward Christ as essential to salvation. At the same time, it spoke of the conversion process in ways Friends had abandoned decades ago. "Those who are sanctified" by Christ, the ministers wrote, "are all of one . . . made Partakers of the Divine Nature" in spirit and flesh. This language echoed Fox's early claims that Quakers would become like perfect "babes of Christ" on earth when saved.[102] But this was the terminology post-Restoration Friends had assiduously avoided and that Thomas Ellwood had worked so hard to purge when he edited Fox's *Journal* for publication in 1694. British Friends no longer wrote of conversion as a bodily transformation.[103]

American Friends' embrace of embarrassing and abandoned theological poses hardly helped convince British Friends of their orthodoxy. But it did inoculate them from the taint of creole degeneracy, in two ways. Post-Restoration British Quakers had moved away from a belief that the sanctified possessed celestial flesh because of its seeming conflict with the notion of perfection and sin as a cyclical process; though Barclay, Penn, and Keith could each envision individual Friends falling away from spiritual perfection after a bout with sin, the notion of a heavenly body degenerating into a worldly one made little sense. But for American Friends desperate to draw sharp lines between themselves and the Indians living in their midst, this concept held tremendous appeal. It justified theologically their desire to see themselves as different bodily and spiritually from Native Americans, and it did so in a way that precluded them from ever becoming like Indians. For how could sanctified (English) flesh ever degenerate and become like unsanctified (Indian) flesh? The former partook of Christ's divine nature, while the latter did not.

Reviving old doctrine served provincial Friends' ends in another way. It allowed them to parry Keith's charge that they had fallen from right Quaker doctrine in America—for it was they, and not the Keithians, who had stayed true to the Society's founding principles. Faced with a crisis of spiritual identity and authority, Pennsylvania's Quaker ministers turned to the movement's early history for sustenance. That British Quakers from Fox down had elected to cover up or revise this history afterward did not matter.[104]

At the heart of these attempts to protect against biological and cultural degeneration lay a wider fear of spiritual as well as corporeal miscegenation. Indeed, anxieties about spiritual miscegenation motivated combatants on both sides of the schism. The Philadelphia Yearly Meeting's early reminder to provincial Friends that "we are but one body of which Christ Jesus is our head" must have seemed to many more of a prescriptive than a descriptive declaration.[105] Indeed, the Yearly Meeting had warned Friends in one of its earliest epistles about the dangers of "wearing Superfluity of apparel" and reminded them that their speech and dress should be "within the limits of Truth, so shall we be to the Glory of God, & the comfort of one . . . another." Without such bodily signifiers, colonial Quakers might lose their identities as individuals and as a community.[106] These concerns emerged on the local level as well. The Falls Men's Monthly Meeting addressed questions of piety and mixture in its very first session, when Thomas Fitzwater and William Biles—one of the twenty-eight Friends who would later sign a letter from the orthodox Meeting condemning Keith—expressed concern about lax discipline in marriage practices among local Friends. Two months after Biles and Fitzwater's investigation into the matter, Jennings and Budd, future opponents in the schism, wrote a letter to the same Monthly Meeting reminding them to take special care that marriages proceeded according to gospel order.[107] And Jennings cosigned Keith's 1688 letter to Whitehead and Fox decrying the state of scriptural knowledge among Friends in New Jersey.[108]

Leading Keithians and anti-Keithians, then, had initially made common cause in the fight against spiritual degeneracy in America. Keith, Budd, Pusey, Fitzwater, and other ministers all worried that migration to Pennsylvania had in some way destabilized or reconfigured Quakerism. Their common concerns showed that they all knew, on some level, the truth behind Keith's more damning accusation. In all likelihood, a majority of Pennsylvania's Friends were "bastard Quakers" of a particular sort. Following the Society's requirements, provincial meetings requested that "friends . . . do bring their Certificates of the respective meetings of friends they belong'd to in other countries" when they migrated to America. The Philadelphia Monthly Meeting insisted upon this practice in its first session; Jennings and Budd later warned the Falls Monthly Meeting to exercise greater vigor in doing the same.[109] Despite this, few Pennsylvania Friends actually provided certificates from British Meetings attesting to their good behavior across the Atlantic during the colony's early years. Indeed, fewer than one in ten Friends in Pennsylvania presented certificates attesting to their membership in British Meetings during the years before the Keithian controversy.[110]

Thus, even accounting for gaps in the documentary record, it appears that only one in three Pennsylvania Quakers during the colony's first decade of settlement had been adult Friends in good standing in Britain, a number that steadily declined. The rest of the colony's Quaker population consisted of converts or those raised from childhood in Pennsylvania—Friends who were, literally and figuratively, born in America.[111] During the formative decades when American Friends were trying to replicate Old World religious institutions in Pennsylvania, as many as two-thirds of all the province's Friends lacked any substantive experience or understanding of British Quakerism. Keith and his opponents each sensed that they lived in something of a creole Quaker community; he was simply more willing to acknowledge that fact, albeit in a way that cast aspersions on the parentage of these new Friends.

Moreover, the spiritual lineage of Keith's "Christian Quakers" appears to have been stronger than that of their orthodox opponents. Judging by certificates received by the Philadelphia Monthly Meeting, a relatively small minority of Keith's supporters had been active Friends in Britain. But by this same measure, they were more than twice as likely as ordinary Friends to have been Friends in good standing before migration.[112] Keith's claim that he and his supporters understood the rudiments of Quaker faith and practice better than their theological foes had a firm grounding in reality.

The Keithian schism, then, erupted during a period in which the Society faced serious internal and external cultural pressures, a fact that contributed to its explosiveness. It happened at a time when encounters with the region's indigenous peoples challenged at least some Friends' conceptions of their spiritual and cultural identities. This encounter with an alien people heightened leading Friends' sensitivity to the presence of "gentiles" within their midst—that population of creole Quaker converts. In Keith's eyes, the Quaker Meeting had reproduced itself by mixing with all the wrong people, and his opponents' impious behavior offered proof. He and his supporters feared that provincial Friends had, by accepting so many new converts into their midst, reduced themselves to the spiritual state of American heathens.

Keith's opponents in the magistracy, meanwhile, felt that his actions threatened their corporate identity. They charged that his time in Pennsylvania had rendered him unmanly as well as unchristian. For a sect that placed such a strong emphasis on the outward embodiment of its piety, Keith's musings on Indian and African spiritual equality and the transmigration of souls represented perhaps the most threatening form of bodily comingling they could imagine. The controversy reinforced the importance of the boundary lines of race, gender, and religion even as it suggested that these lines might be more mutable in America than Friends would have wished.

The schism revealed the brittleness of the colonial structure Pennsylvania's founding Quakers had created. It happened at a time when Pennsylvania's Society of Friends faced the prospect of acculturating a proportionately large number of converts into its fold. It occurred at a moment when, as the trial revealed, Pennsylvanians were confused about which aspects of English law, culture, and authority held sway. The controversy happened when a creolizing provincial elite felt most anxious about its own civil, political, and religious authority. Keith's challenge and their ineffective response dramatized more clearly than any other event in the colony's first decades that Pennsylvania's leaders had no effective means of communicating their authority to those they ruled—and they knew it. The schism made clear to all that provincial institutions were too weak and their legitimacy too contested to maintain order effectively.

The conflict revealed the two faces of the creolization process in early Pennsylvania. The creation of a new, American community of Friends in Pennsylvania involved the incorporation of a large number of outsiders into the fold, a process that in some respects involved the erosion of Quaker values, as Keith so inconveniently noted. But this erosion did not lead to the dissolution of the Quaker community, any more than colonizers' encounters with indigenous peoples turned them into Indians. Instead, it facilitated the emergence of a new, reconfigured, creole Quakerism that drew sharp boundary lines between Friends and "gentiles" without acknowledging overtly the various degrees of cultural difference within the Society itself. George Fox in one of his Revolutionary-era sermons referred to God's Word as a pearl of divine wisdom, buried by the Lord in England, uncovered by Friends, and ready to be shared with the world. Pennsylvania Quakerism was, in its own way, a pearl as well—the product of an endless friction between Friends, would-be Quakers, and others. Creolization worked as a friction that eroded and created simultaneously as Friends struggled to create an imperfect unity out of colonial disunity.[113]

The Keithian schism had a profound impact on Pennsylvania's early development. It laid bare the fault lines in the colony's early history. Keith's aggressiveness "in tongue and in print" exposed the fragility of colonial authority. The province's elites had failed in their efforts to create a unified Quaker community. Yet it also provided a path forward. Keith's success in undercutting his opponents' authority revealed the power that print possessed in the shaping of public opinion. Though this fact had proved damaging to their cause in the short term, it also suggested the possible utility of printed appeals as a force for the consolidation of Quaker authority in the future. And if the ministry's invocation of a Quaker past in their "Antient Testimony" represented the first time colonial elites used history to stabilize their authority, it would not be the last. No matter that the history mentioned in "Ancient Testimony" did not represent the actual past of those "bastard Quakers" born in America; it nonetheless acted as a potent touchstone of identity.

Ultimately, the abiding irony of the Keithian schism lay in the way that Keith himself won by losing. He had initially introduced "Gospel Order Improved" in an effort to teach Pennsylvania's Friends how to be better Quakers. The Meeting's ministers rejected his plan. And yet, within little more than a decade after the schism, the Philadelphia Yearly Meeting had drafted a comprehensive Book of Discipline standardizing faith and practice. Public confessions of faith became more common in provincial Monthly Meetings (even if repentant accounts of former Keithians were the most common genre of such confessions). And leading Friends made more judicious use of print as a didactic tool than they previously had. In all these ways, they imitated the elements of Keith's platform, though they would have vehemently denied any such influence. Keith had indeed taught Pennsylvania's Friends how to be better Quakers, if not in the way he intended.

CHAPTER 5

Narratives of Early Pennsylvania, I

Life on the Colonial Borderlands

ROBERT SUDER HAD bad news. The Anglican clergyman's 1698 report home described a colony in disarray. Desperate to hold on to their power, Pennsylvania's ruling Quakers worked to undermine their Anglican opponents at every turn. One poor soul even claimed that Friends held "Negroes" and other heathens in higher esteem than churchmen. Worse, they denied the power of parliamentary statute and royal prerogative. He also marveled at the colony's lack of military defense and Friends' complete unwillingness to rectify the problem. Provincial politicians had even arrested one colonist who petitioned the king for military aid and bound him over to the peace repeatedly to keep him silent. These actions masked a deeper motive, Suder warned. Colonial Friends did not fear French pirates because they were in league together, with each taking orders from the recently deposed King James.[1]

Suder's letter provides crucial insight not merely into life in fin de siècle Pennsylvania but also into a particular colonial mindset. Some of his descriptions had a ring of truth, as Griffith Jones could attest. But others seem implausible, if not downright risible. How could Anglicans take seriously claims that blacks had been elevated above them? Why did they believe the Quakers had made common cause with Jacobite forces?

The willingness of Suder and other anti-Quakers in America to entertain these fantasies stemmed from the anxiety they felt living on a colonial borderlands.[2] Pennsylvania existed in a culturally and politically contested space "in between." The religious dissenters who populated the colony aroused the ire of Anglicans leading attempts to revitalize the presence of the established

Church in North America. The rumors of Quaker collaboration with French pirates captured the uncertainty of English authority along its imperial boundaries, as had earlier rumors about French and Indian forces massing along Pennsylvania's western frontier. Military indeterminacy mirrored other colonial indeterminacies within Pennsylvania. Suder's acute consciousness of living on the colonial fringe stemmed from his fear that British culture and power might truly unravel there.

Efforts to make order out of this chaos acted as a kind of productive friction that generated new identities among colonists and Native Americans in Pennsylvania. Delaware, Shawnee, and Conestoga Indian peoples created new political realities for themselves as they fended off the imperial ambitions of British colonists to the east and the Iroquois nations to the north.[3] The stories critics told to justify tighter imperial controls in the colony prompted a series of counternarratives by those resisting this imposition of authority. The results roiled provincial law, politics, and diplomacy during the decade and a half after the Keithian controversy.

To "feel the injury of Pennsylvania": Resisting Imperial Control

Francis Nicholson had strong feelings about Pennsylvania that he had no compunctions about sharing. In letters to his superiors in London, the Maryland lieutenant governor listed the faults of his neighbor to the north in exacting detail. Pennsylvanians thumbed their collective nose at royal authority, consorted with England's enemies, invited pirates to visit their ports, and violated imperial laws with impunity. Nicholson had seen colonial intransigence before, having served as lieutenant governor in Virginia as well. But Pennsylvania seemed worse, unrulier and more disruptive, than its Chesapeake neighbors.[4] Other fearful provincials shared Nicholson's views, sending similar accounts back home. It was no wonder that Englishmen hearing these reports believed "That Pennsilvania is become the greatest refuge & shelter for pirates & Rogues in America," as William Penn reported in 1698.[5] These tales of rampant piracy accompanied litanies of frustration at Pennsylvanians' repeated refusals to comply with the Navigation Acts governing trans-Atlantic trade and outrage over a perceived indifference to imperial authority.

At the heart of these complaints lay a single issue: the place of Pennsylvania, a proprietary colony populated and governed by religious dissenters, in an expanding Anglo-Atlantic world. British imperial policy toward its American colonies had been somewhat haphazard during the decades leading up to Pennsylvania's founding. The seventeenth-century English government showed little interest in planting colonies on its own initiative. Nearly all the Anglo-American colonies in 1680 had proprietary or chartered forms of government. Those few with royal governments had either been acquired through conquest, as in the case of colonies like New York and Jamaica, or passed into the Crown's hands following the failure of private endeavors, as in the case of Virginia. Sporadic attempts to increase royal authority in America and bring disobedient colonists to heel only highlighted the imperial bureaucracy's ineffectiveness. Royal commissioners sent to New England in 1664 gathered ample evidence of Massachusetts colonists' proclivities for overstepping their territorial and jurisdictional bounds but ultimately could not force residents of the Bay Colony to change their behavior. Customs officials stationed in Virginia could do little to force Chesapeake planters to comply with Navigation Acts regulating the export of tobacco.[6]

But English policy took a marked turn in the 1680s.[7] Imperial officials in Charles II's reign stepped up their efforts to bring New England's troublesome Puritans to heel, eventually revoking the Massachusetts Bay Company's colonial charter in 1684. His brother James went even further, ordering the consolidation of all colonies north of Pennsylvania into a single political and administrative unity in 1686. Tellingly, James's plan for this "Dominion of New England" placed it under military rule, with no provisions for representative government. His successor, William III, showed this same inclination to expand royal prerogative in America after the Glorious Revolution, even as he made concessions to parliamentary authority at home. The establishment of the Board of Trade in 1696 marked the most serious attempt to exert administrative control over England's burgeoning maritime empire yet.

In the eyes of its critics, Pennsylvania exemplified the problems plaguing colonial rule. The province's inability to contribute to the imperial war effort had led to its royalization in 1692. Its leaders' refusal to take any steps to establish a civil defense force after proprietary control resumed in 1694 led to repeated complaints from all quarters. Royal officials questioned whether the colony would ever fulfill its military obligations, while non-Quaker residents of the Lower Counties pleaded for imperial protection. The Board of Trade cautioned against lodging any power in the hands of Quakers who might, "under pretence of conscience," refuse to defend themselves or others against attack. Pennsylvania's Anglicans concurred, urging permanent royal control.[8]

Imperial officials also complained about chronic smuggling in the

Quaker colony. Philadelphia courted Dutch and Scottish traders, in clear violation of laws granting English vessels exclusive rights to the colonial trade.[9] Far from prohibiting illegal trade, colonial magistrates participated in it. Colonel Robert Quary, stationed in Pennsylvania by the Board of Trade to suppress smuggling, suggested to his superiors that enforcing the Navigation Acts in a growing and increasingly wealthy colony would be "impossible." Another correspondent wondered if anything short of a warship stationed on the Delaware River monitoring merchant ships entering and leaving port would prevent violation of the Acts.[10]

Royal officials fulminated most about Pennsylvania's piracy problem. Pirates, Maryland's Henry Bouton declared, were "protected, harbor'd, aided, and assisted by open force" in Pennsylvania. They walked the streets of Philadelphia "impudently," to the astonishment of visitors and even some Pennsylvanians. Their presence and activity threatened to destabilize trade in the entire region, pushing out more scrupulous traders. Correspondents marveled that Lieutenant Governor William Markham had welcomed a pirate into his own family, his son-in-law James Brown. Markham even secured Brown a place on the Provincial Council, for good measure. Colonial magistrates had no desire to turn away anyone with hard currency to spend, whether ill-gained or not.[11]

When urged to remedy the situation, provincial magistrates proclaimed themselves powerless to check the problem, or worse. Colonial magistrate Robert Snead's quest to bring sailors from the *Fancy* epitomized the absurdity of the situation. In April 1697, Snead presented Lieutenant Governor Markham with a proclamation he had received from the Lords of Justice to apprehend the ship's crew if they came ashore. Markham dismissed the orders on a technicality, noting that they had not been specifically addressed to the provincial government; he thus had no obligation to obey them. Markham proceeded to warn the alleged pirates of Snead's intentions to apprehend them, prompting some of the *Fancy*'s crew to approach the magistrate on the street and denounce him as an "Informer."[12]

Snead found his efforts to bring these men to justice thwarted at every turn. He secured their arrest in April only to watch a fellow member of the provincial government post their bail. A second arrest led only to their prompt escape from jail. Snead's attempt to apprehend the men of the *Fancy* culminated in a visit from the county sheriff, who confiscated Snead's firearm. Apparently, the sheriff had decided that Snead's energetic efforts to enforce the law represented a disturbance of the peace. Only at this point did

Markham raise the hue and cry to bring the supposed pirates to justice. City constables again arrested the pirates, who promptly secured their escape from prison that night. A complaint to Markham about this easy escape elicited the response that, as the lieutenant governor "was neither sherrif nor Gaoler" for Philadelphia County, he had no control over the situation. There the matter ended.[13]

Colonists' seeming belief that they lived outside the law confounded imperial officials. Here, too, officials blamed religion. The Navigation Acts required shipowners and merchants to swear when posting bond to have their cargo cleared but made no provisions for those whose consciences prevented them from taking oaths. Since rigorous enforcement of the Acts would have effectively disenfranchised Quaker merchants, Friends in the government passed a law contravening the Navigation Acts on this score.[14] Nicholson opined that an admiralty court could "be of no use" in Pennsylvania as long as Friends held power. Quakers, he wrote, believed "no law made in England shall be of force in Pennsylvania" if it contradicted their religious scruples.[15]

They also blamed Pennsylvania's anomalous imperial status as a proprietary colony with a reformist legal code. Edward Randolph suggested to the Commissioners of Customs that no proprietary governor could be entrusted with enforcing the Navigation Acts.[16] Quary similarly noted that the colony's liberal naturalization policies complicated his job immensely. Granting Germans, Dutch, Swedes, and Scots the "rights of English" gave them access to a trading system that excluded others of their birth.[17] In other words, granting American colonies the power to naturalize non-English immigrants (a crucial part of the creole legal system Penn and his fellow legislators established) eroded the power of the Navigation Acts in precisely that space where the English government deemed them most necessary—the colonial periphery. The "Pennsylvania Problem" had revealed a structural defect in England's administration of its Atlantic possessions.

The explanations Pennsylvania's politicians and traders gave for their actions confirmed this belief. Governmental officials repeatedly cited problems of conflicting jurisdiction to justify ignoring imperial edicts. The difference between colonists' response to the 1696 revision of the Navigation Acts and their official response to the piracy problem served as a case in point. Provincial Attorney General David Lloyd infuriated his critics when he defended his repeated failure to prosecute individuals suspected of piracy by appealing to Penn's colonial charter. Arguing that colonial courts could hear only cases dealing with infractions committed within the bounds of the proprietary charter and not those dealing with crimes on the high seas, he claimed that Pennsylvania had no sway in the matter. Thus, he could legally take no action against the alleged pirates.[18]

If Lloyd's description of colonial authority represented a form of constitutional minimalism, provincial legislation regulating illegal trade displayed a maximalist understanding of Pennsylvania's constitutional authority. The Assembly responded to news of the 1696 Navigation Acts by passing its own Act of Trade. Pennsylvania's Act of Trade differed from its English counterpart in one crucial respect: it declared that all alleged violations should be tried in a local Court of Quarter Sessions, giving colonial juries the power to decide such cases. English regulations, meanwhile, called for supposed violations to be tried before a Court of Vice-Admiralty, a tribunal overseen by a royal appointee and lacking a jury. Echoing a claim previously advanced by Penn, they justified this action by claiming that the terms of the royal charter gave the proprietor jurisdiction over those waterways leading to and within the boundaries of his grant.[19] These alternating restrictive or expansive understandings of provincial courts' powers led to the same conclusion: imperial authority stopped at the water's edge.

Nothing dramatized this rejection of English authority more than David Lloyd's public mocking of the royal seal in September 1698.[20] Lloyd's previous behavior as attorney general had given the Board of Trade reason to question his suitability for office. He had declared that he served the proprietor only and not King William, and he refused to enforce violations of the Navigation Acts. He even went so far as to act as defense attorney for a ship's captain whose vessel had been seized for violating the Acts. Reviewing his performance, one imperial committee even recommended he be removed from his position as attorney general.[21] Nonetheless, when Quary finalized the establishment of a Court of Vice-Admiralty in the summer of 1698, he asked Lloyd to serve as his deputy, in charge of overseeing the court's operation during his absences from the colony; Lloyd accepted. Quary apparently meant to co-opt this potentially troublesome figure. If so, the futility of the gesture soon became apparent.

The controversy began when John Adams, owner of the *Jacob*, appeared before the Philadelphia County Court of Quarter Sessions. A commissioner of customs at New Castle had seized the ship earlier in the year and Adams sought the return of his vessel. Acting on Lloyd's advice, the Court ruled in Adams's favor. It then ordered the acting marshal of the Vice-Admiralty Court, Robert Webb, to appear in court and explain why the *Jacob* should not be returned to Adams's custody. This decision represented an explicit assertion of colonial legal authority.

Webb appeared at the next meeting of quarter sessions to find Lloyd acting as Adams's counsel. The deputy judge of the Philadelphia Court of Vice-Admiralty thus openly challenged that institution's authority. When Webb produced his royal commission—which contained a seal with effigies of the king and queen of England—to show his right to seize the *Jacob*, Lloyd quickly snatched it away. Acting in "a most insolent & disloyal manner," Lloyd took "the sd Comission in his hand & expos[ed] it" to the assembled onlookers. He then asked Webb, "what is this? do you think to scare us w[i]t[h] a great box (meaning the seal in a tin box) and a little Babie," referring to the royal effigies. Though "fine pictures please children," Lloyd concluded, "wee are not to be frightened" by such a visual symbol of royal authority. If, as one historian has argued, governmental officials in most English colonies in this era "used visual representations of royalty to normalize their authority," then Lloyd's affront carried special potency. Signs of imperial power carried neither the same meaning nor the same weight in Quaker Pennsylvania that they did elsewhere.[22]

But Lloyd justified this attack on monarchical authority as his prerogative as a free-born Englishman. He followed his mockery of the royal seal a year later with a public declaration denying the validity of the Vice-Admiralty Court's commission to operate in Pennsylvania in any capacity. Anyone supporting the court, he warned, was no better than the enemies of freedom who had aided Charles I in his attacks on Parliament in the 1620s.[23] Lloyd drew upon English traditions to defend his stance opposing the execution of parliamentary acts in America. Not surprisingly, officials at Whitehall saw Lloyd's actions in a different light. Declaring him disloyal and incompetent, they insisted that Penn remove him from all provincial offices. Penn complied.[24]

To be fair, provincial politicians exhibited the same disdain for Penn's authority as they did for the king's. Proprietary and antiproprietary factions expended at least as much energy fighting each other as they did fighting royal prerogative. Lloyd and his supporters even managed to force Markham to accept a new Frame of Government in 1696, one that greatly expanded the power of the Assembly.[25] By enduring the hardships of settlement, they argued, they had earned the right to govern themselves. In the eyes of Pennsylvania's Quaker community, the endless tales of colonial intransigence told by their enemies ignored this history of hardship, a past that more than justified their suspicion of outside authority of any type. William Penn thus hoped to resolve both the internal and external problems facing the colony when he set sail for America a second time in 1699.

Accusations and Explanations: Penn's Second Voyage

Penn's arrival in December 1699 promised to bring some measure of stability to the province. During his two-year stay in Pennsylvania, his leadership yielded real results. On the diplomatic front, Penn negotiated a major treaty with several Native American groups in 1701. Easily the largest diplomatic conference Pennsylvania participated in during the colony's first six decades, the 1701 agreement played a major role in securing peace on Pennsylvania's frontiers.[26]

Politically, Penn managed to secure at least a measure of the domestic tranquility that had eluded the province. Both he and his erstwhile opponents showed a renewed willingness to work with each other. This cooperation culminated in the 1701 Charter of Privileges, a new Frame of Government that served as Pennsylvania's constitution until 1776.[27] The Charter marked a major victory for Lloyd and his supporters, who had chafed at the legislative structure the early Frames of Government had established. It established a unicameral legislature, composed of a popularly elected Assembly with the power to initiate laws and sit on its own adjournments. The Charter simultaneously reduced the Provincial Council to a merely advisory body to assist the governor in the performance of his duties. The Charter did reserve the proprietor's appointed governor a veto over laws passed by the Assembly, but it nonetheless represented a significant concentration of power in the hands of the popular branch of the provincial government—exactly the result anti-proprietary politicians had fought for during the previous two decades.

Making peace with his Quaker antagonists allowed Penn to concentrate on other critics of his colony, namely, Anglicans in Pennsylvania and their sympathizers within the imperial bureaucracy. They lamented the colony's moral degeneration, insisting that its lawlessness extended to matters carnal as well as political. They argued that the Assembly's failure to pass laws regulating marriage as rigorous as those in England had led to rampant polygamy, fornication, and bastardy.[28] Defending the Assembly's marriage laws, Penn rejected their calls for the institution of canon law, arguing that "our Circumstances in this licentious Wilderness is our best guide to fitting Remedies" to the problems described. This plea for American rather than English precedents reassured critics on neither side of the Atlantic, however.[29]

Religious developments in the colony emboldened Penn's attackers. Despite its legal position at home, the Anglican Church's authority over settlers in England's colonies had been tenuous at best for most of the seventeenth century. It had a weak foothold in the Chesapeake and almost no presence in New England. But Church leaders moved with a renewed vigor during the 1670s to secure what they saw as their rightful place in the colonial religious landscape. Taking advantage of the Crown's 1684 annulment of the Massachusetts Bay Company's charter, Boston Anglicans founded their first church in that city two years later. The Anglican Church appointed the Reverend James Blair its first commissary to Virginia in 1689, charging him with the task of spreading its reach. Blair's efforts led to a remarkable growth of Anglicanism that took place over the next quarter century. In 1693, New York Governor Benjamin Fletcher convinced the assembly of that colony to pass a law establishing parishes and government-financed salaries for six ministers, leading to the creation of the province's first Anglican churches shortly thereafter. And in 1686, Pennsylvania Anglicans secured a charter for Christ Church in Philadelphia.[30]

Nor did Penn's opponents have faith in the men charged with upholding laws proscribing vice. The minister and vestrymen of Philadelphia's Christ Church wrote of one trio of "remarkable" provincial judges who managed, on a single 1700 circuit, to help a Bucks County man who had committed an act of bestiality with a mare go free on a technicality and to release a New Castle woman who admitted to having killed her infant child. They also failed to prosecute the scion of an eminent Quaker family accused of rape.[31] This lack of effective leadership resulted from "premeditated design" on Penn's part to promote Quaker politicians, judges, and sheriffs ahead of Anglicans. This conspiracy brought disastrous consequences to those provincials who were not members of the Society of Friends.[32]

Anglicans also faulted the treatment of oaths in the colony's legal code. Pennsylvania's laws allowed for affirmations in lieu of oaths at every part of the legal process: officers of the court could affirm their fidelity to Crown and proprietor, jurors could affirm their commitment to uphold their offices faithfully, and witnesses could affirm the veracity of their testimony. Defendants thus faced the prospect of having their "lives, liberties, and estates taken from [them], contrary to law and rights of English subjects, by judges, juries and witnesses not sworn," horrifying Pennsylvania's non-Quaker residents.[33]

For provincials outside the Meeting, there could be no fair trials—no justice at all—in a colony that allowed Quaker conscience to impinge on the lives and liberties of others.

Of course, Penn denied these charges, pointing out that many of the "church party" held positions of authority.[34] The proprietor argued that the Anglican campaign against Pennsylvania's rulers represented an assault on the liberties of Friends, as limiting public offices to oath swearers and bringing marriage under the sway of canon law would dramatically weaken them politically and legally. The Anglican campaign threatened to disenfranchise Quakers in a colony in which they comprised nearly three-quarters of the population.[35]

Moreover, these efforts threatened to strip Friends of their collective property: the province. "It was never intended," Penn wrote, "that Pensilvania should be a Ch[urch] Plantation," only a Quaker one.[36] Political, not economic, motives attracted migrants: "It was not Land but Government of Such as should live in that land that was our chief inducement to undertake such a Chargeable[,] hazardous[,] & toilsome Affair."[37] Friends had earned the right to keep Pennsylvania as their own: "wee have buried our blood & bones as well as estates to make it what it is," Penn wrote.[38] Those who had taken the "Charge trouble & interest requisite" to secure a colonial charter had a special claim to the land, and those who had transformed a "desart 3000 miles off from England" deserved full legal and political privileges.[39]

This strategic language represented a crucial, if subtle, innovation. On both sides of the Atlantic, English authors had long argued that American lands only acquired value through settlement. According to this colonial labor theory of value, so-called wilderness became property only after migrants "improved" it by building houses, erecting fences, and cultivating farms. The English saw their colonies as "plantations."[40] Penn's Quaker critics had invoked this trope when they reminded him of the travails they had endured in the colony's first years: they had planted the colony while he remained in England.[41]

To Penn's mind, though, this formulation missed the bigger picture. Throughout his career as American promoter and proprietor, Penn firmly believed that the worth of overseas English settlements lay in their people: industrious settlers reaped benefits for themselves, their respective colonies, and the Crown.[42] Policies and individuals that encouraged immigration to America were thus the true agents of wealth creation. Pennsylvania's liberal system of government offered unmatched protection of liberties and privileges that acted as such a magnet for prospective settlers. Penn's governance theory of value emphasized the importance of institutions before improvement. Individuals made property through their labor, but constitutions made territories that could attract immigrants in numbers enough to enrich the wider good. Thus, imperial policy should favor those who framed the institutions that gave value to colonial settlements.

This alternative explanation of the colony's value supported the proprietor's political interests. He had undertaken the trouble and expense of securing a colonial charter; he had drafted multiple Frames of Government designed to secure the liberties of those dissenters who traveled to America; and he had taken the lead in protecting the rights of these dissenters from their political enemies. In linking the constitution of Pennsylvania's government with the composition of its first settlers in this manner, Penn subtly redefined the colony's character. He made Pennsylvania more than just a colony with Quakers, a province whose pioneers just happened to be Friends. Rather, it became instead a Quaker colony, a settlement whose Quaker-ness defined its identity.[43] The tens of thousands of Friends who had voted with their feet by coming to America ratified this conception of the colony, at least in the eyes of its founder. Having embraced with Penn the power "to rule our selves," immigrant Friends seemed willing coparticipants in the venture. As latecomers and outsiders, colonial Anglicans were not.[44]

This fusion of historical memory, political economy, and religious dissent created a potent narrative of identity that would play an increasingly large role in Pennsylvania's civic culture. Symbolically appropriating the efforts of his fellow founding Friends, Penn could rebuke Parliament for failing to appreciate how "our" efforts in America had benefited the empire. He thus turned struggles for power in Pennsylvania into matters of tribal importance. Political conflict became a way of building a cohesive Quaker identity. This formulation also functioned as a narrative of identity in another sense, blurring—if not effacing—the distinction between the colony's history and that of its founding members. Provincial Friends found this narrative useful as they tried to convince those inside and outside the Meeting that the province's future depended on the future of its founding political elite. Quaker leaders drew upon this rhetoric with increasing frequency as Pennsylvania endured serious military and legal crises in the decade after Penn's departure in 1701.

Dramatizing Patriotism: The Problem of Civil Defense

Pennsylvania's civil defense problem seemed less pressing when William Penn left for England in October 1701 than it had previously been. The province's non-Quakers still expressed alarm at the lack of a colonial militia, but the end of King William's War in 1697 reduced the threat of imminent French invasion.[45] Closer to home, the "Great Treaty" the proprietor had negotiated in 1701 with the major Indian peoples in the region removed potential military threats on Pennsylvania's frontier.[46] Nonetheless, Penn urged the colonial Assembly in his farewell address to that body to establish a militia.[47] The proprietor saw the formation of a provincial defense force as good politics and good policy, a means of protecting himself from the Board of Trade while protecting the colony from attack. The militia question "is all they have to hitt us with."[48] Solving that would strengthen Penn's hand immeasurably.

This brief period of peace ended with the outbreak of "Queen Anne's War" in 1702. This conflict saw a shift in French military strategy. France adopted a more aggressive posture toward England's American possessions, launching major offenses into New York and New England.[49] The peace agreement New France negotiated with the Iroquois Confederacy in 1701 increased the threat England's colonies faced. The end of this twenty-year struggle with the Iroquois freed the French to devote more resources to their assaults on English colonists. This turn of events placed the colony in a uniquely vulnerable situation. While New York or Massachusetts could rely on Indian allies to provide military assistance in times of war, Pennsylvania could not. As Proprietary Secretary James Logan informed Penn, the province was "destitute of Indians." Pennsylvanians would shoulder the costs of any attack directly.[50]

Newly installed Lieutenant Governor Andrew Hamilton responded to the war's outbreak with a call for a publicly funded militia. Recognizing that a "Religious Tye" enjoined Friends from bearing arms themselves, he urged them not to "be a Barr to others [that] not only have freedom but think it their duty to put Inhabitants in a posture, under God, to Protect themselves from an unlawful force." He warned Quaker politicians against "Invad[ing] the principles of others" by forcing the entire colony to conform to their pacifist beliefs.[51] Quakers in the Assembly, however, again balked at raising money for defense, citing conscience and finance. They further argued that the English government should assume the burden of colonial defense. One or two warships, they claimed, could far more effectively protect the colony than a small group of citizen-soldiers.[52]

Hamilton's other appeals to civic spirit also fell on deaf ears. Given a commission by Hamilton to captain a volunteer company from Philadelphia, George Lowther sent subordinates through the city beating drums to rally prospective militiamen. The captain "found himself much disappointed" upon meeting his recruits for the first time, for they were few and "a much meaner sort than he expected." Many fighting-age men feared enlistment in the militia as tantamount to signing on for duty in England's Canadian campaigns and kept their distance. Provincial Quakers "laughed at" Lowther and his men "for their labour." Many Anglicans also fought the establishment of a provincial militia, precisely because it would ultimately make the colony safer. Aware of the Board of Trade's qualms about letting pacifists rule during a time of war, they believed that forming "a Militia would be the Readiest way to secure the Quakers' government" and thus alleviate the Board's fears. Better, they thought, to leave Pennsylvania helpless, put ruling Friends in an impossible situation, and force the Board to remove these dissenters from power.[53]

This pattern continued after John Evans replaced Hamilton as lieutenant governor in 1704.[54] Worried that God would punish the colony for abetting any form of provincial militarization, pious Friends prevented Evans from publishing a proclamation ordering the formation of new militia companies. Anglican leaders lamented "the want of a Militia to defend them in time of Danger, & then strenuously endeavour[ed] to defeat the Means of obtaining & settling it" through a variety of obstructionist tactics.[55] The governor, meanwhile, blasted Quaker and Anglican politicians for failing to fulfill their sacred duty to protect the province.[56] This bickering extended beyond the colony's elite. City constables arrested members of Philadelphia's militia companies for shirking their service in the city's night watch, leading to street fighting between the two groups.[57] Meanwhile, French privateers renewed their attacks on the Lower Counties and edged closer to Philadelphia.[58] Pennsylvanians fought while the towns of Delaware burned.

Then, on the morning of 16 May 1706, the first day of the spring fair held on Society Hill in Philadelphia, New Castle Sheriff John French arrived in the city to warn the lieutenant governor that a half-dozen French ships had entered the Delaware Bay.[59] Some had attacked the town of Lewes, burning it to the ground. Others had begun to move north and could arrive in the city at any minute. The news spurred Evans to action. He rode about the city with sword drawn, commanding all who could bear arms to gather at Society Hill. Three hundred men in the city responded with a chaotic enthusiasm, gathering to pass powder and shot among themselves.[60]

Others exhibited less civic spirit. The militiamen forgave the women who took ill in distress, but they found the actions of Philadelphia's Quaker men borderline treasonous. Many Friends fled, after securing their goods— some by throwing them down city wells to retrieve later, others by sending them upriver. Their avarice disgusted the militiamen, who declared them traitors and threatened to shoot them. A handful of Friends did arm themselves, further angering militiamen who had suspected that Quaker pacifist principles were flexible in a pinch.

The event confirmed Evans's complaints that the colony lacked an adequate civil defense, making a publicly funded militia essential. It also showed the willingness of the colony's non-Quaker population to take responsibility for their own safety. Finally, it discredited the lieutenant governor's Quaker opponents by demonstrating their religious hypocrisy. Women, at least, had a valid excuse for fainting and fleeing in the face of danger; Quaker men did not.

But the crisis was all a ruse. Hoping to get more information about the attack, James Logan had sailed downriver while Evans rode throughout the city, whereupon the secretary learned Sheriff French's report to be false. Further investigation in the days subsequent revealed Evans to be the originator of the scheme; what is more, he had fabricated earlier warnings from Maryland and New Jersey out of whole cloth—even counterfeiting a letter from the former colony's governor to stoke Pennsylvanians' fears. In the short term, Evans's call for the province's men to muster during that tumultuous market day was for naught; no external enemy threatened.

The alarm, however, did reveal threats within the colony. Political opponents became dangerous enemies as the religious divide in the province deepened. Friends, convinced Evans had manufactured the scare to discredit their leadership, renewed their determination to resist the lieutenant governor's pressure and fund a militia. Their opponents, on the other hand, felt more compelled than ever to press the issue. In a private conference with Evans shortly after the scare, the colony's leading Anglican politicians reiterated their desire for a militia and threatened to appeal to the queen for protection if the Quaker-dominated Assembly did not meet their request.

Evans's behavior following the false alarm deepened this rift. Not wanting to wait until the next session of the Assembly to resolve the problem, he

Figure 8. Portrait of James Logan (1831). Thomas Sully (1783–1872) after Gustavus Hesselius (1682–1755). Courtesy of the Library Company of Philadelphia.

endeavored to send out warrants compelling legislators to meet and deal with the issue. Although dissuaded by Logan and the rest of the Provincial Council from this action, Evans adopted a strategy similar to that of Pennsylvania's non-Quaker politicians, raising the prospect of royalization to get his way. He planned, Logan wrote, to give the Assembly a chance to rectify the civil defense problem and, if it refused, "lay [it] at their door" in his next report to the queen.[61] Not for nothing did some Friends see the alarm as a "coup d'etat," albeit a very "ill-contrived and undigested one."[62] Many believed Evans had planned the scare to force the Crown to take over the colony—after which the imperial government would promptly install him as the royal governor, a supposed promotion from his position as a proprietary lieutenant governor.[63]

Despite this pressure, the legislature took no steps to create a publicly funded militia. Many of the "church party" similarly renewed their efforts to block the formation of an elective militia in the face of Friends' intransigence.[64] Friends recognized their predicament. Committed to maintaining an adherence to pacifist beliefs strictly defined, they realized that they could no longer govern an American colony in a time of war without a militia; they could have one or the other but not both. Logan suggested that Friends revisit their views on nonviolence, for he found absurd Friends' willingness to use force to punish violent criminals within the colony's boundaries while rejecting the use of force in self-defense against invading enemies.[65]

Relations between Quakers and non-Quakers grew increasingly antagonistic after privateers stepped up their attacks on the Delaware coast in 1709 after a brief hiatus. Some Anglicans began to grumble that they would just as soon shoot a Quaker dead as a Frenchman. By 1710, some Friends resigned themselves to—or even welcomed—Penn's surrendering the colony to the Crown.[66]

To Tell the Truth: Legality in the Quaker Colony

Andrew Hamilton was annoyed when he met with the Provincial Council in April 1702. Appointed by Penn to act as Pennsylvania's lieutenant governor, Hamilton had been in the colony for five months but had yet to assume his office. Instead, he had spent the winter and early spring of 1702 waiting for someone—anyone—to administer the oath of office. Hamilton had arrived during a power struggle between the Provincial Council and royal commissioners in the colony over who had the right to qualify appointees for provincial office. Members of the Council argued that in a proprietary colony, they possessed that authority. Imperial officials disagreed, noting that they had received their commissions from King William. Royal prerogative, they argued, should prevail over proprietary prerogative. Though Council members prevailed in this jurisdictional struggle, they won a pyrrhic victory at best. Hamilton—not a Quaker—wanted to be sworn in to his office, while nearly all the councilors were Friends whose religious scruples prevented them from swearing or administering any oaths. And so Hamilton waited, until he finally insisted in the spring that the non-Quaker members of the Council take action. And on 21 April 1702, Hamilton swore an oath to become Pennsylvania's first lieutenant governor under the 1701 Charter of Privileges.[67]

What might have seemed (to Hamilton at least) a minor, if irritating, matter of protocol in fact encapsulated the rampant dysfunction in Pennsylvania's governing institutions during the first decade of the eighteenth century. The problem had procedural and cultural dimensions. Hamilton and then John Evans fought incessantly with the Assembly over that body's privileges and prerogatives. And although they offered different answers, each side grappled with the same question: what did it mean to be a colonial legislature in England's American empire? They also struggled to understand the relationship between culture and authority on the imperial periphery: how would and should power be displayed? These questions had vexed politicians, judges, and litigants in Pennsylvania's legislatures and courts during the colony's first decade. However, they took on a new importance as England's imperial bureaucracy grew after the Glorious Revolution. By 1710, the breakdown of the colony's political and legal institutions was almost complete. One issue hastened this collapse more than any other: oaths.

For nearly all Englishmen, oaths made things true. They verified the truth of words a speaker uttered "under oath," as in a court of law. Other oaths certified the past and present allegiance of the speaker to his monarch. And some oaths bound their utterer to uphold certain future obligations faithfully and truly, whether it be the duties of his appointed office or his service to the Crown. As such, oaths carried powerful weight. Failure to swear fealty to the monarch constituted, in nearly all cases, a treasonous offense punishable by fine, imprisonment, or worse. Oaths could be a matter of life and death in the courtroom as well, because conviction for capital crimes like murder required sworn testimony from at least two witnesses. Thus, oaths fulfilled a crucial function in a system that valorized the "rights of Englishmen" above all else. Swearing took on a potent symbolic charge because of its procedural significance.

Friends, of course, saw things differently, for the rejection of oaths was, for Quakers, a major tenet of their religious faith. Christ had enjoined his follows never to swear. Thus, demanding or offering oaths of allegiance meant privileging worldly over spiritual power—something Friends could not do. They also found the notion that swearing made certain professions more truthful than others problematic; did that not imply that unsworn statements were somehow less trustworthy? Christ's followers should pledge to tell the truth always and not establish different categories of speech with different levels of truthfulness.

These differences shaped how Quakers and Anglicans variously responded to the Privy Council's efforts to bring Pennsylvania's laws and courts in line with those of the rest of the colonies. Although Penn's charter empowered him to set up a provincial legislature, it also declared that the Assembly could pass no laws "repugnant" to those of England. The charter also mandated that Penn send the colony's laws to London every five years for review, where imperial lawyers could disallow those deemed unreasonable or inappropriate.[68] Provincials honored this requirement more often in the breach than the observance during the colony's first fifteen years, but the newly formed Privy Council informed them in 1696 that the bills had come due, so to speak.[69] The Council stepped up its pressure on Penn to comply with this requirement in his charter, motivated in part by Pennsylvania's selective compliance with imperial directives regarding trade. Indeed, the Council first exercised its disallowance power to strike down the colony's Act of Trade. The Board of Trade, the Council declared, and not Pennsylvania's legislature, possessed the power to set such policy.[70] When Penn sailed for England in 1701, he took with him a compilation of the colony's laws for the imperial government to review.

The Privy Council's actions emboldened the church party's efforts to attack statutes they felt unjust. Anglicans embarked on a campaign to undermine the functioning and even legitimacy of colonial courts. The conflict began in 1702 with a disagreement about the use of oaths in provincial courts. Anglicans argued that Queen Anne's accession that year required all colonial officeholders, including judges, to take an oath of abjuration professing their support for the new monarch and repudiating the right of any Stuart claimant to the throne. At a summer session of Philadelphia's Court of Quarter Sessions, Griffith Jones, a member of a bench, refused either to take such an oath or administer one to jurors or deponents. Jones, a Keithian, insisted that provincial justices need only offer an affirmation to serve on the court, as laws imposing the oath of abjuration on legal officials applied in England but not America. When the Anglicans insisted that Jones swear, he withdrew from the session. Other Quakers on the court swiftly followed.[71]

The conflict grew more severe over the next several months as courts in Bucks and Chester, the colony's two most heavily Quaker counties, essentially shut down over the matter. Ironically, the counties' Quakerness proved to be the problem. Because Friends comprised an overwhelming proportion of the judiciary there, many sessions lacked a single justice to administer oaths to those who requested them.[72] In 1703, John Guest, the colony's attorney general, declared that no capital cases could be tried in provincial courts, arguing that no Englishman should lose his life except on the basis of sworn testimony. He proposed instead the creation of a court of oyer and terminer, as existed in England, to hear these cases.[73] Guest's efforts failed, however, blocked by provincials wanting to check the proliferation of courts that existed in England.[74]

Paradoxically, royal efforts to accommodate Quaker rule made matters worse. In 1702, Queen Anne issued a proclamation declaring that all who scrupled against taking oaths could be qualified for office via affirmation, a clear effort to facilitate the participation of dissenters in colonial government. The form of the royal affirmation, however, differed from that prescribed by Pennsylvania law. Moreover, it very clearly insisted that an oath must be tendered to all whose conscience allowed them to take it, without exception. The proclamation put provincial Friends in a difficult position. Following the provincial law on affirmations and oaths might assuage their conscience, but it also meant an open rejection of imperial decree.[75]

Those challenging the court system had mixed motives. Some, to be sure, treated the swearing issue in purely instrumental terms, as it gave them a useful tool to undermine the Quaker proprietary government. Anglican claims that they had "laid the Government on its back . . . unable to move hand or foot" convinced many Friends that the church party's true goal was to throw the colony into such chaos that the queen would have to seize control.[76] While rural courts closed, many Friends sitting on the Philadelphia bench resigned, believing they could not comply with the new directives regarding oaths.[77] Evans's decision to throw his weight behind these machinations threatened to destroy the colony's legal structures. His proclamation in the fall of 1704 rendering all court proceedings in which oaths had not been properly administered null and void "shut [Friends] out of the judicature" and severely impaired attempts to stamp out "vice, looseness, and immorality" among the citizenry.[78]

The church party had more than mere partisan concerns. Or, more accurately, its partisanship and patriotism went hand in hand. Many of those eager to see Pennsylvania royalized believed that they acted as any true Englishman would have done. After all, Pennsylvania's legal system deviated substantially from English precedent, something Penn pointedly reminded the Privy Council of as it reviewed the colony's statutory code.[79] But the beauty of his reforms lay in the eye of the beholder. While Penn believed he had retained the best aspects of the English legal system and purged its most odious, others disagreed. They recoiled at the creole system Penn and others had created and pushed for the installation of a more traditional system in this New World colony. Evans's decision to side with the church party reflected political calculation, to be sure, but his declaration that the colonial government could best secure "Justice by Law in this Province" by ensuring that it was "dispensed [as] in all the Rest of [Queen Anne's] Dominions" expressed his sincere beliefs. Litigants agreed, as evidenced by the woman who appealed a case to the Provincial Council on the grounds that she could receive no fair trial where Quaker jurors were involved.[80] In an English culture that valorized rights, adherence to traditional procedures conferred authority on the government—innovation did not. The Board of Trade's review of Pennsylvania's laws strengthened Quaker critics' doubts, and the Board eventually overturned outright more than half the laws Penn had submitted.[81]

These attacks accelerated ongoing changes in Pennsylvania's court system. The colony's early leaders had designed its legal system to encourage particular forms of civic behavior. Relying on promises of good behavior (peace bonds) instead of corporal punishment for bad behavior, Quaker jurists tried to cultivate an interior civic subjectivity analogous to the inner piety gospel order generated within the Meeting. This emphasis on reform, instead of punishment, set Pennsylvania's legal system apart from those of other colonies.

The province's legal distinctiveness slowly faded after Penn resumed control of the colony in 1695. Some aspects of Quaker jurisprudence remained, albeit in a muted form. Judges still showed a greater proclivity to bind offenders to the peace than to inflict corporal punishment. Over time, however, this tendency became less pronounced as judges administered whippings and other coercive forms of punishment more often.[82] The ratio of peace bonds issued to whippings administered decreased markedly after 1695. Between 1680 and 1695, the ratio in Chester, Sussex, and Bucks Counties was 2.3:1; between 1696 and 1710 it dropped to 1.5:1.[83]

In some counties, the change was especially dramatic. In Chester, for instance, approximately one in fourteen convicted criminals received a public whipping during the 1680s and 1690s; between 1700 and 1710, one in four did.[84] Quaker distinctiveness ebbed in other areas as well. Litigants relied less on the simplified legal procedures Pennsylvania's early legal code had prescribed and more on common law civil procedures, making Latin the legal language of the land after 1710.[85] As a result, lawyers, once banned from the colony's courts, became common after the turn of the century.

Hierarchies of identity and authority became more heavily gendered as a result of these trends. The rise of common law forms of action in civil cases favored plaintiffs and defendants with more legal experience, an overwhelmingly male subsection of the total number of legal participants. This mirrored the experience of women in other colonies who saw their legal authority diminish as common law superseded reformist legal experiments in their colonies.[86] Similar changes occurred in the criminal justice system. Corporal punishment became increasingly gendered and racialized. Before 1696, three in five criminals sentenced to a public whipping were white men. Between 1696 and 1710, only one in three were. Black men and all women, but especially white women, bore the brunt of magistrates' increasing willingness to punish bodies instead of disciplining selves.[87]

Meanwhile, William Biles's 1705 conviction for slander made a mockery of the notion that the courts could effectively protect the reputation of public officials.[88] At the final session of the 1704–5 Assembly in May, Biles, a representative from Bucks County, said of the lieutenant governor, "He is but a boy he is not fitt to be our Governour we'll kick him out we'll kick him out." Taking offense, Evans sued Biles for slander, seeking £2,000 in damages. The case degenerated into a semantic farce, much as the Keithians' trial had a decade before. Biles and his attorney, David Lloyd, argued that he had spoken as William Biles the assemblyman, which would have protected his words from prosecution. No Englishman could deny a representative's authority to criticize his government during a legislative session. Evans, on the other hand, argued that he had spoken as Biles the man, thus disrespecting the highest official in the land.

Evans secured a pyrrhic victory. The court found Biles's words slanderous and awarded Evans £300 in damages—a sum far greater than any plaintiff had ever received but also far less than he had wanted. It also exceeded what Biles, a middling farmer, could pay. Ignoring pleas to accept his vindication in court but forego monetary damages, Evans ordered Biles imprisoned for his failure to make restitution. The assemblyman remained in prison for a month before Evans allowed his release, alienating even some of Evans's staunchest supporters. The sight of women Friends nursing the ailing Biles in prison brought back memories of their sisters in the faith aiding male Friends imprisoned during the worst years of persecution. Biles's sufferings showed that Evans was unfit to rule the colony. A parody of earlier attempts to punish criticism of Pennsylvania's ruling elite, the trial and its aftermath did far more damage to the lieutenant governor's reputation than the assemblyman's words ever could have, starkly revealing the legal system's inability to regulate the province's speech economy.

Pennsylvania's legal system had not unified the populace in the way that its creators had intended. William Penn and his fellow provincial founders had developed a specific set of legal sanctions designed to promote a particular kind of civic subjectivity. These prescriptions and prohibitions operated on the level of personal performance. Magistrates expected litigants to enact rituals affirming the power of the colony's government. Through the use of tools like the peace bond, they encouraged citizens to perform these behaviors outside of court as well. These civic rituals had Quaker roots. The regulation of everyday habits of speech and dress, suitably monitored by Meeting elders, allowed ordinary English Friends to perform their relationship to God and each other. Moreover, these practices carried particular weight because they existed within a broader spiritual world that included a thriving Quaker print culture and a powerful sense of tribal identity—again, fostered by Meeting orthodoxy. English Friends took for granted the fact that their personal spiritual practices took place within a collective whole. Friends in Pennsylvania hoped that the legal system would play a role in provincial society analogous to that played by Meeting discipline.

By 1710, however, Quaker leaders knew that these efforts had failed. Anglican pressure meant fewer court sessions. Thus, citizens could no longer attend county court days to witness public performances of submission and affirmation that authorized government power. The campaign to shut down the courts meant that ordinary Pennsylvanians felt the presence of the law far more lightly after 1700 than they had before. Moreover, the courts increasingly resembled those of other colonies, not something that could effectively inculcate a form of Quakerized civic habits within the populace at large.

Moreover, provincial Friends realized that Pennsylvania's distinctive legal system could never serve as a tool for political and cultural unification. Provincial legal rituals existed in a different cultural field than Quaker religious practices did. Pennsylvanians could not assume that the idiosyncratic elements of their colony's legal culture reflected shared notions of a social order. Rejecting the legal order they encountered, provincial Anglicans proffered an alternative vision, one reflecting imperial, not Quaker, values. Before 1695, Penn berated colonists for failing to live up to the civic rules he had established. After 1695, Pennsylvania's non-Quakers challenged the legitimacy of the rules themselves. Particular civic rituals—the taking of an affirmation in lieu of an oath, the sentence of a peace bond instead of a whipping—dramatized the deep sectarian divisions that existed in the colony. They afforded provincials an opportunity to perform their differences. So long as imperial officials insisted on bringing order to the colony and so long as Anglicans in Pennsylvania supported these efforts, the greatest truth the colony's legal rituals revealed was the tenuousness of Quaker power.

Friends' authority was a contested truth in other spaces as well, most notably the colonial frontier. Provincials fought with various Indian groups over the nature and exercise of authority on this colonial borderland in ways that resembled the conflicts to the east. The struggles revolved around the signs and symbols of diplomatic legitimacy, just as Anglicans and Quakers argued over the merits of oath and affirmation. Conestoga, Delaware, and Shawnee Indians fought to resist the extension of both Iroquois and English power, attempting to maintain some relative autonomy in the face of expansionist desires. Living at the interstices of empire had a profound effect on the evolution of Native American political and cultural identities.

Space and Sovereignty: Redefining the Limits of Colonial Authority

On 12 and 13 September 1700, the "Susquehannah" and Shawnee Indians met with provincial officials in Philadelphia to negotiate two agreements. One of these agreements was intended to meet Indian demands, the other to meet colonial demands. The treaty signed on 12 September "at the Request of the said Indians" had been instigated in response to an incident that had befallen the Conestoga Indians the previous winter. Two traders had visited the Conestogas' winter quarters, "produced a paper with a large seale and

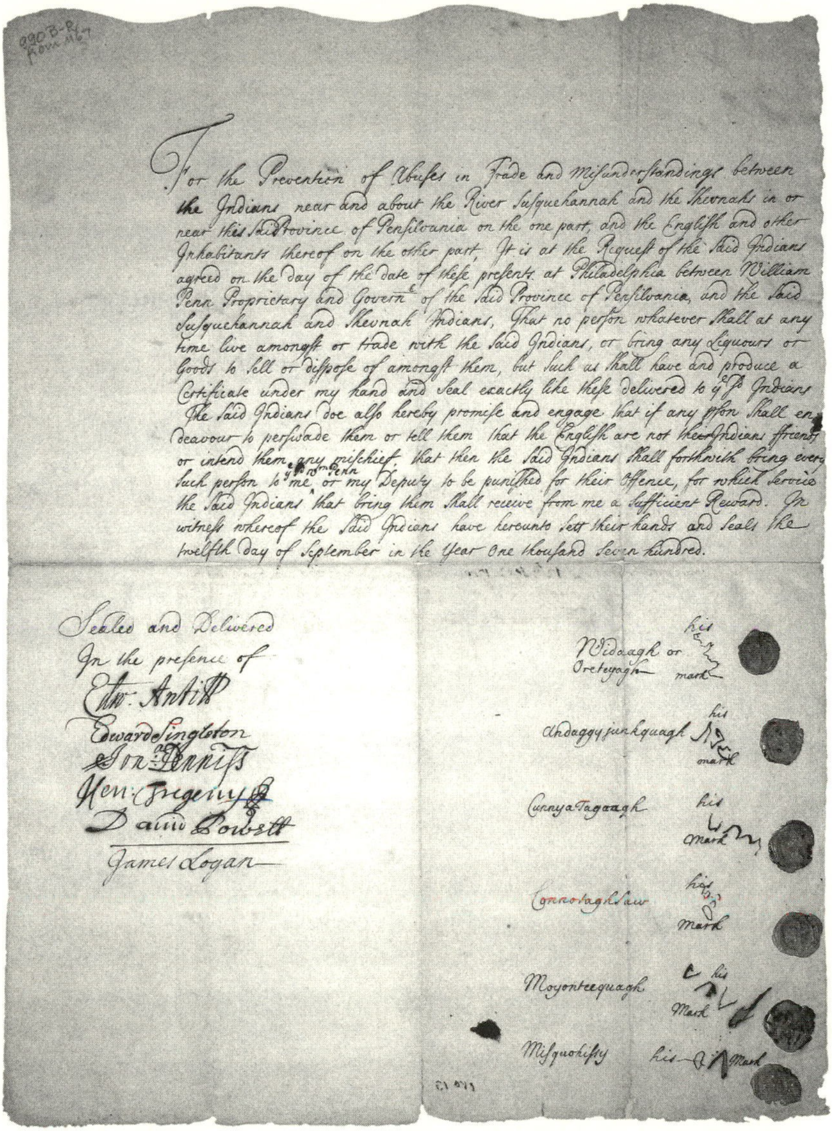

Figure 9. "Treaty with the Susquehannah Indians, 12 September 1700," George Vaux Collection of Correspondence and Documents #1167, Quaker Collection, Haverford College. Courtesy of the Quaker Collection, Haverford College.

pretended it was a warrant from the Governor to require them" to deliver four "strange" Indians who had recently defrauded the traders. When the Conestogas refused, the two traders returned with a third companion, again made their demand, and this time insisted that if the Conestogas failed to comply, the English would "come againe with 600 men" to attack their "families for they had refused the Governors order"—a threat that this time yielded the desired result. Two Conestoga sachems, Conodahto and Mecalloua, recounted the story in a petition to William Penn, noting that the proprietor had shown "love, good will and favour" toward Indians as well as Christians and asked to "receiuve at least an equal share of Favour and protection under him as the rest of our Brethering" in the region.[89]

As a result of this encounter, the 12 September treaty mandated "That no person whatsoever Shall at any time live amongst or trade with the Said Indians, or bring any Liquors or Goods to Sell or dispose of amongst them but Such as Shall have and produce a Certificate under my hand and Seal exactly like these delivered to the sd Indians"—eliminating (it was hoped) the possibility of frauds such as the one the Conestoga had suffered.[90] Modifying the protections for Indians that William Penn and other legislators had built into the colony's first legal code, this provision made the boundaries between native and colonial society somewhat less porous than they had been. It made the provincial government responsible for keeping immoral individuals out of Indian country, using the same means by which Penn had hoped to keep immoral individuals from entering Pennsylvania: passes, seals, and licenses. Moreover, it bore a remarkable resemblance to the Quaker practice of requiring Friends joining a new meeting to produce a certificate attesting to their piety from the one they had just left.[91] Faced with difficulty protecting their own borders, the "Susquehannah Indians" had turned to the colonial government for help and accepted a colonial mechanism to police the boundary.

The next day, the parties negotiated the agreement the colonial government sought—the transfer of land. The treaty was part land sale, part ratification of an earlier sale. At issue was Penn's continuing effort to expand into the Susquehanna Valley. New York's Governor Thomas Dongan had previously blocked his efforts in 1683 by discouraging the Mohawks from selling to Penn, then maneuvering to purchase the land on the upper Susquehanna himself.[92] But Penn eventually prevailed upon Dongan in the latter's retirement to sell him the land in 1696 for £100—a price suggesting that both Dongan and Penn found the former governor's land claim somewhat

dubious.[93] So on 13 September 1700, Widaagh Orytyagh and Andaggy Junk-
quah, "Kings or Sachems of the Susquehannah Indians, and of the River
under that name, and lands lying on both sides thereof," sold Penn the
Susquehanna Valley "in Consideration of a Parcel of English Goods, unto us
given," a cheap price indeed. But the sachems also assented to Dongan's sale
of the upper Susquehanna Valley, giving Penn's earlier purchase a patina of
legality it previously lacked.[94]

This treaty had a counterintuitive air. Title to the land had passed from
the Iroquois to Dongan to Penn. Yet when Pennsylvania's government
wanted to confirm Penn's possession of the land, it turned not to the powerful confederacy of Indian nations that had sold New York's governor the
property but instead to a handful of small bands of Indians living in loose
settlements with little centralized political authority. Moreover, colonial leaders had chosen "strange" Indians as partners for this deal in a literal sense, as
the Shawnee and "Susquehannah" who signed the treaty had arrived in the
river valley region only recently. That Pennsylvania's government felt the
need to secure the newcomers' approval of the sale of large tracts of Susquehanna Valley lands conducted before their arrival likely struck some contemporary observers as odd.

The logic of this seemingly illogical negotiation lay in the changing demographics of the Susquehanna River Valley. The Beaver Wars of the 1670s
had led to the conquest of the Susquehannock Indians at the hands of the
Iroquois Confederacy. The Susquehannocks scattered in the wake of this
defeat. Some went south to the mouth of the Potomac River, while many
migrated north to become adoptees of the Iroquois. These migrations marked
the end of the Susquehannocks' territorial integrity as a politically autono-
mous people. They became a people without sovereignty over their home-
land, a particularly deep blow given the important role collective land
ownership played in defining Indian identities in the colonial world. This
scattering also wrought major cultural changes, as migrants began to assimilate into the new communities within which they lived. Finally, it led to the
depopulation of the Susquehanna River Valley in the 1680s. Penn's early
optimism about the ease of colonizing the region reflected this fact. The
second settlement along the Susquehanna that Penn hoped to establish would
have required the displacement of fewer Indians than the creation of the
initial settlement among the Delaware had.[95]

Various Indian groups began to resettle the valley in the early 1690s.
Some Delaware Indians resettled west in the face of colonial growth. Bands

of Susquehannock, Seneca, Oneida, Cayuga, and Tuscarora Indians moved into the valley and founded the town of Conestoga, an ethnically mixed settlement roughly fifty miles west of Philadelphia. Numerous Conoy Indians came north from Maryland following extended conflict with colonizers in that province. A band of Shawnee Indians founded a town along Pequea Creek just west of the Susquehanna River.[96] Delaware negotiators first mentioned the arrival of "strange Indians" in the valley in 1693, and by 1694 negotiators from the new settlements in the valley had begun to attend conferences with provincial diplomats.[97] The social, cultural, and political boundary lines between these Indian tribes were extremely fluid during this period, as evidenced by the composition of settlements like Conestoga. When provincial diplomats wrote about "Susquehannah" Native Americans in their treaty conferences, they described the Indians' residence rather than their tribal identity.

Resettlement and its resultant cultural reconfigurations produced no dominant political authority in the region, however, motivating the provincial government and the Shawnee and Susquehanna Indians to broker those two agreements in September 1700. Provincial diplomats found these Indian bands appealing partners because of their status as newcomers. Without an established claim to authority in the valley, these "strangers" had little leverage to broker a hard deal. The provincial government, thus, enlarged its sovereignty in two key ways. First, it secured its territorial claim to the upper Susquehanna Valley. Second, it secured the Susquehanna and Shawnee Indians' acceptance of colonial signs of authority—licenses—as the symbols of legality for whites moving into and out of Indian country.

For their part, the Indians on the Susquehanna scored two crucial victories in these accords. By conceding the extension of colonial power deeper into the backcountry, they secured some measure of protection from unscrupulous traders attempting to use forged or fraudulent passes to take advantage of them. More importantly, they gained a measure of respect. The colonial government had, in essence, ratified the Susquehanna Indians as an important player in a complicated system of regional politics. In allowing the provincial government a greater measure of control over space and sovereignty on the frontier, they had also strengthened their own relationship to colonial authorities. Taking advantage of jurisdictional uncertainties along Pennsylvania's borderlands, the Susquehanna and Shawnee Indians gained by losing.[98] Provincials and (some) Indians had found common cause in their desire to bring order to the backcountry.

By the time Penn negotiated his more well-known Articles of Agreement with the Susquehanna, Shawnee, and North Potomac Indians seven months later in April 1701, there was at least some reason to believe Penn's rhetoric that "all the English and Christian Inhabitants" of Pennsylvania and "all the several people of the Nations of Indians" attending would "forever hereafter be as one head and one heart, and live in true Friendship and Amity as one People."[99] The Articles, after all, contained several provisions to which both sides had already agreed, including those contained in the September 1700 accords. They also included the Indians' willingness to "behave themselves . . . according to the Laws of This Government when they live near or amongst the Christian Inhabitants thereof," a somewhat elastic provision given the rapid westward movement of colonial settlement. Penn, for his part, promised equal justice if any English subject under his authority committed any wrong against any of the said Indians.[100] The Articles of Agreement of 1701 represented Penn's efforts to enact his utopian vision of native-colonial relations while conceding the realities of contemporary regional politics.

These treaties illustrate the evolving relationship between discourse, space, and sovereignty as English and Indians redefined colonial authority on Pennsylvania's frontier in the first decade of the eighteenth century. Seeking to expand their authority over the frontier, colonial magistrates attempted to make their rules for handling conflict into the law that would govern interactions between provincials. Indians of various tribes, meanwhile, reacted differently to this trend.

Both colonists and Indians in this period grappled with sovereignty and jurisdiction in ways that mirrored fights over political authority in provincial institutions. First, colonists and Indians struggled with the very basic question of whose rules would be law in conflicts involving parties on each side.[101] Second, they argued over personal and territorial jurisdiction. Who would be subject to colonial writ? How far would it extend?[102] Third, they struggled to define the very forms and symbols that displayed legality, debating the meaning of licenses, passes, certificates, and wampum. Finally, they argued over the ends to which the alliances formed in these meetings would be put. If diplomatic conferences created "chains of friendship" between Indians and colonists, what did these friends owe each other? As colonial negotiators endeavored, in halting and often unsuccessful ways, to have diplomatic councils serve the same legitimating functions on the frontier that courtrooms, theoretically at least, served at home, native negotiators attempted to retain some of their own autonomy and authority vis-à-vis the colonial government and other Indian groups.

At times it seemed as if questions of form dominated the discussion, as colonists and Indians of various backgrounds struggled with the signs and symbols of diplomacy. Colonial officials hoped that treaty councils might parallel the function of English courtrooms in their relations with indigenous peoples, thus serving as sites where Indian peoples might perform allegiance to the colonial government. They soon learned, however, that these diplomatic encounters were very different discursive spaces, where participants performed authority in a very different fashion. Sessions of colonial county courts opened with invocations of the Crown's and Penn's authority, legitimating magistrates through their relationship to these centers of political authority. Indian diplomats displayed their authority at the outset of treaty conferences not simply through performative speech but also through the offering of gifts and a display of material signs of legitimacy, specifically wampum.[103] In 1705, Logan and his party were greeted by Indians that, though they were poor, "presented us with some skins."[104] Lieutenant Governor John Evans received gifts of skins, pipes, and tobacco during a trip along the Susquehanna to quell tensions between the Indians living in the valley and the Iroquois Confederacy.[105] Colonial diplomats realized only slowly the importance of gift-giving in establishing their own legitimacy to Indian negotiators, a fact that irked Pennsylvania's native peoples. Although by 1709 Lieutenant Governor Charles Gookin was cognizant enough of this custom during a council with "Mingo," or Ohio country Iroquois Indians, to remind the Assembly of "the immediate necessity . . . for a supply to make them a reasonable present," provincial officials honored this custom irregularly.[106]

Wampum was perhaps the most critical gift exchanged at these diplomatic councils. Indian negotiators used the sacred shell beads to establish their authority to provincial diplomats. Other goods helped construct a relationship through which negotiation could occur. Building social ties provided the primary rationale for gift exchange in Indian culture more generally. Wampum, however, served as a sign of diplomatic and political authority. A gift of wampum was a public claim of one's worthiness to give it and the recipient's worthiness to accept it.[107]

Provincial clerks noted this practice almost from the beginning of diplomatic exchanges; the first Lenape to meet Governor Benjamin Fletcher in 1693 opened negotiations by "la[ying] a belt of Wampum at his Excellency's feet."[108] The Lenape sachems that came to Philadelphia a year later did the same, depositing a belt of wampum before Fletcher so that he might address the governor "in the name of the rest of the Delaware Indians."[109] This practice was common to other eastern Indians as well. In February 1708, for example, the Conestoga interpreter Indian Harry opened a council that he had initiated at Philadelphia by "laying upon the board Six loose strings of white Wampum for his Credentials" so that his message to the Provincial Council might be trusted.[110] Eight months earlier, a Nanticoke negotiator from the Susquehanna Valley had similarly showed Evans belts of wampum as evidence both of his people's peaceful relations with Maryland, Pennsylvania, and the Iroquois and of his authority to negotiate with the province.[111]

Wampum sometimes acted not only as a sign of an Indian negotiator's authority to deliver a message but as the message itself. At the 1709 council in Philadelphia, a Mingo speaker rose before assembled diplomats and magistrates, "laid on the Board a Belt of Wampum, as a Token to Confirm what he had to Speak," and then relayed information about tensions between Maryland Indians and the Iroquois Nations.[112] The wampum was, in this instance, no different from the provincial Great Seal over which colonists fought so bitterly. Nine representatives from the Tuscaroroas, Conestogas, Senecas, and Shawnees similarly "spoke on" eight belts of wampum sent both to break off hostilities on the Pennsylvania frontier and to solicit Lieutenant Governor Gookin's help in negotiating a more stable peace.[113] Nor were Indians the only diplomats who granted wampum such authoritative power; provincial officials increasingly grasped this aspect of its meaning as well. In sending the Conestoga man Kneeghnyaskoate as a messenger to the Onondagas in 1705, Evans made sure that the emissary carried "a small Parcell of wampum for his Credential" to empower him to inquire in Evans's name about rumored strife between these two groups.[114] In the same way, a wampum belt sent by the Iroquois to New Castle by way of Indian Harry was enough to convince Gookin of the credibility of rumors of Iroquois aggression on the frontier.[115]

Other tactile signifiers of cultural authority became subjects of discussion at treaty conferences as well. Negotiators on all sides saw unscrupulous traders bandying about counterfeit passes and seals and acting in the government's name as a problem. This sense of the danger posed by such counterfeit symbols of authority merely underscored the importance that Native and Euro-Americans alike placed on symbols such as wampum, warrants, passes, seals, and licenses. Provincials and Indians debated frontier traders' licenses and certificates on several occasions. Evans, for example, reassured the Sus-

quehanna Indians who arrived at Philadelphia in June 1706 that the government "had made a Law to prevent any injuries to them from the Christians,
. . . and had also enacted in that Law, that no person should trade with them,
but such as should first have a License from the Governor under his hand
and Seal."[116] The question of traders without licenses or with fraudulent ones
was also the main topic of discussion at the February 1708 conference between Indian Harry and the Pennsylvanians.[117] And perhaps most preposter-
ously, Gookin, at a 1710 meeting, suggested that those Indians who wanted
to immigrate into the river valley should be required to produce licenses
before moving, just as traders traveling to Indian country or Quakers moving
to another meeting were supposed to bear certificates of good behavior:

> We acquainted them . . . that if they intended to settle and live amiably
> here, they need not Doubt the protection of this Government in such
> things as were honest and good, but that to Confirm the sincerity of
> their past Carriage toward the English, and to raise in us a good opinion
> of them, it would be necessary to procure a Certificate from the govern-
> ment they leave, to this, of their Good behaviour, and then they might
> be assured of a favorable reception.[118]

Negotiators on both sides, then, allotted power to material markers of
authority in their attempts to construct "neutral" cultural spaces such as
treaty councils and to control movement across boundaries between Anglo-
American and Indian societies. The treaty council relied on mutually recog-
nizable material signs to legitimate its proceedings both to those present and
to those to whom news of the event would circulate. Employing political
rituals that were truly indigenous to none of the participants involved, the
treaty council was an attempt to craft a political site that was, culturally
speaking at least, creole to both natives and newcomers. Moreover, the same
material signs that awarded authoritative entrée to diplomatic discussions—
trade goods, wampum, licenses, seals, passes—also gave entrée to Indian
country for traders and later even for other Indians. That displays of such
symbols of authority operated as frames for the negotiations revealed that
Indian diplomats and provincial officials agreed on their importance; that
such signs proved bones of contention revealed that each side occasionally
disagreed with how the other employed them. Controversies arose less over
the need for material signs of power in mediating the boundary between
Pennsylvania and Indian country than over *whose* signs—Indians' or Euro-

Pennsylvanians'—would wield the most power. This push and pull over the symbols of legitimacy in treaty councils was part of a creolization process through which a shared hybrid Indian-colonial civic culture could have emerged.

Conflict over signifiers of authority manifested deeper divisions between provincials and Indians over space and sovereignty, however. Magistrates showed interest not simply in forcing natives to accept passes, seals, and licenses as authoritative signs but also in forcing Indians to accept the larger political, social, and conceptual edifice that went along with them. Their willingness to accord wampum a central role in diplomatic negotiation did not mean they granted Indian standards of legality precedence when it came to matters of jurisdiction and sanction. William Penn and his successors held firm in the proprietor's previously stated belief that equal justice on the frontier meant English justice. Before his journey back to England in 1701, Penn reiterated his intention to punish harshly those colonizers who harmed Indians. To do so, "the Governor Desire[d] that when ever any Transgressed the said Law, and Came, Contrary amongst them, to agreement they would forthwith take Care to give information thereof to the Government, that the offenders might be duly prosecuted."[119] Penn thus elucidated an ambiguous aspect of the Articles of Agreement ratified six months earlier, which had promised swift justice against any Christians who harmed an Indian but had not specified which brand of justice would be applied.[120] Five years later, Evans likewise emphasized to local Indians that applying Anglo-American law on the frontier would "prevent any injuries to them from the Christians." He also added that if colonials did harm Indians, the government would lay "greater Punishments on those that should Committ them, than if they were done to the English themselves."[121] For Evans, the principle of exemplary justice, with the goal of convincing Indians to submit to colonial law, outweighed the principle of equal justice.

Perhaps not surprisingly, therefore, the region's indigenous peoples showed little interest in the "protective" power of Anglo-American law. At a council one month after Gookin's proposal for certificates, the Onondaga spokesman Connessoa met the deputy governor's proposal with a strong claim for natives' authority to mete out justice in their own way. Through the interpreter Indian Harry, he presented provincial negotiators with a series of demands that he felt essential for the preservation of peace in the region. In particular, Connessoa insisted upon Indians' ability to punish those colonials who had wronged them; natives believed "that (notwithstanding our hearty desyres of peace) yet if any Man affronts You, be not daunted, but revenge Your Selfes."[122]

Indian negotiators, however, asked not for political, legal, protection. Although they accepted, and in some ways even encouraged, the encroachment of Pennsylvania's authority further west on the frontier, natives wanted it on their own terms. Aware of the Iroquois' increasing attempts to extend their political dominance southward and the resulting threat of violence, Indian groups along the Susquehanna more than once sent messengers to enlist the provincial government's support against the Iroquois Confederacy.[123] Thus, Indians and colonials could no more agree on these crucial questions of how the provincial government's authority should best be used than they could agree on whose signs and symbols of authority should take precedence in diplomatic rituals.

These debates over space and sovereignty took place within a slowly developing discourse of friendship and allegiance. Both sides used treaty councils as a means of keeping close ties. For provincials, these conferences also proved a means of securing and maintaining alliances with various Indian groups in the region—a matter of paramount importance during a time of war.[124] Provincials used diplomatic councils to dispel rumors of war, to determine if reports of attempts to "debauch all" England's Indian allies to the French cause were true, or to ensure simply that those Indian peoples with whom Pennsylvania was at peace remained happy with the English side during time of war. For their part, Native Americans asked for reassurances that their allies would offer military aid should French forces invade the colony. In a larger sense, for Indians maintaining political links was a raison d'être for the councils themselves.[125] The process (the council) and the product (renewed ties) were intricately intertwined.[126]

Both Indians and colonials spoke of maintaining a "chain of friendship" that would bind each to the other. But this term carried different meanings for the parties involved. Native diplomats described friendship as a chain that might need to be polished periodically and "brightened" but if cared for properly would remain strong.[127] No bonds could exist without renewal. Provincials used it to remind their Indian counterparts of the agreements Penn had made with native leaders during his first and second visits to Pennsylvania. Colonists envisioned a perpetual friendship that needed no renegotiation.[128]

Even native references to their bond with Penn had contested meanings. Negotiators from the tribes living around Conestoga repeatedly reminded colonial diplomats of their "ancient friendship" with Penn and his successors, even though the colony's establishment predated their settlement in the Susquehanna Valley. Lenape diplomats similarly emphasized the longevity of their relationship with the Christian inhabitants of the region. This friendship, they noted, predated the alliances Pennsylvania had formed with Shawnees and Conestogas in the area. Ritualistic invocations of their relationship to the proprietor became strategic attempts to claim a status as the preeminent Indian entity in the colony.[129] Defining their relationship to the colony, Lenape, Conestoga, Shawnee, and other Susquehanna Indians helped define their relationship to each other—and thus, in a roundabout way, helped them define themselves.

These variations in language, however slight, revealed the difficulties that colonists and Indians had in creating a creole diplomacy. When each side invoked the language of friendship, they spoke the same language—almost. But differences in interest as well as understanding separated them. The Susquehanna Indians gained no political or economic advantage from being tied to Pennsylvania in a permanent alliance; in emphasizing the need for constant renewal, they asserted their independence of colonial authority. Colonial negotiators, meanwhile, emphasized a perpetual bond for strategic reasons. When James Logan lamented to William Penn that the colony was nearly "destitute of Indians," he did so not out of ethnographic interest but of fear: he worried that the colony would have no Indian allies to protect it in the event of a French attack on the western frontier.[130] Claims of "ancient friendship," then, served the cause of the European contest for North America, rather than the creation of a truly hybrid diplomatic culture.[131]

The differences between colonial and Indian understandings of the "chains of friendship" that had been forged epitomized the difficulties both sides faced in establishing a diplomatic culture native to each side. Pennsylvanian politicians frequently demonstrated good intentions in their dealings with Native Americans. But good faith could not overcome competing interests. That treaty councils gradually over Pennsylvania's first three decades took on the appearance of a hybrid culture—through the agreed-upon use of wampum and other material signifiers of political authority—masked deeper divisions. In essence, colonists and Indians used common cultural symbols to tell opposing political stories. The failure of colonial negotiators to craft a truly creole diplomacy with natives in the region would lead to increased tension over the following decades, as the Iroquois Confederacy increased its efforts to expand its authority southward into the Susquehanna and Delaware Valley region.

Pennsylvania's founders had designed an elaborate set of political and legal rituals that they hoped might accomplish two ends: to creolize newcomers to the colony and to naturalize Quaker power. They failed on both counts. Moreover, their efforts to secure a Quaker utopia in Pennsylvania had fostered the development of a self-conscious Anglican community that opposed Friends' rule in principle as well as practice. The stories anti-Quaker authors told about Friends' malfeasance as provincial fathers coalesced into a larger narrative about the cultural and institutional need for imperial order on the North American borderlands.[132] Pennsylvania was one of only two British colonies that saw vocal cries for the imposition of more royal authority. The other colony that had witnessed such agitation, West Jersey, had been royalized in 1702 and merged into the colony of New Jersey, a testament to the vulnerability of Quaker colonial efforts in America.[133] This resistance to Quaker authority from their fellow colonists mirrored efforts by Native Americans to assert their own power. Arguments about form and precedent in treaty councils generated new political and cultural identities simultaneously.

Coming on the heels of the Keithian controversy, these challenges threatened Pennsylvania's existence as a distinctive colony on the fringes of the British empire. The creolized civic culture Friends had created was as weak as the creole Quakerism the Keithians had decried. But the uncertainties of life on the colonial borderlands ultimately spurred provincial Friends to develop a particularly New World religious culture. This, in turn, allowed them to reconstitute Pennsylvania as a Quaker colony in the face of external pressure.

PART III

Triumph

CHAPTER 6

Narratives of Early Pennsylvania, II

The Founding of Pennsylvania

BY 1709, WILLIAM PENN had reached a state of utter despair about the fate of his American colony. Political opponents like David Lloyd stood firm in their perverse opposition to him at every turn. Worse, voters repeatedly rewarded Lloyd's behavior. What governor, he asked his secretary James Logan, "would care one jot w[ha]t comes of such a foolish (if not wicked) people"? Logan concurred, wondering why Penn had not shed himself of the colony long ago. Acknowledging Penn's fear that Friends would suffer political and legal disabilities were the colony royalized, Logan believed Quaker disenfranchisement a "singularly just" outcome. Quaker ingrates needed "to deal to their Portions Crosses[,] Vexation[,] & Disappointments to convince them of their Mistakes and own Inconsistancy." Penn needed no further convincing. After all these years of bickering, he was finally ready to surrender his colony to the Crown.[1]

And yet only fourteen months later, Penn found himself thanking Pennsylvania's Quaker community for "the eminent Zeal and Concurrence for the Publick Good & therein for my service," still convinced the two went hand in hand. He assured them that he would make every effort to "take care of your Property and Privileges . . . as Christians & Englishmen" against any and all imperial encroachments. For their part, leading provincial politicians, having removed Lloyd and his supporters in the October 1710 elections, pledged their support for Penn and their gratitude for his efforts on their behalf. Three decades of conflict had given way to harmony between proprietor and colonists.

This remarkable political turnaround culminated a long process of religious and cultural consolidation. After years of conflicts between proprietary and antiproprietary factions, imperial and local officials, and struggles between Quakers and non-Quakers, provincial Friends finally came to terms with their history in America. This allowed them to create the workable political identity that had previously eluded them. Decades after Penn received his charter from Charles II, they established Pennsylvania as a firmly Quaker colony.[2]

In one sense, this outcome was deeply ironic. For years, Penn and his opponents had blamed their inability to create community on infighting within Pennsylvania's Quaker governing class. Provincial politics would have been harmonious and amicable, if only Quaker leaders treated themselves with the same love and unity Friends exhibited within the Meeting. Quaker leaders could easily "season" new settlers and bring non-Quakers into the civic fold if only they embraced their common tribal identity as Friends. And American Quakerism would have flowered if only the Keithian "weeds" had not despoiled the spiritual landscape. Penn and his newfound allies each wrote of the election of 1710 as the triumph of these hopes. It represented the fulfillment of Pennsylvania's initial promise.

But these persistent religious and political frictions had not prevented Friends from achieving the coherent civic order they constructed in 1710. Rather, they provided Pennsylvanians numerous opportunities to define what it meant to be a Quaker in America. They helped them to work out the relationship between Friends and non-Friends in a Quaker colony. And they allowed them to come to terms with what it meant to live in a proprietary colony within the English empire. Provincials needed to have these arguments as they built a workable political language they all found legitimate. In other words, Pennsylvania's political stabilization did not happen *in spite* of the internal strife that had plagued the colony in the decades after its founding; it happened *because* of it. Years of cultural friction enabled the creation of a creole civic culture.

Histories of Pennsylvania: The English Inheritance in America

On 12 April 1704, Lieutenant Governor John Evans addressed Pennsylvania's legislature for the first time. He reminded the Assembly and Provincial Council that a good society required a "well Regulated Legislative Power" in which those empowered to govern had the respect of the governed. He asked them to look on the motherland as an example, for its glory derived in no small part from the harmony that prevailed in Parliament, its legislative body. Evans's words must have seemed uncontroversial, if not cliché, to the audience. They were, after all, "blest with the Priviledges of English men," just as he and their compatriots on the eastern side of the Atlantic were.[3]

But while the speaker and the audience both spoke the language of "English rights," they disagreed about what it meant to have English rights in America. They debated, at great length, points of procedure and executive and legislative prerogative. Though these arguments at times represented instrumental grabs for political power, they also contained substantive assessments of the legal merit of the other side's competing claims. At root, Evans and his Quaker opponents fought over the English legal and political inheritance in North America, a critical issue for provincials struggling to create a stable creole civic identity.

Military concerns quickly ended any honeymoon Evans and the Assembly might have otherwise enjoyed. The lieutenant governor moved immediately after assuming his position to request money for England's war effort. To his astonishment, the legislature rebuffed his request for constitutional as well as religious reasons. After conferring with selected members of the Provincial Council to discuss the issue, Quaker assemblymen informed Evans that they would pass no law contributing money for public safety because they objected to a clause in his commission granting him the power to confirm or reject laws before transmission to England for Penn's approval. This stipulation, they argued, represented an usurpation of their power. The Council's argument that Evans's commission merely followed the procedures laid out in the 1701 Charter failed to move the Assembly.[4]

This served as an opening salvo in a constitutional war. Assemblymen denounced Evans's veiled threats to prorogue the Assembly as a violation of the Charter of Privileges granting them legislative power "according to the Rights of the free born subjects of England, and as is usual in any of the King's Plantacons in America."[5] They also chafed at his refusal to negotiate over bills he had rejected. This preemptory conduct went against "the practice of England"—the Crown would never so treat Parliament. Evans angrily replied that their "unnecessary Scrutinies" into their constitutional authority had caused legislators to lose sight of their "real Privileges as Englishmen," namely, securing the happiness of the people of Pennsylvania.[6] Stuck at an impasse, this session of the Assembly went by without a revenue bill. The failure foreshadowed the legislature's level of activity during the lieutenant governor's stay in the colony. The Assembly passed no new legislation during Evans's tenure.[7]

During this prolonged standoff, legislators developed an increasingly elaborate justification of their position, grounded in their historical status as immigrants and Englishmen. When asked to contribute money to alleviate Penn's financial distress, they informed Evans that, as the first settlers and "real adventurers" in the province, they had done as much or more than the proprietor had for Pennsylvania.[8] This language was not limited to Quakers, as evidenced by a 1706 petition of 150 Germantown residents for naturalization. Residents of one of the colony's oldest towns, the petitioners argued that their industry had transformed "uncultivated Lands . . . into good settlem[en]ts." These improvements, accompanied by declarations of allegiance to the monarch, entitled them to the rights of natural-born Englishmen. Concurring, the Provincial Council asked Penn to encourage the Board of Trade to naturalize the Germantown settlers and "all others in their Circumstances." Their travails in the wilderness gave them a claim to English rights, regardless of their birth.[9]

The conflict between Evans and the Assembly over his bid to establish Courts of Chancery and Equity generated the most detailed narratives and counternarratives about Pennsylvanians' proper place in the English Atlantic world. For Evans the story was simple: provincials did not understand the proper nature of their own colony. Pennsylvania, he argued, resembled a monarchy in which sovereignty rested with William Penn. Consequently, freemen of the province had "the right of concurring in making Laws," but nothing further. Moreover, they had gone beyond claiming rights missing from the 1701 Charter; they claimed broader rights than any other colonists in English America. Only deluded provincial politicians, Evans sneered, could believe that their legislature possessed all the powers and privileges of Parliament. In the end, Pennsylvanians were mere colonials living "in one of the least of her Majesty's Dominions." Living in the New World had given them a factious humor, a physical deficiency that caused faulty political logic.[10]

Agreeing with the lieutenant governor that their rights should follow their condition, his Quaker opponents differed wildly about the nature of that condition. Against Evans's assertions of their coloniality, they affirmed their Englishness. They argued that Pennsylvania's status within the realm more closely resembled that of Wales than Virginia, New York, or Massachusetts. Such a claim, if true, would have precluded the establishment of any courts without a royal order, which Evans lacked.[11] Echoing the language Joseph Growden used against William Penn in 1689, they added that they had more than mere "dative" rights granted by their proprietor: they also retained all their "native" English rights. Like the radical Parliament of 1641, they simply wanted the privileges enjoyed by the legislative branch under the English constitution.[12] They concurred with Evans that they asked for more expansive liberties than enjoyed elsewhere in English America but argued that their situation justified it. Other colonies had been established "at the Charge of the Crown" or through private investment and were "peopled with the purges of English prisons." Pennsylvania's founders were "men of Sobriety and Substance" from many nations who had come to America at their own expense, drawn by their desire to obtain privileges unavailable at home. They had secured these rights through a compact with the proprietor at the moment of settlement, meaning that all privileges and liberties promised Penn under the 1681 royal charter had been extended to them. The liberties enumerated in the 1701 Charter supplemented, but did not override, the initial compact. If they claimed an unusual constellation of liberties, that merely reflected their unique place within the empire.[13]

Beneath these arguments with the lieutenant governor lay a metanarrative of Pennsylvania exceptionalism. More than colonial, more than English, the province stood out from the rest—even from the utopian settlement in Massachusetts Bay the Crown had recently seized.[14] David Lloyd even questioned, in a moment of hubris, whether laws passed by Parliament after Pennsylvania's founding even reached its shores. At the very least, he argued, they would need modification before enactment since "we are under such different Circumstances" here.[15] They were exempt, however, from the physical infirmities that threatened other American colonists and that Evans accused them of. Though the colony occupied a lower latitude than the mother country, "the people [here] are generally averse to any but an English Constitution," in both senses of the term. Their place in the English Atlantic, geographically and administratively, had led to neither legal nor bodily degeneration.[16]

These stories contained apparent contradictions. The narratives cast colonials as innately culturally conservative, clinging to their collective pasts to protect themselves from outside aggression. Yet their appeals to both the ancient past of English law and the recent past of an American founding exhibited more than a little cultural creativity. They rejected the either/or dichotomy Evans used to describe their Englishness and Americanness in favor of a both/and formulation. These brief histories of settlement insisted that Pennsylvania's first settlers brought their English liberties with them as they traveled across the Atlantic, while noting that the first adventurers came from several "native Countreys."[17] In arguing that they had settled the colony, they wrote William Penn out of the history of Pennsylvania's founding—a neat rhetorical trick. Evans found these shifting lines of argument maddening, the histories they told revisionist, and the logic strained for convenience.

And yet the contradictions had an odd consistency. By evoking old and new identities to justify their political rights, the assemblymen, like other colonists in British America, sought to replicate traditional English forms in a new environment but created new cultural landscapes unlike anything in the "mother" country. Meanwhile, their description of their own role in Pennsylvania's founding mirrored Penn's defense of his proprietary rights before the Board of Trade. The proprietor and his colonists each appropriated the others' labor in their accounts of Pennsylvania's founding. Their fights with the lieutenant governor led provincials to anticipate a new identity shaped by their fear of imperial power, a jealousy of their political rights, and an intense concern with the colony's origins, no matter how recent. For Evans's Quaker antagonists, the logic of their illogic lay in the recognition of their anomalous position within the English Atlantic and their need to explain this difference to themselves and others.[18]

Pennsylvanians' concerns over their status explained their increasingly strict attention to protocol in their dealings with Lieutenant Governor Evans and Proprietary Secretary Logan. Logan proved a particular irritant to Lloyd, the speaker of the Assembly for most of Evans's tenure, leading to several unusual conflicts. During a visit to the Assembly to convey Evans's demands to establish chancery and equity courts forthwith, Logan jokingly asked one of the legislators if the Assembly's obstinacy had not made him ashamed to look the provincial secretary in the face. The Assembly promptly complained to the lieutenant governor that his remark represented a "Breach of Privileges." Evans felt obliged to call Logan and Samuel Richardson, the allegedly offended legislator, before him, whereupon the latter "declared he was not at all affronted."[19] Lloyd later tried to have Logan impeached and arrested for scandalous libel because he had the temerity to criticize the speaker in public.[20] Though neither the impeachment nor the attempted arrest succeeded, they revealed the Assembly's heightened sensitivity to matters of cultural and institutional honor. The most absurd conflict occurred at a conference between several assemblymen and Evans in 1707, when the former insisted on sitting when speaking to the latter. Interpreting this as a claim by legislators to equality with the head of the executive branch, the lieutenant governor ordered Lloyd, as speaker, to stand when addressing him. Refusing, Lloyd marched out of the conference, with other legislators in tow, rather than pay deference to Evans.[21] "The Air of Grandure & sacred care for the honour & Dignity of the house that runns thro Everything [was] too Vissible" for any who cared to look.[22]

On the face of it, the many arguments between Evans and his Quaker opponents were simply fights over prerogative and power. At the same time, however, they were about culture and identity as well. Pennsylvanians never resembled their fellow colonials in the Americas more than when trying to resolve the thorny question of what it meant to be a provincial in an Atlantic empire. In the short term, Quaker politicians told histories about themselves and their colony to strengthen their resolve against the lieutenant governor. In so doing, they increased the political chaos besetting Pennsylvania. Over time, however, these narratives would play a central role in checking the province's rampant factionalism.

Betrayal and Abandonment: Penn and His Quaker Opponents

William Penn had barely set sail for England before his colonists rebelled. Between 1702 and 1710, they attacked Penn's government and his deputies, often in personal terms. Penn wrote in his letters of speaker of the Assembly David Lloyd as an ungrateful villain who failed to appreciate all Penn had done for his colonists. For his part, Lloyd complained that Penn treated his political opponents in Pennsylvania as the "Vilest of Men."[23] The fighting between opposing Quaker factions brought the province's government to a standstill more than once, and nearly convinced Penn to surrender it to the Crown, terminating his "Holy Experiment."

That the proprietor and the settlers would risk the future of their colony demands explanation not only of the origin of these conflicts but of their intensity as well. What could cause such animosity among Friends? The answer was religion, for the political battling owed its rancor to the shared spiritual identity of its participants. Penn had named his colony's capital city Philadelphia—the city of brotherly love. It may seem tempting to see this name as ironic given the partisan fighting that took place there during the first decade of the eighteenth century. In fact, it was only because the contending parties loved each other, as brethren within a religious fellowship, that they could see each other's actions as a series of betrayals and abandonments.

When Penn arrived in England in December 1701, he found his finances in worse shape than he had expected. He had engaged in a long-running dispute over money with Philip Ford, his financial agent, since his first voyage to Pennsylvania, when Ford presented him with a bill of £2,581 for expenses incurred managing Penn's Irish affairs and promoting his American colony. This initial debt had ballooned to nearly £11,000 by the end of the seventeenth century, the result of both Penn's financial ineptitude and Ford's "sharp practice." Desperate to raise cash and settle his accounts, he turned to what he believed the most reliable source of income: colonial quitrents. Provincial landowners already owed Penn approximately £5,000 in rents. Collecting these back payments would have greatly reduced, but not eliminated, his considerable debt. In 1702, he wrote Logan instructing him to redouble his efforts to collect the overdue payments, as well as a £2,000 property tax passed before Penn's departure in 1701.[24]

Penn's timing, however, could hardly have been worse. The collapse of the West Indian grain trade in 1702, as a consequence of the outbreak of Queen Anne's War, devastated the provincial economy. A downturn in the tobacco market choked off the coastal trade between Pennsylvania and its Chesapeake neighbors to the south, making life for Pennsylvania farmers and merchants even harder. Even had colonists wanted to pay Penn, they were unable to do so. Consequently, Logan's efforts met with disdain, anger, and resentment. Penn could hardly have adopted a more counterproductive strategy. By the beginning of 1703, he had failed to clear his debts yet succeeded in embittering colonists against himself and Logan.[25] Lieutenant Governor Andrew Hamilton's efforts to raise a provincial militia further antagonized provincial Quakers, while the affirmation controversy deepened divisions between Friends and Anglicans in the colony. Haggling between Pennsylvanian officials and the residents of the Lower Counties over a proposed split between the colonies delayed the election of a new legislature until fall 1703.

The 1703–4 session of the Assembly proved contentious. As speaker, Lloyd instituted new procedures based on the rules of order used in England's House of Commons. These rules put an end to the disorder that had frequently plagued the colonial legislature before, with representatives speaking over each other, out of turn, or off topic. They also gave the speaker unprecedented power. Lloyd could now set the terms of legislative debate, choosing the topics to be discussed and the speakers who could discuss them.[26]

Lloyd used this power to guide a number of controversial bills through the legislature. One bill contained a form of affirmation to substitute for the one prescribed by the queen and provisions to remove effective authority over the courts from Penn's hands and place them under local control. The measure seemed designed to antagonize royal and proprietary authority simultaneously.[27] More provocatively, he submitted for the Assembly's consideration a bill ostensibly confirming the Charter of Privileges and the Philadelphia city charter but which, in fact, included substantial revisions to each. Because of Evans's effective opposition, the Assembly adjourned in August without Lloyd's achieving any of his major legislative goals.

Lloyd's response reshaped the nature of the conflict between Penn and his opponents. In August 1704, he sent Penn a letter, ostensibly on behalf of the entire Assembly, rebuking the proprietor for his treatment of Pennsylvania's Quaker settlers. This "Remonstrance" had a decidedly religious tone, casting Pennsylvania's troubles as the result of the colony's fall from grace. Penn, the letter argued, had wooed "thy First Purchasers & Adventurers to Embark with thee to Plant this Colony" under false pretenses, offering them not only land but also great privileges if only they supplied Penn with the quitrents he requested; he needed these fees, he told them, to defray the considerable expenses he incurred as colonial governor. For a time things were good. The 1682 Frame of Government granted those who came "All the Temporall Felicity and happiness Mortalls could be Capable of Enjoying in this Life," and its fame induced many to move to America.[28]

Penn, however, quickly reneged on his promises. By uniting Pennsylvania and the Lower Counties in a common government, he weakened Friends' authority. And, "by a Subtil Contrivance And Artifiace," he secured the repeal of the 1682 Frame and replaced it with a constitution that increased his power at the expense of the freemen. Then, in 1684, Penn returned to England. He nonetheless continued to demand his rents, although as "Proprietary only" and not a resident governor, he needed no such revenues. Pennsylvania's Quaker settlers thus found themselves shortly after the province's founding deprived of promised rights, forced to share power with outsiders to the south, and burdened with heavy taxes. The "Remonstrance" ended by calling on Penn to honor his obligations to "thy Friends & particularly thy First Purchasers" by keeping the colony under his control; surrender would be nothing less than a betrayal of those he had lured into the American wilderness.[29]

The language of the "Remonstrance" greatly resembled the letters of admonition Penn and other Friends sent to schismatics in post-Restoration England, not simply in its style but also in its audience; Lloyd wrote the "Remonstrance" not to Penn the politician but to Penn the Friend. The contrast between Lloyd's letter and the 1690 petition colonists delivered to Governor Benjamin Fletcher was remarkable. The authors of the earlier petition, a mix of Quakers and non-Quakers, presented their case to Fletcher publicly via a handwritten appeal and a printed tract. On the other hand, Lloyd elected not to print the "Remonstrance", present it in open session to the Assembly, nor even make it available to Lieutenant Governor Evans. Instead, he presented it to Penn—and a select group of London Friends. Lloyd sent a copy of the "Remonstrance" in an October 1704 letter to George Whitehead, William Mead, and Thomas Lower. This letter detailed a range of political grievances. Lloyd beseeched its recipients to take note of these facts and to use "such Christi[an] measures as you shall see meet, to Oblige him to Do the People Justice" as a proprietor and a Friend.[30]

The "Remonstrance" provoked predictably strong responses in America and England. Evans doubted that it represented the views of the entire Assembly. Meanwhile, Friends in Pennsylvania challenged the implication that "the body of Friends" in the colony endorsed Lloyd's charges, as its style and tone suggested. Both the lieutenant governor and the Philadelphia Men's Monthly Meeting requested copies of the "Remonstrance"; Lloyd rebuffed each.[31] Penn also saw the dispute through a largely religious lens, expressing his sincere desire that gospel discipline in Pennsylvania would deal with those "illegitimate Quakers" who abused him despite all he had suffered in "purse & pains" for them. Lloyd was no better than an ungrateful villain who suffered from the "Excess of Vanity" that had crept up among too many Friends in Pennsylvania. Apparently, migration to America had led to a moral degeneration similar to the fall from grace of proud Quakers in England. In each case, it produced division and weakness within the Society.[32]

Lloyd continued his attack on Penn politically and personally, spreading rumors that Ford had taken possession of the colony, which engineered a major defeat of Penn loyalists in the 1705 Assembly election.[33] That summer he sent the proprietor a letter, even more scathing than the "Remonstrance," in which he chastised Penn for abandoning those people who "Exposed themselves . . . to the danger of a Savage Nation." Lloyd invoked the memory of George Fox, reminding the Quaker founder that Fox had asked Penn to "mind the poor Friends" in America. Lloyd warned Penn about accommodating too much the queen's demands for the establishment of a militia, increased royal oversight of legislation, and more liberal use of oaths in colonial legal and political life. Such acquiescence, he argued, had proven disastrous to Friends in West Jersey. His correspondence revealed equal parts anger, hurt, and fear.[34]

West Jersey served as the backdrop for both Lloyd's attacks on Penn and the proprietor's response. West and East Jersey had been unstable societies during their first quarter century of existence—religiously polarized, economically fractious, and politically dysfunctional. In 1702, the Crown declared the proprietary experiment ended and royalized the two territories, which it then combined to form the single colony of New Jersey. The Crown appointed Edward Hyde, Viscount Cornbury, to serve as governor of both New York and New Jersey. No ally to the Quakers, Cornbury worked to reduce their power, tipping the balance in the political conflict between Friends and Anglicans. Friends faced disenfranchisement on several levels, as Anglicans worked to remove their exemption from militia duty and to reduce the use of the affirmation in government affairs. In juxtaposing the myth of Pennsylvania's founding with the specter of West Jersey, Lloyd reminded Penn of Pennsylvania's early promise and the nightmarish possibilities of its end.

Penn shared Lloyd's fears, even as he considered surrendering his province to the Crown. He also knew the anxiety West Jersey's royalization had engendered within Pennsylvania's Quaker community. Although he hoped that a royal New Jersey would not diminish Quakers' rights, he expected the worst.[35] Two forces shaped Penn's thinking on surrender as the situation deteriorated in New Jersey. On the one hand, he endeavored to secure Friends' liberties in the event that Pennsylvania passed into imperial hands. He reminded the Board of Trade more than once that Friends had transformed the province's "meer wilderness . . . into a usefull and beneficiall Colony," making it only natural that they should retain their liberties in a royal Pennsylvania.[36] "I went thither," he argued, both "to lay the Foundation of a free Colony for all Mankind, that should go thither," and to secure a refuge for persecuted Friends. A royal government that imposed oaths, shut Friends out of certain civil offices, or imposed a "Coercive" militia would render Friends "Dissenters in our own Countrys; a Design Barbarous as well as unjust."[37] But Penn feared that his colonists' behavior might force a surrender on unfavorable terms. Failure to stoop to royal authority, he fretted, would be the surest way to convince the Crown to impose its will quite forcefully, as it had done in West Jersey.[38]

Quaker West Jersey's fall intensified political conflict in Pennsylvania. Lloyd's antiproprietary faction repeatedly warned voters that Penn had already lost Pennsylvania to the queen.[39] Lloyd and his supporters hoped to establish important precedents each time they resisted efforts to bring the colony under tighter control. Better, they felt, to defend their political and legal privileges now, as these liberties would certainly come under assault later. They attacked Penn so fiercely because they perceived that he would not protect them from such an assault on the colony, whether due to weakness, malice, or venality. His mounting debts to Ford and his seemingly boundless desire for taxes made them suspect the latter. They chafed at the anachronistic "semifeudal privileges" (like quitrents) Penn demanded, but they knew that Pennsylvania's continued existence as a haven for dissenters depended upon his influence in the upper reaches of the British political system.[40] The proprietor's sense of betrayal, the litany of complaints about his opponents' ingratitude, his supporters' disbelief at the turn provincial politics had taken—all proceeded from this same fundamental premise: that Penn's protection would be necessary, but not sufficient, to prevent Pennsylvania from sharing West Jersey's fate. The same narrative thread ran through the arguments of Quaker proprietary and antiproprietary forces. Each side shared a vision of what Pennsylvania might have been and what it might become while trying to determine who was to blame for what it was.

By 1709–10, Penn and many of his supporters appeared resigned to the end of the Quaker experiment in Pennsylvania. Logan wondered if the fault lay in Friends' attempts to govern. Could, he asked Penn, a religion based on "denying the World, Living out of it, & acting in opposition to its depraved wayes" prepare a people to rule a colony within an English empire? Or did their historic and spiritual experiences as Friends render them unfit for such a position? The Quaker political order looked as fractured in 1710 as its religious order had seemed in the immediate aftermath of the Keithian schism. If the schism revealed the fragility of Quaker identity in America, its ultimate resolution revealed how to create a creole Quaker identity in the wake of massive disruption.

Decline and Redemption: Remembering the Keithian Schism

The Keithian controversy had been both a traumatic and formative movement for the Quaker orthodoxy in Pennsylvania. The schism had ended formally with the London Yearly Meeting's disownment of Keith in 1695. The struggle to define the schism's meaning, however, continued for years afterward. This fight had begun during the controversy's early years, as each faction tried to narrate its version of events in ways that evoked the Society's past. The Keithians produced and circulated printed tracts, much like the prolific Quaker pamphleteers active in Interregnum and Restoration England. Meanwhile, their opponents assiduously circulated manuscript certificates of condemnation and epistles cataloging the sufferings of Pennsylvania's orthodox Friends throughout the English Atlantic, much as the Society's founding mothers and fathers had. The Keithians "exposed" their experiences in print "to the view of the World" to sway Quakers and non-Quakers alike. Their opponents relied on a strictly Quaker communicative network, on the other hand, to "hold fast the head by which the whole body receiving nourishment—as by joints and bands—is Knit-together."[41] The Keithians urged public argumentation, while weighty Friends in the Meeting urged silence.

Debate over the controversy's meaning stretched through the first decade of the eighteenth century, even as its terms shifted. Although William Bradford's move to New York in the wake of the schism left Pennsylvania temporarily without a printer, controversial literature continued to circulate. George Keith himself published attacks in New York and London following his disownment.[42] The most prominent polemicist was Daniel Leeds, the ex-Quaker who had run afoul of the Meeting for publishing esoteric literature. Leeds published six anti-Quaker tracts from 1697 to 1705, including his *News of a Strumpet Co-Habitating in the Wilderness; or, A Brief Abstract of the Spiritual and Carnal Whoredoms and Adulteries of the Quakers in AMERICA.*[43] He focused—"obsessed" may be a better word—on exposing the contradictions and hypocrisies inherent in "Fox-craftian" faith and practice (as he called Quakerism). Leeds delighted in pointing out each instance of faulty logic in Robert Barclay's, Penn's, or especially Fox's writings, noting whenever possible Fox's lack of formal education. He also criticized Friends for their selective adherence to principle as rulers of the colony, echoing charges Keith had made during the schism. Quaker politicians in Pennsylvania, he claimed, showed a greater love for power than for Christ.[44] Pennsylvania, Leeds argued, exemplified an age-old story in which an initially pious sect of believers fell into apostasy as it gained adherents and influence.

These attacks on orthodox Friends' public authority did not go unchallenged. Ministers had refused to print any responses to Keith's pamphlets while the Philadelphia Yearly Meeting weighed the matter and assailed Keith

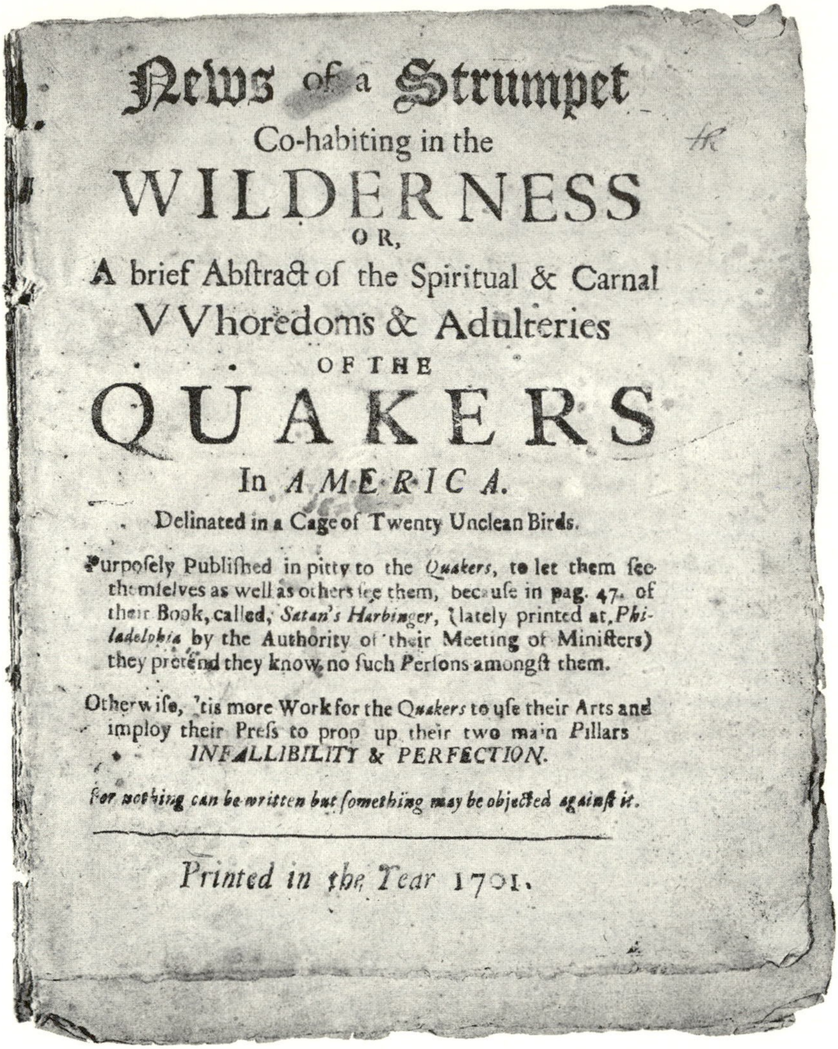

News of a Strumpet
Co-habiting in the
WILDERNESS
OR,
A brief Abstract of the Spiritual & Carnal
VVhoredoms & Adulteries
OF THE
QUAKERS
In AMERICA.
Delinated in a Cage of Twenty Unclean Birds.

Purposely Published in pitty to the *Quakers*, to let them see
themselves as well as others see them, because in pag. 47. of
their Book, called, *Satan's Harbinger*, (lately printed at *Philadelphia* by the Authority of their Meeting of Ministers)
they pretend they know no such Persons amongst them.

Otherwise, 'tis more Work for the *Quakers* to use their Arts and
imploy their Press to prop up their two main Pillars
INFALLIBILITY & PERFECTION.

For nothing can be written but something may be objected against it.

Printed in the Year 1701.

Figure 10. *News of a Strumpet Co-Habiting in the Wilderness . . .* Title page of Daniel
Leeds's 1701 pamphlet. Reproduced by permission of The Huntington Library, San
Marino, California.

for doing so. Once the matter moved to London, however, they had no such compunctions. Orthodox Friends' first published accounts of the schism, Samuel Jennings's *State of the Case* (1696) and Caleb Pusey's *Modest Account* (1696), saw print in London and soon made their way to Pennsylvania.[45] Bradford's exit hampered Friends' ability to respond to Keith and Leeds until the Philadelphia Yearly Meeting purchased a press and installed Reynier Jansen as the colony's new printer in late 1698. Jansen may not have been "a Person that well understands printing," as his critics charged, but he provided Jennings and Pusey an American press from which to respond.[46] Especially prolific, Pusey authored eight responses to Leeds from 1700 to 1706.[47] But he exhibited curious timing, with most of his publications appearing just as the last Keithian congregations disappeared.[48] Why did Pusey continue to attack his opponents in print even after he had seemingly won the battle?

Certainly Keith's reappearance on the scene provided some motivation for Pusey. The Scottish schismatic had engaged English Friends in a number of public debates in the years after his disownment from the Society, delighting in any opportunity to expose the contradictions and errors in Quaker theology. He also published several works ridiculing the Society and warning readers about its evils.[49] His concerns about the evils of Quakerism soon morphed into a more general concern about the dangers of separatism, prompting him to embrace the Church of England. In 1700, he converted to Anglicanism, joining the ranks of its clergy soon thereafter.[50]

Keith wasted no time enlisting in the Church of England's efforts to counter dissent at home and abroad. This push roughly coincided with his conversion. Concerned that spiritual ignorance left believers susceptible to heretical preachers, the Anglican minister Dr. Thomas Bray founded the Society for the Propagation of Christian Knowledge (SPCK) in 1699. This organization dedicated itself to publishing religious tracts, catechisms, and other forms of doctrinal literature to spread right religious thinking among the English public. Bray's time as the Church's commissary in Maryland in the 1690s convinced him of the need for a comparable effort for the American colonies; in 1701, he founded the Society for the Propagation of the Gospel in Foreign Parts (SPG) to spread the Anglican faith in England's overseas dominions. Where the SPCK sent books in the service of the cause, the SPG aimed to send men. In 1702, the organization appointed Keith as its first missionary to North America.[51]

Arriving in America in 1702, Keith took to his task with gusto. He worked to reach unchurched audiences from North Carolina to Maine dur-

ing a two-year trip; in some instances, his marked the first real presence of
Anglicanism in a particular community. But he took special delight in tor-
menting his former brethren in the mid-Atlantic, making multiple visits to
Pennsylvania and New Jersey and publishing three anti-Quaker books. Each
return visit by "that lump of scandal," as James Logan called him, revived
the schism. It also reminded Friends of their vulnerability as dissenters in the
face of the Church of England's newly aggressive stance in the colonies.[52]
Pusey held a personal as well as theological animus against Keith, as Keith
had openly mocked Pusey's modest education in a London publication.
Keith's decision to issue two anti-Pusey publications in 1703 provided ample
incentive for the Chester County farmer to keep the fight alive.[53]

Pusey had a larger, more important motivation, however: explaining the
death of the Keithian movement. Pusey believed that the seeds of the movement's death had been present at its origins. The difference between the
Keithians and orthodox Friends, he argued, was that the former belonged to
a creole religious community and the latter did not. Pusey rejected the notion
proffered by some Quakers that Keith split with the Meeting because he had
never been a true member of the Society.[54] In Keith, Pusey saw not a false
Friend but a fallen one. Keith's principles only deviated from Quaker orthodoxy after his arrival in Pennsylvania, when his renewed interest in the salvation of Native Americans led him to believe in the revolution of souls after
death.[55] This spiritual change disordered the former Quaker minister's thinking and led him to organize a community of confused souls with similarly
misguided beliefs, a "strange *Babel*" spouting spiritual nonsense.[56] The Keithians, then, were a specifically American religious movement in origin, one
whose preoccupations only made sense in a New World environment.

This understanding of the schism's creole origins explained Pusey's response to Leeds, the most vocal of the Keith's adherents. Pusey's writings
remained remarkably consistent. He paid little attention to Leeds's scurrilous
charges about Quaker sexual immorality. Instead, he endeavored to refute,
on both theological and factual grounds, the almanac maker's claims about
the incompatibility of Quakerism and civil government. Leeds's assertion
that Penn had relied on ungodly means to secure a colonial charter had no
basis in reality, Pusey argued, nor did the claim that Quakers had taken up
arms to combat a privateer in the 1690s.[57] Moreover, Pusey denied that
Quaker principles prohibited involvement in worldly affairs. Robert Barclay
had not warned Friends not to meddle in government altogether but merely
to refrain from using "Revenge and War" as tools of statecraft. For Leeds to

write otherwise signified his ignorance of the movement's most important theologian.[58] Quoting Pennsylvania Friends' sacred texts against them, Leeds had merely shown his own ignorance of the true meaning of their traditions.

Beneath these arguments, however, lay a powerful cultural imperative to turn Leeds's (and Keith's) narratives of Quaker decline back onto the accusers by casting the Keithian movement as the product of creole degeneration. Where Leeds argued that the Keithian schism epitomized that "Ancient Story" about the downfall of a once pious people as they learned to compromise with the world, Pusey saw the controversy as a thoroughly "modern story" about the rise and fall of an upstart sect "within the space of about seven years." The self-styled Christian Quakers, supposed avatars of primitive Christianity in Pennsylvania, were creole moderns, their American birth the cause of their sudden death.[59] Leeds's degeneration into a *"Strumpet* Man" worse than any *"Atheist, Turk,* [or] *Jew"* only proved his point.[60]

Pusey's writings "made" history on several levels. They retold the origins of the controversy so as to place the burden of separation on Keith. They retold the history of Quakerism to create a usable spiritual past that allowed, even justified, Friends' efforts to create a godly colonial government. Moreover, defining the Keithian movement as an aberrant form of Quakerism and framing Keith as a fallen Friend allowed Pusey to pull a narrative sleight of hand. It let him write the Keithians out of the history of Anglo-American Quakerism while exempting Pennsylvania Friends from the historical process of creole degeneracy that had corrupted the Keithians. Pusey thus enacted a unified Quaker identity whose existence had seemed so tenuous only a few short years before, a literary performance that would shape the future history of Quakerism in Pennsylvania.

Quaker authors refought the Keithian schism because they had to. Retelling the story of the schism allowed them a way to reaffirm their Quakerness. This process gradually gathered a momentum of its own. Continually exhuming the controversy so that they might rebury it only increased its symbolic power—thus making careful management of its meaning even more imperative.

Pennsylvania Friends used institutional as well as literary means to keep the memory of the schism alive. The Philadelphia Men's Yearly Meeting delighted in detailing the Keithians' declining fortunes. For eight years after the schism, its annual epistles to the London Yearly Meeting reported dissension among "Christian Quakers." The Women's Yearly Meeting merely celebrated the fact that most of those whom Keith had led astray saw the error of their ways and chose to return to the fold.[61] These epistles framed the affair within the longer history of the Quaker movement, a story of a people collectively overcoming backsliding and disunity as they moved forward toward end times. In other words, the Meeting's retellings of the Keithian schism increasingly resembled other Quaker tales of persecution, suffering, and redemption. Monthly and Yearly Meetings also revisited the schism through ritual readings of condemnation from former Keithians asking forgiveness for their earlier errors. Although monthly meetings regularly listened to letters of self-condemnation from penitent Friends guilty of all manner of transgressions, the Yearly Meeting in this era only heard those relating to the Keithian controversy.[62] The Philadelphia Women's Monthly Meeting rebuked a deceased dissident a dozen years after Keith's disownment. The Women's Monthly Meeting refused Griffith Jones's offer of a £20 gift his wife Frances had left "as a legacy of [her] love" for Friends because she had not "given public satisfaction to Frds for going into separation with George Keith." It did, however, "accept . . . her Love therein."[63] The Yearly Meeting even approved the publication of a former Keithian's account of his disillusionment with and rejection of "Christian Quakerism." That the author in question ended his spiritual journey as a Seventh Day Baptist mattered less than his antipathy toward Keith.[64]

Quaker elites also worked to suppress contrary views of the schism. Although they could not prevent Leeds from publishing anti-Quaker tracts in New York, their ownership of Pennsylvania's only press meant that they could prevent the printing of comparable tracts in their colony. Quaker overseers of the press, appointed first by the Philadelphia Yearly Meeting and then by the Philadelphia Monthly Meeting, worked assiduously to prevent the local publication of anti-Quaker works. When the Yearly Meeting sold its press, it reminded those conducting the sale that they should take "Care that the printer be restricted from printing anything against Frds."[65] Although Quaker polemicists appreciated the value of using print against their opponents, the schism had not given them a faith in the necessity of public debate for a vibrant holy society. The Keithians' trial revealed the power Quaker memory and mythology had for provincial Friends. It also revealed that the laity could use this cultural power against leaders within the Meeting. Having once allowed dissidents to garner popular sympathy by invoking collective memories of persecution, the Quaker elite vowed never to let it happen again. If Meeting leaders could not control how the "public"—

Pennsylvania's ordinary citizens—remembered the affair, they could at least control how Friends spoke of it in public.

The schism prompted leading Friends to take other steps to build a coherent religious identity in the colony beyond their efforts to manage the schism's afterlife in public memory. Under the Meeting's guidance, Reynier Jansen restarted the tradition of publishing Quaker devotional literature that had faded in the early 1690s. He published a brief tract by George Whitehead containing the dying words of three young Quaker men, one of whom lamented "the Looseness, Pride, and vanity" he had witnessed since coming to America; he offered American Friends these "Chastisements" because without such warnings "we [are] Bastards and not Sons" of Christ.[66] Jansen also republished works by George Fox, including a children's primer that explained, among other things, why Friends wore their hats before all worldly authorities. He also published a sermon delivered three decades earlier to Barbadian Friends describing the duties Christian leaders had toward white, black, and Indian families in a godly colony.[67]

The Meeting also made other changes in the wake of the schism intended to preserve order. It appointed Quaker "overseers" in each monthly meeting to monitor individual Friends' behavior. It also established "preparative meetings," in which overseers and other "weighty" Friends gathered before each monthly meeting to determine the subjects to be discussed that month.[68] Not satisfied with these institutional changes, Quaker leaders then took steps to outline a general code of conduct for all provincial Friends, appointing fifteen members of the Philadelphia Yearly Meeting to scan early Quaker writings and compile them into "One Paper." This resulted in the 1704 manuscript "Rules of Discipline of the Philadelphia Yearly Meeting," issued to all the monthly meetings under Philadelphia's purview.[69]

This compilation of rules articulated a well-regulated vision of a pious life within a Quaker society. It contained instructions governing marriages and weddings, training and disciplining children and servants, settling personal differences, and dealing with sinners. The introduction articulated a grander vision of the Meeting's place in a temporal and religious order, exhorting Friends to remember the Apostle Paul's injunction to "sett in Order the Things that are wanting and Ordain Elders in Every City." Reminding Friends that "God . . . is a God of Order and not of Confusion," it assured them that the new structures of authority created after the schism were essential to lead the Meeting back to "its Primitive Purity . . . after the long night of Apostasy." This greater measure of order and discipline served "the honour

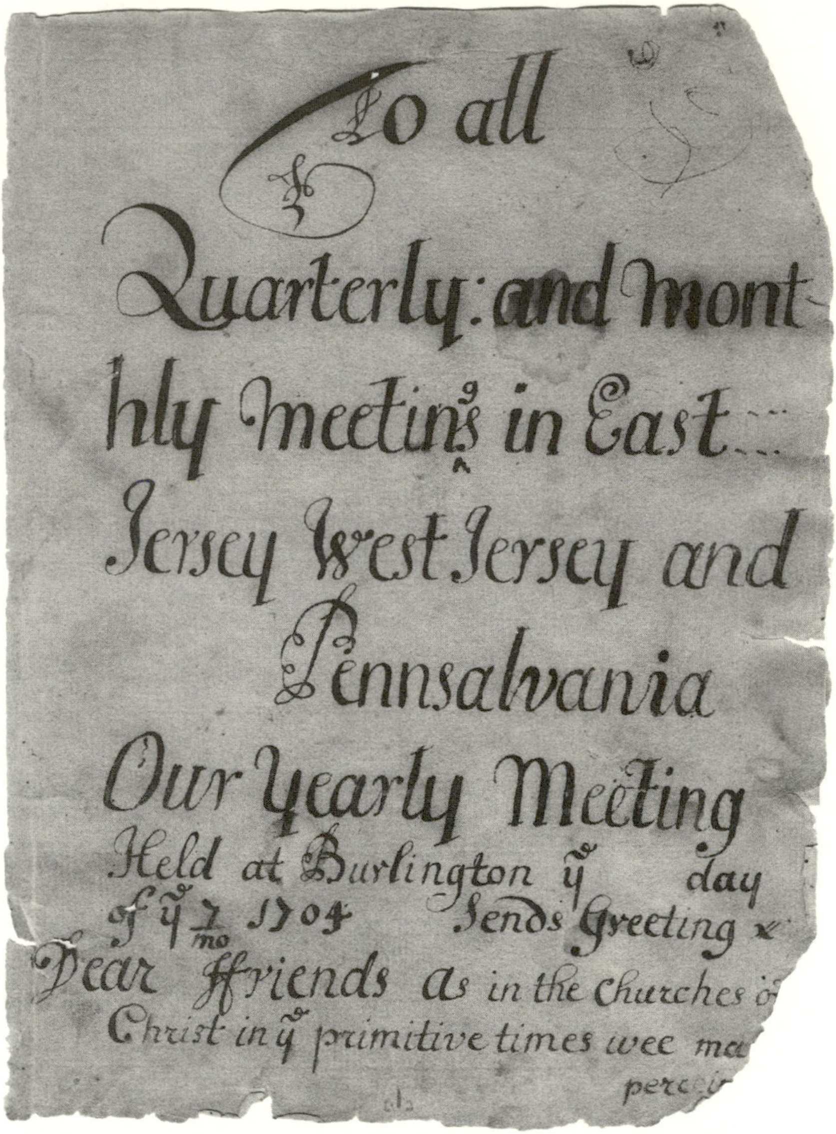
To all
Quarterly: and mont
hly Meetings in East
Jersey West Jersey and
Pennsalvania
Our Yearly Meeting
Held at Burlington ye day
of ye 7 mo 1704 Sends Greeting
Dear ffriends as in the Churches of
Christ in ye primitive times wee ma
perc

Figure 11. First page of the "Rules of Discipline of the Phila. Yearly Meeting," 1704, Manuscript Copy, Call #976, Quaker Collection, Haverford College. Courtesy of Quaker Collection, Haverford College.

of God[,] the Reputacon of his precious Truth and The good of one another both of soul and Body."[70]

This celebration of Meeting order contained a warning as well. The "Rules" quoted approvingly the notion that "the Church is the Body of Christ and that the members thereof should have the same care one of another that there be no Schism in the Body." None who rebelled against Christ's body in any way would be excused for his "disorderly practices"; he would instead be purged. Citing Paul a final time, the "Rules" asked, "Know ye not that little Leaven Leaveneth the whole Lump?" Preserving gospel order meant that it was better to "Purge out the old Leaven" so that Friends might become a "New Lump."[71] This metaphor of fall, purgation, and rebirth—the cycle of perfection at the center of Quaker notions of redemption—made the purpose of the manuscript clear: its authors intended the "Rules of Discipline" it outlined to inculcate unity and uniformity among Friends as well as piety. Just as the adoption of Pauline doctrine suggested that piety was inseparable from unity and uniformity, Friends' pious care of their own bodies and their own souls through adherence to these "Rules of Discipline" would allow the Meeting to remain one body of believers.

The Philadelphia Yearly Meeting followed this initial effort at regularizing religious practice with a revised and expanded "Book of Discipline" in 1719. Tellingly, however, these two compilations represented a major innovation in Quaker practice. No other Friends in Britain or America felt the need to issue a comparable code of conduct until the London Yearly Meeting issued its "Book of Discipline" in 1738.[72] Pennsylvania Friends had a motivation other Anglo-American Friends lacked. They created formalized codes of conduct to acculturate American converts and creoles into the Quaker fold, reflecting their anxiety that Keith's denunciation of his enemies as "bastard Quakers" had hit too close to home. The rhetoric of the 1704 "Rules of Discipline" offered orthodox Friends a way of writing the Keithians out of their religious community and provided them with a means of keeping future dissidents out.

The controversy ultimately became a critical cultural touchstone in early Pennsylvania. The circulation and recirculation of stories about the affair through printed screeds and manuscript epistles revealed how much the schism reverberated in the collective memory of provincial Friends, particularly their anxiety over Keith's warnings of creole degeneracy in the infant colony. With these narratives, Friends created a usable history of American Quakerism, one that would have made no sense without Keith. Pusey, for instance, could dispel the fear that orthodox Friends were "bastard Quakers" by pointing to the example of the American-born "Christian Quakers." The controversy also motivated leading Friends to develop new mechanisms for promoting cultural cohesion. The schism had been caused by a fear of Quaker declension, yet it spurred, more than any other event in early Pennsylvania, the process of creolization through which orthodox Friends mixed new cultural languages and practices with old ones to create a new "tradition."

No individual better exemplified this complicated process than Francis Daniel Pastorius, a former Mennonite who joined the Society of Friends as an adult. One of Pennsylvania's cultural leaders, he had a distinguished career, helping found Germantown, cosigning the first petition against African slavery in North America, and serving as a stalwart defender of the Quaker orthodoxy during the Keithian controversy. Most significantly, Pastorius was the greatest promoter of public education in the colony, serving as a school master and authoring works as diverse as a primer to teach the rudiments of the English language and a handbook to train prospective lawyers.

Pastorius's writings betrayed the anxiety and trauma many provincials felt in the aftermath of the Keithian schism. He hoped his *New Primmer* (1698) would impart "things necessary & useful both for the youth of this province, and likewise for those, who from foreign countries and nations are come to settle amongst us." Following cursory lessons in spelling, reading, and writing, he focused primarily on the "General and Particular Duties of True Christians" with respect to doctrine and conduct. Children owed respect to their parents and elders, who, in turn, needed to lead their families and communities in a respectful and righteous manner. All Christians, young and old alike, needed at all times to "present their Bodies as a living Sacrifice" to God and abstain from worldly vanity in speech, apparel, or comportment.[73] Pastorius presented a "particular" doctrine indeed, with specific passages on the nature of God's seed in man and the properties of God's regenerate body—two of the major issues at stake in the Keithian schism. Tellingly, Pastorius's views on this subject hewed more closely to early Quaker doctrine than later attempts at rationalization and refinement within the English Meeting.[74] In other words, Pastorius elected to embrace a theological originalism in the wake of a controversy marked by fears of American degeneracy, just as Pennsylvania's Quaker ministers had in their 1695 declaration of orthodox doctrine.[75]

The *New Primmer* also showed Pastorius's ambivalence about assimilation and cultural adaptation. He frequently stressed the need for his fellow German immigrants to adapt to Anglo-American society. He insisted when writing Germantown's founding legal code that ignorance of the English language or custom could never excuse violations of provincial statutes. In one letter to his children, he reminded them that as they had been "born in an English Colony, consequently each of you [are] *Anglus Natus*, an Englishman by Birth. Therefore it would be a shame for you if you should be ignorant of the English Tongue, the Tongue of your Countrymen."[76] In the *New Primmer*, a work intended for children and non-English immigrants, Pastorius advised his readers to look for wisdom in vernacular proverbs. "Proverbs," he wrote, were "*delightful words of Truth*" and "precious Monuments & Reliques of antient Times." The "wrinkled and gray hair'd sayings of our most experienced and judicious Ancestors," they "often contain[ed] a whole and wholesome Sermon in seven words."[77]

But whose ancestors should his readers remember? Would the words of these ancients sound different in translation? In some respects, Pastorius's primmer helped pave the way for a new, creolized colonial culture because he elected not to answer these questions. Greater specificity might have limited its potential audience and thus made the knowledge contained therein less "useful," not only for individual readers but for the colony writ large. At the same time, the ambiguity in Pastorius's call to hold on to the old ways implicitly acknowledged the coming loss of those traditions he asked his readers to mind, revealing a certain nostalgia for the cultural loss creolization entailed.

Pastorius's efforts at public education also led to his authoring the schism's most poignant echo. His manuscript compilation, the "Young Country Clerk's Collection," was the first practical legal treatise written in America. It provided templates of a variety of different legal forms and writs, explaining the meaning of each one. Recognizing the low level of legal literacy in the colony, Pastorius wrote the "Young Country Clerk's Collection" to help train provincial lawyers and encourage the development of a more coherent legal system in the colony.[78] He included in this compilation a standard writ of mittimus, a document directing a sheriff to arrest a suspected criminal. The sample mittimus Pastorius included called for the seizure of "AB printer & CD Taylor . . . upon information of publishing and spreading a malitious and seditious Paper to the disturbance of the Peace & Subversion of the present Government."[79]

Although presented as a generic writ—with the suspects' names transposed into the initials "AB" and "CD"—Pastorius had in fact transcribed the writ of mittimus issued against the Keithians William Bradford and John McComb almost verbatim.[80] Written nearly two decades after the Keithians' trial, the writ testified to the place the schism occupied in Pastorius's memory.[81] Consciously or not, the Quaker jurist had made the Keithian schism the epitome of seditious or subversive political activity and the individuals involved the archetypal examples of provincial criminals. During their trial, the Keithians had called the very foundations of Pennsylvania's colonial legal order into question. Through this evocative exemplary mittimus, Pastorius reclaimed the legitimacy of the colony's creole legal system, if only in retrospect.

Leading Friends learned several lessons in the aftermath of the Keithian schism. It showed them the power of history as a tool in consolidating their cultural power. It also convinced them of the power of print as a means of projecting their authority to the province at large. The type of public discourse that emerged after the purchase of a Quaker press in 1699 strongly resembled Meeting discourse, where all Friends spoke with a single voice. The strategies pursued in creating a workable, creolized Quaker religious culture would prove valuable when Quaker politicians, many of whom held positions of leadership within the Society, looked to stabilize Pennsylvania's fractious political order.

Pennsylvania Quakers Found Penn's Colony

In 1710, Penn reopened negotiations with the Board of Trade for the sale of Pennsylvania, convinced that he could no longer sustain his colony. Although he had managed to settle his accounts with the Ford family, Penn remained in massive debt, even landing briefly in debtor's prison.[82] Meanwhile, the situation in North America had deteriorated. The Lower Counties suffered repeated attacks at the hands of French warships.[83] Similarly, the political situation seemed to be worsening. Having condemned the assemblies elected in 1707 and 1708 as collections of wicked, vile, and foolish people, Penn became thoroughly disheartened to learn that voters in 1709 elected representatives with the same "unaccountable humour (almost become a Custom now) of Straining and resenting Everything[,] of Creating monsters & then Combating them."[84]

Penn made one final endeavor to woo his people back to his side. In

June 1710, he wrote a letter to "Friends in Pennsylvania" to plead his case. In founding the colony, he had hoped to do good and do well, creating a "flourishing Countrey blest with Liberty Ease & Plenty" that might also provide him with "a small comfort from the Services done to so many hundreds of People." He had tried to protect the liberties of the people from an overweening executive. Unfortunately, he argued, the colonists had abused their liberties, practicing licentiousness under the cover of protecting their privileges. These actions had destabilized the society, as "good Order . . . may be equally broke in upon the turbulent Endeavours of the People, as well as by the overstraining Power in a Govr." Penn called the colonists to remember the exceptional opportunity Pennsylvania offered. "The People of many Nations in Europe look on that Countrey as a Land of ease & Quiet, wishing to themselves in vain the same blessings they conceive you may enjoy," despite the province's political turmoil. He feared that "the kind hand of Providence that has so long favour'd & protected you" would leave them. So, he begged them to reject in the upcoming election those men who fostered division. Instead, they should select individuals committed to bringing a spirit of "Peace Love & Unity" to Pennsylvania.[85]

For the first time, Penn made a political appeal in providential language. In his eyes, Pennsylvania's future success lay in understanding its place in history. This meant remembering its past and the utopian possibilities that had existed at its founding. The colony stood at its inception outside history, a settlement exempt from forces that corrupted other nations. The men who allowed their "Spirit of Contention & Opposition" to infect colonial politics threatened to insert Pennsylvania into that same historical trajectory that afflicted those other nations so jealous of its liberties. In one sense, these appeals were nothing new; various authors, including Penn, had characterized the Quaker "Holy Experiment" in such grandiose terms. None, however, had so carefully linked such narrative accounts to a political platform. Penn essentially argued that antiproprietary forces had, in attacking him, bitten the hand of Providence that had blessed the colony. A vote for proprietary politicians in the 1710 election, he wrote, would return Pennsylvania to its status as the most exceptional place on earth and in history.

Unfortunately, Penn's letter did not reach Pennsylvania until November, too late to influence the fall elections. Leading Friends within the Philadelphia Meeting, however, had come to share his point of view. Isaac Norris worried in February 1710 that church and state had corrupted each other, to the detriment of each. He blamed "Keithians or such as stand Loose from

Friends" for the political strife that had troubled the colony, a sentiment Logan and Penn had long shared.[86] Their actions threatened to undo the careful steps Friends had taken to unify the Quaker community in the fifteen years since the schism. "This Unhappy Difference in State," he feared, "will affect the peace of the Church, one frd opposing another" privately and publicly. Such division in the Meeting would then undercut any efforts to resist encroachments by outside forces—the fate that befell Quakers in West Jersey earlier in the decade.[87]

Anxiety led the leaders of Pennsylvania's Quaker community to take action. The Meeting had previously done little to interfere with colonial politics; it had offered a vague condemnation of those who "have been too Factious and Troublesome in the Government" in "Seditious Words, Insinuations, & Practices" and had requested of David Lloyd a copy of his "Remonstrance" in 1704 so that it might determine if Lloyd's letter violated gospel order, but nothing further.[88] In 1710, however, it directly appealed to both Quaker and non-Quaker audiences. In September, the Philadelphia Yearly Meeting approved an epistle to Friends in Pennsylvania to stand against "Self-Seekers, Self-Exalters, Self-Revengers, and Self-Deckers" who acted contrary to accepted Quaker practice by sowing public dissention with other Friends. Voters should instead select men who "fear[ed] and lov[ed] god" and "aim[ed] at Righteousness, Truth, and Peace, in all their Consultations and actings therein."[89] Never before had the Meeting involved itself so directly in partisan politics.

More importantly, the Philadelphia Meeting appealed publicly to an extra-Quaker audience for the first time. In September 1710, shortly before the October 1 elections, Isaac Norris published *Friendly Advice to the Inhabitants of Pennsilvania*, with the support of the Yearly Meeting.[90] The pamphlet represented a major shift in Quaker public rhetoric. Norris disavowed any intent to encourage division or faction; instead, the tract was "designed for short hints, not a Contest." In *Friendly Advice*, Norris argued that while supporting the proprietor sometimes conflicted with vigorously defending the rights and privileges of the people, Pennsylvanians could achieve both politically. Condemning the "Men of *Design*" who spent their time in the Assembly "to no viable purpose, but to shew . . . their Abilities to play with words" and "Create Quarrels, & then Remonstrate finely," Norris suggested that voters should look beyond the "very good & talking Face" these scheming men exhibited and vote for men of a deeper character, men who showed their "Designs" through "plain Indications." Norris called on his fellow citi-

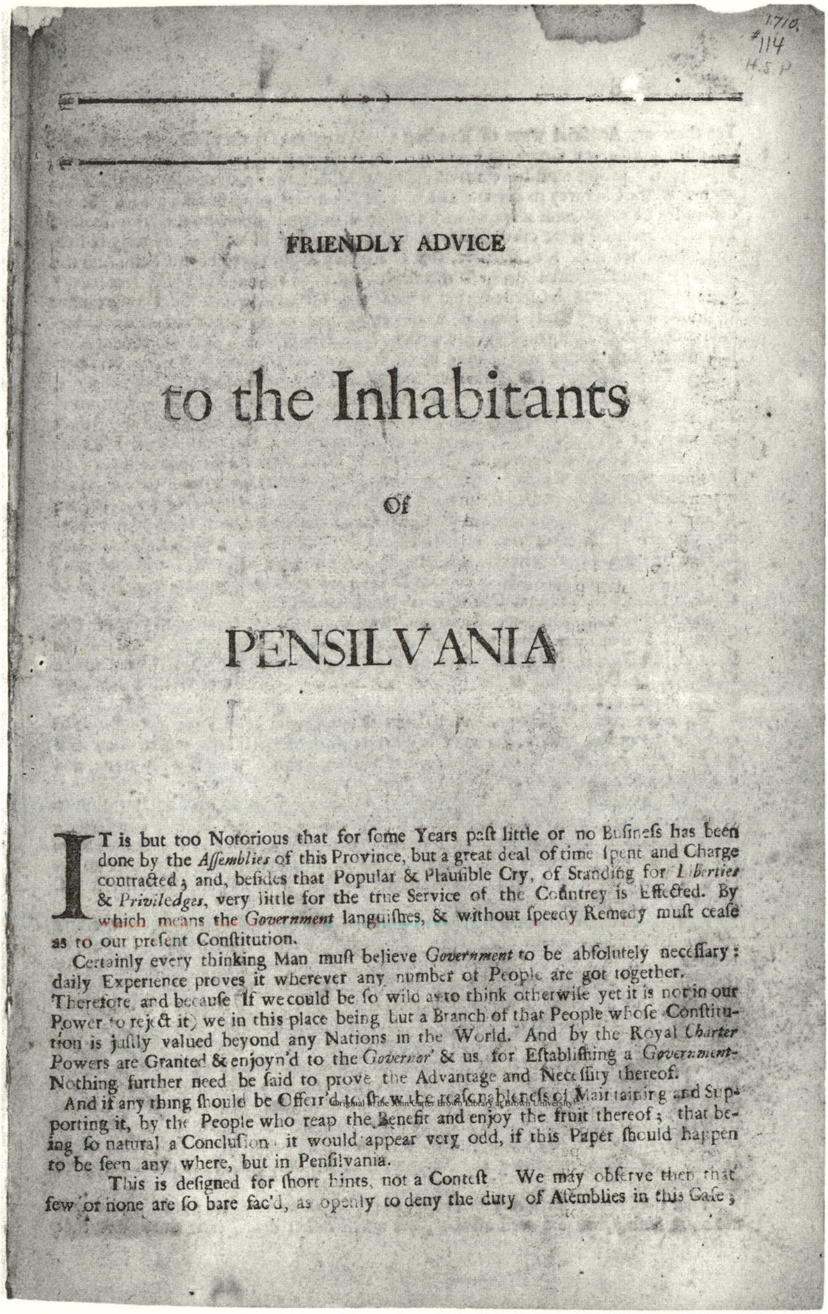

FRIENDLY ADVICE

to the Inhabitants

Of

PENSILVANIA

IT is but too Notorious that for some Years past little or no Business has been done by the *Assemblies* of this Province, but a great deal of time spent and Charge contracted; and, besides that Popular & Plausible Cry, of Standing for *Liberties* & *Priviledges*, very little for the true Service of the Countrey is Effected. By which means the *Government* languishes, & without speedy Remedy must cease as to our present Constitution.

Certainly every thinking Man must believe *Government* to be absolutely necessary: daily Experience proves it wherever any number of People are got together. Therefore, and because If we could be so wild as to think otherwise yet it is not in our Power to reject it; we in this place being but a Branch of that People whose Constitution is justly valued beyond any Nations in the World. And by the Royal *Charter* Powers are Granted & enjoyn'd to the *Governor* & us, for Establishing a *Government*. Nothing further need be said to prove the Advantage and Necessity thereof.

And if any thing should be Offer'd to shew the reasonableness of Maintaining and Supporting it, by the People who reap the Benefit and enjoy the fruit thereof; that being so natural a Conclusion it would appear very odd, if this Paper should happen to be seen any where, but in Pensilvania.

This is designed for short hints, not a Contest. We may observe then that few or none are so bare fac'd, as openly to deny the duty of Assemblies in this Case;

Figure 12. *Friendly Advice to the Inhabitants of Pensilvania.* Title page to Isaac Norris's 1710 election appeal. Courtesy The John Carter Brown Library at Brown University.

zens to choose assemblymen "of such Honor & Truth, that they will Stand firmly & truly" for the people "whom they represent & With whom they are so Linkt as to Stand or Fall."[91]

Even as Norris stressed the equality between the electors and elected, he did not suggest that the people would best be represented by choosing from a cross-section of colonial society. Rather, "daily Experience shews us even in our private Affairs (and much more in the Public) That where there is a good understanding between the concern'd Parties, Business is most easily done, and our desires & advantages there, more easily gained."[92] Norris concluded by arguing that "impartial" readers of "sense & judgment" would have to admit that despite the work of some scheming men, God had favored Pennsylvania "beyond any province in America, with . . . respect of Government." Working with Penn, he noted, could preserve the province's special place in the world, by allowing people and proprietor to defeat attempts to royalize the colony.[93] He closed with a condemnation of unruly discourse and a call for public moderation, asking his readers to end the "Remarkable & Scandalous" state of Pennsylvania's politics by being "sober and moderate" at the ballot box.[94] Indirectly, Norris urged his readers to support the slate of Quaker merchants and ministers vying to remove the Lloydians from office.

Friendly Advice legitimated a particular type of Quaker political rule by redefining how public figures should speak authoritatively to and on behalf of the public. Norris called on voters to read politicians' motives through their words and demeanor and suggested that "honest" speech and "plain indications" signified true character and public spirit. In so doing, he cast Quaker techniques of religious discourse as standards of political credibility. By emphasizing his desire for unity and his attachment to Pennsylvanian society, he cast his own verbal style as reflective of the public interest. All other modes of public discourse—remonstration, quarreling, or simple word play—became antagonistic to the province's interest. Rejecting the notion that public opinion could be represented through alternative political styles, Norris implied that Quaker speech was uniquely capable of articulating the public good. *Friendly Advice*'s claims to public authority were not grounded in its adoption of the "people's"—any people's—words, but rather in the claim that Quaker speech, with its plain and noncontentious style, bore a greater similitude to provincial public opinion than any other speech genre.[95] *Friendly Advice* marked the first time that a Quaker politician had applied speech practices developed to communicate order within the Meeting to a political contest involving a significant non-Quaker audience.

Friendly Advice also articulated a historical argument in favor of Quaker rule. Norris's call for selecting men of "good understanding" to rule Pennsylvania highlighted two of the colony's virtues: first, he reminded his readers of the unmatched privileges they enjoyed. Second, he noted Pennsylvania's bountiful nature, implying that this reflected God's favor. Each of these points called attention to the central role Penn and other Friends played in shaping Pennsylvania's development. *Friendly Advice* involved a form of rhetorical appropriation, as Norris—who had not even settled in Pennsylvania until 1694—wrote Quaker politicians into the history of Pennsylvania's founding. He thereby ensured that they shared credit with the proprietor for the colony's original shape and form. His invocation of "English liberties" reiterated the oft-repeated claim that England was truly a nation above all others while also casting Quaker Pennsylvania, with its even more generous liberties, as a special nation within a nation.[96] Pennsylvania, Norris argued, occupied a special place in history, thanks to its founders. Leaving ambiguous the question of whether others could adopt Quaker political styles and rule legitimately, *Friendly Advice* pioneered a political discourse that implicated historical myth, Quaker speech, and a Quaker-inflected notion of communal consensus as the bases for civic power in Pennsylvania.[97]

Whether Pennsylvania's voters accepted Norris's celebration of Quaker modes of public discourse in toto, his calls for sobriety and moderation succeeded at the polls. The "mask of the designers" had been ripped off, Norris later claimed, allowing the people to "see their true interest."[98] Every legislator in the 1710 Assembly met defeat in the October elections, including speaker David Lloyd.[99] More than half those elected in October 1710 were first-time legislators, the least experienced group of legislators since Benjamin Fletcher's brief reign as governor of the province and the least experienced ever elected under the Charter of Privileges.[100] This more conservative coalition of Friends still opposed Penn on certain issues (most notably quitrents) but governed more quietly than Lloyd had. They reached a state of relative accord with the proprietor and his lieutenant governors Charles Gookin and Sir William Keith from 1710 to the early 1720s. This group of Quaker politicians, which included leaders within the Philadelphia Yearly Meeting such as Isaac Norris, Caleb Pusey, and Richard Hill, stayed in power with little turnover through 1723. The composition of the Provincial Council also reflected this newfound political stability. Whereas the Council and Assembly had been sharply opposed during Lloyd's tenure as speaker, men such as Norris, Hill, and Pusey frequently held positions in both bodies simultaneously in the 1710s.[101] Not surprisingly, tensions between the two bodies disappeared during this period.

The election also marked a new direction in relations between provincial politicians and the proprietor. Indeed, the triumphant party trumpeted their embrace of Penn as a way of bolstering their political legitimacy. Once in power, they published Penn's June 1710 letter. Though disappointed that it had not arrived before the elections, when it "might have facilitated" the peaceful revolution that took place, they certainly appreciated Penn's sentiments.[102] Penn reciprocated in a letter, thanking provincial Friends for electing an Assembly sympathetic to his aims. Their earlier unruly behavior, he wrote, had attracted the attention of the ministry at Whitehall, raising the likelihood that Pennsylvania would suffer West Jersey's fate. Guided by the hand of providence, Friends' prudence had forestalled that possibility, however. Penn promised, for his part, to do his utmost to protect their privileges as "Christians & Englishmen." Colonists and proprietor shared the same goal: protecting their God-given promised land, "that Copious & good Countrey so we may enjoy it & ours from Generation to Generation" of Friends.[103] Penn validated provincial Friends' efforts to claim equal credit for the province's founding as a uniquely blessed place. He participated in this narrative construction of Pennsylvania so that Quakers on both sides of the Atlantic might speak as one voice.

Pennsylvania's position on the cultural and imperial borderlands of England's Atlantic empire made this cultural transition possible. Dissenters living in a proprietary colony, provincial Quakers were outliers in the English empire religiously and politically. The growing number of non-Quakers in their colony—strangers in the Quaker realm, so to speak—threatened their civic identity. Besieged by outside forces, Friends renewed their efforts to protect their specialness. They also renewed their efforts to define, or at least explain, their specialness—hence the development of a founding mythology that combined the languages of provincial history, Quaker rhetoric, and a celebration of liberties Pennsylvanian and English. The result was a distinctive political system made legitimate by an authentically creole political discourse.

The larger political and cultural forces that shaped creolization in Pennsylvania spurred the creation of a creole self-consciousness throughout the colonial Atlantic. Intellectuals everywhere fostered a sense of historical self-consciousness that helped define the contours of social identity in their respective settlements. Authors in English colonies like Massachusetts, Barbados, Georgia, and Virginia wrote histories intended to deflect charges of creole degeneracy and celebrate their ancestors' achievements.[104] Political factors certainly influenced these writers. Caribbean elites railed against imperial regulations that treated them like "*Aliens*" in large part because of settlers' mean origins.[105] Creoles in New Spain and Peru, meanwhile, attacked the way the Spanish crown had stripped from them the privileges their ancestors, the conquerors of America, had earned. According to one seventeenth-century chronicler, imperial policy had rendered creoles "strangers in their own land," a sentiment later echoed by Norris and Penn.[106]

Pennsylvania's experience most resembled that of Massachusetts. Late seventeenth-century New England experienced a series of shocks that occasioned a bout of significant cultural creativity. A long-running religious conflict over church membership culminated in 1662 in a compromise allowing the children of full church members to become partial members of their parents' congregation, a move an embittered and vocal minority believed corroded the fabric of provincial society. King Philip's War, waged against a confederation of Indian tribes, destroyed dozens of towns and killed a thousand colonists, making it the deadliest Indian war in the region's history. And the imperial government's displeasure with the colony's independence culminated in the revocation of the Bay Company's charter in 1684. Massachusetts seemed as if it were in constant peril in the decades after the Restoration.

Their struggles to account for this series of existential crises led New England clergymen to create a new cultural form: the jeremiad. The first authentically American literary genre, the jeremiad followed a strict formula, whether delivered as a sermon or in print. First, Puritan ministers laid out for their audience the ways in which the people had failed in their obligations to God, using appropriate citations from scripture. Next, they recounted the afflictions visited upon the colonists as a result. They concluded by instructing the faithful on how to reform in order to make things right with the Lord. This deceptively simple structure proved remarkably adaptable. The growth of heretical sects like the Quakers and Baptists, the devastating war, the troubles with the Crown—all these could be explained by the colonists' collective sins. Repentance, moreover, might obviate future suffering. Implicit or explicit comparisons to New England's founders ran through these jeremiads, issued with increased frequency and intensity over the years. If providence had blessed the efforts of the first generation with success, then any subsequent tribulations reflected the sins of the second generation. New

England Puritans used the jeremiad to understand their past and lay out a plan for their future in an uncertain colonial world. In the words of Perry Miller, it offered them a "way of conceiving the inconceivable, of making intelligible order out of the transition from European to American experience."[107]

These stereotypical stories of decline and redemption helped define the creole culture that second generation New Englanders created. Ministers encouraged the people to embrace their heritage, even while admonishing them for their failure to live up to it. Ritual castigation built a sense of tribal identity across generational lines. This collective identity helped settlers in Massachusetts as they made the transition from being a self-governed colony with a well-defined religious mission to being an imperial province with a royal governor after they received a new charter in 1691. This particular approach to cultural heritage also infused the major histories written at the end of the seventeenth and the beginning of the eighteenth centuries. Cotton Mather's two-volume opus *Magnalia Christi Americana* subsumed all New England's history to the logic of the jeremiad with a narrative in which the only agency was providential. For good measure, he included numerous hagiographic accounts of the founders to remind the present generation of their faults.[108] New England authors took the development of this newfound sense of colonial memory as their central mission, and they proved remarkably adept at the task.

The Quaker creole consciousness that emerged in Pennsylvania expressed itself differently, however. The development of narratives about the colony's past did not coincide with the rise of a colonial literary culture. The province produced no authors as noteworthy as those in other colonies. While Virginia had Robert Beverly, Massachusetts had Cotton Mather, Peru had the "Inca" Garcilaso de la Vega, New Spain had Carlos de Sigüenza y Góngora, and Barbados had Richard Ligon, Pennsylvania had . . . Caleb Pusey, the man whom George Keith had described as a "miller-philosopher" with a "dull stone."[109] Moreover, no Pennsylvanian published a history of the province until Robert Proud in 1797. Historical self-consciousness in Pennsylvania, so central to the colony's nascent creole culture, grew out of political conflict rather than literary endeavors. Where colonists in Peru and Massachusetts read great works of art written by Garcilaso and Mather, respectively, Pennsylvanians got a set of political parables that used history as a means of sanctifying the present.[110]

Notably, the Quaker leaders most responsible for cultivating this provincial creole identity wrote about the issue of "criolian degeneracy" in a markedly different way than their counterparts elsewhere in the colonial Atlantic world did. In their public discourse, they exhibited little of the overt anxiety about their colonial status that pervaded the works of other American authors. Addressing European audiences as much as American ones, men like Ligon, Garcilaso, and Mather wrote as "dominated yet privileged colonial subject[s]," elites desperate to demonstrate that their provinciality did not render them inferior politically or culturally.[111] Pennsylvania Quakers, meanwhile, cared far less about metropolitan approval. And while Puritan divines warned about degeneration within their own spiritual community, Friends did not. Provincial Quakers externalized the sources of the colony's religious troubles. Orthodox Friends' failure had not brought about the schism; the Keithians' fall from grace had. This allowed them to externalize the colony's political troubles as well. Norris and other leading Friends did blame Quakerism's decline for the province's political strife, but blame lay with those who "stood Loose from Friends." The formulation allowed ruling Friends to define both those out of unity with the Meeting and non-Quakers in the province as outside Pennsylvania's history, a potent political tool. Their experience creating a creole religious identity in the aftermath of the Keithian schism enabled them to create a coherent, distinctly creole political coalition.[112]

Drawing their cultural power from their appropriation of the colony's origins, the men who assumed provincial leadership in 1710 were, in a very real sense, Pennsylvania's charter generation. Thirty years after the fact, they made Pennsylvania's origins as a Quaker colony a central part of colonial political and cultural identity. If 1682 marked the year of Pennsylvania's settlement, then 1710 marked the year of its founding. Provincial Friends would have scoffed at this statement, of course. Their political, cultural, and religious identity required them to deny any such assertion. Making Pennsylvania Quaker involved spinning yarns that omitted as much, if not more, than they included.

Penn, nonetheless, continued his negotiations with the English government for Pennsylvania's surrender for two years after the 1710 election. Characteristically, his decision to do so reflected both self-interest and benevolent paternalism. Settling his accounts with Ford had not removed all of Penn's financial difficulties; he remained deeply in debt, albeit to a different, and less difficult, set of creditors. Selling Pennsylvania promised to solve these problems, provided the government made a generous offer.[113] Political considerations also entered into Penn's thinking. He feared royalization's consequences for colonial Friends. A negotiated surrender, he believed, would allow him to shape the terms of the post-surrender settlement. Before any deal could be finalized, however, Penn suffered two debilitating strokes in 1712. He never recovered, and neither his widow nor his sons shared his interest in selling the colony. The Penn family would retain control of Pennsylvania until the American Revolution.

Thus, colonists had to find their place within the empire. This meant negotiating efforts by the Board of Trade to bring Pennsylvania in line with the rest of Britain's colonies. It also meant dealing with new waves of Atlantic immigration. Having consolidated their political power within the colony in 1710, Quakers would have to find a way to hold on to it as they became a minority in the colony after 1720.

CHAPTER 7

The Parables of Pennsylvania Politics

The Power of Quaker Mythology

ON OCTOBER 1, 1726, supporters of Sir William Keith, erstwhile lieutenant governor of Pennsylvania, gathered in honor of his election to the provincial Assembly. The celebration grew raucous; Keith's followers staged bonfires, while ships anchored along the Delaware fired their guns in his honor. Keith marked his victory in an even more dramatic manner two weeks later. On the first day of the new legislative session, he led a triumphant procession of dozens of followers through Philadelphia. He intended to cap this parade with his selection as speaker of the Assembly, having already planned a victory party, complete with trumpets and guns, at a country estate later that evening.[1]

Keith's electoral victory and the popular celebrations that accompanied it represented the most significant test ruling Friends faced in the aftermath of their consolidation of power in 1710. His actions threatened Quaker power in multiple ways. Most obviously, a new political coalition threatened the nascent system of one-party rule that Quaker assemblymen had created. His partisan appeals to provincial artisans and newly arrived immigrants encouraged the discontent many felt against elite Friends in the colony. Moreover, Keith's tactics, which drew on a rich Anglo-American tradition of "popular" politics, challenged the ways Friends justified their own authority.[2] Facing organizational and rhetorical opposition under the guidance of an able politician, ruling Friends worried that the province would return to the political chaos that had characterized its early years.

Keith's challenge, moreover, came at a time when the colony faced trou-

Figure 13. Portrait of Sir William Keith, Lieutenant Governor of Pennsylvania, 1718–1726. Courtesy of the Capitol Preservation Committee of Pennsylvania and Brian Hunt.

ble on the frontier. Provincial diplomats became increasingly involved in conflicts between Indian tribes as the Iroquois Confederacy moved to extend its power southward through the Susquehanna Valley. They found themselves confronted with the difficult choice of ratifying Iroquois claims to the region—a move that would anger the Conestoga, Mingo, Delaware, and Shawnee Indians on their borders—or rejecting Iroquois authority, which would likely alienate the most potent Indian group in northeastern North America. The consequences these decisions carried inevitably made Indian policies an issue in provincial politics.[3]

Yet Quaker power in Pennsylvania emerged stronger than ever by the 1730s, even as Friends become a smaller minority in the province. On the frontier, provincial rulers adopted the mantle of Penn's successors, drawing on the legacy of his friendship with Native Americans as they navigated Indian politics. Their self-description as the founder's heirs justified the westward expansion of colonial power. In the province proper, Quaker politicians closed ranks against non-Quaker challengers. In the wake of these threats, they elaborated on the story of the province's founding used to justify the government turnover in 1710. They told a series of political parables about Pennsylvania's origins that bridged the past and present in ways that effaced the history of creolization that created the colony's civic culture.[4] In doing so, leading Friends articulated a political discourse that incorporated aspects of Quaker religious culture, the language of English rights, and appeals to their status as the colony's founding fathers. The voice they adopted was neither disinterested nor disembodied. In defending themselves from external threats, Quaker leaders spoke as Friends in a political style that granted them a privileged public authority, implying that they were uniquely capable of representing the public's interests politically and discursively. That the electorate supported them so overwhelmingly suggests the power of these modes of persuasion.[5] Both challenge and response served to rework definitions of civic authority in Pennsylvania, further inflecting it with a Quaker character.

The Calm Before the Storm: Pennsylvania in the 1710s

Political and social tensions in Pennsylvania eased dramatically after the end of Queen Anne's War in 1713. The coming of peace removed civil defense as a pressing concern, quelling anger against pacifist Quaker politicians. It also fueled an economic boom. The defeat of French forces in North America

removed possible military threats to the colony, while the cessation of hostilities in the Caribbean opened valuable markets for provincial wheat. Exports
rose dramatically, offering farmers and merchants a measure of prosperity
after years of economic insecurity. The value of goods imported from England more than doubled. Driven largely by the Caribbean market, the colonial economy continued to grow throughout the decade, despite persistent
fluctuations in wheat prices.[6]

More significantly, provincial legislators managed to come to terms with
their place in the postwar empire. The Assembly had clashed with the Board
of Trade several times over the colony's legal code. Penn's Charter stipulated
that the proprietor submit colonial statutes to the board so that it might
determine if they were "repugnant" to the laws of England. The Assembly's
efforts to comply with this clause were half-hearted at best; at one point they
repealed and repassed over one hundred laws in a single session in an effort
to evade the requirement that statutes be conveyed to the Board within five
years of their passage. The Board responded in kind, repealing twenty-one of
these laws in 1705.[7]

Relations proved more cordial thereafter, as the legislature made a concerted attempt to meet the imperial government's requirements. Their efforts
paid off; the Board of Trade approved provincial legislation at a much higher
rate after 1705.[8] In 1711, the Assembly took steps to alleviate another point of
conflict, amending the provincial law governing affirmations and oaths. This
new law protected dissenters' rights to give an affirmation but mandated that
an oath be administered to all who requested it when assuming office or
giving testimony in court. This key concession rendered moot a major colonial Anglican complaint against the Quaker government. Though the Board
of Trade took issue with the exact wording of the affirmation the legislature
prescribed, it ultimately approved this compromise in 1719.[9]

But to gain royal approval of their law regarding affirmations, provincial
politicians had to compromise on one of the issues nearest and dearest to
the hearts of seventeenth-century Quaker legal reformers: the penal code.[10]
Pennsylvania's first legal code had placed a heavy emphasis on rehabilitation
with a relatively light emphasis on corporal punishment. Most notably, it
called for capital punishment only for premeditated murder.[11] Statutory revisions in 1700 expanded the number of offenses meriting corporal or capital
punishment. Legislators introduced branding and castration as penalties for
several offences, and mandated that African Americans convicted of raping a
white woman be executed.[12]

Even after these changes, however, Pennsylvania's penal code was far milder than England's, a fact that irked some members of the Board of Trade. In 1718, the legislature passed "An Act for the Advancement of Justice and More Certain Administration Thereof," the most significant reform of Pennsylvania's legal code before the American Revolution.[13] The Act expanded the number of crimes punishable by death to a dozen. Arsonists, burglars, and those guilty of bastardy now faced the gallows. These revisions to the penal code assuaged the imperial government's fears and helped convince the Board to yield on affirmation, but they did so at the cost of Pennsylvania's legal distinctiveness. Quaker legislators had ended one of Penn's boldest experiments to maintain their hold on political power. Learning to live in the empire had come at a price.

Colonial political debate died down in this period as well. Pennsylvania had lacked a printer since Reynier Jansen's death in 1706. The Philadelphia Yearly Meeting, which inherited Jansen's press, showed little inclination to publish, issuing a total of eight titles during the seven years it owned the press. Caleb Pusey's rabid anti-Keithian campaign between 1700 and 1706 outstripped the colony's entire output during the years immediately following Jansen's demise.[14] This meager output led the Assembly to issue a public call for a full-time printer. Andrew Bradford, son of Keithian publisher William Bradford, responded, moving to Pennsylvania in 1713.[15] Bradford started slowly but soon increased his pace, issuing on average more than five titles annually between 1716 and 1720.

This period saw qualitative as well as quantitative changes in Pennsylvania's print culture, especially after Bradford's arrival. Religious polemics, the most common publication genre in the years following the Keithian schism, disappeared almost entirely after Pusey's crusade ended. The few that did see print were reissues of British works.[16] Moreover, while these newer works addressed contemporary religious and political issues, they refrained from direct criticism of the government, of governmental opponents, and certainly of the Quaker Meeting.[17] The Pennsylvania press hardly acted as an agent for political debate in the aftermath of ruling Friends' consolidation of power.

Print became an increasingly significant vehicle for dissemination of public authority during this period. Though the colony's early statutory code mandated regular publication of the colony's laws, the Assembly made almost no effort to do so until 1714. From 1714 to 1722, however, Bradford's press issued eleven titles compiling the province's laws, including tracts detailing treaties with local Indians.[18] He published a variety of other government documents as well. From his arrival in 1717, Lieutenant Governor Sir William Keith displayed a notable proclivity for the printed word, using Bradford's press as a platform from which to issue a steady stream of speeches, particularly his addresses to the Provincial Council.[19]

The press had thus begun to take on the role Penn wanted Pennsylvania's legislature to play at the colony's inception, with one crucial twist. Penn had invited the people to attend a public session of the Assembly and "hear what shall be spoken unto them" as a means of increasing government authority over its citizens. In giving their silent assent to their rulers, they participated in a legislative ritual that ratified the legislature's legitimacy.[20] Government publications during Bradford's tenure served the same function, albeit in an impersonal way. They enacted a form of political discourse designed to convey authority, not elicit response. Through the publication of provincial laws and official proclamations and addresses, the Assembly and lieutenant governor had turned to print as a way of textually representing their legitimacy to a provincial reading public. Colonial rulers invited the people to show their assent imaginatively, not personally. Where Penn asked the people to hear the voice of their rulers, later politicians asked them to read what their rulers had declared unto them. In conjunction with Bradford, provincial rulers fostered a print culture that located authority in the public utterances of the provincial government.

In the years after the political revolution of 1710, Pennsylvania experienced the greatest harmony it had ever known. But economic calamity after 1720 showed that the Quaker consolidation of power had merely quelled colonial factionalism, not eliminated it.

Sir William's Challenge

The collapse of the South Sea Bubble in 1720, together with a contraction of the West Indian trade, marked the beginning of a period of economic decline. Imports and exports declined precipitously. These economic troubles hit Philadelphia particularly hard. Urban merchants felt the pinch first. According to one wit, "several Gentlemen who kept their Coaches before they dipt in to the South Sea, are now forced to walk on Foot. By the same Turn of Fortunes wheel, Footmen and Cook Maids loll in their guilded Chariots and smile at the Fate of their quondam Masters."[21] The economic pain quickly spread throughout colonial society, driving the colony into a serious depression. Arriving in the city in 1723, Benjamin Franklin noted that the number of buildings available for rent "made me think then that the inhabitants of the city were one after another deserting it."[22] This economic crisis coincided with a major wave of immigration from Ireland, as thousands of Ulster Scots came to the colony after 1718. The arrival of these newcomers, many destitute, raised social, economic, and political tensions.[23]

Some provincials urged the government to alleviate the economic crisis by emitting a paper currency. The depression had caused a significant drainage of specie from Pennsylvania, leaving many colonists stripped of cash. Unlike their counterparts in New England, provincial lawmakers had never authorized printing paper currency, limiting the colonial money supply.[24] The question became a major issue in the 1721 elections, a contest James Logan described as "very mobbish, and carried by a Levelling spirit."[25] Despite broad popular support, the Assembly defeated a paper money bill in 1722.[26]

The bill's defeat elicited strong criticism. Hoping to benefit from the Assembly's unpopularity, Keith encouraged criticism of the Quaker ruling party. He formed two political organizations, the Tiff or Leather Apron's Club, and the Gentlemen's Club, in which his political followers from different ranks of society could congregate. This broadened political participation significantly.[27] The lieutenant governor's efforts to focus this public discontent proved effective, as all but two of the assemblymen who had voted against the paper-money bill went down to defeat in the fall elections.[28] Ruling Friends feared the worst. "All Encouragement," Isaac Norris lamented, "hath lately been given & all ways taken to Insult Creditors and render men of ability . . . obnoxious, in mobbish discourses and wretched argument."[29]

Keith and his supporters heightened these concerns. The lieutenant governor fanned the flames of discontent in his Assembly address at the opening of the January 1723 session: "We all know it is neither the great, the rich, nor the learned that compose the body of any people, and that civil government ought carefully to protect the poor, laborious, and industrous part of mankind in the enjoyment of their just rights and equal liberties and privileges with the rest of the fellow creatures."[30] The Assembly responded with a bill authorizing the printing of £15,000, hoping to alleviate the financial straits of constituents and followed up the next year with a bill for another £30,000.[31] Paper-money advocates also convinced David Lloyd, retired from colonial politics since his 1710 defeat, to reenter public life in support of their cause. After writing a May paper in favor of another emission of currency, Lloyd stood for provincial election in October 1723. He won handily and was promptly named speaker of the Assembly.[32]

These populist efforts represented a curious amalgam of tradition and novelty masquerading as tradition. On the one hand, Keith encouraged voluntary associations more than previous partisan groups, such as the short-lived antiproprietary "Charter Club" of 1689–90, ever had.[33] He also broke new ground rhetorically. His January 1723 address articulated a novel vision of provincial society, distinguishing groups within Pennsylvania and suggesting that they had distinct economic and political interests. Such a conception of society stood at odds with the notion of public unity Quaker politicians had embraced during the relative harmony of the preceding decade. In doing so, Keith offered a new standard by which political leaders could be judged: their protection of the liberties of the greater part of society.

But if Keith broke new ground in how he spoke *of* the public, he showed little novelty in how he spoke *to* them. He directed his celebration of Pennsylvania's "poor, laborious, and industrious" people to the colony's leaders, not to the people themselves. Though Keith adopted a more contentious tone than Quaker assemblymen often did, he nonetheless delivered the speech to the legislature. He spoke *for* the people to other colonial leaders. Moreover, he elected not to reprint the address, though previous Assembly addresses had appeared in the *American Weekly Mercury*. In effect, he argued that political leaders should be judged by how they served the people, without inviting the people themselves to judge their rulers.

Keith's actions put leading Quakers in a bind. He had proven a capable administrator willing to defend Friends' rights. He had played a significant role during negotiations with the Board of Trade over the affirmation issue and repeatedly stood with Friends when Anglicans attacked them on religious grounds.[34] Keith represented a known quantity the Society could trust to respect Friends' rights to liberty of conscience. Given the conflict Quakers had endured with previous Anglican governors, they were grateful for his steadfast support.[35]

Keith's actions nonetheless disturbed conservative Quaker leaders such as Norris and Logan. In their eyes, his push to legitimate sites of public discourse outside Quaker authority threatened the colonial political order. Likewise, his attempts to divide the body politic came during a crucial demographic shift. Friends' percentage of Pennsylvania's overall population had been shrinking since the 1690s; by 1720, they were a minority in the province.[36] Keith's language called into question Friends' ability to speak for

Pennsylvania as a whole. The sense among Keith's opponents that he drew the bulk of his support from recent immigrants made his language more threatening.³⁷ They saw Keith's new rhetoric, audience, and modes of communicating as part of an innovative political style that threatened the relative monopoly on public authority Friends claimed.

James Logan responded to Keith's challenge in 1723 by publishing his *Charge* to the Philadelphia grand jury.³⁸ In some respects, the *Charge* was an unremarkable example of its genre. It enjoined the grand jury to "*Inquire* with *Diligence*" into all disorderly conduct and "to *Present*, with *Truth* and Uprightness" whatever it found. Logan asked the juror to pay careful attention to instances of rioting, counterfeiting, acts of "*Petty-Treason*, When a Servant Kills his or her Master or Mistress, a Woman killing her Husband, or an Ecclesiastic his Superior," and crimes of "uncleanness" such as "adultery, fornication, rape, and attempted rape, bigamy, incest, sodomy and bestiality" that were "nott fitt to be explained."³⁹ Justices in seventeenth- and eighteenth-century Anglo-America routinely made similar appeals to grand juries.

Even where Logan strayed from the typical form of the genre, he hewed closely to a Quaker line. He used the *Charge* as an occasion to offer a general inquiry into the sources of governmental authority, articulating a political philosophy that resembled that of William Penn. Government, he argued, existed to curb the "Motions of natural Passions such as Ambition, Avarice, Lust, and Revenge" among those in society likely to prey upon the weak. This required the enforcement of fixed laws by virtuous magistrates with "a sense of GOD's Omnipresence, and Omniscience." Great Britain stood alone among nations in its commitment to the rule of law, a quality that had preserved order at home and throughout its colonial possessions.⁴⁰

Rulers could not rule solely by law alone, however. The governed needed to fulfill their social obligations as well. Each part of society needed to play its proper role. Good subjects, Logan argued, needed to work assiduously to cultivate habits of justice, industry, frugality, wisdom, and especially sobriety. While the first four qualities were essential in maintaining order and prosperity, they ultimately rested on the fifth. Sobriety, Logan wrote, was "the Ornament of a good man," giving "Health and Strength" to the Body" and peace to the mind. But the cultivation of individual sobriety served public as well as private ends. Properly developed, "it most effectually prevent[ed] those innumerable Disorders, which spring from Debauchery and Riot."⁴¹ Here, too, Britain offered an important example. Its system of mixed government diffused social tensions by allowing different social ranks to participate in ways appropriate to their station. Harmony ensued as long as rulers and ruled remembered their respective duties.

The political philosophy Logan laid out in the *Charge* blended Enlightenment ideas about the "passions," Protestant political ideology, and British patriotism with Quaker social thought. It represented a more elaborate expression of the type of secular civic Quakerism Penn had hoped to instill among colonists in Pennsylvania. Logan believed that government should encourage "sincere LOVE FOR OUR COUNTRY" in the heart of every citizen. Once this had taken hold, the people would "endeavour to learn the true interest of our Country, abstracted from its private Ones." For Logan, following the public interest meant deferring to provincial rulers so that they might better guard public tranquility. This, he argued, fulfilled Penn's original vision for Pennsylvania, the establishment of "a Government, on the enduring Ties of Unity and Love," where provincials cared for each other as brethren.[42]

However, the *Charge* broke new ground in a way that reflected the dramatic social and legal changes Pennsylvania had recently experienced. Logan was the first justice in British North America to publish a grand jury charge. His true audience was not the grand jury but the province at large.[43] Pennsylvania's colonial status and large immigrant population, Logan argued, motivated him to publish a call to patriotism: "The lateness of this our Settlement indeed will scarce allow many, to account it their Country because they can remember, that they were born and bred in another." "Evil Communication" in print made this acculturation process tougher. Logan saw his *Charge* as a means of countering this "Vicious Education."[44]

Logan's decision to transpose a traditional oral performance of authority into a new medium also represented an adaption to new legal realities in Pennsylvania. Penn and his fellow founders hoped that the provincial legal system would serve an important educative function; courts and magistrates could teach citizens the practices of good citizenship. The breakdown of the legal system in the early eighteenth century revealed the impossibility of this strategy. The 1718 penal code reform signified that they had abandoned these efforts altogether. Unable to compel Pennsylvanians to enact certain civic performances through the legal system, Logan could at least exhort them to do so in print. He could assert Quaker cultural power even after they lost their legal power. The *Charge* articulated a novel civic language, constructed from a variety of sources but heavily Quaker in influence, intended to help immigrants embrace Pennsylvania as "their Country." It was, in other words, a thoroughly creolized political language designed to creolize new colonists and quite literally authorize Quaker power.

The publication of the *Charge* did little to stem the political tide Logan feared. Paying little heed to the proprietary secretary's enjoinders, voters returned to office the pro-Lloydian and Keithian legislators who had displaced the Quaker old guard the year before. These legislators reciprocated with another paper-money bill.[45] Fearing Keith's rise as a demagogue after this electoral success, Logan left for England to advise Hannah Penn, William Penn's widow and proprietor of the province, to remove Keith from office. As unhappy with Keith's conduct as Logan, Penn began the process of finding a new lieutenant governor.[46]

The Genteel Radicalism of David Lloyd

Logan returned in mid-1724 with written instructions from the proprietrix communicating her displeasure with Keith in no uncertain terms. She expressed particular distress with his governing style and directed him to make specific changes. She admonished Keith for ignoring the Provincial Council and directed him to consult with the Council before consenting to any law passed by the Assembly or even addressing the Assembly in spoken or written form. Moreover, she wanted Keith to appoint more Friends to the Provincial Council, believing that their status as Pennsylvania's principal settlers merited them a greater leadership role.[47] In essence, Penn wanted a return to the political order that had prevailed over the past decade, offering the appeal to history that Isaac Norris, Caleb Pusey, and others had when they assumed power in 1710.

Penn's directives set off a fierce debate involving Keith, Logan, and Lloyd. Keith rejected the implication that he promoted factionalism, arguing that he had always promoted civic harmony and worked carefully to secure the colonists' liberties as English subjects and "Dutiful Tennants" of the proprietors. The lieutenant governor's decision to make his correspondence with the proprietrix public belied these disavowals, however.[48] Over the ensuing weeks, he continued to defend his conduct in print, casting himself as a humble servant of the people.[49] Logan defended Penn's instructions in a memorial to the Assembly but eschewed any printed appeal. The secretary made a case for the legality and desirability of Penn's directions. If the proprietrix had the authority to appoint and remove a lieutenant to govern the colony in her stead, he argued, it only made sense that she could compel him to exercise his powers in ways consonant with her wishes. Besides, Logan noted, colonial governors in every other colony in the British Atlantic ruled with the advice and consent of their councils; in Virginia, for example, a governor could scarce fire a justice of the peace without his council's permission.[50] The Assembly, under Lloyd's guidance, flatly claimed that Penn's instructions violated the 1701 Charter: "The Representative Body of this Province," and not the Provincial Council, was "the Guardian of the People's Rights and Liberties." This response, unlike the memorial that prompted it, appeared in the colony's only newspaper. The Assembly also voted to post the minutes of sessions in which they debated these issues in the city's coffee-house, ensuring that their views reached the largest audience possible.[51]

Speaker Lloyd elaborated his position in his *Vindication of the Legislative Power*, a curious hybrid of populist appeal, constitutional analysis, and religious discourse. Lloyd warned that Logan's efforts to enforce Penn's instructions threatened not only to violate the people's traditional "English Rights," which he celebrated as "the greatest rights, liberties, and privileges thereby granted"; it also imperiled those distinctive rights granted in the 1701 Charter, as evidenced by Logan's suggestion that the government should become more like that of other colonies. He called on his audience to be mindful of their freedom, invoking English traditions and the colonial Charter to appeal to their patriotism as Britons and Pennsylvanians. Lloyd also refuted what he saw as the prevailing wisdom among many elite Pennsylvanians: that men of wealth and learning possessed a unique capacity to protect those rights. "According to my experience," he wrote, "a mean man, of small interest, may do more good to the State than a Richer or more Learned Man, who by his ill Temper and aspiring mind becomes an Opposer to the Constitution by which he should act."[52]

The *Vindication* hardly represented a paean to egalitarianism, however, for Lloyd then suggested how these mean men might best help serve the public good. He did not suggest that these men should rule directly. "An Interest in the Colony" he argued, was an essential "Qualification to act for the good of the Publick." He simply believed that heritage, not wealth, determined interest. The province should be ruled by an Assembly "consisting of some Ancient Settlers . . . and others, who are descended from such as brought considerable estates into the Province, and went through great Difficulties in the first Settlement of this Wilderness, to the hazard of their Lives and Estates, amongst the Indian Natives." The labor of these settlers

A Vindication of the Legislative Power,

Submitted to the Representatives of all the Free-men of the Province of *Pennsylvania*, now sitting in Assembly.

May it please this Honourable House,

Aving perused *James Logan*'s Memorial and other Papers lately published by your Authority, I find the Governour hath vindicated the Powers of our Legislature and the method you are now in, with such convincing Arguments, urged with so much clearness and good reasoning, that it seems needless to say any more; yet, I hope, it will be no offence to offer some legal Authorities to prove what has been so Excellently advanced in favour of the Rights and Liberties of the Subject, as well as the regular Powers and Franchises of Government in the Points now under Consideration.

It is Evident to me, that the Royal Charter granted to our late Proprietary *William Penn*, under the great Seal of *England*, may safely be deemed the Fundamental Constitution of our Legislative Authority, by which Charter the late King *CHARLES* the second, in a very gracious and bountiful Manner, was pleased to signify his Royal Will and Pleasure in these Words, *to wit*, "That we, reposing special Trust and Confidence in the Fidelity, "Wisdom, Justice and provident Circumspection of the said *William Penn*, for Us, Our "Heirs and Successors, *Do Grant* free, full and absolute Power by Virtue of these presents, "to him and his Heirs, to his and their Deputies and Lieutenants, for the good and happy "Government of the said Country, to Ordain, Make and Enact, and, under his and their "Seals, to publish any Laws whatsoever, for the raising of Money for the Publick uses "of the said Province, or for any other End, appertaining either unto the publick State, "Peace or Safety of the said Country, or unto the private Utility of particular Persons, "according unto their best Discretion, *By and with* the Advice, Assent and Approbation "of the Free-men of the said Country, or the greater part of them, or of their Delegates "or Deputies, *Whom*, for the Enacting of the said Laws, when and as often as need shall "require, We will, That the said *William Penn* and his Heirs shall Assemble in such sort "and form as to him and them shall seem best."

By Virtue of this Clause the Proprietor had Power to make Deputies and Lieutenants, in which Case (as it is in all other Cases where a Deputy may be appointed) the Law says, he has full Power to do any act or thing which his Principal may do: And that is so essentially incident to a Deputy, that a Man cannot be a Deputy to do any single act or thing, nor can a Deputy have less Power than his Principal, and if his Principal make him *Covenant, That he will not do any particular thing which the Principal may do*, the Covenant is void and repugnant; as if the Under-Sheriff Covenant, that he will not Execute any process for more than *Twenty Pounds* without special Warrant from the High-Sheriff; this is void, because the Under-Sheriff is his Deputy, and the Power of the Deputy cannot be restrained to be less than that of his Principal, save only that he cannot make a Deputy, because it implies an Assignment of his whole Power, all which was adjudged by the Court of King's Bench, the 13 *William* 3. in the Case of *Parker* and *Kett*, where the Debate arose concerning the Steward of a Mannor-Court.

The Case of the Under-Sheriff here cited by *Holt*, is reported by the late Lord Chief Justice *Hobart* thus, *viz.* If a Sheriff will make an Under-Sheriff, *Provided* that he shall not serve Executions above 20 *l.* without his special Warrant, this *Proviso* will be void: For, tho' he may chuse whether he makes an Under-Sheriff at all, or may make him at his will, and to remove wholly, yet he cannot leave him an Under-Sheriff, and yet abridge his Power, *no more than the King may in Case of the Sheriff himself*: But it was said, that the Case here was not so, that the restraint of Executions above 20 *l.* grew not on the part of the Sheriff, but on the part of the Under-Sheriff by his Covenant, which might stand for good, notwithstanding the repugnancy to his Office; but the Covenant here was holden void, as being against *Law* and *Justice*. For since by being made Under-Sheriff, he is liable by Law to Execute all Process, he could, no more than the the Sheriff himself, Covenant not to Execute Process without another's special Warrant, for that is to *deny or delay Justice*.

This last Case was that which Governed the opinion of the Council (when Judge *Mompesson* assisted) to declare that part of Col. *Evan*'s Commission void, which reserved to the Proprietor the final Assent to all such Bills as he passed into Laws in this Province. Therefore, I admire how *James Logan* (being not only present at those Debates, but either drew up or copy'd and signed that solemn Resolution of the Council, and knows how it was approved of by the Assembly at the same time) can so strenuously insist upon the Restriction now in Debate; which is as much against *Law* and *Justice* as the Instances in the above quoted Cases could be.

The next thing observable in the above recited Clause of the Royal Charter, is the Right and Power of Legislation, granted to the Proprietor and his Heirs and to his and their

A   Deputies brought the favor of "Divine Providence" and made Pennsylvania prosperous. The speaker urged his readers to entrust the colony's political future to those who had, by that ancestry, "great reason to lay the good of the Publick and its true Interest as close to Heart as any others."[53]

Lloyd thus championed the political capabilities of common men while simultaneously suggesting that political power should be concentrated in the hands of the few. He rejected the notion that wealthy elites should dominate the political order. But rather than making a case for a more egalitarian system, he argued for the establishment of a political order dominated by a different sort of elites: men distinguished by their civic spirit. Moreover, in claiming that descendents of the province's "Ancient Settlers" could best safeguard the public interest, Lloyd gave provincial Quakers a singularly important public legitimacy. The *Vindication* feinted toward greater political participation, as the speaker ratified readers' power to choose their leaders, but it ultimately suggested that political participation involved assenting to the power of elite Friends who exercised well the authority that was their birthright. The *Vindication* thus redefined the nature of civic performance in a multicultural society, making it inclusive and exclusive at the same time. It explicitly appealed to the political judgment of non-Quakers but effectively excluded them from power. Lloyd had articulated a new form of imaginative civic participation, using print to encourage the people to hear what was spoken to them by their leaders. The secretary's authoritative charge from the bench and the speaker's genteel radicalism both led to the same logical conclusion: the naturalization of Quaker civic power.

Lloyd achieved this rhetorical end by way of a massive act of radical historical revisionism. William Penn would likely have been bemused by Lloyd's championing of the 1701 Charter, given the vehement attacks the latter leveled against it in his correspondence with the proprietor in 1704 and 1705.[54] This revisionism betrayed a deeper cultural conservatism, however. Lloyd's invocation of the Charter differed little from his use of the 1681 royal charter against Penn in 1704–5; he had simply chosen a new "founding moment" to justify rhetorically his political position. Quite literally, he had rendered Pennsylvania Quakers the colony's "charter" group. In that sense, Lloyd's *Vindication* represented a variation on a theme; whatever their partisan differences, Norris, Penn, and Lloyd all naturalized Quaker political power by grounding their appeals in a historical mythology that defined the colony as a Quaker place. Indeed, Lloyd relied so heavily on this authorizing narrative because of the *Vindication*'s populist overtones: the broader the scope of his non-Quaker audience, the harder he needed to work to "make" Pennsylvania Quaker if he and his brethren were to keep power.

By the time Logan responded with a pamphlet of his own, this political metanarrative had been firmly cemented in the minds of Quaker politicians.[55] Logan's *Antidote*, like Lloyd's *Vindication*, presented its author's case on both constitutional and historical grounds. Recapitulating the argument laid out in his memorial to the Assembly, Logan argued that Penn was well within her rights to compel Keith to consult the Council when consenting to legislation; this provision of Penn's instructions left Pennsylvania no different from any other proprietary colony.[56] He extolled the colony's exceptional character in other ways, however. Pennsylvanians, he reminded his readers, had been blessed with "mighty Privileges" beyond those possessed by other freeborn English subjects, a fact for which all provincials should be thankful. He also embraced Lloyd's suggestion that founding Friends had a unique capacity to govern.

But, he asked, what right did Lloyd, who was not one of Penn's first purchasers, have to speak for this planting generation? Penn and those first adventurers had endured extreme hardship to make Pennsylvania the "wonder" of the colonies around it. One man had shattered that amicable unity: "*George Keith*, the Grand *Apollyon* of this Country's Peace. . . . Hence the minds of Numbers were tainted and soured," touching off years of dischord.[57] Thankfully, Logan concluded, provincial freemen had voted in 1710 to return Pennsylvania to the state of tranquility in which it once lived; they had it in their power to do so again, if only they turned the Lloyd-Keith faction out of office.[58] Logan's invocation of the founding relied on historical trickery. If the fact that Lloyd came to the colony in 1695 had disqualified him from speaking on behalf of Pennsylvania's first generation, then Logan's 1699 arrival would seem to have given him even less claim.

Lloyd's and Logan's dueling tracts served two functions in Pennsylvania's tumultuous political culture. On the one hand, they each advanced a specific agenda with major implications for the colony's constitutional order. Instituting Penn's directives would have substantively reduced the power of the Assembly, the province's only elected branch of government. They also acted as a kind of theatrical performance that solidified Quaker identity across the partisan divide. The lines of argument they pursued purposely left several key assumptions about political authority in Pennsylvania unquestioned.[59] The secretary and the speaker each operated in a particular field of opinion that silently excluded other perspectives. They disagreed about which founding moment should be remembered and protected, with Lloyd claiming 1701 and Logan 1682, and they quarreled about which Quaker founders should be valorized. Neither, however, questioned the notion that the freemen should evaluate political leaders' claims to authority in terms of these politicians' relationship to Pennsylvania's founders. They employed print as a form of ritual practice that naturalized Quaker discourse as the dominant language of power in a creole society, just as Norris had done in his *Friendly Advice* in 1710. These Quaker antagonists resembled each other far more than they would have liked to admit.

Lloyd's and Logan's exchange happened during a transitional moment in the province's print culture. The arrival of Samuel Keimer as the colony's second printer helped spur three interrelated trends. First, the number of political tracts published in Pennsylvania rose sharply after 1725, with both Keimer and Bradford getting into the action.[60] Electioneering that year was good for business. Some of the tracts carried only indirect political meanings, such as Keimer's publication of the 1701 Charter, which had never before appeared in print. The Charter gave Lloyd and his supporters a founding text to rally around as the speaker made his pseudopopulist appeals.[61] Others took a more overt approach. Keith weighed in shortly before the election with a tract defending Lloyd's interpretation of the Charter and attacking Logan's.[62] Logan published a pamphlet contrasting the behavior of demagogues stirring up resentment against the "Men of good Stocks" in the colony with the "Honesty, Sobriety, Industry, religious Concern of Mind, and Openness of Heart" that characterized Pennsylvania's "first Settlers" and "seem[ed] . . . to have gone to the Grave with them."[63] Other authors weighed into the debate before the election, primarily on the Keithian-Lloydian side.[64]

Second, Bradford and Keimer expanded the range of political writings produced in the colony, ushering in a qualitative as well as a quantitative change in the relationship between print and politics. They published the first political satires. They also exposed their readers to contemporary British political thought. Andrew Bradford ran the first American printings of John Trenchard and Thomas Gordon's enormously influential *Cato's Letters* series in the *American Weekly Mercury* in February 1722; its popularity prompted Keimer to respond by issuing the first American imprint of Trenchard and Gordon's *Independent Whig* in 1724.[65] All these changes led to a widening of the colony's political sphere, as more voices, writing in a variety of styles, appealed to an expanding audience. The Quaker old guard, then, faced a cultural as well as electoral challenge.

Third, the Quaker Meeting's role in the print sphere also evolved during the 1720s, as the overseers of the press stepped up their efforts to print confessional literature. In 1722, the Philadelphia Yearly Meeting printed hundreds of copies of its annual epistle to local Quarterly and Monthly Meetings for the first time since 1701. It repeated this practice in 1723, 1724, 1727, and 1729.[66] Friends supported the publication of other Quaker texts as well, reissuing classic seventeenth-century tracts originally printed in England along with those produced locally. The Yearly Meeting underwrote publication of 2,000 copies of Robert Barclay's *The Antient Testimony of the People called Quakers* in 1723 and a reprint of his catechism in 1726.[67] These titles generally found a ready audience.[68] The Meeting also supported printing contemporary tracts published by British Friends and, for the first time, conversion narratives by and memorials of American Friends.[69]

The Yearly Meeting's increasing willingness to publish doctrinal literature paralleled a renewed concern among Quaker leaders with policing the boundary between those within and outside the Society, epitomized by the dissemination of an expanded "Rules of Discipline" in 1719. The expansion of Quaker print culture as Friends became a minority in the province they founded thus reflected cultural confidence and anxiety at the same time. Meeting elders no longer feared the possibility that public discussion of religious issues would lead to an open rift similar to the Keithian schism; at the same time, they sensed the need for didactic literature to acculturate their children into the Quaker faith during a period in which Friends comprised an ever smaller proportion of Pennsylvania's population. The confluence of these three trends—the ferocity of the campaign between proprietary and antiproprietary factions, the increasing complexity of colonial political discourse, and the increasing willingness of Quaker leaders to participate in provincial print culture—contributed to the fracture of the Lloyd-Keith political alliance in 1726.

"A Great Regard for Our Ancestors": The Triumph of Quaker Political Mythology

The Lloyd-Keith faction courted the electorate heavily before the 1725 elections. In addition to printed appeals, Keith assembled "Night Meetings and Entertainments" where he "cajol[ed] the people with very particular familiarities . . . Representing himself as their Champion and Deliverer" against

Logan's machinations.[70] His efforts succeeded, as the faction again won victory at the polls. Logan credited the lieutenant governor's popularity with colonial artisans and journeymen and those "vast Crowds of bold & indigent Strangers" who had recently settled in the colony.[71] Keith appeared before the newly elected Assembly on October 15 to announce his desire to work with the assemblymen to promote liberty and good order; the Assembly concurred, declaring peace and unanimity with the lieutenant governor. Each address appeared in the *American Weekly Mercury*, cementing the alliance between the executive and legislature as a textual as well as a political one.

In 1726, however, the political scene shifted against Keith. Penn began the steps to remove the lieutenant governor from office, accusing him of lying in his correspondence with her, ruining Pennsylvania's economy, and "animating the common people against the merchants to a very great degree." In March, the Privy Council approved her petition to replace Keith with Major Patrick Gordon, and Gordon arrived in Pennsylvania in June. Hoping to discredit Keith further, Logan published Penn's case against her former deputy.[72] Keith responded in kind, launching a satirical attack on the proprietary secretary. In it, he employed the same language of creole degeneracy against Logan that Quaker polemicists in the 1690s and early 1700s had. Keith lamented the contrast between English Friends, who were "a very plain, honest Good People in all their dealings," and American Friends, whom "nature" had deprived of good sense and judgment. William Penn, he suggested, would be bitterly disappointed in their actions. He also denied Quaker claims to be Pennsylvania's first settlers, noting that "great Numbers of *Swedes*" and Indians lived in the colony well before Friends' arrival.[73] In his final address to the Assembly before Gordon's installation, Keith trumpeted his service to the colony, declaring that Pennsylvania flourished more under his leadership than ever before. He had served the people and always taken pains to look with "Favour [upon] the People called *Quakers*."[74]

The Assembly's response revealed the fissures in the Lloyd-Keith alliance. Keith credited the colony's prosperity to his leadership; the legislature credited God, who had showered the colony "with many inestimable Blessings ever since it was settled." The Assembly thanked Keith for his work on behalf of Friends during negotiations with the crown over affirmations; his assistance helped restore Friends' ability to give affirmation in lieu of an oath, "a Right which they ought to have enjoyed, as at their first Settlement of this Country," before Anglican chicanery. The implications of the representatives' message were clear: Keith was their ally, not their leader. He had merely helped them return to a position of authority that was their due, as descendents of the province's founders. Keith noted the slight, declaring their address a "Dissimulation of the Truth" for minimizing his accomplishments as leader.[75] Both leaders of this faction understood the crucial role historical narrative played in legitimating power in Pennsylvania, particularly narrative pasts that invoked Penn or the province's Quaker founding. Lloyd and his supporters hoped to claim this creolized political discourse for themselves, while Keith desired to supplant it.

The 1726 election exposed these tensions, when Keith chose to run for a seat in the Assembly. Confronted with challenges on two fronts, old-guard Friends who had held power before Lloyd's reemergence resigned themselves to the fact that they would have to make some accommodation to the popular speaker. Logan summed up the feelings of many when he doubted Lloyd's ability ever to cooperate fully with the proprietary family; "the Ethiopian" could not, he wrote, "change his skin." Nonetheless, "Rather than leave any chance to S[i]r W[illiam], of those evils, one would choose the least."[76] In other words, tribal identity offered some hope of overcoming political disunity. They saw their worst fears realized on election day, when "numbers of Vile people" who "may Truly be call'd a Mob" turned out to vote for Keith and his allies. Staging "Bonfires[,] Gunns[,] and Huzzas" and shouting "Keith forever," they voted the former lieutenant governor into office. They proceeded to burn down the pillory, stock, and butcher stalls in downtown Philadelphia for good measure.[77] Keith's campaign had unleashed a leveling spirit among the people.

And then the threat receded at what seemed its high point. On 15 October the opening of the first session of the newly elected Assembly, Keith arrived in Philadelphia leading a procession of "Eighty Horses composed of Butchers[,] Taylors[,] Blacksmiths, Journeymen[,] Apprentices[,] Porters[,] and Carters marching two by two." This display, he believed, was merely prelude to his selection as speaker of the Assembly. The legislature soon dashed Keith's hopes when, "to his great Mortification [he] was not so much as proposed" for the post by any assemblyman.[78] Returning Lloyd to his position, the representatives left "the great Sir William . . . dwindled down to the low Degree of an Assembly man in common with other members."[79] Keith's march had celebrated "Triumphantly his Gradations Downward from a Governor to an Equal with Every plain Country Member" of the legislature.[80] The majority-Quaker Assembly backed one of its own over the man they now treated as a usurper.

Patrick Gordon, Keith's replacement as lieutenant governor, ratified the political mythology Lloyd and Logan championed. Having expressed in his first address to the Assembly his great regard for the Penn family, Gordon informed the legislature after the election of his certainty that Pennsylvanians "may be a happy people, if we can but act worthy of those Blessings, which seem to have attended . . . those sober Good People who have joined their Endeavour's to the Settlement of this Colony."[81] Gordon conceded Friends' cultural authority as provincial founders as the price of doing politics in Quaker Pennsylvania.

Conflict between Keith's faction and the Quaker political elite continued throughout 1727, but the former lieutenant governor's fortunes faded rapidly following his failed bid for the post of speaker in 1726. Keith made another run for the Assembly in 1727, with his supporters making similar appeals on their leader's behalf. Isaac Norris countered with a paper reminding the voters how honored Pennsylvania was to have been first settled by Friends with a unique sense of "vertue, wisdom, and ability" as well as "a sincere Zeal for God." Voting to keep Quakers in office, he argued, would show sincere love of country: "By such a conduct, we shall show ourselves worthy successors of those valuable persons, the first settlers of this province, and may leave our prosperity the like examples."[82] Pennsylvania's freemen could secure the virtue and prosperity of their descendents by deferring to the authority of the descendants of the founders.

Norris's argument won the day. Voters reelected Keith, but he again failed to unseat Lloyd as speaker. He left Pennsylvania for England in early 1728, leaving his supporters without a champion.[83] The publication of a pamphlet revealing Keith's plans to turn Pennsylvania into a royal colony further weakened his faction.[84] Lloyd's public accusation, issued on behalf of the entire Assembly, that Keith had instilled in his followers the same "Wild and Daring" spirit that had driven Jacobites to rise up against the Hanovarian monarchy completely discredited the insurgent party's legitimacy.[85]

Leading Friends in Pennsylvania thus approached the 1728 elections with a spirit of unanimity that they had lacked for some years. Lloyd turned tactics he had used against Logan and the proprietary family against his former allies. When protestors challenged Lloyd's decision to leave Keith's seat vacant after the latter left the colony, he issued a paper defending his power to do so. The protestors lacked Lloyd's "great Regard our Ancestors have always had for fundamental Laws," one of which guaranteed a legislature's right to determine the qualifications of its own members. Lloyd cited nearly every conceivable ancestral authority to make his case: reason, Sir Edward Coke's *Institutes*, William Penn's several writings on liberty and property, the 1682 royal charter, and the 1701 Charter of Privileges. He even drew on James Logan's 1725 "memorial" to the Assembly, the very document that had spurred him to write his *Vindication*. "Our" ancestors, he reminded the public, were English and Quaker, even as the colony became less English and less Quaker with every boatload of immigrants. Members of the newly resurgent Quaker party, Lloyd argued, were the true heirs to the province's political tradition and uniquely capable of protecting the English and Pennsylvanian rights the colonists possessed.[86]

The imperative leading Friends felt to rewrite provincial history once again reflected the overriding need that had shaped politics in Pennsylvania from its inception: the problem of articulating a civic discourse that Quakers and non-Quakers alike found legitimate. Lloyd, Logan, and Norris drew on several legal and political traditions to create a new civic language. They subsumed this political discourse, however, within a broader mythic history of Pennsylvania as a special place thriving under the leadership of wise stewards.[87] And yet the persuasiveness of this creolized civic discourse relied on the same denial that defined Quaker identity in Pennsylvania. Orthodox Friends had responded to dissent during the schism by turning George Keith's accusations of creole degeneracy against him. They needed to believe that they had not changed in America; they needed to believe that their collective identity as Friends had remained constant as they adjusted to the entire host of challenges colonization presented.

Admitting the possibility that Quakerism had creolized would have undercut the very basis of Friends' claims to political authority. What right did they have to rule if they had deviated from the example set by their brethren who had settled the colony? Friends had not changed in the four decades since Pennsylvania's founding, even if the colony around them had. In their printed appeals, they offered non-Quakers a chance to reverse the political degeneracy that plagued the province: voters could recognize Friends' claim to power and keep them in office. By accepting the legitimacy of this political narrative, "the people" could become coparticipants in Pennsylvania's special mission.

The malleability of this creole civic discourse was what made it successful. After all, there was nothing inevitable about Sir William Keith's defeat. His political appeals, which stressed popular political participation, obeisance to royal authority, and economic reform seemingly fit Pennsylvania's mood in the 1720s more than the conservative Quaker platform did. Quaker leaders proved more adaptable, however. Confronted with the fact that the old civic discourse they used no longer carried the same legitimacy it once had, they first created a new civic lingua franca to win the approval of the province's freemen and then developed it into a more elaborate set of practices and languages. Each time they told political parables of Pennsylvania's founding, they added new details and told the stories in new ways—all the while denying that anything had changed. These parables connected the present and past of Quaker power in such a manner as to make its truth not merely unquestioned but unquestionable. The constant reiteration of these stories made and remade Quaker Pennsylvania politically and culturally.

The Quaker coalition prevailed at the polls in 1728, keeping Lloyd and his allies in power. Friends would dominate the Assembly for the next quarter century, comprising between 50 and 90 percent of the legislature in every year but one during that period.[88] Moreover, their legislative power increased even while their portion of the colonial population decreased, as immigration from northern Ireland was supplemented by the arrival of tens of thousands of German migrants.[89] The electorate, in other words, found this Quaker narrative more compelling as the population grew more diverse. This language of Quaker power shaped the acculturation of successive waves of immigrants into Pennsylvania's political system. These stories of Pennsylvania's Quaker past were the political fables they learned as they became provincial citizens.

A tract under the name Constant Truman nearly a decade after Keith's defeat perhaps best captured Friends' success in naturalizing their own legitimacy. Published before the 1735 elections, this *Advice to the Free-holders and Electors of Pennsylvania* exemplified the power and ambiguity of Quaker political rhetoric, celebrating equality and Quaker power simultaneously. The *Advice* opened with a celebration of English liberties, declaring how happy Pennsylvanians were to live in a society where "we are at Liberty to Declare our Thoughts freely to one another, concerning *Publick Affairs.*" A Pennsylvania freeman did not suffer under an arbitrary government with "his Mind enslaved, his Tongue tied, his Hands fettered and his Legs chained, just as the Humour or Wantonness of a Great MAN, without any Regard to Justice and the Laws," saw fit to appoint. Truman denounced deference, warning readers that "if you can once be frightened by the Threats & Frowns of great men, from speaking your Minds freely . . . you are no longer Freemen, but Slaves, [and] Beasts of Burden" to those at the top of the social hierarchy.[90]

Truman linked this attack on deference to Quaker control, arguing that "as long as we have the Descendants of the late Honourable *WILLIAM PENN* among us. . . . We'll laugh at any insolent Fellow that shall pretend to tell us, that we must say as he says, and do as he doth, . . . because he hath a greater Estate than some of us have, or the like." Urging voters to elect "worthy honest" leaders, he challenged his readers to stand up to grasping individuals, asking them "What (my Friends) are you afraid to act like Men . . . ?" For Truman, deferring to Quaker leadership was the ultimate way Pennsylvania's voters could fight deference toward social elites and fashion themselves as virtuous civic men. Truman's appeal epitomized the political discourse of the period, as Friends' political power reached its zenith in the 1730s and 1740s.[91]

These stories of Pennsylvania's founding carried weight on the province's boundaries as well. Provincial leaders in the 1710s and 1720s faced an increasingly unstable diplomatic world, as new native groups jockeyed for power on the province's borders. The struggle for power in the backcountry heightened colonial and Indian negotiators' desire to find a workable, legitimate diplomatic culture that each side might find legitimate.

Folktales of Justice: The Death of Sawantaeny

In early January 1722, near the Pennsylvania-Maryland border, Sawantaeny, a Seneca man living in an ethnically mixed Indian settlement with his Shawnee wife Weynepeeweyta, was killed by the English trader John Cartlidge. The short version of the story is really quite simple.[92] Sawantaeny died after a drunken argument with Cartlidge in which the former accused the latter of failing to deliver all the rum he was owed. Sawantaeny may or may not have gone back to his cabin to get his rifle, but in any case the disagreement quickly became physical. Cartlidge, thinking his life was endangered, assaulted Sawantaeny, eventually kicking him to death. With the help of Civility (Tagotolessa), a Conestoga Indian who had served as a translator and go-between on the Pennsylvania frontier, John and his brother Edmund—another trader present—arranged a hurried condolence ceremony and burial for Sawantaeny in the hope that authorities in Philadelphia would not discover what had transpired.

The Cartlidges' attempts to keep this death on the Monocacy River a secret were in vain. Word of the Seneca man's death reached Philadelphia, and the Provincial Council sent officials James Logan and Colonel John French to the frontier town of Conestoga to investigate in March. Finding substantial evidence of Cartlidge's responsibility, they decided to try him according to English law. French and Logan realized, however, the impracticality of "get[ting] such a Number of Christians to undertake that Journey [to Conestoga] as would constitute a legal jury." Thus, they had John and Edmund taken to Philadelphia to face a criminal court there. After releasing the Cartlidges on bail, the Provincial Council sent word to Conestoga to try to recover Sawantaeny's body so that the trial could proceed.

The spring and summer brought several councils between the provincial government and diplomats representing Delaware, Shawnee, Conestoga, and Iroquois Indians, with each tribe offering its own take on what the Cartlidges' fate should be and how Sawantaeny's death should be resolved. Finally, in September, the Iroquois diplomat Tanachaha asked Pennsylvania's lieutenant governor William Keith for clemency for John Cartlidge. Against the wishes of provincial legislators who wanted to try him for murder, Keith set Cartlidge free and gave the Iroquois a £110 gift.[93] Relations between Indians and Pennsylvanians along the frontier returned to normal—for the early eighteenth century. Edmund even obtained a license from the legislature to buy and sell Indian lands years later.

That is the short version of the story of Sawantaeny's death. But this version raises as many questions as it answers. Why was it so difficult to convene a jury on the frontier? Who would have composed the jury in a case such as this? Why did representatives from two Indian groups ask that Cartlidge be granted clemency? Why was Pennsylvania's government so hesitant to grant that request? It also raises questions about the significance Sawantaeny achieved in death. Why did this particular instance of frontier violence come to involve representatives from so many different nations—Conestogas, Shawnees, and Delawares as well as Iroquois?

Answering these questions means investigating the folktales of justice the participants used to resolve the jurisdictional conflicts the case presented. All the parties involved told stories about the relationship between Pennsylvania's government and various Indian nations to justify why their particular rules of order should be used to resolve the dispute. They told these folktales of justice to make their rules law.[94]

The Indians and colonists faced with the task of burying Sawantaeny looked to precedent to plot their actions and rewrote the past to explain the meaning of these actions. Moreover, both natives and colonists invoked narratives of the past to justify the sovereignty of their legal claims over competing ones. In other words, the diplomatic councils convened in the spring and summer of 1722 to discuss how to handle Sawantaeny's death were themselves contests over legal myths and historical accounts. The various sides in the negotiations told very different stories of recent events on the frontier, accounts they contextualized in different ways.[95] Both the Indians living on the Susquehanna and the Iroquois justified their authority on this matter by invoking idealized histories of their friendship with William Penn, the province's founder.

Lieutenant Governor Keith's position relied on a very different understanding of Penn's history with the Indians, one that cast the proprietor's relationship with the natives as benevolent paternalism, not a reciprocal friendship. Settling the jurisdictional questions surrounding Sawantaeny's death meant adjudicating these different narratives. The debate over legal authority at the time of the Seneca's death created an arena of conflict for natives and newcomers alike. Understanding this incident involves understanding the context in which it occurred; it means looking at evolving legal boundaries on a shifting frontier and exploring the ways the handling of such episodes changed over time. This intercultural homicide provides a window onto the changing dynamics of law, authority, and power among and between Native Americans and the immigrants who had settled in Pennsylvania.

Investigating the Cartlidges

On 14 March 1722, James Logan and Colonel John French, representing the proprietary government, held a council at Conestoga with leaders from the Conestoga and Delaware Indians. The provincial records noted the presence of "divers English and Indians."[96] Logan, addressing the Indians as his "Friends and Brethren," opened the meeting by invoking the memory of William Penn and the "firm League of Friendship and Brotherhood" the founder had established with Pennsylvania's native peoples. "Agree[ing] that both you and his People should be as one Flesh and Blood," Penn and the Indians' predecessors had covenanted that neither side should suffer injury to the other. Having heard, then, "that one of our Brethren had lost his Life by some Act of Violence, alledged to be done by some of our People," Logan had called the council "so that Justice may be done." He concluded his address with a final call for friendship, noting that "We shall suffer no Injury to be done to any of you without punishing the offenders according to our Laws."[97]

Through translators, including Civility, Logan interviewed witnesses at Conestoga. Despite conflicting reports, some elements of the case quickly became clear. The Cartlidges, assisted by two servants, William Wilkins and Jonathan Swindel, had traveled to the frontier hoping to trade rum for furs; they found a ready market for their wares. All agreed that Sawantaeny had received quite a bit of rum and been drinking through the night before his run-in with John Cartlidge. That morning "the Sinnekae said he must have more Rum, for that he had not received all he had bought." After Cartlidge refused him, the Indian went back to his cabin to retrieve his gun.[98] When he emerged, Edmund Cartlidge and Wilkins managed to grab Sawantaeny's gun, and, after "stripping off his clothes," John Cartlidge assaulted him. Following repeated blows, Sawantaeny managed to crawl back to his cabin, where he died the next day.[99]

By 17 March, Logan and French had heard enough to send John and Edmund Cartlidge to Philadelphia in sheriff's custody "for suspicion of Killing the Indian mentioned in their report."[100] They decided to try the Cartlidges in the provincial capital, not on the frontier. This choice was not perfect, for it meant that the jury would be unable to see a key piece of evidence—the body of the dead man. As the two Pennsylvania commissioners noted, Sawantaeny's corpse had been buried in the woods, "three days thence" from Conestoga, making it "impracticable" for the commissioners "to get such a Number of Christians to undertake that Journey as would constitute a legal Jury."[101] Despite this problem, the Cartlidges arrived in Philadelphia on March 22 and were granted bail two days later.

Sawantaeny's case did not pose new jurisdictional problems. Legal boundaries had been one of the first issues William Penn had addressed at Pennsylvania's founding, when the legislature passed laws regulating the conduct of sailors and other travelers to the colony. Penn also called for the creation of "mixed" juries in criminal cases involving colonists and Indians, with "six on each side" to settle the matter.[102] No evidence exists, however, that such a mixed jury was ever called. Moreover, although colonials frequently discussed Indians in provincial courts—with some colonists tried for violating laws regulating Indian affairs—Indians themselves rarely appeared before the bar. And while there had been instances of interracial homicide on the Pennsylvania frontier before, Sawantaeny's death was the first time the

Provincial Council had concerned itself with a homicide in which an Indian was the victim.[103]

Thus, Logan and French had little precedent to guide them in deciding the Cartlidges' fate. There is no direct evidence that either was aware of the province's early statute calling for mixed-jury trials, but in any case, it would have been difficult—if not impossible—to apply.[104] This law stated that when an Indian had been wronged, the provincial government was required to contact "the king to whom such Indian belonged" so that he could summon an appropriate group of Indian peers to be impaneled in the jury. Given Sawantaeny's ambiguous ethnic and political affiliations, however, Logan and French would have had a difficult time determining his "king." As a Seneca man living on the Pennsylvania frontier—outside Seneca and Iroquois country—with a Shawnee wife amid bands of Delaware, Shawnee, and Conestoga Indians, under whose jurisdiction was Sawantaeny living? To whom did he belong?[105]

Faced with the prospect of entering legally uncharted territory, the two councilors fell back on a familiar legal system: their own. But their decision to apply English law to settle the murder of an Indian man may have resulted less from their legal reasoning than from their interpretation of changing political relationships on the frontier. Sawantaeny's death occurred during a period in which the rhetoric of Pennsylvania's diplomats toward their Indian counterparts was changing. While Pennsylvanians continued to mention the peace and harmony that had existed between them and the Indians, they also increasingly stressed the importance of using European methods of conflict resolution to maintain that amity. The Provincial Council had warned the Conestoga Indians in 1715 that they should "be very careful on their parts that no difference should arise between any of their and our people, or if there should that they would acquaint us with it immediately, that we might duly inquire into it, and Justice should be done them if they were in any way wronged."[106] Keith gave a similar warning to Conestoga diplomats two years later.[107]

Sawantaeny's death presented Pennsylvania's government with a test case, an opportunity to increase the authority of the colonial legal system over the province's Indians by ensuring that "Justice" would be determined according to European rules. Provincial magistrates may have disagreed sharply over matters of policy and power, as the feud between Keith and Logan demonstrated. Yet neither Logan nor Keith questioned the appropriateness of applying English laws to the Sawantaeny affair. Provincial officials who had never before made any attempt to bring Indians into provincial courts suddenly became interested in the prospect in the aftermath of this murder. They realized that providing equal justice to Indians and colonists provided the colonial government a means of expanding provincial sovereignty farther west.[108]

Brother Miquon Versus Brother Onas

The colonial government continued to negotiate with the province's Indians to determine the Cartlidges' fate after the court released them at the end of March 1722. Governor William Keith, in a council at Civility's cabin in Conestoga in early April 1722, reiterated his government's commitment to equal justice. Addressing the "Chiefs of the Mingoes, the Shawanois, and the Ganaway," Keith reminded them "that if any one hurts an Indian He will be tryed and punished in the same manner as if he had done it to an English Man."[109] He then asserted that he thought he had "acted herein like a true Friend and Brother," adding that he expected the Indians to "look upon me even as a child would respect and obey the Words of a tender father." Keith noted that he anticipated the Cartlidges would be tried "as soon as . . . any . . . Proof can be had that the Indian is dead or was actually killed by them."[110]

For Keith, inheriting Penn's mantle meant protecting natives with benevolent paternalism. Aquila Rose, Keith's court poet, captured the lieutenant governor's self-image as a great lawgiver in a poem after a June 1721 treaty conference at Conestoga:

> To *Indians* thou [Keith] shalt a *Lycurgus* be,
> Who Ages hence shall almost worship thee. . . .
> The *Indian* Children shall be taught thy Name,
> And Woods and Rivers Echo with thy Fame:
> . . . The *Indian* Nations round thy Name applaud,
> And call thee, not unjustly, like a God.[111]

Civility did not share Rose's view of Keith, however. Responding to Keith's attempt to assume Penn's mantle, he noted that the local Indians were "ready to receive [Keith's] Words, and . . . willing and content to follow his Advice: For they know the Governour to be Absolute Rule[r], and it becomes them to submit." Yet Indians revered the memory of William Penn, Civility argued, precisely because the proprietor did not "Call them Children or Brothers only: For often Parents would be apt to whip their Children too severely; and Brothers sometimes differ." In an oblique reference to the role of alcohol in Sawantaeny's death, Civility concluded by reminding Keith that Penn himself had hoped to prohibit the sale of rum to Indians. If Keith wanted to act paternal, he could take more useful steps to protect them. Natives would prosper, he argued, without the rum that came among them contrary to Penn's promise. The Conestoga diplomat punctuated his invocation of Penn's memory by "Holding a Parchment in his Hand which they received from William Penn."[112] In the end, while Keith agreed to check the amount of rum that reached the Indians, the question of the Cartlidges' fate—and the reach of English law on the frontier—had not been settled.

After the April meeting at Conestoga, negotiation regarding the Cartlidges continued. In May, messengers from the Iroquois Confederacy and the Conestoga Indians arrived in Philadelphia to discuss Sawantaeny's death and the provincial government's response.[113] Keith reminded the Iroquois that the Cartlidges must be tried "by the Laws of our Great King." Once he had finished trying the Cartlidges according to English law, he continued, he would be happy to meet with more Indian delegates. While Indian custom called for those who killed another to make monetary or material reparations to the family of the deceased, English law could not be "alter[ed] or disobey[ed] . . . in the least point" and could not allow such a form of justice; instead, a jury would have to determine if John Cartlidge acted in the heat of passion or in cold blood. If the latter, he would be executed. In other words, neither the Iroquois nor the Indians on the Susquehanna should concern themselves with the Cartlidges' fate.[114]

Keith continued to meet with representatives of the Iroquois nations throughout the summer, reiterating his desire to punish the Cartlidges "in the same manner as if they had killed an Englishman."[115] The Iroquois, however, steadfastly urged John Cartlidge's release. In August, their messenger Satcheechoe told Keith that the Iroquois "desired John Cartlidge might be released out of Prison, and the injury done to [their] Kinsman be forgot."[116] During a September council at Albany, Tanachaha told Keith that "we think it hard the persons who killed our friend and Brother should suffer, and we do in the name of all of the five Nations forgive the offence, and desire You will likewise forgive it, and that the men who did it may be released from Prison and set at Liberty, to go wither they please."[117] Tanachaha used Sawantaeny's status as a Seneca to press his claim, as they were brothers in the Iroquois league. Deferring to Tanachaha, Keith told him that, on his return to Philadelphia, the Cartlidges would be set free. The next day, the Iroquois surrendered to Pennsylvania all claims to the lands around Conestoga where Sawantaeny was killed; Tanachaha's profession of authority over his fellow Iroquois had been transformed overnight into a declaration of Iroquois sovereignty over the entire region and the Indians who lived in it. Following this, the lieutenant governor and the Indians exchanged gifts, cementing Pennsylvania's position as a treaty partner in the Iroquois Covenant Chain.[118] The Sawantaeny incident was, for all intents and purposes, over.

Retelling the end of *l'affaire Sawantaeny* does not, however, answer one of the central questions the negotiations raised: why did both the Iroquois nations and the Indians on the Susquehanna work for the Cartlidges' release? Iroquois motives differed from those of the Conestoga, Delaware, and Shawnee Indians on whose behalf Civility negotiated, but they seem relatively straightforward. The Six Nations appear to have gotten what they wanted. Although Keith refused to call his £110 gift at the Albany conference a "condolence payment" to atone for Sawantaeny's death, it appears to have functioned as such in everything except name. Moreover, Keith's decision to grant the Iroquois request for clemency after he had denied similar requests from the Indians on the Susquehanna effectively recognized the Iroquois as the dominant Indian power in the region.[119] While both Indian groups had claimed Sawantaeny as a "brother," Keith's selective gift-giving and treaty-making legitimated only the Iroquois claim. The Iroquois used the Seneca man's death as an occasion to display their affection toward Keith, seizing the opportunity to strengthen their diplomatic ties to the province and weaken those between Pennsylvania and the Indians on the Susquehanna.

This may summarize the Iroquois' motives, but it does not explain why Civility would have worked for the Cartlidges' release on behalf of the other Indian groups along the Susquehanna. Civility hinted at their thinking in the statement he made to Keith at that conference at Conestoga in April 1722. Recalling the founder's words about Europeans and Indians being of "one Blood," Civility challenged Keith's attempt to play the "Father" to his native "Children," with all the inequality these terms implied. This objection to familial language suggests that he rejected the terms on which Pennsylvania had hoped to incorporate the indigenous people around Conestoga into a political and legal system in which justice meant European justice. The absence of natives in provincial courts, then, was a result of Indian as well as colonial choices.

Civility's invocation of Penn also served as a reminder that the colonists had not lived up to all their agreements to live in harmony with the Indians. Embedded within Civility's acquiescence to the lieutenant governor's "Absolute Rule," then, was a critique of the ways in which that rule had been enforced. By retelling the story of Penn's treaty with the Indians, Civility challenged the legal narrative in which Keith contextualized European-Indian relations, framing them instead within the local history of Pennsylvania's frontier.[120] This narrative of friendship and alliance, not metaphors of bodily or familial interconnection, provided the dominant linguistic frame for Civility's claims.[121] He justified his political claims with reference to a mythic history of Pennsylvania, one in which those people he spoke for had played a crucial role.

Civility's response to Keith's speech was not unique. Sawantaeny had died during a period in which colonial-Indian negotiations waged semantic battles over terms of address. While European negotiators often referred to Indians as "Brothers" or, less often, "Children," Indians stressed, as Civility did, that Indians and Europeans were of "one Blood" in "two parts."[122] Provincial-Indian negotiators also fought over interpreting recent diplomatic history. During the decade before Sawantaeny's death, Indian negotiators had invoked Penn's promises to Conestoga and Delaware Indians to critique what they viewed as illegal and unethical encroachments by settlers and traders on native lands. In 1715, for example, Sassoonan, speaking for the Delawares, informed Lieutenant Governor Charles Gookin during a meeting at Philadelphia that his people had come "to renew the former bond of friendship that William Penn had, at his first coming," made with them, implying that Penn's successors had not filled the founder's shoes. Three months later Sotyriote, speaking for the Conestogas, also used Penn's example to chastise Gookin mildly.[123]

These negotiators' claims to a special relationship with "Miquon"—the Delaware name for Penn—were pointed challenges not only to Pennsylvania's government but also to Iroquois diplomats who invoked their old relationship with "Onas," as the Iroquois named him.[124] They also represented some jockeying for position between the Delawares and Conestogas, as each tried to make itself the premier group among Indian nations along the Susquehanna. By grounding the negotiations within mythohistoric narratives of peace, Indian diplomats such as Civility, Sassoonan, and Sotyriote shifted the discussion away from Euro-American frames of justice and legitimacy into a moral context more familiar to Delaware Valley Indians.[125]

Civility revealed the motivations behind this frame switch in a speech at a treaty council in May 1723. When told by Keith that English "Laws make no distinction between our people and yours," Civility, speaking on behalf of the Indians on the Susquehanna, dissented. He told Keith that "The Indians well approve of all the Governor Had said except where he told them that the English Law made no difference between the English and the Indians, for they should not like, upon an Indian's committing a fault, that he should be imprisoned as they had seen some Englishmen were."[126]

This statement demonstrated the stakes involved in managing Sawantaeny's death. Civility asked the Pennsylvania government to grant John Cartlidge clemency because the Indians wanted to remain independent of European laws in the face of colonial expansion. Equal justice under English law implied acceptance of English sovereignty. He simultaneously fought Iroquois efforts to adjudicate the affair because he hoped to stem the Confederacy's influence southward. Civility wanted to bury Sawantaeny immediately because he felt that this outcome best secured a measure of autonomy for the Indians on the Susquehanna, even as the Delaware, Conestoga, and Shawnee maneuvered among each other for status and influence.[127]

Keith's decision to make restitution to the confederacy for Sawantaeny's death thus represented a partial victory for the assorted Indian nations on the Susquehanna. On the one hand, it temporarily checked the expansion of English law. The colonial government was not able to make its rules law, despite its best efforts. But this outcome did sanction Iroquois claims to rule the Susquehanna Valley. Pennsylvania's Indians found themselves increasingly vulnerable to encroachment from the north, even as they resisted encroachment from the east.[128]

Equal Justice on the Colonial Frontier

The resolution of Sawantaeny's death did not settle the problems underlying the difficult negotiations of 1722 and 1723. A series of unrelated homicides in 1728 brought these thorny jurisdictional problems to a head. In early May, Walter and John Winter, two brothers living on Skippack Creek on the Pennsylvania frontier, received a report—incorrect, as it turned out—that Indians had killed two nearby colonials. Having recently heard rumors of an impending invasion led by foreign or "Spanish Indians," the Winters decided to take matters into their own hands. Electing to "defend" themselves against attack, they grabbed their rifles and went immediately to a nearby cabin where a Delaware man, Tacocolie, lived with his family. There they opened fire, killing Tacocolie, his wife Quilee, and their son and wounding their two daughters.[129]

Lieutenant Governor Gordon responded immediately, apprehending the Winter brothers for murder. He convened a council at Conestoga to meet with Conestoga, Shawnee, Delaware, and Conoy diplomats to tell them he was "grieved . . . exceedingly" by the news of the Winters' actions. He assured the Indian diplomats that the murderers had been captured "and are now in Irons in a Dungeon to be tried by the Laws of the Great King of all the English, as if they had Killed so many of his Subjects." Gordon also noted that provincial officials had found the bodies of the Winters' victims "who by my order were laid in a Grave and covered with Shirts and Strowds."[130] The Winters were hanged that July, in Philadelphia. Their corpses became a sign, to Indians and provincials alike, of Gordon's punitive legal potency. Their gallows confessions appeared in the *American Weekly Mercury*, a warning to all citizens to avoid their example.[131]

But Gordon's concerns went beyond the death of Tacocolie and the punishment of his murderers. He also used this council as an occasion to bring up another killing. Eight months earlier, Gordon had received a report that some Indian warriors had murdered an Englishman named John Burt in Snake Town. Now he "expect[ed] the Indians will doe us Justice by apprehending the Murtherers that they may be punished."[132] Their obligations to reciprocate in the wake of the Winters' execution demanded as much. Through this appeal, Gordon not only denominated provincial jurisprudence as the appropriate standard for "equal" justice, but he also claimed "Onas"— Pennsylvania's government—as the only sovereign capable of meting out equal and appropriate punishment to Indian and colonist alike. While he accepted the Indians' collective refusal to pursue the accused on the grounds that the murder at Snake Town had been committed by an Indian "of another Nation," he did not relent from his initial position that equal punishment meant Anglo-American punishment.

Gordon made his position even clearer later that year when he received a report that a servant named Timothy Higgins had died at the hands of Shawnee warriors.[133] Calling a council at Philadelphia with Delaware, Iroquois, and "Brandywine" Indians, Gordon reminded his assembled guests of the speed with which he meted out justice against the Winters.[134] Accordingly, he hoped these Indian leaders might locate the Snake Town murderer as well as the Shawnees who had killed Higgins. Gordon cited his actions after Tacocolie's death again at treaty conferences in 1731 and 1735.[135] Civility had tried to bury Sawantaeny quickly and without fanfare. Gordon, on the other hand, felt compelled to exhume the Winter brothers symbolically so he could ostentatiously kill them over and over again. This was part of his relentless campaign to convince Native Americans that English law should prevail on the frontier.[136] And at every step, Gordon took pains to invoke Penn's ancient friendship with the Indians, much as Civility, Tanachaha, and Sassoonan used narratives of their peoples' relationships with the proprietor. Both sides found historical narratives of Pennsylvania's founding useful in advancing their political claims.

The Iroquois took advantage of this situation to build their own relationship with Pennsylvania. Since the early 1720s, the Iroquois had pressed their claim to rule the Susquehanna by right of conquest with increasing frequency and vehemence. They moved in the 1730s to cement an alliance with colonial officials predicated on the disenfranchisement of the Indians on Pennsylvania's western boundary. In 1732, negotiators from the confederacy acquiesced to Gordon's demand to return any fugitive slaves owned by Pennsylvanians. That the Iroquois lacked any means of enforcing these agreements was largely irrelevant to the Conestoga, Delaware, and Shawnee Indians. What mattered was the colonial government's willingness to accept Iroquois claims that they had the right to alienate their sovereignty over the region.

Iroquois diplomats found a ready partner in Gordon, who had sweetened his demands about harboring fugitive slaves with an acknowledgment of Confederacy sovereignty over the Shawnee in the Susquehanna Valley.[137] In 1735, at the lieutenant governor's last treaty conference, Civility invoked the 1700 and 1701 treaties between Penn, his representatives, and the Conestoga and the Shawnee Indians as a sign of these tribes' political independence from the Iroquois. Gordon not only rejected the Conestoga negotiator's claims to political independence, he denied the Susquehanna Indians any autonomy at all. He insisted that from that moment forward, if these assorted Indian nations wanted to remain in Pennsylvania's good graces, they must treat as enemies all other natives "without some sufficient Credential from this Government to show that they come as Friends." Gordon effectively denied the Conestoga and Shawnee Indians the right to determine their allies and enemies.[138]

Historical narratives mattered in Indian politics just as they did in provincial politics. Native and colonial diplomats alike appropriated the mantle of William Penn for strategic purposes; agents on all sides hoped that invoking their (fictitious) relationship with him might lend authority to their claims. Ultimately, one particular narrative prevailed: that of Penn the lawgiver. The counternarrative put forth by Civility and others, in which Penn and local Indians were coparticipants in creating a harmonious, reciprocal colonial space, lost. Ironically, perhaps, Civility's vision more closely resembled the political fables put forth by Logan and Norris, stories that insisted that Penn and the colonists, having settled the colony together, bore credit and responsibility for its success, than those put forth by Keith and Gordon. Keith and Gordon were Penn's heirs in one particular respect: where Penn claimed to be the lawgiver who secured colonial rights through his heroic endeavors, his successors as lieutenant governor adopted the mantle of lawgiver and justice providers for local Indians. These lieutenant governors succeeded, in a sense, where Penn had failed. They managed to impose their sovereignty over Indians living to their west, even as the natives questioned the legitimacy of the folktales of justice they told.

The "Walking Purchase" and William Penn's Legacy

Perhaps nothing encapsulated this complex dynamic more than the Indian policy of William Penn's children. Thomas, Richard, and John Penn inherited Pennsylvania after their mother Hannah's death in 1725 and assumed control over the province in 1732. They swiftly showed that they possessed all their father's defects as a proprietor but nothing of his good intentions. In particular, they shared their father's tendency to live beyond their means. By 1734, they were deeply in debt and at the mercy of their creditors.[139]

They turned to their only potential source of revenue: sale of provincial lands. Thomas Penn, who had moved to America to become the colony's resident governor, instructed James Logan to start surveying lands along the forks of the Delaware, on the colony's northeastern edge. His brothers, meanwhile, began to secure buyers in Britain. The Penn brothers had one major problem, however. They had not secured title to the land from the Delaware Indians who lived there. Furthermore, Delaware leaders rebuffed Logan's efforts to purchase the land in 1735.

Desperate to extricate themselves from this quandary, the Penns developed a two-pronged strategy. First, they looked to the past, specifically, a 1686 agreement between William Penn and the Lenape Indians. The Lenape, Logan argued, had sold a tract of land between the Delaware River and Neshaminy Creek, "extend[ing] . . . back into the Woods as far as a Man can go in one day and a half." Though the proprietor had paid for the land, Logan argued, the purchase had never been finalized; no one had yet made the walk determining its final boundaries. Logan's claims were of dubious provenance, as the original deed did not exist. He did, however produce a supposed copy of this agreement, albeit one which lacked signatures. Delaware leaders challenged the veracity of the document. The sachem Nuntimus questioned Logan's ability to vouch for the deed, noting that the secretary "was not born in this Country."[140] Nonetheless, Delaware leaders eventually relented, signing a deed in August 1737 confirming the original sale.

The provincial government engaged in a good degree of power politics as well, looking to the Iroquois to enlist their aid in this attempt to acquire the land on the forks of the Delaware River. Logan expected Iroquois assistance. The Six Nations had been "highly pleased with our Conduct towards them" since "the great Treaty at Albany in 1722"—the council held to settle Sawantaeny's death.[141] His prediction proved accurate. Citing their long friendship with "Brother *ONAS*," the Six Nations entered into three agreements with Pennsylvania in September 1736. First, provincials formally declared that the Iroquois were sole sovereigns, by right of conquest, of the Indian tribes in Pennsylvania and that no sachems from these tribes could sell land without the Confederacy's permission. Second, the Iroquois sold all land on both sides of the Susquehanna River to Pennsylvania and relinquished all claims to land between the Delaware River and the Kittatiny Mountains—precisely the territory the government was hoping to buy from the Delaware Indians. Finally, the Iroquois agreed to recognize Pennsylvania's legal jurisdiction over the frontier, promising to turn any Indian thought to have harmed a colonist over to provincial magistrates for prosecution.[142] These agreements represented the culmination of the provincial government's long campaign to deny Indians along the Susquehanna River their sovereignty, a process that facilitated expansion of colonial settlements westward. The Six Nations, for their part, found these treaties beneficial politically and financially.

These negotiations also secured Iroquois consent for the justifiably infamous "Walking Purchase" of September 1737.[143] The provincial government and the Delaware selected September 19 and 20 as the days when the boundary line would be walked off and the 1686 purchase finalized. The Penns prepared well for the event. They selected three walkers, sent out an advance party to mark a path, readied supply horses, and promised 500 acres to the one who covered the most territory. The pace proved too much for two of the three men; one dropped out after the first day, while another exerted himself so strenuously that he died a few weeks later. Edward Marshall, however, the third individual sent into the woods, managed to cover more than sixty miles in a day and a half. Marshall having done his job, colonial surveyors then did theirs. Through a creative interpretation of the 1737 deed confirmation, they drew expansive boundaries around the new tract. Moving from the agreed-upon starting point on the Delaware River, the surveyors proceeded northwest more than sixty miles inland along the line Marshall had laid out. Then they made a 90-degree turn and traveled another sixty-plus miles northeast toward the border with New York and New Jersey. All told, the "Walking Purchase" covered around 1,110 square miles, slightly less than the entire colony of Rhode Island, larger than the plot the Delaware thought they were selling by several orders of magnitude.

The Penns, with Logan's assistance, had proven the power of the myth of "Onas." Privileging the narrative of the founder's friendships with the confederacy over his relationships with the Delaware, Conestoga, or Shawnee Indians, they ratified a dubious myth of conquest. The Penn sons transformed his desire to treat Indians with justice into a means of extending their legal authority far into the colonial hinterlands. And they invoked a falsified treaty, negotiated in William Penn's name, to justify one of the largest and most fraudulent land sales in the history of British North America. Their ability to reshape Pennsylvania's Indian policy relied on the steadfast support of the "traditions" laid down by their father. Their use of the past ratified proprietary power in their present.

Caleb Pusey, Miller Philosopher and Man of Letters

ON 25 FEBRUARY 1727, Caleb Pusey died in his home in Marlboro Township, Chester County. He was seventy-six. Pusey left 200 acres of land and other financial legacies to various children, stepchildren, grandchildren, and nephews. He also left behind his final unfinished literary project: a "historical account of the first settling and continuance of the Christian people called Quakers in the provinces of Pennsylvania and West Jersey," the first such history ever attempted.[1] Pusey's "Account" began by giving thanks to God for having visited England during its "long night of apostacy" to awaken the inner Christ, "the true light that lighteth every man that cometh into the world," within Friends. Through God's love, an "abundance were convinced in our native country," encouraging Friends to spread God's Word in America as well: Barbados, Jamaica, Carolina, Virginia, Maryland, New York, Rhode Island, and Massachusetts all saw Quaker missionaries. Some settled in West Jersey after its formation in 1676, and some even settled on the western banks of the Delaware River.

But it was not until 1681, when Penn received a royal charter "to erect a new colony here," that Friends truly found their home. Under Penn's guidance, many "antient stock or of very early convincement" Friends settled in America. They quickly set about establishing meetinghouses to worship the Lord, and God blessed their endeavors. God brought his people over to America to prosper, not die.[2]

Pusey showered special praise on Penn. He celebrated the proprietor's efforts to create a legal code "adapted to the circumstances of the people and

Figure 15. Caleb Pusey House. The Chester (now Delaware) County house, built c. 1683, is believed to be the oldest English-built house in Pennsylvania. Sources reveal that it is also one of the few surviving buildings that William Penn visited. This nineteenth-century photograph shows it before restoration in 1964. Courtesy of the Library of Congress, Prints and Photographs Division, Historic American Buildings Survey (HABS PA, UPLA, 1-16).

nature of a wilderness country" while still offering unparalleled protections to liberty of conscience. Penn's wisdom and justice convinced the Dutch, Swedish, and Finnish peoples who had previously colonized the region to welcome Quaker rule. Provincial Assemblymen worked diligently with the proprietor in the province's first three decades to secure liberty of conscience and other "temporal privileges" for all Pennsylvania's settlers; despite efforts from the imperial government to infringe on their liberties, Penn and his colonists succeeded.[3]

As for Pennsylvania's Indians, Penn had "so greatly engaged their love and nearness" that they cherished his memory still. Pusey cited as evidence a treaty conference in 1722 in which a speaker representing the natives present announced that they "should never forget . . . our proprietor's justice and kind regards toward them." Their affection for Pennsylvania's founder was so great that they even forgave the recent death of a Seneca man killed by traders on the frontier. "Sensible of the innocency of both our government and people in the matter" and satisfied that Penn's successors had "wiped away and covered the blood of our dead friend and brother," Indian negotiators noted that "we desire the same may be forgotten so as it may never be mentioned or remembered."[4] Quaker settlers and Native Americans in Pennsylvania harbored love and affection for each other and especially for William Penn.

Only one thing, Pusey noted, marred this picture: George Keith. Once a leader in the Society, in America Keith "came to disown what before he had largely defended" and to preach heretical doctrines. When confronted with his errors, Keith "grew very hot and angry," launching a vituperous campaign against the Meeting. Though "judicious wise" Friends like Thomas Lloyd worked to resolve the situation, it soon moved out of control, leaving the Quaker colony to face its first major test. Thankfully, however, the crisis passed with Keith's banishment. With the traitor in its midst removed, Pennsylvania could continue as the "Holy Experiment" in America.

Pusey's "Account" had a long afterlife. It first passed to Friend John Smith, a member of the Philadelphia Yearly Meeting; a year later the Meeting asked Smith to pass the manuscript to Isaac Norris and David Lloyd so that they might collaborate on a history of the colony. Unable to complete this project, Lloyd passed Pusey's papers to James Logan in 1734, who gave them to John Kinsey. Pusey's "Account" eventually made it into the hands of Philadelphian Quaker Robert Proud, whose 1797–98 two-volume account of Pennsylvania was the first published history of the province.[5] Though never published, Pusey's "Account" made history in a very real sense, exerting a strong influence on subsequent versions of Pennsylvania's past.

The power of Pusey's "Account" lay in its narrative simplicity. He presented Pennsylvania's success as the inevitable product of God's favor, Penn's wisdom, and the tireless efforts of the colony's virtuous founding Friends. His Pennsylvania was tolerant, diverse, and harmonious. Most of all, it was a Quaker colony, one whose Quakerness defined its identity and ensured its success. It corresponded neatly with stories about Pennsylvania that had already begun to take hold in Europe and America. Setting an example for the nations of the world, Quaker Pennsylvania could redeem the promise of the New World after centuries of colonization.[6]

The simplicity of Pusey's "Account" was deceptive, however. Its omissions spoke volumes. Nowhere in his discussion of Penn's relationship with his colonists did Pusey mention the proprietor's exasperated pleas for them to pay their rents or comply with his directives, nor did he mention that

Lloyd—singled out for praise—had played the principal role in antiproprietary conflict in the 1680s and 1690s. Nowhere in his celebration of Pennsylvania's original Frame of Government and the liberties it protected did he mention that Pennsylvania's first Assembly rejected the 1682 Frame, nor that provincial agitation led to the ratification of new Frames in 1696 and 1701.

Perhaps most strikingly, Pusey failed to mention his own role in shaping this history. In his condemnation of the apostate Keith, Pusey chose not to reveal himself as the most vocal anti-Keithian author. His readers did not learn that Chester County voters had sent him to the legislature in twelve of Pennsylvania's first eighteen elections and sixteen times overall, nor that he was appointed to serve on the Provincial Council every year between 1700 and his death. His detailed accounts of Penn's relations with Native Americans omitted his own presence at two of the most important treaty conferences of this era. Pusey signed the 1701 "Articles of Agreement" between Pennsylvania and the several Indian tribes in the region, justly celebrated as one of the high points in European-Indian relations. He even joined Sir William Keith on the 1721 trip to Conestoga that inspired Aquila Rose's poem to the lieutenant governor.

Pusey's willingness to efface his own agency in shaping Pennsylvania's history epitomized the mixture of remembering and forgetting that ran throughout his "Account." In emphasizing the inevitability of Pennsylvania's rise, his story maximized Quakers' accomplishments and minimized their struggles. Remembering the difficulties provincial Friends overcame in creating a thriving colony in too great detail might have involved remembering the challenges they faced in establishing a solid Quaker community. Admitting the contingency of Pennsylvania's success would have raised the possibility that the charter group most responsible for the colony's development was itself the creation of a contingent historical process. Pusey thus had powerful incentives to forget these possibilities. (These tensions even shaped Pusey's discussion of Indian relations, as his draft copy included the following notation before his account of Sawantaeny's death: "Query, whether anything should be said here about the Indian lately killed, seeing these nations desired it might never be mentioned nor remembered more." Remembering that the Iroquois Indians wished to erase the event from history helped Pusey extol Quakers' peaceful relationship with Native Americans.) These gaps allowed him to draft a text that acted, in effect, as an autobiographical account of a colonial elite that denied the historical process that created it. Pusey's "Account," in other words, was a creole Quaker document, the product of a colonial culture defined at least in part by a refusal to acknowledge its own creolization.[7]

Pusey's history thus fit perfectly into the arc of seventeenth- and early eighteenth-century Quakerism. Early Friends had a deeply ambivalent relationship to history. Despite having built a sect deeply rooted in a Protestant pietistic tradition, they could never bring themselves to acknowledge any debt to other Christian groups. This historical sensibility reflected the broader cultural dynamics that shaped Quakerism from its inception. The founders of the Society created a very adaptable and flexible religious movement capable of incorporating influences from several sources while developing institutional mechanisms that constructed Quaker identity. This institutional structure—the combination of a Meeting system, a network of itinerant ministers, and liberal use of the press—ensured the growth of the Society in its early years far more than any other element of their practice did. A commitment to Quaker ritual, rather than to any particular article of faith, guided the development of every new Quaker, whether convert or birthright Friend. The process through which Quaker culture spread was intrinsic to Quaker culture itself.

This cultural sensibility had a profound impact on William Penn's American endeavor. Two overriding imperatives shaped Penn's colonial project: his desire to create a society that encouraged political participation for all while protecting Quaker privileges and power. To that end, the proprietor introduced practices designed to create a "Quakerized" civic culture to help acculturate immigrants. But problems of transplantation and transmission undermined his scheme from the start. The liberties Penn cherished could not, it turned out, simply be moved across the Atlantic and established in Pennsylvania. A colonial population not wholly English, living outside England, needed to be educated on their rights as Englishmen, especially given that Pennsylvania's legal and political system differed so dramatically from what existed at "home." How, then, could the provincial elite Penn hoped would "season" new colonizers transmit these values to those they ruled? Similar problems beset the establishment of Quakerism in Pennsylvania, as leading Friends found daunting the task of incorporating into the fold individuals who had only come to the faith in America.

Thus, provincial political, legal, and religious institutions were fundamentally creole from the start, born out of Penn's desire to build a "Holy Experiment" without precedent in human history and a need to adapt cultural inheritances to a New World environment. This creolization process failed numerous times; efforts to build workable civic discourses in legal, political, and diplomatic realms met with rejection. The Quaker community itself shattered, revealing that it needed to "Quakerize" itself before it might "Quakerize" others. Consequently, leading Friends adopted alternative strategies for stabilizing the colony and maintaining their order. Increasingly willing to abandon the effort to inculcate Quaker civic habits through reformist institutions, they focused on cultivating a public provincial history through print: through subsequent retellings of political fables they defined themselves as they defined the colony. The net result was texts like Pusey's "Account" that drew on a historical identity that never existed to explain their political authority; Friends made Pennsylvania Quaker the same way they "Quakerized" themselves.

The triumph of a creolized Quaker political culture in the 1720s did not last forever, of course. Challengers would offer competing visions of civic virtue that justified access to political power on different grounds during the 1730s, 1740s, and 1750s as tens of thousands of Scots Irish and German immigrants flooded the colony, the Great Awakening swept through the province, and the long British peace that had begun after Queen Anne's War ended. The notion that Friends' status as provincial fathers gave them a particular claim to speak for the public was generally discredited after the outbreak of the Seven Years' War, replaced by a civic discourse that defined martial masculinity, not ancestry, as the key component of civic virtue.[8] The underlying dynamic shaping political and cultural struggles changed little, however; each new wave of settlement led to renewed efforts by civic actors on all sides to develop new political habits, languages, and practices comprehensible to all groups and individuals.[9]

Pusey's "Account" obscured more than it revealed in some respects. Certainly, it hid the cultural changes that created it. But it is difficult, if not impossible, to imagine Pusey writing anything different. Creolization is, after all, a historical process that responds to and makes history at every turn, as it works old cultural forms into new ones and shapes the new social realities in which groups and individuals act. Consciously or unconsciously, every instance of history making is itself an act of creolization inasmuch as it weaves older strands of discourse, practice, myth, and symbol into a new narrative. Just as every act of creolization is necessarily selective in what it includes and excludes, so too is historical narration. Creole culture in Pennsylvania had been marked from its inception by refusal to acknowledge the process that created it. A product of its environment, Pusey's "Account"—simultaneously creole and creolizing—reflected this cultural imperative.

As scholars such as Michel-Rolph Trouillot have reminded us, however, creolization (including history making) happens in a social context: creole cultures come *from* somewhere, as do the historical narratives that both describe and help create them.[10] The "anguish, nostalgia, and resentment" that characterized creole consciousness in seventeenth- and eighteenth-century Latin America reflected in large part the particular dynamics of Spanish imperial rule. The systematic exclusion of creoles from positions of governmental and ecclesiastical authority prompted the creation of colonial narratives valorizing the role creoles and their ancestors had played in the temporal and spiritual conquest of the Americas. Creole intellectuals met European theories about the biological inferiority of native-born Americans with their own scientific accounts asserting the New World's superiority. Spanish American creoles developed their own historical self-consciousness out of a particular set of cultural and political conflicts.[11] To the north, New Englanders' memorials to those who arrived in the "Great Migration" began in the 1680s, a period marked by both a demographic transition and the imposition of imperial power. A powerful sense of nostalgia for the founding and anxiety about the future, reiterated through jeremiads and histories, offered ways of maintaining a regional culture as the fabled "New England Way" that ensconced ministerial power crumbled.[12] Creole identities in New Spain and New England reflected the social histories of these two regions, as well as the motives and means through which colonials understood these histories. Creole understandings of their respective pasts had a powerful effect on their "presents" and futures.[13]

Charter groups came from somewhere as well. Here it is instructive to compare the histories of two such groups: the "Atlantic creoles" who shaped the creation of African American culture and the so-called "first families" of Virginia. Each had a distinct historical trajectory that shaped its influence on later generations. The first Atlantic creoles emerged in West and West Central Africa in the late sixteenth and early seventeenth centuries as European explorers, missionaries, and merchants attempted to establish roots along the coast. Born of a process of European expansion, Atlantic creoles played a crucial role mediating European colonial efforts and African cultural responses. Multilingual go-betweens on the coast acted as middlemen between European and African traders, while those inland shaped economic relationships, the Atlantic slave trade, and even to some degree the penetration of

Catholicism into the interior. In other words, they fostered the syncretism that shaped these cultural encounters. This, in turn, helped account for their relative influence in colonial American society. Throughout the Atlantic rim, enslaved creoles navigated colonial legal systems, contributed to the rise of staple agriculture, and oft times secured a measure of freedom, "official" or otherwise. Individuals like Anthony Johnson, who named his plantation on Virginia's eastern shore "Angola," maintained aspects of their African background while integrating into colonial society.[14]

And yet the long-term influence of Atlantic creole charter generations was uneven in different parts of the Americas. In places where they maintained some limited forms of authority, such as the Latin American slaves who maintained religious confraternities that practiced a syncretic Afro-Catholicism or autonomy as in the maroon communities in Louisiana, creole charter generations shaped the acculturation of later immigrants. In these instances, early arrivals shaped the re-creation of African "nations" in America, helping build ethnic identities that blended old and new influences. But in other instances, Atlantic charter generations had a much smaller impact. The transition from a "society with slaves" to a "slave society" in the Chesapeake in conjunction with the dramatic increase in slave imports reduced Atlantic creoles' independence and their numbers relative to the black population as a whole. In the British West Indies, the eighteenth-century creation of intercultural creole societies reflected particular trends in the slave trade, not the legacy of Atlantic charter groups. With limited means of maintaining and transmitting cultural power, Atlantic creoles could do little as hundreds of thousands of new arrivals "re-Africanized" slave communities in the colonies. The hybrid cultures creole charter generations exhibited reflected common experiences along the Atlantic littoral. But their ability to shape the creolization of African-born slaves and the relative pace of this process varied according to local conditions and histories.[15]

By contrast, English Chesapeake charter groups formed decades after settlement and yet had a significant durable impact. Social and political instability marked Virginia's early decades, exacerbated in no small part by demographic instability. Deaths outnumbered births through nearly all the seventeenth century; immigration, not natural increase, drove population growth. Virginia's legal order suffered from general instability as well, driven by weak institutions and difficulty coming to terms with the rise of chattel slavery in the colony. Only with the rise of a creole elite in the last decades of the seventeenth century did Virginia's leaders solidify their status as a ruling class with a seemingly natural claim to "power and dignity." These "countrie-born" provincials developed a new political style that was responsive to their constituents while keeping power firmly in their own hands. They also remade the colony's legal order. The legislature passed the colony's first slave code in 1705. Meanwhile, courts increasingly enforced legal regulations prohibiting interracial marital and sexual liaisons. Semipermeable boundaries of race and slavery had become hard and fast lines by the beginning of the eighteenth century. Charter group formation in Maryland followed roughly the same chronology.[16]

These two southern groups stood in revealing contrast. An African charter group arrived early but exerted little long-term influence. An English elite took decades to establish itself as a charter group but then wielded tight control over Virginia's development through the Revolution and beyond. From this position, it shaped the creolization of tens of thousands of immigrants, free and enslaved, in the eighteenth century.[17] Being first did not guarantee longevity or influence. Being able to establish creole institutions did.

These charter groups differed in another major way as well. Atlantic creole culture exuded a syncretic quality. Atlantic creoles in Africa and America embraced multiculturalism out of choice and necessity; it allowed them to survive, and sometimes prosper, in a turbulent colonial world. Their ability to forge new identities that incorporated elements from European and African sources gave them a social currency, even if their liminal status made them a vulnerable minority; their cultural creativity was both a source of power and a sign of their lack of access to formal social and political power.[18]

Virginian elites rejected the prospect of hybridization at every turn. Their virulent denunciations of Native American and African American peoples denied the possibility of racial and cultural mixture in America. While they failed to prevent the former, they had greater success forestalling the latter.[19] They strove to emulate metropolitan ideals, though they failed here as well; men whose power and status derived from their position as slave masters could never Anglicize themselves the way they hoped to. Ultimately, English provincials in the Chesapeake built a society whose institutions and cultural patterns were definitely creole—the 1705 Virginian slave code had no English precedent—but not mixed. Power played a significant role in determining the extent to which creolization involved syncretism.

That slaveholders had exerted more control over the creolization process than did the enslaved seems a banal point. But the comparison between these

ruling and subaltern charter groups is revealing for what it says about Quakers in colonial Pennsylvania. Anglo-American Friends resembled each group
at different moments of the Society's development. The religious culture
English Quakers created bore a marked similarity to the Atlantic creole culture created in West Africa—each was hybrid out of necessity, born in a
social whirlwind. The product of a revolutionary world in motion, Quakers
developed a syncretic system of faith and practice, even as they denied any
outside influences. But the Quaker experience in America resembled that of
Virginia's "first families" more than it did that of a black charter generation.
Friends showed no desire to embrace hybrid legal, political, or religious practices as they created a creole civic order. They did so only under duress, and
with great ambivalence. And at every step, they denied that they had ever
countenanced innovation, hybridity, or syncretism. Their status as provincial
founders and rulers allowed them to adopt this stance. Friends had the power
to "Quakerize" immigrants while retaining a strong tribal identity among
themselves.

This comparison helps place Pusey's "Account" in context. It was a text
written by an influential member of Pennsylvania's charter group solidifying
its identity as Friends consolidated their political power as a ruling minority.
The narrative of Quaker Pennsylvania that seems so familiar is a story written
at Friends' moment of triumph by a man partly responsible for that victory.
Pusey could hide his role in creating a creole Pennsylvania because his side
won.

These evasions within the authorizing narrative of Pennsylvania's founding group typify the historical stories of the American—United States-ian—
nation in one crucial respect: the denial of a creole identity or a creolized past
has long been a central motif in Anglo-American history. Racial and ethnic
"others" in the Americas—Africans, Spanish, Portuguese, French, even
Anglo-Caribbeans—were creoles, but never mainland English colonizers.
Anglo-Americans were exceptional, outside the processes that shaped the experiences and identities of other Americans. This denial has removed the
history of colonial British America from its historical context. It has prevented a thorough discussion, scholarly or otherwise, about cultural similarities and differences along the Atlantic rim.

Nowhere, then, was Pusey's narrative more American than in its silences.
Confronting the refusals in Pusey's comforting, creole-and-creolizing history,
then, means addressing the silences and refusals in American history more
generally. It also requires dropping the analytical boundaries that have too

often divided the history of Anglo-American colonizers from the history of other peoples in the colonial Atlantic world. Only after we begin to examine the role creolization played in the creation of political and religious culture in England's American colonies and the ways in which creole societies in English America obscured the circumstances of their birth can we start to recover the meaning of Anglo-American civic habits and practices and the influence they exert even today.

ABBREVIATIONS

THE FOLLOWING ABBREVIATIONS are used in the notes:

AHR	*American Historical Review*
AWM	*American Weekly Mercury*
Bucks Courts	*Records of the Courts of Quarter Sessions and Common Pleas of Bucks County, Pennsylvania, 1684–1700* (Meadville, Pa.: Tribune Publishing Company, 1943)
Cable, *Statutes*	Robert L. Cable, ed., *The Statutes at Large of Pennsylvania*, vol. 1, *1682–1700* (Harrisburg: Legislative Reference Bureau, 2001)
Chester Courts	*Record of the Courts of Chester County Pennsylvania, 1681–1697* (Philadelphia: Patterson & White, 1910)
CSPC	Karen Ordahl Kupperman, John C. Appleby, and Mandy Banton, eds., *Calendar of State Papers, Colonial Series, America and West Indies, 1574–1739 CD-Rom* (New York: Routledge, 2000)
EAS	*Early American Studies*
EHR	*English Historical Review*
Gospel-Truth	George Fox, *Gospel-Truth Demonstrated, in a Collection of Doctrinal Books, Given Forth by That Faithful Minister of Jesus Christ, George Fox: Containing Principles, Essential to Christianity and Salvation, Held among the People Called Quakers* (London: Thomas Sowle, 1706)
HL	Huntington Library

HSP	Historical Society of Pennsylvania
INLB, I	Isaac Norris Letterbook, 1709–16, HSP
INLB, II	Isaac Norris Letterbook, 1716–30, HSP
JLLB, I	James Logan Letterbook, 1701–9, HSP
JLLB, II	James Logan Letterbook, 1702–9, 1716–20, 1724–26, HSP
LCP	Library Company of Philadelphia
Journal	*The Journal of George Fox*, ed. John L. Nickalls (New York: Cambridge University Press, 1952)
LLP	Craig W. Horle, ed., *Lawmaking and Legislators in Pennsylvania: A Biographical Dictionary* (Philadelphia: University of Pennsylvania Press, 1991–97); vol. 1, *1682–1709*; vol. 2, *1710–1756*
Mitchell, *Statutes*	James T. Mitchell, Henry Flanders, et al., eds., *The Statutes at Large of Pennsylvania from 1682 to 1801* (Harrisburg: Clarence M. Busch, 1896)
MPCP	Samuel Hazard et al., eds., *Minutes of the Provincial Council of Pennsylvania*, Colonial Records (Philadelphia: J. Severns & Co., 1852–56)
NEP	Albert Cook Myers, ed., *Narratives of Early Pennsylvania, West New Jersey and Delaware, 1630–1707* (New York: Scribner's Sons, 1912)
PLC	Edward Armstrong, ed., *Correspondence Between William Penn and James Logan, Secretary of the Province of Pennsylvania, and Others, 1700–1750 from the Original Letters in Possession of the Logan Family*, 2 vols. (Philadelphia: HSP, 1870)
PMHB	*Pennsylvania Magazine of History and Biography*
PMMM	Philadelphia Men's Monthly Meeting of the Society of Friends, Minutes located at QCHC
PPOC	Penn Papers Official Correspondence, HSP
PWP	Mary Dunn and Richard S. Dunn, eds., *The Papers of William Penn*, 5 vols. (Philadelphia: University of Pennsylvania Press, 1981–86)
PWP (Micro)	*The Papers of William Penn (Microfilm)*, 14 reels (Philadelphia: HSP, 1975)
PWMM	Philadelphia Women's Monthly Meeting of the

Society of Friends, Minutes located at the
QCHC

PYMM   Philadelphia Men's Yearly Meeting of the Society
of Friends, Minutes located at QCHC

QCHC   Quaker Collection, Haverford College

Sussex Courts   Craig W. Horle, ed., *Records of the Courts of Sussex
County, Delaware, 1677–1710* (Philadelphia:
University of Pennsylvania Press, 1991)

Votes   Gertrude Mackinney and Charles F. Hoban, eds.,
*Pennsylvania Archives, Ser. 8: Votes and
Proceedings of the House of Representatives of the
Province of Pennsylvania, 1682–1776*, 8 vols.
(Harrisburg, 1931–35)

WMQ   *William and Mary Quarterly*

WWP   *World of William Penn*, ed. Richard S. Dunn and
Mary Maples Dunn (Philadelphia: University of
Pennsylvania Press, 1986)

WPFP   Jean R. Soderlund, ed., *William Penn and the
Founding of Pennsylvania, 1680–1684: A
Documentary History* (Philadelphia: University of
Pennsylvania Press, 1983).

INTRODUCTION

1. Thomas M. Stephens, "Creole, Créole, Criollo, Crioulo: The Shadings of a Term," *SECOL Review* 7, 3 (1983): 28–39. Of course, I am speaking here about general usage, which did not always mirror social reality. The dynamics of colonial society in Portuguese and Spanish America meant that many individuals had both African and European ancestry.

2. Charles Stewart, "Introduction: Creolization: History, Ethnography, Theory," in *Creolization: History, Ethnography, Theory*, ed. Charles Stewart (Walnut Creek, Calif.: Left Coast Press, 2007), 7.

3. Joyce E. Chaplin, "Creoles in British America: From Denial to Acceptance," in *Creolization: History, Ethnography, Theory*, ed. Stewart, 52; Gwendolyn Midlo Hall, *Africans in Colonial Louisiana: The Development of Afro-Creole Culture in the Eighteenth Century* (Baton Rouge: Louisiana State University Press, 1992), 157–58.

4. On Latin America, see Anthony Pagden, "Identity Formation in Spanish America," in *Colonial Identity in the Atlantic World, 1500–1800*, ed. Nicholas P. Canny and Anthony Pagden (Princeton, N.J.: Princeton University Press, 1987); D. A. Brading, *The First America: The Spanish Monarchy, Creole Patriots, and the Liberal State, 1492–1867* (New York: Cambridge University Press, 1991); Jorge Cañizares-Esguerra, *How to Write the History of the New World: Histories, Epistemologies, and Identities in the Eighteenth-Century Atlantic World* (Stanford, Calif.: Stanford University Press, 2001). The seminal works on African American creolization are Kamau Brathwaite, *The Development of Creole Society in Jamaica, 1770–1820*, rev. ed. (Miami: Ian Randle, 2005); Sidney W. Mintz and Richard Price, *The Birth of African-American Culture: An Anthropological Perspective* (Boston: Beacon Press, 1992). On the evolution of this concept within the field, see Richard Price, "The Miracle of Creolization: A Retrospective," *New West Indian Guide/Nieuwe West-Indische Gids* 75, 1 (2001): 35–64; Stephan Palmié, "Creolization and Its Discontents," *Annual Review of Anthropology* 35 (2006): 433–56; Palmié, "Is There a Model in the Muddle? 'Creolization' in African Americanist History and Anthropology," in *Creolization: History, Ethnography, Theory*, ed. Stewart, 178–200.

5. Hume: J. G. A. Pocock, *Barbarism and Religion*, vol. 2, *Narratives of Civil Govern-*

ment (New York: Cambridge University Press, 1999), 196; Montesquieu: Charles de Secondat Montesquieu, *The Spirit of the Laws* (New York: Cambridge University Press, 1989), 37; Jefferson quoted in J. William Frost, "Wear the Sword as Long as Thou Canst: William Penn in Myth and History," *Explorations in Early American Culture* 4 (2000): 41.

6. Voltaire, *Letters Concerning the English Nation*, trans. John Lockman (London: Printed for C. Davis and A. Lyon, 1733), 29.

7. Jack D. Marietta and G. S. Rowe, *Troubled Experiment: Crime and Justice in Pennsylvania, 1682–1800* (Philadelphia: University of Pennsylvania Press, 2006), 3.

8. J. William Frost, *A Perfect Freedom: Religious Liberty in Pennsylvania* (University Park: Pennsylvania State University Press, 1993); Alan Tully, *William Penn's Legacy: Politics and Social Structure in Provincial Pennsylvania, 1726–1755* (Baltimore: Johns Hopkins University Press, 1977); Tully, *Forming American Politics: Ideals, Interests, and Institutions in Colonial New York and Pennsylvania* (Baltimore: Johns Hopkins University Press, 1994); Sally Schwartz, *"A Mixed Multitude": The Struggle for Toleration in Colonial Pennsylvania* (New York: New York University Press, 1987); Barry Levy, *Quakers and the American Family: British Settlement in the Delaware Valley* (New York: Oxford University Press, 1988).

9. Much of this has focused on Penn's famed treaty with the Delaware Indians: Frost, "Wear the Sword as Long as Thou Canst," 28. William Penn appears in *Sid Meier's Civilization IV: Colonization*, a game about European colonization of the Americas during the early modern period. The player who secures Penn as a "Founding Father" in his "Continental Congress" increases his likelihood of peaceful relationships with Indians and attracting immigrants from Europe.

10. See Richard Cullen Rath's description of creolization as a "way of forming a 'native' identity in a situation where there is no natal society." Rath, "Drums and Power: Ways of Creolizing Music in Coastal South Carolina," in *Creolization in the Americas*, ed. David Buisseret and Steven G. Reinhardt (College Station: Texas A&M University Press, 2000), 99. Megan Vaughan has similarly described it as the process by which multiple cultural influences "merge, take root, and 'naturalize'" in a new land. Vaughan, *Creating the Creole Island: Slavery in Eighteenth-Century Mauritius* (Durham, N.C.: Duke University Press, 2005), 2. Here I take a somewhat broader view of the creolization process than Jack P. Greene, who defines creolization an "adjustment of inherited forms and practices to make them congruent with local conditions." Greene, *Pursuits of Happiness: The Social Development of Early Modern British Colonies and the Formation of American Culture* (Chapel Hill: University of North Carolina Press, 1988), 169. As I show below, I see creolization as a creative and generative process as much as an adaptive one.

11. My approach here is heavily influenced by anthropological efforts to understand cultural and linguistic creolization. Linguistic anthropologists generally write of creolization as a two-stage process. The first stage, called pidginization, involves, in anthropologist John Holm's words, the creation of a "reduced language that results from extended contact between groups of people with no language in common." The creation of this lingua franca, called a pidgin, usually involves the reduction, simplification, and sometimes—but

not always—hybridization of the native languages of the various groups involved. The second stage, creolization, involves expansion rather than reduction, resulting in the creation of a full-blown creole language. This process most commonly occurs as a former pidgin acquires native speakers. John A. Holm, *Pidgins and Creoles*, vol. 1, *Theory and Structure* (New York: Cambridge University Press, 1988), 5–6, 7. See also the discussions and definitions of this process in Dell H. Hymes, ed., *Pidginization and Creolization of Languages: Proceedings of a Conference Held at the University of the West Indies, Mona, Jamaica, April, 1968* (New York: Cambridge University Press, 1971), 84; Derek Bickerton, "Pidgin and Creole Studies," *Annual Review of Anthropology* 5 (1976): 171–73; Suzanne Romaine, *Pidgin and Creole Languages* (New York: Longman, 1988), 2–3, 24, 32, 39; Christine Jourdan, "Pidgins and Creoles: The Blurring of Categories," *Annual Review of Anthropology* 20 (1991): 191–92.

Cultural anthropologists, meanwhile, have frequently relied on linguistic terminology to explain the relationship between African and African American cultures and the creation of African American creole cultures. Melville Herskovitz argued that communities throughout the African diaspora were connected to each other and West Africa through a common cultural grammar. Melville: Herskovitz, *The Myth of the Negro Past*, cited in Palmié, "Is There a Model in the Muddle?" 185. Sidney Mintz and Richard Price likewise adopted a linguistic metaphor in their analysis of social and cultural evolution among enslaved African peoples: Mintz and Price, *Birth of African-American Culture*, 9, 21, 52–53. Palmié, however, has recently argued that historians and anthropologists have generally applied linguistic models too literally, resulting in misleading accounts of African American communities and peoples. Palmié, "Creolization and Its Discontents," 443–47; Palmié, "Is There a Model in the Muddle?"

In this book, I hew more closely to the Mintz/Price approach, treating cultural creolization as analogous to linguistic creolization but without applying the pidginization-creolization processual model directly. Although I believe that the creolization paradigm as generally considered holds a great deal of explanatory power, I do not believe (following Palmié) that the historical record justifies the use of a technical linguistic approach here.

12. Hamilton: Alexander Hamilton, *Gentleman's Progress: The Itinerarium of Dr. Alexander Hamilton, 1744*, ed. Carl Bridenbaugh (Chapel Hill: University of North Carolina Press, 1948), 8. Byrd: Kenneth A. Lockridge, *The Diary and Life of William Byrd II of Virginia, 1674–1744* (Chapel Hill: University of North Carolina Press, 1987), 81–82; Ralph Bauer, *The Cultural Geography of Colonial American Literatures: Empire, Travel, Modernity* (New York: Cambridge University Press, 2003), 179–99; Michael Zuckerman, "Endangered Deference, Imperiled Patriarchy: Tales from the Marchlands," *EAS* 3, 2 (2005): 235–44.

13. Cotton Mather, *The Wonderful Works of God Commemorated Praises Bespoke for the God of Heaven in a Thanksgiving Sermon Delivered on Decemb. 19, 1689 . . .* (Boston: Printed by S. Green & sold by Joseph Browning, 1690), 34; John Canup, "Cotton Mather and Criolian Degeneracy," *Early American Literature* 24, 1 (1989): 20–34; Canup, *Out of the Wilderness: The Emergence of an American Identity in Colonial New England* (Middle-

town, Conn.: Wesleyan University Press, 1990), 198–235. On early fears of creole degeneracy in Anglo-America, see also Joyce E. Chaplin, *Subject Matter: Technology, the Body, and Science on the Anglo-American Frontier, 1500–1676* (Cambridge, Mass.: Harvard University Press, 2001), 137; Kariann Yokota, "To Pursue the Stream to Its Fountain: Race, Inequality, and the Post-Colonial Exchange of Knowledge Across the Atlantic," *Explorations in Early American Culture* 5 (2001): 173–229; Bernard Bailyn, *Education in the Forming of American Society: Needs and Opportunities for Study* (Chapel Hill: University of North Carolina Press, 1960), 81–82; Jack P. Greene, "Search for Identity: An Interpretation of the Meaning of Selected Patterns of Social Response in Eighteenth-Century America," in Greene, *Imperatives, Behaviors, and Identities: Essays in Early American Cultural History* (Charlottesville: University Press of Virginia, 1992), 161–62. On these fears in Spanish America, see Pagden, "Identity Formation in Spanish America," 80–81; Brading, *First America*; Cañizares-Esguerra, *How to Write the History of the New World*, 180, 211; Jorge Cañizares-Esguerra, *Puritan Conquistadors: Iberianizing the Atlantic, 1550–1700* (Stanford, Calif.: Stanford University Press, 2006), 22–23; Bauer, *Cultural Geography*, 129–34.

14. For a discussion of this historiographic tradition, see Jack P. Greene, "Interpretive Frameworks: The Quest for Intellectual Order in Early American History," in Greene, *Interpreting Early America*, 292–93; and David Armitage, "Greater Britain: A Useful Category of Historical Analysis?" *AHR* 104, 2 (1999): 434–35. The phrase "Greater Britain" is J. G. A. Pocock's; on the history of the term, see Pocock, "The New British History in Atlantic Perspective: An Antipodean Commentary," *AHR* 104, 2 (1999): 490–500. For case studies exploring continuities in Anglo-America, see David Grayson Allen, *In English Ways: The Movement of Societies and the Transferal of English Local Law and Custom to Massachusetts Bay in the Seventeenth Century* (Chapel Hill: University of North Carolina Press, 1981); Stephen Foster, *The Long Argument: English Puritanism and the Shaping of New England Culture, 1570–1700* (Chapel Hill: University of North Carolina Press, 1991). See also the historiographic review in James P. P. Horn, *Adapting to a New World: English Society in the Seventeenth-Century Chesapeake* (Chapel Hill: University of North Carolina Press, 1994), 8–10.

15. Frederick Jackson Turner, "The Significance of the Frontier in American History" and "The First Official Frontier of the Massachusetts Bay," in Turner, *The Frontier in American History* (Huntington, N.Y.: R.E. Krieger, 1975), 38, 65; Michael Zuckerman, "Tocqueville, Turner, and Turds: Four Stories of Manners in Early America," *Journal of American History* 85, 1 (1998): 18–19. Louis Hartz has offered a modified version of this thesis, arguing that Turner's study is one variant of a larger process in which European ideological "fragments" flourish in new societies freed from the social constraints of old Europe. Hartz, *The Founding of New Societies: Studies in the History of the United States, Latin America, South Africa, Canada, and Australia* (New York: Harcourt, Brace, 1964), 6–7, 10. The historiographic discussion in Horn, *Adapting to a New World*, 8–10, is especially useful here. Historical geographers have placed a somewhat stronger emphasis on environmental factors in shaping the processes of reduction and simplification in European settlements in North America. R. Cole Harris, for example, has essentially argued

that the material environment alone determines what survives the simplification process and what does not; see, for instance, Harris, "The Simplification of Europe Overseas," *Annals of the American Association of Geographers* 67, 3 (1977): 470, 474. Robert D. Mitchell, while arguing against a strict materialist interpretation, likewise places as strict an emphasis on environmental forces as Turner; see Mitchell, "The Formation of Early American Cultural Regions: An Interpretation," in *European Settlement and Development in North America: Essays on Geographical Change in Honour and Memory of Andrew Hill Clark*, ed. James R. Gibson (Toronto: University of Toronto Press, 1978), 67; Robert D. Mitchell, Adrian Pollack, and R. Cole Harris, "Commentary: The Simplification of Europe Overseas," *Annals of the American Association of Geographers* 69, 4 (1979): 474–75; Mitchell, "American Origins and Regional Institutions: The Seventeenth-Century Chesapeake," *Annals of the American Association of Geographers* 73, 3 (1983): 404. See also Jack Greene's adoption of this approach: "Interpretive Frameworks," 285, 303.

16. Bernard Bailyn, *The Peopling of British North America: An Introduction* (New York: Vintage, 1988), 112–13, 114; Oscar Handlin, "The Significance of the Seventeenth Century," in *Seventeenth-Century America*, ed. James Morton Smith (Chapel Hill: University of North Carolina Press, 1957), 4.

17. This is true even of scholars who try to present value-neutral interpretations of the social development of colonial British America. Jack Greene, for example, has presented a model of colonial social development that traces the interplay of creolization and metropolitanization in Britain's American colonies. Greene's model, however, assumes that American physical environments caused each colonial settlement to undergo a process of "social simplification . . . characterized by much unsettledness and disorientation." Greene, *Pursuits of Happiness*, 165.

18. Definition of charter group: T. H. Breen, "Creative Adaptations: Peoples and Cultures," in *Colonial British America: Essays in the New History of the Early Modern Era*, ed. Jack P. Greene and J. R. Pole (Baltimore: Johns Hopkins University Press, 1984), 204–5. On charter groups in New England and Virginia, see Breen, "Persistent Localism: English Social Change and the Shaping of New England Institutions," "The Covenanted Militia of Massachusetts Bay: English Background and New World Development," and "Looking Out for Number One: The Cultural Limits on Public Policy in Early Virginia," in Breen, *Puritans and Adventurers: Change and Persistence in Early America* (New York: Oxford University Press, 1980), 3–23, 24–45, 106–26; David Hackett Fischer, *Albion's Seed: Four British Folkways in America* (New York: Oxford University Press, 1989). German immigrants: A. G. Roeber, *Palatines, Liberty, and Property: German Lutherans in Colonial British America* (Baltimore: Johns Hopkins University Press, 1993), 6 and passim. Enslaved Africans: Ira Berlin, "From Creole to African: Atlantic Creoles and the Origins of African-American Society in Mainland North America," *WMQ* 53, 2 (1996): 251–88.

19. Gary B. Nash, *Quakers and Politics: Pennsylvania, 1681–1726*, new ed. (Boston: Northeastern University Press, 1993); Schwartz, *"Mixed Multitude"*; Levy, *Quakers and the American Family*; Fischer, *Albion's Seed*, 409–603; Tully, *Forming American Politics*, 287.

20. David Buisseret, "Introduction," in *Creolization in the Americas*, ed. Buisseret

and Reinhardt, 6; Roger Bastide, *Les Religions afro-brésiliennes: Contributions à une sociologie des interpenetrations de civilizations* (Paris: Presses Universitaires de France, 1960), cited in Richard Price and Sally Price, "Shadowboxing in the Mangrove," *Cultural Anthropology* 12, 1 (1997): 7. Kamau Brathwaite's discussion of creolization in Jamaica epitomizes this approach; see Brathwaite, *Development of Creole Society*, 296; also xxv, 101, 224, 226, 298, 303, 308.

21. Mintz and Price, *Birth of African-American Culture*, 10; Michel-Rolph Trouillot, "Culture on the Edges: Caribbean Creolization in Historical Context," in *From the Margins: Historical Anthropology and Its Futures*, ed. Brian Keith Axel (Durham, N.C.: Duke University Press, 2002), 199, 200; Palmié, "Creolization and Its Discontents," 440, 442.

22. Writing that "There is *no creolization without conflict* between affirmed contrasts and the movement toward unity," Françoise Vergès has argued that creolization in different contexts may lead to multicultural mixing or, to the extent to which this cultural pluralism exacerbates social tensions, ethnic antagonism and separatism. Creolization, in other words, is inseparable from its social and historical context. Vergès, "Indian-Oceanic Creolizations: Processes and Practices of Creolization on Réunion Island," in *Creolization: History, Ethnography, Theory*, ed. Stewart, 144, 148–49. On creolization as a slow falling away from cultural norms, see Jack Greene's argument that creolization was largely the result of a "slowly accumulating expertise arising out of inhabitants' learning" how best to create societies suited to American physical and social environments. Greene, *Pursuits of Happiness*, 169. See also Robert Olwell's and Alan Tully's definition of creolization as "a centrifugal force that worked to create cultures defined by their surroundings rather than by their origins." Olwell and Tully, "Introduction," in *Cultures and Identities in Colonial British America*, ed. Olwell and Tully (Baltimore: Johns Hopkins University Press, 2006), 10.

23. In this sense, I see this study of creolization in colonial Pennsylvania as an archetypal example of what David Armitage and Michael J. Braddick have termed "cis-Atlantic" history, which they define as "the history of any particular place—a nation, a state, a region, even a specific institution—in relation to the wider Atlantic world." Armitage, "Three Concepts of Atlantic History," in *The British Atlantic World, 1500–1800*, ed. David Armitage and Michael J. Braddick (New York: Palgrave Macmillan, 2002), 22.

24. I am drawing here on Marshall D. Sahlins's insight that all "cultural schemes are historically ordered," with meanings constantly "revalued as they are practically enacted." Sahlins, *Islands of History* (Chicago: University of Chicago Press, 1985), vii.

CHAPTER 1. QUAKERISM'S ENGLISH ROOTS

1. Fox, *Journal*, 27.

2. On historians' willingness to overlook Fox's early activities, see especially H. Larry Ingle, "George Fox, Historian," *Quaker History* 82, 1 (1993): 31.

3. A note on usage: throughout the text I use the unmodified term "Meeting" to refer to the network of monthly, quarterly, and yearly meetings that comprised the ecclesi-

astical structure of the Society of Friends and as shorthand for the general body of Friends as a whole. I use the lower case "meeting" to refer to unspecified congregations ("monthly meetings") and the upper case "Meeting" when referring to particular congregations ("Falls Monthly Meeting" or "Philadelphia Yearly Meeting").

4. David Cressy, "Revolutionary England 1640–1642," *Past & Present* 18, 1 (2003): 50; Cressy, "The Protestation Protested, 1641 and 1642," *Historical Journal* 45, 2 (2002): 251–79.

5. Michael R. Watts, *The Dissenters* (Oxford: Clarendon Press, 1978), 100–2, 106, 115–16; Christopher Hill, *The Century of Revolution, 1603–1714* (New York: Norton, 1982), 142.

6. J. F. McGregor, "The Baptists: Fount of All Heresy" and "Seekers and Ranters," in *Radical Religion in the English Revolution*, ed. Barry Reay and J. F. McGregor (New York: Oxford University Press, 1984), 23–64, 121–24; Christopher Hill, *The World Turned Upside Down: Radical Ideas During the English Revolution* (New York: Viking, 1972), 184–85, 187, 191–92, 259–68; Watts, *Dissenters*, 121–24; B. S. Capp, *The Fifth Monarchy Men: A Study in Seventeenth-Century English Millenarianism* (Totowa, N.J.: Rowman and Little-field, 1972); Capp, "The Fifth Monarchists and Popular Millenarianism," in *Radical Religion*, ed. McGregor and Reay, 165–90.

7. Christopher Hill, Barry Reay, and William M. Lamont, *The World of the Mugglet-onians* (London: T. Smith, 1983); A. L. Morton, *The World of the Ranters: Religious Radicalism in the English Revolution* (London: Lawrence & Wishart, 1970), 70, 92; Brian Manning, "The Levellers and Religion," in *Radical Religion*, ed. McGregor and Reay, 60, 72–73; Watts, *Dissenters*, 117; Hill, *World Turned Upside Down*, 102.

8. Morton, *World of the Ranters*, 21; Barry Reay, "Radicalism and Religion in the English Revolution: An Introduction," in *Radical Religion*, ed. McGregor and Reay, 13–14; Hill, *World Turned Upside Down*, 98; Watts, *Dissenters*, 111–15.

9. Watts, *Dissenters*, 116.

10. Watts, *Dissenters*, 124.

11. Watts, *Dissenters*, 183; McGregor, "Seekers and Ranters," 132–34. J. C. Davis has argued that no Ranter movement existed, claiming that it emerged from sensationalist "yellowpress" authors in 1650 and 1651. Davis, *Fear, Myth, and History: The Ranters and the Historians* (New York: Cambridge University Press, 1986), 92; Davis, "Fear, Myth, and Furore: Reappraising the 'Ranters'," *Past & Present* 129, 1 (1990): 79–103. Other historians have rebutted Davis's claims, arguing that the abundant anti-Ranter tracts demonstrate the existence of Ranterism. See J. F. McGregor, Bernard Capp, Nigel Smith, and B. J. Gibbons, "Debate: Fear, Myth, and Furore: Reappraising the 'Ranters': I," *Past & Present* 140, 1 (1993): 155–94. I do not think it necessary here to weigh in on this debate; if nothing else, the fear of Ranterism testifies to the supercharged religious atmosphere of the late 1640s and early 1650s and the anxieties this engendered among many English men and women.

12. There is some debate among historians regarding the origins of the Society of Friends, specifically whether partisans have exaggerated Fox's leadership role in the early

years; accounts of both seventeenth-century Friends and modern historians suggest that Fox was the leader of the Society from its rise in the early 1650s to his death in 1691. For accounts that corroborate Penn's assertion that Fox was "the first instrument by whom God was pleased to gather" Friends, see Melvin B. Endy, *William Penn and Early Quakerism* (Princeton, N.J.: Princeton University Press, 1973), 54–55; William C. Braithwaite, *The Beginnings of Quakerism*, 2nd ed. (New York: Cambridge University Press, 1955), 28–50; Hugh Barbour and J. William Frost, *The Quakers* (New York: Greenwood Press, 1988), 25–35; H. Larry Ingle, *First Among Friends: George Fox and the Creation of Quakerism* (New York: Oxford University Press, 1994). Ingle argues that Fox's leadership was as much organizational as spiritual, crediting him with creating the Meeting structure; many non-Friends (and some Friends) saw James Nayler as the Quakers' spiritual leader. For accounts stressing Nayler's importance in the early movement, see Hill, *World Turned Upside Down*, and Barry Reay, *The Quakers and the English Revolution* (New York: St. Martin's, 1985); "First Publishers of Truth": William Penn, *A Brief Account of the Rise and Progress of the People Called Quakers . . .* (London: T. Sowle, 1694), in Penn, *A Collection of the Works of William Penn*, 2 vols. (London: J. Sowle, 1726), 1: 878.

13. Fox, *Journal*, 1, 11; Ingle, *First Among Friends*, 18–40. Fox's *Journal* was selective in its account of his relationship to other prominent Friends in the early days of the movement; see Ingle, "George Fox, Historian."

14. George Fox, *A Collection of Many Select and Christian Epistles, Letters and Testimonies Written on Sundry Occasions, by That Ancient, Eminent, Faithful Friend and Minister of Christ Jesus, George Fox; the Second Volume* (London: T. Sowle, 1698), 2; Braithwaite, *Beginnings*, 42; Ingle, *First Among Friends*, 48.

15. Fox, *Journal*, 14, 15, 17.

16. Braithwaite, *Beginnings*, 44, 51–77; Watts, *Dissenters*, 186; Ingle, *First Among Friends*, 54; Rosemary Anne Moore, *The Light in Their Consciences: Early Quakers in Britain, 1646–1666* (University Park: Pennsylvania State University Press, 2000), 117.

17. Braithwaite, *Beginnings*, 102–4, 155–62; Ingle, *First Among Friends*, 91–94.

18. Braithwaite has estimated approximately 35,000–40,000 Friends in the British Isles and American colonies in 1660 (*Beginnings*, 512); later historians have tended to agree. Reay has argued for Braithwaite's estimate (*Quakers and the English Revolution*, 27); Ingle, without offering an estimate, has implied it may be on the high side (*First Among Friends*, 328n60).

19. Fox, *Journal*, 7–8; Fox, *The Following PAPER Was Publish'd 1654 . . .* (1654), in *Gospel-Truth*, 23–24; James Nayler, *A Discovery of the Man of Sin . . .* (London: Giles Calvert, 1654), 38; Kate Peters, *Print Culture and the Early Quakers* (New York: Cambridge University Press, 2004), 163; Melvin B. Endy, "Puritanism, Spiritualism, and Quakerism: A Historiographical Essay," in *WWP*, 289.

20. Fox, *Vials of Wrath Upon the Man of Sin* (1654), in *Gospel-Truth*, 15, 16, 19; Fox, *To All That Would Know the Way to the Kingdom* (1653), in *Gospel-Truth*, 3; Fox, *The Pearl Found in England . . .* (1658), in *Gospel-Truth*, 137; Fox, *For the Emperor of China* (1660), in *Gospel-Truth*, 207; Fox, *Journal*, 15–16.

21. George Bishop, *Jesus Christ, the Same to Day, as Yesterday* . . . (London: Giles Calvert, 1655), 4; Moore, *Light*, 149; Francis Howgill and George Whitehead, *A Testimony Concerning the Life, Death, Trials, Travels and Labours of Edward Burroughs That Worthy Prophet of the Lord Who Dyed a Prisoner for the Testimony of Jesus, and the Word of God, in the City of London, the 14th of the 12th Month, 1662. F. H.* (London: William Warwick, 1663), 5.

22. Thomas Aldam, *False Prophets and False Teachers Described, 1652* (London: 1652), 4; Fox, *Journal*, 78; Fox, *Following PAPER*, 25.

23. George Fox, *To All That Would Know the Way to the Kingdome* . . . ([London]: 1654), in *Gospel-Truth*, 16, 19; Fox, *A Visitation to the Jew* . . . (London: Giles Calvert, 1656), in *Gospel-Truth*, 39; Fox, *The Priests Fruits Made Manifest* . . . (London: Thomas Simmons, 1657), in *Gospel-Truth*, 117; Fox, *A Declaration of the Difference Between Ministers of the Word, from Ministers of the World* . . . (1656), in *Gospel-Truth*, 66; Fox, *Following PAPER*, 26; Fox, *Journal*, 10, 247; Moore, *Light*, 52, 54, 55; Peters, *Print Culture*, 78; Siddall and Crook cited in Reay, *Quakers and the English Revolution*, 34, 52.

24. Fox, *The Woman Learning in Silence; or the Mystery of the Womans Subjection to her Husband* . . . (1656), in *Gospel-Truth*, 77; Fox, *Journal*, 668.

25. Phyllis Mack, *Visionary Women: Ecstatic Prophecy in Seventeenth-Century England* (Berkeley: University of California Press, 1992), 1.

26. Fox, *Journal*, 27; Mack, *Visionary Women*, 151; Richard Bailey, *New Light on George Fox and Early Quakerism: The Making and Unmaking of a God* (San Francisco: Mellen Research University Press, 1992), 30, 44, 77–84, 90–97. Here I would modify Michelle Lise Tarter's argument that the Quaker belief that they might transcend their fleshy bodies and inhabit divine ones "prophetically challenged the prevalent notions of woman as inferior and the body as contaminated." Tarter, "Quaking in the Light," in *A Centre of Wonders: The Body in Early America*, ed. Janet Moore Lindman and Tarter (Ithaca, N.Y.: Cornell University Press, 2001), 152. Although Friends did not believe women spiritually or bodily inferior to men (see below), they most certainly found unregenerate bodies contaminated.

27. William Dewsbury, *A true Prophecy of the Mighty day* . . . (London, 1654); Ingle, *First Among Friends*, 122; Peters, *Print Culture*, 107–10; Braithwaite, *Beginnings*, 180; Bailey, *New Light*, 86.

28. Peters, *Print Culture*, 93, 98–101, 104–6; Richard Bauman, *Let Your Words Be Few: Symbolism of Speaking and Silence Among Seventeenth-Century Quakers* (New York: Cambridge University Press, 1983), 70, 88–94.

29. John Gratton, *A Journal in the Life of that Ancient Servant of Christ* (London: J. Sowle, 1720), 44; William Dewsbury, *Discoverie of the Great Enmity of the Serpent against the Seed of the Woman* (London: Giles Calvert, 1655), 16–17; Fox, *Following PAPER*, 27; Mack, *Visionary Women*, 153–55.

30. James Nayler, *The Power and the Glory of the Lord Shining out of the North* . . . (London: Giles Calvert, 1653), 21; Fox, *Journal*, 24. On the distinction between the visible and invisible churches, see Edmund Sears Morgan, *Visible Saints: The History of a Puritan Idea* (New York: New York University Press, 1963), 3–4, 10–11, 13–14, 20–32.

31. Samuel Fisher, *Rusticus ad Acedemicos in Exercitationibus Expostulatoriis, Apologeticis Auatuor The rustick's Alarm to the Rabbies, or, The country Correcting the University and Clergy . . .* , in Fisher, *Testimony of Truth Exalted by the Collected Labours of . . . Samuel Fisher who Died a Prisoner for the Testimony of Jesus and Word of God, anno 1665* (London: s.n., 1679), 30; Watts, *Dissenters*, 203.

32. Fox, *Journal*, 22; Bailey, *New Light*, 38–39.

33. Michael J. Braddick, "Civility and Authority," in *The British Atlantic World, 1500–1800*, ed. David Armitage and Braddick (New York: Palgrave Macmillan, 2002), 93, 100.

34. William Penn and George Fox, *The Preface, Being a Summary Account of the Divers Dispensations of God to Men from the Beginning of the World to That of Our Present Age, by the Ministry and Testimony of His Faithful Servant George Fox, as an Introduction to the Ensuing Journal* (London: T. Sowle, 1694), xxxiv; Hill, *World Turned Upside Down*, 231.

35. Norman Penney, ed., *Experiences in the Life of Mary Penington* (London: Friends Historical Society, 1992), 38.

36. Ingle, *First Among Friends*, 37–38; Braithwaite, *Beginnings*, 66–68; Fox, *To the High and Lofty Ones* (1655), in *Gospel-Truth*, 29; Fox, *A Warning to all Merchants*, in *Gospel-Truth*, 127–30; Fox, *The Serious Peoples Reasoning, and Speech . . .* (1659), in *Gospel-Truth*, 158–59, 61. On plain clothing, see also Frederick B. Tolles, "'Of the Best Sort but Plain': The Quaker Esthetic," *American Quarterly* 11 (1959): 482–502; Joan Kendall, "The Development of a Distinctive Form of Quaker Dress," *Costume* 19 (1985): 58–74; David Hackett Fischer, *Albion's Seed: Four British Folkways in America* (New York: Oxford University Press, 1989), 475–81, 544–52.

37. On Quaker speech ways, see also Bauman, *Let Your Words Be Few*; Hugh Ormsby-Lennon, Peter Burke, and Roy Porter, "From Shibboleth to Apocalypse: Quaker Speechways During the Puritan Revolution," in *Language, Self, and Society: A Social History of Language*, ed. Burke and Porter (Cambridge: Polity Press, 1991), 72–112; Mack, *Visionary Women*, 137–42.

38. Thomas Howsegoe, *A Word from the North, Sounded into the South, Heard, and Received of Many . . .* (London: Giles Calvert, 1657), 2; Thomas Symonds, *The Voyce of the Just Uttered . . .* (London: Thomas Simmons, 1656), 6; Moore, *Light*, 121.

39. Bauman, *Let Your Words Be Few*, 45. Under the "Old Style" calendar, the year began on 25 March.

40. See Bauman, *Let Your Words Be Few*, 63–83, for the best analysis of the cultural dynamics of Friends' aggressive proselytizing.

41. Braithwaite, *Beginnings*, 152, 162, 186, 196, 440, 487–95.

42. Braithwaite, *Beginnings*, 139, 175; Bauman, *Let Your Words Be Few*, 95–119.

43. Edward Burrough, *A Message for Instruction, to All the Rulers, Judges, and Magistrates, to whom the Law is Committed* (1657), in Burrough, *The Memorable Works of a Son of Thunder and Consolation: Namely, That True Prophet, and Faithful Servant of God, and Sufferer for the Testimony of Jesus, Edward Burroughs, Who Dyed a Prisoner for the World of*

God, in the City of London (London: 1672), 343–61; George Fox, *To the Parliament of the Comon-Wealth of England Fifty Nine Particulars Laid Down for the Regulating Things, and the Taking Away of Oppressing Laws, and Oppressors, and to Ease the Oppressed. By G. F.* (London: Thomas Simmons, 1659), 14–23; Fox, *To the Rulers of the Earth* (1655), in *Gospel-Truth*, 32; Fox, *To Both Houses of Parliament* (1660), in *Gospel-Truth*, 220, 236.

44. Anthony Pearson, *A Few Words to All Judges, Justices, and Ministers of the Law in England. From Anthony Pearson* (London: Giles Calvert, 1654), 6–7; Dorothy White, *Friends, you that are of the Parliament, hear the Word of the Lord as it Came Unto Me . . .* (London, 1659), 1; Moore, *Light*, 169.

45. Mark Kishlansky, "The Case of the Army Truly Stated: The Creation of the New Model Army" *Past & Present* 81 (1978): 51–74.

46. Watts, *Dissenters*, 209.

47. Braithwaite, *Beginnings*, 136, 346, 446, 445; Barry Reay, "Quakerism and Society," in *Radical Religion*, ed. McGregor and Reay, 157.

48. Moore, *Light*, 92; Peters, *Print Culture*, 180; Braithwaite, *Beginnings*, 214. Braithwaite records numerous instances, most notable perhaps the brutal treatment accorded Friends in Oxford (295–99).

49. Alan Cole, "The Quakers and the English Revolution," *Past & Present* 10 (1956): 41.

50. Isaac Penington, *The Fundamental Right, Safety and Liberty of the People* (London: John Macock, 1651), 2, 12, 20, 29. See also Burrough, *Declaration*, in Burrough, *Memorable Works*, 442.

51. Edmund Morgan has argued that Penington was "One of the most perceptive" authors on the topic of Parliamentary authority, even if not entirely original. Edmund S. Morgan, *Inventing the People: The Rise of Popular Sovereignty in England and America* (New York: Norton, 1988), 84–85, 92.

52. Edward Burrough, *A declaration of the present sufferings of above 140. persons of the people of God (who are now in prison,) called Quakers with a briefe accompt of about 1900* (London: printed for Tho. Simmons at the Bull and Mouth near Aldersgate, 1659), 28; Reay, *Quakers and the English Revolution*, 39; Fox, *To All That Would Know the Way to the Kingdom*, 7; R. Michael Rogers, "Quakerism and the Law in Revolutionary England," *Canadian Journal of History* 22, 2 (1987): 156.

53. Pearson, *A Few Words*, 6, 7; Edward Billing, *A Mite of Affection* (London: G. Calvert, 1659), 3, 10; Burrough, *Declaration*, 442; Rogers, "Quakerism and the Law," 168.

54. Fox, *A Few Plain Words By way of Query, and Information, to the Teachers and People of the Nation*, in *Gospel-Truth*, 220.

55. Billing, *Mite of Affection*, 2, 3, 5; Burrough, *Declaration*, 442; Rogers, "Quakerism and the Law," 159; William Tomlinson, *Seven Particulars . . .* (London: Giles Calvert, 1657), 17–18.

56. Burrough, *Declaration*, 441–42; Fox, *Instruction*, 20; Fox, *The Law of God, the Rule for Lavv-makers, the Ground of all Just Laws, and the Corruption of English Laws and Lawyers Discovered* (London: Giles Calvert, 1658), 26; Rogers, "Quakerism and the Law,"

151. Rogers has argued that this reflected a Quaker belief in "natural law," as defined in Catholic theology. Given that no Quaker author uses the term "natural law," this assertion seems questionable.

57. Penn and Fox, *The Preface,* xlix.

58. Braithwaite, *Beginnings,* 40–41, 202; Henry J. Cadbury, "Early Quakerism and Uncanonical Lore," *Harvard Theological Review* 40, 3 (1947): 183–87, 192–95; John L. Brooke, *The Refiner's Fire: The Making of Mormon Cosmology, 1644–1844* (New York: Cambridge University Press, 1994), 25–29.

59. Murray Tolmie, *The Triumph of the Saints: The Separate Churches of London, 1616–1649* (New York: Cambridge University Press, 1977), 73; McGregor, "Baptists," 29.

60. Braithwaite, *Beginnings,* 247.

61. See Hill, *World Turned Upside Down,* 232, for a similar argument.

62. I am very grateful to Roger Abrahams for helping me formulate this point.

63. Fox, *Journal,* 174; Braithwaite, *Beginnings,* 155, 176–205, passim; Moore, *Light,* 31–35.

64. On Fell's central role in coordinating Quakerism's early growth, see Moore, *Light,* 23–28; Braithwaite, *Beginnings,* 135–37, 317–26.

65. William Dewsbury, *The Faithful Testimony of That Antient Servant of the Lord, and Minister of the Everlasting Gospel William Dewsbery His Books, Epistles and Writings, Collected and Printed for Future Service* (London: Andrew Sowle, 1689), 1; Braithwaite, *Beginnings,* 140–41; Ingle, *First Among Friends,* 102–4; Moore, *Light,* 129–41.

66. Braithwaite, *Beginnings,* 138–42.

67. Braithwaite, *Beginnings,* 721.

68. George Fox, *The Vials of the Wrath of God Poured Forth Upon the Seat of the Man of Sin . . .* (London: Giles Calvert, 1654), 14; Martin Mason, *The Proud Pharisee Reproved: Or, the Lying Orator Laid Open . . .* (London: 1655), 10; Peters, *Print Culture,* 34, 35.

69. William Tomlinson, *A Word of Reproof to the Priests or Ministers, Who Boast of their Ministery and Ordinances, and yet Live in Pride, Disdain, Persecution, &c . . .* (London: Tho. Wayte, 1653), 17; Bauman, *Let Your Words Be Few,* 74–78; Peters, *Print Culture,* 26, 29, 31.

70. Hugh Barbour and Arthur O. Roberts, eds., *Early Quaker Writings, 1650–1700* (Grand Rapids, Mich.: Eerdmans, 1973), 14; Peters, *Print Culture,* 21.

71. Peters, *Print Culture,* 21–22, 50–60; Braithwaite, *Beginnings,* 317.

72. Adrian Johns, *The Nature of the Book: Print and Knowledge in the Making* (Chicago: University of Chicago Press, 1998), 186.

73. Peters, *Print Culture,* 26.

74. Peters, *Print Culture,* 63, 67, 69.

75. Dewsbury, *Faithful Testimony,* 3.

76. Peters, *Print Culture,* 117–23.

77. Francis Howgill, *The Inheritance of Jacob Discovered. After His Return out of Aegypt . . .* (London: Giles Calvert, 1656).

78. In Burrough, *Memorable Works*, 77–81.

79. On the medieval and early modern Christian Church's traditional antipathy toward itinerants, see Timothy D. Hall, *Contested Boundaries: Itinerancy and the Reshaping of the Colonial American Religious World* (Durham, N.C.: Duke University Press, 1994), 22–25, 28.

80. On the "accelerative" nature in some cultures that spurs the creation of pathways that facilitate their dissemination, see Greg Urban, *Metaculture: How Culture Moves Through the World* (Minneapolis: University of Minnesota Press, 2001), 18, 47, 49.

81. Bauman, *Let Your Words Be Few*, 9.

82. Cole, "The Quakers and the English Revolution," 46.

83. Fox, *Journal*, 358; Gerardus Croese, *The General History of the Quakers . . .* (London: Printed for John Dunton, 1696), 123–24. On the history of Quaker pacifism, see Meredith Baldwin Weddle, *Walking in the Way of Peace: Quaker Pacifism in the Seventeenth Century* (New York: Oxford University Press, 2001).

84. Fox, *Collection of Many Select and Christian Epistles*, 137; James F. Maclear, "Quakerism and the End of the Interregnum: A Chapter in the Domestication of Radical Puritanism," *Church History* 19, 4 (1950): 269.

85. Watts, *Dissenters*, 221–22; Braithwaite *Beginnings*, 476–77; Fox, *Journal*, 391–94.

86. Watts, *Dissenters*, 222; Braithwaite, *Beginnings*, 9, 12–13.

87. Moore, *Light*, 186.

88. Tim Harris, *Restoration: Charles II and His Kingdoms, 1660–1685* (London: Penguin Global, 2006), 76–77.

89. Moore, *Light*, 187.

90. William C. Braithwaite, *The Second Period of Quakerism*, 2nd ed. (New York: Cambridge University Press, 1961), 223.

91. Braithwaite, *Second Period*, 225–31.

92. Moore, *Light*, 194–95.

93. "Testimony of the Brethren" cited in Moore, *Light*, 224–25; Braithwaite, *Second Period*, 254.

94. Fox, *Collection of Many Select and Christian Epistles*, 276–93; Braithwaite, *Second Period*, 264.

95. "The Dissatisfactions of William Rogers and Others," 1 February 1678, in *PWP (Micro)*, 2: 636–37, 639.

96. Ingle, *First Among Friends*, 261–62; Braithwaite, *Second Period*, 309–10; John Pearson, *Antichristian Treachery Discovered and Its Way Block'd up in a Clear Distinction Betwixt the Christian Apostolical Spirit, and the Spirit of the Antichristian Apostate . . .* ([London]: 1686), 74–78.

97. Fox, *Collection of Many Select and Christian Epistles*, 175; J. F. McGregor, "Ranterism and the Development of Early Quakerism," *Journal of Religious History* 9, 4 (1977): 361.

98. For concise accounts of the Nayler incident, see Moore, *Light*, 35–49; Braithwaite, *Beginnings*, 251–67.

99. Christopher Hill, *The Experience of Defeat: Milton and Some Contemporaries* (New York: Viking, 1984), 129–60, emphasizes the political aspects of the Quaker movement and thus the political consequences of the Restoration, unnecessarily deemphasizing the spiritual impact of the Restoration.

100. Robert Barclay, *A Catechism and Confession of Faith . . .* ([London]: 1675), in Barclay, *Truth Triumphant through the Spiritual Warfare, Christian Labours, and Writings of That Able and Faithful Servant of Jesus Christ, Robert Barclay, Who Deceased at His Own House at Urie in the Kingdom of Scotland, the 3 Day of the 8 Month 1690* (London: Thomas Northcott, 1692), 123, 133; Barclay, *An Apology for the True Christian Divinity . . .* ([Aberdeen?]: 1678), in *Truth Triumphant*, 313, 311–12.

101. Barclay, *Apology*, 334,

102. Barclay, *Catechism and Confession of Faith*, 133; Barclay, *Apology*, 263.

103. Barclay, *Apology*, 263, 388, 264; see also Barclay, *Catechism and Confession of Faith*, 136–38.

104. Barclay, *Apology*, 260.

105. George Keith, *Truth's Defence . . .* (London: Benjamin Clark, 1682), 63. See also John Whiting, *Truth the Strongest of All . . .* (London: J. Sowle, 1706), 22; Whiting, *An Account How George Keith Became a Quaker, and a Preacher Amongst Them* (1715), 7. The latter tract was bound together with a copy of Whiting, *Persecution Expos'd in Some Memoirs Relating to the Sufferings of John Whiting, and Many Others of the People Called Quakers . . .* (London: J. Sowle, 1715), located in Friends Historical Library, Swarthmore College.

106. Barclay, *Apology*, 260.

107. Isaac Penington, "Some Misrepresentations of me concerning Church Government" (1675?), in Penington, *The Works of the Long-Mournful and Sorely-Distressed Isaac Penington . . .* (London: Benjamin Clark, 1681), Part II: 435. The date is approximate, as Penington wrote in response to a proseparatist tract of that same year: John Pennyman and Isaac Penington, *This Is for the People Called Quakers Being a Collection of Several Passages Taken out of Isaac Penington's, Edward Burrough's, and Other Men's Writings: Whereunto Are Added Three Letters Sent to Some of the Said People / by John Pennyman* (London: Fr. Smith, 1675). On the date of this writing and its importance in the schism, see Braithwaite, *Second Period*, 348.

108. Robert Barclay, *The Anarchy of the Ranters and Other Libertines . . .* ([London]: 1676), in *Truth Triumphant*, 217, 27.

109. Barclay, *Anarchy*, 222–23, 228.

110. Barclay, *Anarchy*, 217.

111. The phrase is from Sacvan Bercovitch, *The Puritan Origins of the American Self* (New Haven, Conn.: Yale University Press, 1975), 30.

112. I am borrowing from Mikhail M. Bakhtin here: "The word in language is half someone else's." Bakhtin, *The Dialogic Imagination: Four Essays*, ed. Michael Holquist, trans. Caryl Emerson and Holquist (Austin: University of Texas Press, 1981), 293.

113. For a discussion of Barclay's thoughts on this, see Braithwaite, *Second Period*, 341–46. My understanding of the role of discipline in defining Quaker identity is influ-

enced by Brigitte Miriam Bedos-Rezak's discussion of the semiotics of medieval seals. Bedos-Rezak, "Medieval Identity: A Sign and a Concept," *AHR* 105, 5 (2000): 1489–1583.

114. See Greg Urban, *A Discourse-Centered Approach to Culture: Native South American Myths and Rituals* (Austin: University of Texas Press, 1991), 1, 2, for what such an approach to culture entails.

115. "On Creating Quaker History," in *PWP*, 1: 363, 364–65.

116. Donald Veall, *The Popular Movement for Law Reform, 1640–1660* (Oxford: Clarendon Press, 1970); J. G. A. Pocock, *The Ancient Constitution and the Feudal Law: A Study of English Historical Thought in the Seventeenth Century* (New York: Cambridge University Press, 1987).

117. Mary Maples Dunn, *William Penn, Politics and Conscience* (Princeton, N.J.: Princeton University Press, 1967), 114–17, 122–23; Tim Harris, *Revolution: The Great Crisis of the British Monarchy, 1685–1720* (London: Penguin Global, 2008), 214–18.

118. Dunn, *William Penn, Politics and Conscience*; Andrew R. Murphy, *Conscience and Community: Revisiting Toleration and Religious Dissent in Early Modern England and America* (University Park: Pennsylvania State University Press, 2001), 168–80.

119. On the relationship between order and ordering, see John Smolenski, "Introduction: The Ordering of Authority in the Colonial Americas," in *New World Orders: Violence, Sanction, and Authority in the Colonial Americas*, ed. Smolenski and Thomas J. Humphrey (Philadelphia: University of Pennsylvania Press, 2005), 1–16, esp. 14.

120. Hugh Barbour, "The Young Controversialist," in *World of William Penn*, 15. On Penn's early career as a Quaker, see Mary K. Geiter, *William Penn* (New York: Longman, 2000), 1–23; Mary Maples Dunn, "The Personality of William Penn," in *World of William Penn*, 6–8; Braithwaite, *Second Period*, 55–64.

121. My account of the trial is taken from Penn, *The People's Ancient and Just Liberties*, in *Works*, 1: 7–18 (indictment 9). On the terms of the 1670 Conventicle Act, see Harris, *Restoration*, 53.

122. Penn, *People's Ancient and Just Liberties*, 12, 14–16.

123. William Wirt Blume, "Origin and Development of the Directed Verdict," *Michigan Law Review* 48, 5 (1950): 555–57; Dunn, *William Penn, Politics and Conscience*, 17–18; Dunn and Dunn, "The Personality of William Penn," 6; William Pencak, "What Is a Fair Trial? The Case of Penn and Mead," in *Law and the Conflict of Ideologies: Ninth Round Table on Law and Semiotics*, ed. Roberta Kevelson (New York: Peter Lang, 1996), 199–209; Craig W. Horle, *The Quakers and the English Legal System, 1660–1688* (Philadelphia: University of Pennsylvania Press, 1988), 116–18.

124. Though the tract has been included in early modern and modern collections of Penn's writings, such as Joseph Besse, *A Collection of the Sufferings of the People Called Quakers . . .* (London: L. Hinde, 1753), and Penn, *The Political Writings of William Penn*, ed. Andrew R. Murphy (Indianapolis: Liberty Fund, 2002), Penn himself denied authorship. Mary Maples Dunn has suggested that while "the point of view and language of the speeches are [certainly] Penn's," the tract was likely authored by Thomas Rudyard, Penn's lawyer (Dunn, *William Penn, Politics and Conscience*, 14). *People's Ancient and Just Liberties*

was reprinted on its own in 1682, 1710 (two editions), 1771, and 1794 in England. It was also reprinted in the 1726 edition of Penn, *Works*; Penn, *The Select Works of William Penn: To Which Is Prefixed a Journal of His Life* (London: s.n., 1771), 159–69; Penn, *The Select Works of William Penn*, 5 vols. (London: J. Phillips, 1782), 1: 79–147; Besse, *Sufferings*, 1: 416–36. On Quaker trials as "social dramas" embodying Friends' rebellion against political authority and their importance to Quaker identity, see Bauman, *Let Your Words Be Few*, 95–119.

125. Penn, "Exceptions Against the Procedure of the Court," in *PWP*, 1: 175; Penn, *People's Ancient and Just Liberties*, 12.

126. As Andrew Murphy has pointed out, Penn did argue that Catholics who renounced the Roman Church's political authority should be granted the freedom to worship as they chose (*Conscience and Community*, 179–80).

127. Penn, *People's Ancient and Just Liberties*, 16.

128. These phrases are taken from Clifford Geertz, "Local Knowledge: Fact and Law in Comparative Perspective," in Geertz, *Local Knowledge: Further Essays in Interpretive Anthropology* (New York: Basic Books, 1983), 175.

129. Penn, "The Dissatisfactions of William Rogers and Others," 1 February 1678, in *PWP (Micro)*, 2: 628–47; "Result of a Meeting Between John Story and William Penn," c. 12 February 1678, in *PWP (Micro)*, 2: 650.

130. Horle, *Quakers and the English Legal System*; Braithwaite, *Second Period*, 55–77; Dunn, *William Penn, Politics and Conscience*, 19–22.

131. Penn, *The Great Case of Liberty of Conscience Once More Briefly Debated & Defended . . .* (London: 1670), in *Works*, 1: 447.

132. Penn, *Great Case*, 448, 449, 451.

133. Penn, "Narrative of the Sufferings of Quakers in the Isle of Ely" (November 1671?), in *PWP*, 1: 223. On "antient constitution," see Pocock, *Ancient Constitution*, 16 and passim.

134. Penn, Concerning Tythes" (1675?), in *PWP (Micro)*, 2: 14; Penn, *Great Case*, 453; Penn, "Narrative," 224.

135. Penn, *Great Case*, 453.

136. William Penn, *England's Present Interest Discover'd . . .* (London: 1675), in *Works*, 1: 675. On the centrality of law to English identity, see Jack P. Greene, " 'By Their Laws Shall Ye Know Them': Law and Identity in Colonial British America," *Journal of Interdisciplinary History* 33, 2 (2002): 247–60.

137. William Penn to J[ohn]. H[awtrey?]. and Companion, 31 March 1674, in *PWP*, 1: 280. On the importance of the ancient constitution in Penn's political thought, see Murphy, *Conscience and Community*, 171; Dunn, *William Penn, Politics and Conscience*, 30–31, 49, 56 (on fundamental and superficial law, see 56).

138. Penn, *Great Case*, 456; Penn, "Narrative," 224; Penn, "Concerning Tythes," 14; Dunn, *William Penn, Politics and Conscience*, 59–61. Penn's interest in locating the origin of English liberties in the deep Anglo-Saxon past differed from that of contemporaries who wrote about the "antient constitution." Legal reformers such as Gerrard Winstanley

and John Lilburne argued for the restoration of the customary liberties guaranteed under the ancient constitution as a means of eradicating the so-called Norman Yoke, the feudal system of property holding imposed by William the Conqueror and sustained by common law. Winstanley and Lilburne emphasized the preconquest origins of the constitution to attack contemporary social and economic structures, not England's religious establishment (Pocock, *Ancient Constitution,* 319–20).

139. Penn to J.H., *PWP,* 1: 279–80; and see Penn, *Great Case,* 455.

140. Penn, *An Address to Protestants of All Perswasions More Especially the Magistracy and Clergy, for the Promotion of Virtue and Charity: In Two Parts / by W. P. A Protestant,* 2nd ed. (London: T. Sowle, 1692), in *Works,* 1: 797; Penn, *England's Present Interest,* 688. The 1692 edition of Penn's *Address* was originally published (minus some prefatory material) as Penn, *An Address to Protestants Upon the Present Conjuncture in II Parts / by a Protestant, William Penn* (London: 1679).

141. Penn, *England's Present Interest,* 674–76 (quote at 675), 689; Penn, *Address,* 738.

142. Penn, *Great Case,* 453; Penn, *England's Present Interest,* 673.

143. Penn, *Great Case,* 445.

144. Penn, *Address,* 733.

145. Penn, *One Project for the Good of England That Is, Our Civil Union Is Our Civil Safety: Humbly Dedicated to the Great Council, the Parliament of England* (London: 1679), in *Works,* 2: 682. On the centrality of civil interest in Penn's political philosophy, see Murphy, *Conscience and Community,* 177–79.

146. Penn, *England's Present Interest,* 686.

147. Penn, *Great Case,* 455; Penn, *England's Present Interest,* 693.

148. Penn, *Address,* 810.

149. Penn, *England's Present Interest,* 688, 690, 691, 692.

150. Penn, *Address,* 797.

151. Penn, *England's Present Interest,* 674, 690, 705 (quote at 690).

152. Murphy has argued that this generalized notion of reason is one of Penn's central arguments for toleration (*Conscience and Community,* 174). In suggesting that Penn's constitutional theory was based at least as much in history as in reason, I differ from Jane E. Calvert's argument that Penn believed man's knowledge of fundamental law came primarily through "synteresis." Calvert, "The Quaker Theory of a Civil Constitution," *History of Political Thought* 27, 4 (2006): 589–90. Though Penn invoked synteresis when describing reason and natural law (see *England's Present Interest,* 675; *Great Case,* 453), those are the only times he used the term in his political or constitutional writings; his appeals to reason were much more general, and his appeals to history more frequent.

153. Dunn, *William Penn, Politics and Conscience,* 57; Morgan, *Inventing the People,* 101–6; Harris, *Restoration,* 155–56.

154. Penn, *England's Present Interest,* 683.

155. Penn, *England's Present Interest,* 688.

156. Penn, *Address,* 797 (foundation), 799 (faith).

157. Penn, *Address,* 701, 703.

158. Penn, *Address*, 703, 705, 733, 738, 740.

159. William Penn to William of Orange, 26/12mo/1679[80], in *PWP*, 2: 27.

160. Penn, *England's Present Interest*, 679.

161. John Edwin Pomfret, *The Province of West New Jersey, 1609–1702: A History of the Origins of an American Colony* (Princeton, N.J.: Princeton University Press, 1956), 54. Charles had awarded James a charter to the territory before the conquest, providing the impetus for the invasion (52); Richard P. McCormick, "Introduction," in *The West Jersey Concessions and Agreements of 1676/77: A Round Table of Historians* (Trenton: New Jersey Historical Commission, 1979), 9.

162. Pomfret, *Province of West New Jersey*, 65.

163. Pomfret, *Province of West New Jersey*, 65–85; Joseph E. Illick, *William Penn, the Politician: His Relations with the English Government* (Ithaca, N.Y.: Cornell University Press, 1965), 12–13.

164. This was the assessment of eminent early twentieth-century historian Charles McLean Andrews, who wrote that "The plans drawn up for the government of this Quaker colony are of conspicuous importance. . . . None are as worthy of study as these." Andrews, *The Colonial Period of American History* (New Haven, Conn.: Yale University Press, 1934), 3: 167–68. A roundtable of historians commemorating the Concession's bicentennial concurred; see John Murrin's assessment that the Concessions were "easily the most radical document about politics accepted by any American colony before the Revolution" (Murrin, "The Ideas and Principles of the Concessions and Agreements," 42); Mary Maples Dunn's assertion that, in comparison to Pennsylvania's 1682 Frame of Government "the greater of these was the Concessions" (Dunn, "Did Penn Write the Concessions?" 28); and Paul G. E. Clemens's assertion that "The drafters of the Concessions were clearly among the more advanced political thinkers of their era" (Clemens, "The Concessions in Relation to Other Seventeenth-Century Colonial Charters," 32), all in *The West Jersey Concessions and Agreements*. See also John E. Pomfret, "The Problem of the West Jersey Concessions of 1676/7," *WMQ* 5, 1 (1948): 95; Caroline Robbins, "Laws and Governments Proposed for West New Jersey and Pennsylvania, 1676–1683," *PMHB* 105, 4 (1981): 373–92; and the editors' note to "The West New Jersey Concessions," in *PWP*, 1: 387. All references to the Concessions are from the version in *PWP*, 1: 387–410.

165. Though some of Penn's more generous biographers once described him as the sole author of the Concessions, it now seems extremely unlikely. At this point, historians generally agree that it was a collaborative work, with Billing playing the most prominent authorial role and Penn a lesser but still substantial one. See Pomfret, "Problem of the West Jersey Concessions," 100–101; Robbins, "Laws and Governments Proposed for West New Jersey and Pennsylvania"; Dunn, "Did Penn Write the Concessions?"

166. "West New Jersey Concessions," in *PWP*, 1: 396–97.

167. "West New Jersey Concessions," 403–5.

168. "West New Jersey Concessions," 393, 395 (quote 395).

169. Caroline Robbins, "William Penn, Edward Byllynge, and the Concessions of 1677," 16.

170. Pomfret, *Province of West New Jersey*, 107–10, 112, 125, 127.

171. Frederick R. Black, "The Fate of the Concessions, 1677–1702," in *The West Jersey Concessions and Agreements*, 35.

172. This power struggle is detailed in Pomfret, *Province of West New Jersey*, chap. 8.

173. *CSPC*, 10: 544. For narrative accounts of Penn's applications, see Joseph E. Illick, "The Pennsylvania Grant: A Re-Evaluation," *PMHB* 86, 4 (1962): 375–96; Illick, *William Penn, the Politician*; and Mary K. Geiter, "The Restoration Crisis and the Launching of Pennsylvania, 1679–81," *English Historical Review* 112, 446 (1997): 300–18. See also Stephen Saunders Webb, "'The Peaceable Kingdom': Quaker Pennsylvania in the Stuart Empire," in *World of William Penn*, 173–83.

174. Illick, "The Pennsylvania Grant," 380.

175. William Penn to James Harrison, 28/6mo/1681, in *PWP*, 2: 108.

176. See the OED entry for *experiment* and its usages in the seventeenth century.

177. William Penn to T[homas] J[anney], 21/6mo./[16]81, in *PWP*, 2: 106.

CHAPTER 2. WILLIAM PENN SETTLES HIS COLONY: THE PROBLEM OF LEGITIMACY IN EARLY PENNSYLVANIA, 1681–1691

1. Richard S. Dunn, "Penny Wise and Pound Foolish: Penn as a Businessman," in *WWP*, 37–54.

2. William Penn, *Some Account of the Province of Pennsylvania in America* (London: 1681), in *NEP*, 197–215.

3. Penn, *Some Account*, 203.

4. Penn, *Some Account*, 210.

5. Peter C. Mancall, *Hakluyt's Promise: An Elizabethan's Obsession for an English America* (New Haven, Conn.: Yale University Press, 2007), 153; David Cressy, *Coming Over: Migration and Communication Between England and New England in the Seventeenth Century* (New York: Cambridge University Press, 1987), 37–38.

6. Penn, *Some Account*, 210. On Penn's desire to make government a "nursery of virtue," see Chapter 1 above.

7. William Penn, *England's Present Interest Discover'd* . . . ([London]: 1675) in William Penn, *A Collection of the Works of William Penn*, 2 vols. (London: J. Sowle, 1726), 1: 679.

8. Penn, *Some Account*, 208.

9. I am drawing these terms from Paul W. Kahn, *The Cultural Study of Law: Reconstructing Legal Scholarship* (Chicago: University of Chicago Press, 1999), esp. 45–86.

10. Christopher L. Tomlins, "Introduction: The Many Legalities of Colonization: A Manifesto of Destiny for Early American Legal History," in *The Many Legalities of Early America*, ed. Tomlins and Bruce H. Mann (Chapel Hill: University of North Carolina Press, 2001), 2–3.

11. See Robert Blair St. George's discussion of a "colonial project" as an effort to establish colonial rule both through the creation of historically specific imperial knowledge

and the development of particular imperial institutions. St. George, "Introduction," in *Possible Pasts: Becoming Colonial in Early America*, ed. St. George (Ithaca, N.Y.: Cornell University Press, 2000), 6.

12. For a fuller discussion of the ideological depth of these founding documents, see John Smolenski, "As the Discharge of My Conscience to God: Narrative, Personhood, and the Construction of Legal Order in 17th-Century Quaker Culture," *Prospects* 24 (1999): 132–40.

13. See Chapter 1 above.

14. Penn, "Fundamentall Constitutions of Pennsylvania," in *PWP*, 2: 142, 141.

15. Penn, "The Frame of Government and the Laws Agreed Upon in England," in *PWP*, 2: 212.

16. Penn, "Fundamentall Constitutions of Pennsylvania," in *PWP*, 2: 142.

17. Martyn Thompson, "The History of Fundamental Law in Political Thought from the French Wars of Religion to the American Revolution," *American Historical Review* 91, 5 (1986): 1103–28; Donald R. Kelley, "'Second Nature': The Idea of Custom in European Law, Society, and Culture," in *The Transmission of Culture in Early Modern Europe*, ed. Anthony Grafton and Ann Blair (Philadelphia: University of Pennsylvania Press, 1990), 131–72.

18. Penn, "The Frame of Government," in *PWP*, 2: 213; Penn, "Fundamentall Constitutions of Pennsylvania," in *PWP*, 2: 142.

19. Penn, "The Frame of Government," in *PWP*, 2: 213.

20. Penn, "The Frame of Government," in *PWP*, 2: 212.

21. Sir William Blackstone, *Commentaries on the Laws of England: In Four Books*, 4th ed. (Philadelphia: Robert Bell, 1771), 1: 56. Modern scholars writing about law, discipline, and power have tended to draw most heavily on the writings of Michel Foucault, without appreciating his argument that Quakers, with their notion of the inner light, played a key role in shaping innovative techniques of discipline and power in Euro-American culture: Foucault, *Discipline and Punish: The Birth of the Prison*, 2nd Vintage Books ed. (New York: Vintage, 1995), 116, 239. On his understanding of the productive nature of power relations, see also Foucault, *The History of Sexuality*, trans. Robert Hurley, vol. 1, *An Introduction* (New York: Vintage, 1990), 87, 144. I discuss this issue at greater length in John Smolenski, "Introduction: The Ordering of Authority in the Colonial Americas," in *New World Orders: Violence, Sanction, and Authority in the Colonial Americas*, ed. Smolenski and Thomas J. Humphrey (Philadelphia: University of Pennsylvania Press, 2005), 16.

22. Gary B. Nash, *Quakers and Politics: Pennsylvania, 1681–1726*, new ed. (Boston: Northeastern University Press, 1993), 48–89; Edwin B. Bronner, *William Penn's Holy Experiment: The Founding of Pennsylvania, 1681–1701* (New York: Temple University Publications, 1962), 49; Richard Alan Ryerson, "William Penn's Gentry Commonwealth: An Interpretation of the Constitutional History of Early Pennsylvania, 1681–1701," *Pennsylvania History* 61, 4 (1994): 415–19. Much of the documentation detailing this period is contained in *PWP*, 2: 297–507.

23. Here I depart slightly from other narratives of early Pennsylvania—most notably

by Nash and Ryerson—that stress disagreement between Penn and the colonists over the Frame of Government and early governance. Although I would hardly deny conflict in Pennsylvania politics—or what Penn called the colonists' "litigious, & brutish" spirit—I would argue that shared cultural assumptions regarding politics and law were more significant in shaping early Pennsylvania's civic culture than were disagreements.

24. "The Frame of Government of the Province of Pennsylvania (1683), in *WPFP*, 267. For Harrington's influence on Penn, see Mary Maples Dunn, *William Penn, Politics and Conscience* (Princeton, N.J.,: Princeton University Press, 1967), 81–87; Ryerson, "William Penn's Gentry Commonwealth," 402, 412, and Chapter 1 above. On Harrington's belief that a well-structured government should separate "debate" and "result," see J. G. A. Pocock, *The Machiavellian Moment: Florentine Political Thought and the Atlantic Republican Tradition* (Princeton, N.J.: Princeton University Press, 1975), 394–95.

25. "Benjamin Furly's Criticism of the *Frame of Government*," in *WPFP*, 134–40.

26. Nash, *Quakers and Politics*, 42. See also Ryerson, "William Penn's Gentry Commonwealth," 407, who argues that Penn's goal in creating a powerful Provincial Council was to install a colonial aristocracy similar to the English court that had treated him well.

27. Penn to Commissioners of State, 27 December 1687, in *PWP*, 3: 170.

28. Penn to Commissioners of State, 1 February 1687, in *PWP*, 3: 145.

29. Penn to Thomas Lloyd, 17 November 1686, in *PWP*, 3: 128.

30. Penn to Thomas Lloyd, 21 September 1686, in *PWP*, 3: 117.

31. Penn to Provincial Council of Pennsylvania, June 1686, in *PWP*, 3: 94, 96. On the evolution of the term "seasoning," see Joyce E. Chaplin, "Creoles in British America: From Denial to Acceptance," in *Creolization: History, Ethnography, Theory*, ed. Charles Stewart (Walnut Creek, Calif.: Left Coast Press, 2007), 54–55. On its use to describe newly arrived slaves in particular, see Kamau Brathwaite, *The Development of Creole Society in Jamaica, 1770–1820*, rev. ed. (Miami: Ian Randle, 2005), 298.

32. Penn to Comissioners of State, 18 September 1688, in *PWP*, 3: 210.

33. Penn to Provincial Council of Pennsylvania, 11 November 1690, in 3: 285–91.

34. *MPCP*, 1: 85.

35. J. G. A. Pocock has argued that Harrington's description of how this process of recognizing and assenting to a natural set of leaders is deference in its purest form: Pocock, "The Classical Theory of Deference," *AHR* 81, 3 (1976): 517–19. Penn's reliance on a governmental model based so closely on Harrington suggests that deference would have been essential to the proprietor's political plans.

36. See Chapter 1 above.

37. This definition is taken from Richard Bauman and Joel Sherzer, "Introduction," in *Explorations in the Ethnography of Speaking*, ed. Bauman and Sherzer, 2nd ed. (New York: Cambridge University Press, 1989), 6.

38. My definition of speech economy is drawn from Dell Hymes and Anthropological Society of Washington, "The Ethnography of Speaking," in *Anthropology and Human Behavior*, ed. Thomas Gladwin and William C. Sturtevant (Washington, D.C.: Anthropology Society of Washington, 1962), 13–52.

39. See Chapter 1 above.

40. For narrative discussions of Penn's fight with Baltimore, see Dunn, *William Penn, Politics and Conscience*, 100–103, 107, 109; Nash, *Quakers and Politics*, 68, 74–76, 84, 87, 104; Ryerson, "William Penn's Gentry Commonwealth," 414–15; Bronner, *William Penn's Holy Experiment*, 22, 54–67. For the documentary record of Penn's legal troubles, see *PWP*, 3: 256–59, 281–84, 329–33, 344–46, 357–58, 381–437.

41. Pennsylvania's complicated legislative history makes a direct comparison between these two periods difficult but not impossible. Between 1682 and 1684, the legislature passed 153 laws and passed fifty-three (53) laws between 1684 and 1692. These were repealed when the colony was royalized and placed under Governor Benjamin Fletcher's control at the end of 1692. Between 1694, when the colony was returned to Penn, and 1699, the Assembly passed a total of 150 laws. The great majority, however, consisted simply of repassed versions of statutes overturned in 1692. See Cable, *Statutes*. A majority of Pennsylvania's legislators were Quaker during the colony's first two decades. Craig Horle notes that, with the exception of the first session, Quakers comprised a majority of the Assembly (which assented to laws proposed by the Council) throughout the seventeenth century in Pennsylvania. His findings for the Provincial Council (which initiated and proposed legislation) are similar. With the exception of 1694—when royal governor Fletcher appointed his own Council, dismissing those elected under the 1683 Frame—Friends comprised well over 50 percent of Council. See Horle, "Religious Affiliation," in *LLP*, 1: 115–21.

42. See Chapter 1 above.

43. Cable, *Statutes*, 27–28.

44. Cable, *Statutes*, 87 (for murder); 31, 32, 76, 118 (corporal punishment). On relevant legal reforms in New England, see G. B. Warden, "Law Reform in England and New England, 1620 to 1660," *WMQ* 35, 4 (1978): 680, and more generally, William E. Nelson, "The Utopian Legal Order of the Massachusetts Bay Colony, 1630–1686," *American Journal of Legal History* 47, 2 (2005): 183–230.

45. Cable, *Statutes*, 53.

46. Stanley N. Katz, "The Problem of a Colonial Legal History," in *Colonial British America: Essays in the New History of the Early Modern Era*, ed. Jack P. Greene and J. R. Pole (Baltimore: Johns Hopkins University Press, 1984), 476, 480; John Ruston Pagan, *Anne Orthwood's Bastard: Sex and Law in Early Virginia* (New York: Oxford University Press, 2003), 9, 58–59, 67.

47. On the self-conscious legal primitivism of Delaware Valley Quakers, see William M. Offutt, Jr., "The Atlantic Rules: The Legalistic Turn in Colonial British America," in *The Creation of the British Atlantic World*, ed. Elizabeth Mancke and Carole Shammas (Baltimore: Johns Hopkins University Press, 2005), 160–61, 167. On similar phenomena in New England (and the ways legal simplification increased legal hierarchies), see David T. Konig, "A Summary View of the Law of British America," *WMQ* 50, 1 (1993): 49; Warden, "Law Reform in England and New England, 1620 to 1660"; Cornelia Hughes Dayton, *Women Before the Bar: Gender, Law, and Society in Connecticut, 1639–1789* (Chapel Hill: University of North Carolina Press, 1995), 27–28, 42; Richard J. Ross, "Puri-

tan Godly Discipline in Comparative Perspective: Legal Pluralism and the Sources of Intensity," *AHR* 113, 4 (2008): 986–87.

48. Cable, *Statutes*, 28, 34, 39, 69. Notably, the legislature did not pass a single vice law during the next seventeen years.

49. Cable, *Statutes*, 42 (days of the week); 39–40 (sedition).

50. Cable, *Statutes* 41, 88 (scolding); 28 (abusing or deriding other faiths).

51. Cable, *Statutes*, 29, 51–52.

52. The penal code stated that an individual guilty of profaning "Almighty God, Christ Jesus, The holy Spirit, or the Scriptures of truth" received a 5 shilling fine. Cable, *Statutes*, 40, 30.

53. Cable, *Statutes*, 64.

54. Cable, *Statutes*, 43.

55. Cable, *Statutes*, 39.

56. Penn, "Conditions or Concessions to the First Purchasers" and "Laws and Orders the Keepers and Frequenters of Ordinaries," in *WPFP*, 71–76, 206–7.

57. Evan Haefeli estimates that approximately 1,400 non-Quakers lived in the Delaware Valley before 1681: approximately 800 Swedes, 400 Dutch, and 200 non-Quaker English. Given the presence of previous settlements in the English province of West Jersey, this would suggest that perhaps 800–1,000 non-English lived within the boundaries of Penn's charter. See Haefeli, "The Pennsylvania Difference: Religious Diveristy on the Delaware Before 1683," *EAS* 1, 1 (2003): 50n66.

58. Penn to the Inhabitants of Pennsylvania, 8 April 1681, in *WPFP*, 55; Penn to William Blathwayt and Francis Gwynn, 21 November 1682, in *WPFP*, 190–91.

59. The following discussion of denization and naturalization in England and North America is drawn from James H. Kettner, *The Development of American Citizenship, 1608–1870* (Chapel Hill: University of North Carolina Press, 1978), 29–34, 66–71; Polly J. Price, "Natural Law and Birthright Citizenship in Calvin's Case (1608)," *Yale Journal of Law & the Humanities* 9 (1997): 86–96; Marilyn C. Baseler, *"Asylum for Mankind": America, 1607–1800* (Ithaca, N.Y.: Cornell University Press, 1998), 44–45; and Tamar Herzog, *Defining Nations: Immigrants and Citizens in Early Modern Spain and Spanish America* (New Haven, Conn.: Yale University Press, 2003), 184–86. On Pennsylvania's distinctiveness, see Kettner, *Development of American Citizenship*, 86, 104n47.

60. Kettner, *Development of American Citizenship*, 66–67, 69–73; Daniel J. Hulsebosch, "The Ancient Constitution and the Expanding Empire: Sir Edward Coke's British Jurisprudence," *Law and History Review* 21, 3 (2003): 454–58.

61. Penn, *Some Account*, 203. On the political-economy argument that population growth (especially in overseas territories) was crucial to national strength, see Baseler, *"Asylum for Mankind"*, 38–41; David Armitage, *The Ideological Origins of the British Empire* (New York: Cambridge University Press, 2000), 159, 165.

62. William Penn to the Inhabitants of Pennsylvania, in *WPFP*, 55. On the fears of some English authors that overseas colonization would weaken the English republic by encouraging the naturalization of foreigners, see Armitage, *Ideological Origins*, 128, 132; and Hulsebosch, "Ancient Constitution," 448.

63. Penn, *Some Account*, 203.

64. Cable, *Statutes*, 3; Sally Schwartz, *"A Mixed Multitude": The Struggle for Toleration in Colonial Pennsylvania* (New York: New York University Press, 1987), 27–29; Baseler, *"Asylum for Mankind,"* 61–64.

65. On the immediate application of Swedes for naturalization, see "Philadelphia County Court Minutes," in *WPFP*, 197–99. On the appointment of Swedes as justices in the province's first years and the high level of Swedish participation in the legal system, see William Offutt, Jr, "The Limits of Authority: Courts, Ethnicity, and Gender in the Middle Colonies, 1670–1710," in *The Many Legalities of Early America*, ed. Christopher L. Tomlins and Bruce H. Mann (Chapel Hill: University of North Carolina Press, 2001), 375.

66. *CSPC*, 7: 97.

67. Penn to Jasper Batt, 5 February 1683, in *WPFP*, 199.

68. Penn to Batt, in *WPFP*, 200.

69. Ralph Bauer, *The Cultural Geography of Colonial American Literatures: Empire, Travel, Modernity* (New York: Cambridge University Press, 2003); Michael Zuckerman, "The Fabrication of Identity in Early America," in Zuckerman, *Almost Chosen People: Oblique Biographies in the American Grain* (Berkeley: University of California Press, 1993), 21–54; Zuckerman, "Identity in British America: Unease in Eden," in *Colonial Identity in the Atlantic World, 1500–1800*, ed. Nicholas P. Canny and Anthony Pagden (Princeton, N.J.: Princeton University Press, 1987), 159–212; John Canup, *Out of the Wilderness: The Emergence of an American Identity in Colonial New England* (Middletown, Conn.: Wesleyan University Press, 1990); Jack P. Greene, "Search for Identity: An Interpretation of the Meaning of Selected Patterns of Social Response in Eighteenth-Century America," in Greene, *Imperatives, Behaviors, and Identities: Essays in Early American Cultural History* (Charlottesville: University Press of Virginia, 1992), 113–42; Greene, *The Intellectual Construction of America: Exceptionalism and Identity from 1492 to 1800* (Chapel Hill: University of North Carolina Press, 1993), 126–29. For Spanish America, see Anthony Pagden, "Identity Formation in Spanish America," in *Colonial Identity in the Atlantic World*, ed. Canny and Pagden, 51–93; D. A. Brading, *The First America: The Spanish Monarchy, Creole Patriots, and the Liberal State, 1492–1867* (New York: Cambridge University Press, 1991); Jorge Cañizares-Esguerra, *How to Write the History of the New World: Histories, Epistemologies, and Identities in the Eighteenth-Century Atlantic World* (Stanford, Calif.: Stanford University Press, 2001); J. H. Elliott, *Empires of the Atlantic World: Britain and Spain in America, 1492–1830* (New Haven, Conn.: Yale University Press, 2006), 236–45.

70. Penn, *A Further Account of the Province of Pennsylvania and Its Improvements, for the Satisfaction of Those That Are Adventurers, and Enclined to Be So* (London, 1685) in *NEP*, 269. The wide variety of crops that could be grown in Pennsylvania is also described in Thomas Paschall, *An Abstract of a Letter from Thomas Paskell of Pennsilvania to his friend J. J. of Chippenham* (London: John Bringhurst, 1683), in *NEP*, 253. Jack Greene has suggested Penn and his fellow authors typified broader trends in colonial promotional literature; see Greene, *Intellectual Construction of America*, 69–76.

71. Penn, *Information and Direction to Such Persons as Are Inclined to America, More Especially Those Related to the Province of Pensilvania* (London: 1686), 3–7.

72. Thomas Budd, *Good Order Established in Pennsilvania & New-Jersey in America* (Philadelphia: Printed by William Bradford, 1685), 7. The quality of Pennsylvania vineyards is also mentioned in Nicholas More, *A Letter From Doctor More With Passages Out of Several Letters From Persons of Good Credit Relating to the State and Improvement of the Province of Pennsilvania* (London, 1687), in *NEP*, 291.

73. Francis Daniel Pastorius, *Circumstantial geographical description of Pennsylvania* (Frankfurt, 1700), in *NEP*, 399; More, *Letter from Dr. More*, 291; Penn, *Further Account*, 262.

74. William Penn, *A Letter From William Penn Proprietary and Governour of Pennsylvania in America To the Committee of the Free Society of Traders of That Province, Residing in London* (London: A. Sowle, 1683), in *NEP*, 239. This is not exactly true; there was significant conflict between Penn and the Assembly over provisions of the Frame of Government. The Assembly actually rejected Penn's proposed Frame of Government in 1682 and only approved a Frame in 1683 after significant revisions.

75. Penn, *Further Account*, 276.

76. Budd, *Good Order*, 2.

77. Pastorius, *Circumstantial Geographical Description*, 409.

78. Elizabeth Gratton to Penn, 20 March 1684, in *WPFP*, 362.

79. Pastorius, *Circumstantial Geographical Description*, 400; Penn, *Further Account*, 260; Philip Ford, *A Vindication of William Penn, Proprietary of Pennsilvania from the Aspersions Spread Abroad on Purpose to Defame Him* (London: Benjamin Clark, 1683).

80. "The Loyal Protestant, and True Domestick Intelligence, or News both from City and Country," 17 September 1681, in *WPFP*, 81.

81. Ford, *Vindication*, 2.

82. Penn, *Further Account*, 260.

83. Penn, *Further Account*, 260.

84. *Three Letters of Thanks to the Protestant Reconciler. 1. From the Anabaptists at Munster. 2. From the Congregations in New-England. 3. From the Quakers in Pensilvania* (London: Benj. Took, 1683), 20. By contrast, Friends frequently used utopian language to describe Pennsylvania in their private correspondence.

85. Budd, *Good Order*, 14, 15.

86. Budd, *Good Order*, 15.

87. See the discussion of the Keithian controversy in Chapter 4 below.

88. George Keith, *A Plain Short Catechism for Children & Youth: That May Be Serviceable to Such Others, Who Need to Be Constructed in the First Principles and Grounds of the Christian Religion* (Philadelphia: William Bradford, 1690).

89. Society of Friends, *The Christianity of the People Commonly Called Quakers, Asserted by Them, against the Unjust Charge of Their Being No Christians, Upon Several Questions Relating to Those Matters, Wherein Their Christian Belief Is Questioned* (Philadelphia: William Bradford, 1690), 1, 3.

90. Philadelphia Yearly Meeting, *A Loving Exhortation to Friends, from a Yearly Meeting Held at Philadelphia, the 4th of the 7th Month, 1689* (Philadelphia: William Bradford, 1689). For this ritual enjoinder to unity, see also John Burnyeat, *An Epistle from John Burnyeat to Friends in Pennsylvania: To Be Disperced by Them to the Neighbouring Provinces, Which for Convenience and Dispatch Was Thought Good to Be Printed, and So Ordered by the Quarterly Meeting of Philadelphia, the 7th of the 4th. Month 1686* (Philadelphia: William Bradford, 1686), 1.

91. Philadelphia Yearly Meeting of the Religious Society of Friends, William Penn, and Frances Taylor, *A General Epistle Given Forth by the People of the Lord, Called, Quakers: That All May Know, We Own None to Be of Our Fellowship, or to Be Reckoned or Numbred with Us, but Such as Fear the Lord and Keep Faithfully to His Heavenly Power* (Philadelphia: William Bradford, 1686), 18.

92. Keith, *Plain Short Catechism*, 20, 21.

93. Friends, Penn, and Taylor, *General Epistle*, 3, 6, 9.

94. John Willsford, *A Brief Exhortation to All Who Profess the Truth, to Come Clear out of Babylon, and Not to Joyn with Any Hurtful or Unseemly Practice, nor Make Marriages with Unbelievers, but Be a Seperate People from Every Unclean Thing, That God May Receive You* (Philadelphia: William Bradford, 1691), 3–4, 1.

95. Philadelphia Yearly Meeting, *Loving Exhortation*, 1.

96. On Irish Friends' innovations in discipline and observers' responses, see William C. Braithwaite, *The Second Period of Quakerism*, 2nd ed. (New York: Cambridge University Press, 1961), 502, 504, 508. On Scottish development of church discipline—earlier but more rudimentary than within Irish meetings—see 328–35.

97. Michael Zuckerman has argued that the desire to innovate through the transplantation of reified English in America was actually an endemic feature in the production of identity in seventeenth-century English North America. See Zuckerman, "The Fabrication of Identity in Early America," 32.

98. Penn, *The Excellent Privilege of Liberty and Property Being the Birth-Right of the Free-Born Subjects of England* (Philadelphia: William Bradford, 1687), i, iii.

99. See Chapter 1 for a fuller explanation of Penn's thought.

100. Penn, *Excellent Priviledge*, 24.

101. On "legal literacy," see Mary Sarah Bilder, *The Transatlantic Constitution: Colonial Legal Culture and the Empire* (Cambridge, Mass.: Harvard University Press, 2004); William Offutt, Jr. has argued that Delaware Valley Friends possessed a high familiarity with the law, reflecting English Friends' increasing sophistication in navigating the English legal system during the Restoration era. As I hope to demonstrate in this chapter and the next, however, suffering Friends' interaction with the court system in England led to the easy transplantation of an English legal culture in Pennsylvania's early years. Offutt, Jr. "The Atlantic Rules," 167–68. See also Craig W. Horle, *The Quakers and the English Legal System, 1660–1688* (Philadelphia: University of Pennsylvania Press, 1988).

102. Jack P. Greene, "Empire and Identity from the Glorious Revolution to the American Revolution," in *The Oxford History of the British Empire*, vol. 2, *The Eighteenth*

Century, ed. P. J. Marshall and Alaine M. Low (Oxford: Oxford University Press, 2001), 221; Greene, " 'By Their Laws Shall Ye Know Them': Law and Identity in Colonial British America," *Journal of Interdisciplinary History* 33, 2 (2002): 247–60; Greene, "The Cultural Dimensions of Political Transfers: An Aspect of the European Occupation of the Americas," *EAS* 6, 1 (2008): 15–23.

103. Christopher L. Tomlins, "The Legal Cartography of Colonization, the Legal Polyphony of Settlement: English Intrusions on the American Mainland in the Seventeenth Century," *Law & Social Inquiry* 26, 2 (2001): 351, 352; Hulsebosch, "Ancient Constitution," 447–54; Offutt, "Atlantic Rules," 160.

104. Kettner, *Development of American Citizenship*, 103; Hulsebosch, "Ancient Constitution," 457.

105. Tomlins, "Legal Cartography of Colonization," 330 ("all [the] liberties"), 341, 343; Hulsebosch, "Ancient Constitution," 439, 473, 478 (quote). On slavery and the transmission of English law to Virginia, see Pagan, *Anne Orthwood's Bastard*.

106. Penn to Lord North, 24/5mo/1683, in *PWP*, 2: 414.

107. Penn, *Further Account*, 276. For Penn's praise of Lenape government in general, see Penn to the Earl of Sunderlund, 28/5mo/1683, in *PWP*, 2: 417.

108. William Penn, *Letter*, 230. On Williams, see Karen Ordahl Kupperman, *Indians and English: Facing Off in Early America* (Ithaca, N.Y.: Cornell University Press, 2000), 87–88.

109. On the Delaware pidgin (also technically referred to as a "jargon"), see Ives Goddard, "The Delaware Jargon," in *New Sweden in America*, ed. Carol E. Hoffecker (Newark: University of Delaware Press, 1995), 137–49; Goddard, "Pidgin Delaware," in *Contact Languages: A Wider Perspective*, ed. Sarah Grey Thomason (Amsterdam: Benjamins, 1997), 43–97. On its uses, see Goddard, "The Use of Pidgins and Jargons on the East Coast of North America," in *The Language Encounter in the Americas, 1492–1800: A Collection of Essays*, ed. Edward G. Gray and Norman Fiering (New York: Berghahns, 2000), 63–71; James O'Neil Spady, "Colonialism and the Discursive Antecedents of Penn's Treaty with the Indians," in *Friends and Enemies in Penn's Woods: Colonists, Indians, and the Racial Construction of Pennsylvania*, ed. William Pencak and Daniel K. Richter (University Park: Pennsylvania State University Press, 2004), 21.

110. On Quaker speech ways see Chapter 1 above.

111. Stephen Greenblatt, *Marvelous Possessions: The Wonder of the New World* (Chicago: University of Chicago Press, 1991); Greenblatt, "Learning to Curse: Aspects of Linguistic Colonialism in the Sixteenth-Century," in Greenblatt, *Learning to Curse: Essays in Early Modern Culture* (New York: Routledge, 1990), 86–118; Tzvetan Todorov, *The Conquest of America: The Question of the Other* (Norman: University of Oklahoma Press, 1999), esp. 14–33, 63–97, 168–82; Jane Kamensky, *Governing the Tongue: The Politics of Speech in Early New England* (New York: Oxford University Press, 1997), 48–55; Kupperman, *Indians and English*, 79–88; Edward G. Gray, *New World Babel: Languages and Nations in Early America* (Princeton, N.J.: Princeton University Press, 1999), 85–111; Anthony Pagden, *The Fall of Natural Man: The American Indian and the Origins of Compara-*

tive Ethnology, 1st pbk. ed. (New York: Cambridge University Press, 1986), 119–209; Gordon M. Sayre, *Les Sauvages Américains: Representations of Native Americans in French and English Colonial Literature* (Chapel Hill: University of North Carolina Press, 1997), 79–143.

112. Margaret Trabue Hodgen, *Early Anthropology in the Sixteenth and Seventeenth Centuries* (Philadelphia: University of Pennsylvania Press, 1964), 265–94; Gray, *New World Babel*, 8–55; Pagden, *Fall of Natural Man*, 146–209.

113. Greenblatt has argued that the more relevant poles of interpretation for European ethnographers were "a tendency to imagine the Indians as virtual blanks—wild, unformed creatures as naked in culture as they are in body" and "a tendency to imagine the Indians as virtual doubles, fully conversant with the language and culture of the Europeans," an assertion that I believe most of the literature on this topic does not bear out (Greenblatt, *Marvelous Possessions*, 95). On the temporalization of spatial cultural differences, see Hodgen, *Early Anthropology*, 386–478. On native peoples as figures from Europe's barbarian past, see Hayden V. White, "The Forms of Wildness: Archaeology of an Idea" and "The Noble Savage Theme as Fetish," in White, *Tropics of Discourse: Essays in Cultural Criticism* (Baltimore: Johns Hopkins University Press, 1978), 150–82, 183–96; Joyce E. Chaplin, *Subject Matter: Technology, the Body, and Science on the Anglo-American Frontier, 1500–1676* (Cambridge, Mass.: Harvard University Press, 2001), 76–115; Florike Egmond and Peter Mason, *The Mammoth and the Mouse: Microhistory and Morphology* (Baltimore: Johns Hopkins University Press, 1997), 157–82; Sabine MacCormack, "Limits of Understanding: Perceptions of Greco-Roman and Amerindian Paganism in Early Modern Europe," in *America in European Consciousness, 1493–1750*, ed. Karen Ordahl Kupperman (Chapel Hill: University of North Carolina Press, 1995), 179–229; MacCormack, *Religion in the Andes: Vision and Imagination in Early Colonial Peru* (Princeton, N.J.: Princeton University Press, 1991). On European ethnographers treating native peoples as "other," see Kamensky, *Governing the Tongue*, 49, 53. Karen Ordahl Kupperman has suggested that English colonial writers did not see the Indians as irrevocably "other" but emphasized common traits: Kupperman, *Settling with the Indians: The Meeting of English and Indian Cultures in America, 1580–1640* (Totowa, N.J.: Rowman and Littlefield, 1980), 104–40. See also James Axtell, "Imagining the Other: First Encounters in North America," in Axtell, *Beyond 1492: Encounters in Colonial North America* (New York: Oxford University Press, 1992), 25–74.

114. Pauline Turner Strong has suggested that Quaker ethnographers in the colonial period were significantly better at describing a common humanity between themselves and Indians than were other Englishmen, allowing the beginnings of a cross-cultural dialogue between newcomers and natives. See Strong, *Captive Selves, Captivating Others: The Politics and Poetics of Colonial American Captivity Narratives* (Boulder, Colo.: Westview Press, 1999), 152–66.

115. Pastorius, *Circumstantial Geographical Description*, 430; Penn, *Letter*, 230.

116. In this sense, I disagree with Greenblatt's assertion that, for European ethnographers who saw Indians as virtual doubles of themselves, this process "does not lead to

identification with the other, but to a ruthless will to possess" (*Marvelous Possessions*, 98). My argument here is that Quaker ethnography is, in critical ways, apart from the mainstream he describes. Both Karen Kupperman and Nancy Shoemaker, meanwhile, have argued that both Indians and English looked first for similarities rather than differences in their interactions; see Kupperman, *Indians and English*; Shoemaker, *A Strange Likeness: Becoming Red and White in Eighteenth-Century North America* (New York: Oxford University Press, 2004). On the ethnographic of the other as the antithesis to the self, see also Egmond and Mason, *Mammoth and the Mouse*, 60; and Peter Stallybrass and Allon White, *The Politics and Poetics of Transgression* (Ithaca, N.Y.: Cornell University Press, 1986), 128.

117. These were the four most common themes in European anthropology of the Americas as a whole. See Pagden, *Fall of Natural Man*; Hodgen, *Early Anthropology*.

118. See Penn, *Letter*, 230–31; Gabriel Thomas, *An Historical and Geographical Account of Pennsilvania and of West-New-Jersey* (London: A. Balwin, 1698) in *NEP*, 343. This description is from a 1697 letter to Herr George Leohard Model, republished in Pastorius, *Circumstantial Geographical Description*, 435.

119. Penn, *Letter*, 230; Pastorius, *Positive Information from America, Concerning the Country of Pennsylvania, From a German Who Has Migrated thither; Dated Philadelphia, March 7, 1684* (1684), in *NEP*, 401.

120. Gray, *New World Babel*, 13, 28–55; Kupperman, *Settling with the Indians*, 47–48, 108–9.

121. There is, for example, nothing comparable in the British American world to the massive translation efforts led by Fray Bernadino de Sahagún to catalog Nahuatl language and culture or Jesuit efforts to create Algonquian dictionaries. See the essays in Jorge Klor de Alva et al., eds., *The Work of Bernardino de Sahagun: Pioneer Ethnographer of Sixteenth-Century Aztec Mexico* (Albany, N.Y.: Institute for Mesoamerican Studies, SUNY, 1988); Karen Ordahl Kupperman, "Introduction," in *America in European Consciousness*, ed. Kupperman, 18; James Axtell, *The Invasion Within: The Contest of Cultures in Colonial North America* (New York: Oxford University Press, 1985), 108.

122. Penn, *Letter*, 230, 235.

123. Pastorius, *Circumstantial Geographical Description*, 384, 419.

124. Budd, *Good Order*, 31

125. Budd, *Good Order*, 30, 28.

126. Penn, *Letter*, 235. Thomas similarly noted that Lenape Councils were "slow and deliberate . . . in resolving, naturally wise, and hardly to be out-witted" (*Historical and Geographical Account*, 335).

127. Penn, *Letter*, 233.

128. Pastorius, *Circumstantial Geographical Description*, 419, 420.

129. Penn, *Letter*, 234; Penn to the "Kings of the Indians," 10/8mo/1681, in *WPFP*, 86.

130. For examples of this kind of Quaker speculation, see Penn, *Letter*, 236–37; Richard Frame, *A Short Description of Pennsilvania* (Philadelphia: William Bradford, 1692), in *NEP*, 300–305, esp. 302–3; Pastorius, *Circumstantial Geographical Description*,

385. For discussions of this theme among other European anthropologists of America, see Gray, *New World Babel*, 24–25; Hodgen, *Early Anthropology*, 284, 296, 312; Kupperman, *Settling with the Indians*, 107–11.

131. Charles Marshall, "Testimony Concerning John Camm and John Audland" (1689), in Hugh Barbour and Arthur O. Roberts, eds., *Early Quaker Writings, 1650–1750* (Grand Rapids, Mich.: Eerdmans, 1973), 82; Joseph Besse, *A Collection of Sufferings of the People Called Quakers, . . .* (London: L. Hinde, 1753); William Dewsbury, *True Prophecy of the Mighty Day of the Lord* (1655), in Barbour and Roberts, eds., *Early Quaker Writings*, 131, 93, 95.

132. Hodgen, *Early Anthropology*, 386–426.

133. This theme is discussed in Robert Daiutolo, Jr., "The Early Quaker Perception of the Indian," *Quaker History* 72, 2 (1983): 103–19.

134. This demographic transition is discussion in Chapter 5 below.

135. Penn, to the "Kings of the Indians," in *WPFP*, 87–88. Penn was in actuality addressing local leaders of the Lenape Indians; given their decentralized political structure and lack of true "kings," his sentiments are more commendable than his grasp of Lenape customs.

136. Penn, "Instructions Given by Me, William Penn, Proprietor and Governor of Pennsylvania, to My Trusty and Loving Friends, William Crispin, John Bezar, and Nathaniel Allen, My Commissioners for the Settling of the Present Colony This Year Transported into the Said Province," in *WPFP*, 82–86. See Francis Jennings, *The Invasion of America: Indians, Colonialism, and the Cant of Conquest* (Chapel Hill: University of North Carolina Press, 1975), for a critical discussion of English treatment of Native Americans in other colonies in the seventeenth century.

137. Penn to William Markham, 1 September 1683, in *PWP*, 2: 473.

138. Penn, "Additional Instructions to William Markham," 28/10mo/1681, in *WPFP*, 89. For discussions of William Haige's attempts to purchase land in the Susquehanna Valley on behalf of Penn, see "The Mohawk Indians' Answer to William Haige and James Graham," in *PWP*, 2: 481–82; William Haige to Penn, 29 August 1683, in *PWP*, 2: 469–71.

139. Anthony Pagden, "The Struggle for Legitimation and the Image of Empire in the Atlantic to c. 1700," in *The Oxford History of the British Empire*, vol. 1, *The Origins of Empire British Overseas Enterprise to the Close of the Seventeenth Century*, ed. Nicholas P. Canny (New York: Oxford University Press, 1998), 39. See also Pagden, *Lords of All the World: Ideologies of Empire in Spain, Britain and France c. 1500–c. 1800* (New Haven, Conn.: Yale University Press, 1995), 73–91; Robert A. Williams, *The American Indian in Western Legal Thought: The Discourses of Conquest* (New York: Oxford University Press, 1990), 151–57, 174–77; Jennings, *Invasion*, 45.

140. See Chapter 1 above.

141. Pagden, *Lords of All the World*, 77; Williams, *American Indian in Western Legal Thought*, 241–55.

142. For a summary of this English perspective, see Tomlins, "Legal Cartography of Colonization," 315–47.

143. John Locke, *Two Treatises of Government* (New York: Cambridge University Press, 1988), §49, 301.

144. Locke, *Two Treatises*, §36, 293.

145. Richard Tuck, *The Rights of War and Peace: Political Thought and the International Order from Grotius to Kant* (New York: Oxford University Press, 1999), 176.

146. Cable, *Statute*, 64. Penn, "Conditions or Concessions to the First Purchasers," 11/5mo/1681 in *WPFP*, 74. See also Penn, *Letter*, 236. He had also signaled his intentions to create this mixed-jury system in his first letter to the "Kings of the Indians," in *WPFP*, 87.

147. "Deed from the Lenape Indians," 15 July 1682 and 1 August 1682, in *WPFP*, 156–62; see also "Deed from the Lenape Indians," 23 June 1683, in *WPFP*, 287–88.

148. "Deed from the Lenape Indians," 15 July 1682 and 1 August 1683, in *WPFP*, 160.

149. Penn's policies differed from what Patricia Seed has identified as the prototypical "English" approach to colonization—marking territory through solid barriers such as fences and plantings: Seed, *Ceremonies of Possession in Europe's Conquest of the New World, 1492–1640* (New York: Cambridge University Press, 1995), 16–40.

150. Ives Goddard writes that "Chiefs acted as mediators and performed ceremonial functions, but they lacked coercive prerogatives. At times they seem to exercise little power beyond that of persuasion, unable to control the warriors and merely acting as spokesmen for their particular people in dealings with the Europeans." Goddard, "Delaware," in *Handbook of North American Indians: Northeast*, ed. Bruce Trigger (Washington, D.C.: Smithsonian Institution, 1978), 216.

151. More, *Letter from Dr. More*, 292.

152. Penn, *Letter*, 236. For a more skeptical account of Penn's relations with local Lenape, see Spady, "Colonialism and the Discursive Antecedents of *Penn's Treaty with the Indians*."

153. Pastorius, *Circumstantial Geographical Description*, 401.

154. Paschall, *An Abstract of a Letter*, 254.

155. Penn, *Further Account*, 276.

CHAPTER 3. WORDS AND THINGS: CONTESTING CIVIC IDENTITY IN EARLY PENNSYLVANIA

1. William Penn to Thomas Lloyd et al., 18/3mo/1685–17/6mo/1685, in *PWP*, 3: 44.

2. Penn to Lloyd et al., in *PWP*, 3: 44.

3. Penn to Lloyd et al., in *PWP*, 3: 50.

4. *MPCP*, 1: 44 On Blackwell's entrance, see Gary B. Nash, *Quakers and Politics: Pennsylvania, 1681–1726*, new ed. (Boston: Northeastern University Press, 1993), 117.

5. Nash, *Quakers and Politics*, 293.

6. For an attempt to frame this conflict in terms of land policy, see Nash, *Quakers and Politics*, 89–126. For the suggestion of an ingrained Quaker antiauthoritarianism, see

Alan Tully, *Forming American Politics: Ideals, Interests, and Institutions in Colonial New York and Pennsylvania* (Baltimore: Johns Hopkins University Press, 1994), 36–37.

7. For a definition of performative speech, see J. L. Austin, *How to Do Things with Words*, 2nd ed. (Oxford: Clarendon Press, 1975); see also Pierre Bourdieu, "Authorized Language: The Social Condition for the Effectiveness of Ritual Discourse," and "Rites of Institution," in Bourdieu, *Language and Symbolic Power*, ed. John Thompson, trans. Gino Raymond and Matthew Adamson (Cambridge, Mass.: Harvard University Press, 1991), 107–16, 117–26.

8. My understanding of the relationship between manners and deference here is derived from David Graeber, "Manners, Deference, and Private Property in Early Modern Europe," *Comparative Studies in Society and History* 39, 4 (1997): 694–728.

9. See J. G. A. Pocock, "The Classical Theory of Deference," *AHR* 81, 3 (1976): 516–24, esp. Pocock's definition of deference on 516. On Harrington's *Oceana* as a model deferential community, see 517; and Pocock, *The Machiavellian Moment: Florentine Political Thought and the Atlantic Republican Tradition* (Princeton, N.J.: Princeton University Press, 1975), 395.

10. Walter Bagehot, *The English Constitution* (London: Kegan, Paul, Trench, 1882), 4.

11. Bernard Bailyn has argued that the lack of a true aristocratic leadership class was one of the major reasons colonial American politics differed so greatly from English politics: Bailyn, *The Origins of American Politics* (New York: Knopf, 1968), 96–105. He has similarly argued that a political leadership class emerged in Virginia only in the 1680s, nearly eight decades after that colony's founding: Bailyn and James Morton Smith, "Politics and Social Structure in Virginia," in *Seventeenth-Century America: Essays in Colonial History*, ed. Smith (Chapel Hill: University of North Carolina Press, 1959), 90–115. Michael Zuckerman has argued that flimsy claims of Pennsylvania's rulers to social stature rendered any calls for deference risible: Zuckerman, "Authority in Early America: The Decay of Deference on the Provincial Periphery," *EAS* 1, 2 (2003): 3–8.

12. Penn to John Alloway, 29/9mo/1683 in *PWP*, 2: 503–4.

13. *Votes*, 47.

14. Edwin B. Bronner, *William Penn's Holy Experiment: The Founding of Pennsylvania, 1681–1701* (New York: Temple University Publications, 1962), 89–96; Nash, *Quakers and Politics*, 83–114.

15. Penn to John Blayking, Thomas Camm, Thomas Langhorne, and Robert Barrow, 16/2mo/1683, in *WPFP*, 217.

16. *MPCP*, 1: 58–59; Peter Thompson, *Rum Punch & Revolution: Taverngoing & Public Life in Eighteenth-Century Philadelphia* (Philadelphia: University of Pennsylvania Press, 1999), 111.

17. *MPCP*, 1: 59.

18. *MPCP*, 1: 135–37.

19. *MPCP*, 1: 141.

20. *MPCP*, 1: 192; *Votes*, 66–69; *PWP*, 3: 124–26.

21. *MPCP*, 1: 196, 98 For an earlier accusation of treason against Curtis, see 161–62.

22. *MPCP*, 1: 210.

23. *MPCP*, 1: 219 The case is recorded in *Sussex Courts*, 533–34.

24. Penn to Commissioners of State, in *PWP*, 3: 168.

25. Penn to Commissioners of State, in *PWP*, 3: 170.

26. Thomas Holme to Penn to 24/1mo/1688, in *PWP*, 3: 180–81.

27. On these two events, see Chapter Five below.

28. *Votes*, 13–43, 85; William Markham to Penn, 21/5mo/1688, in *PWP*, 3: 196–97, 286; Nash, *Quakers and Politics*, 67–73, 80–81, 87, 103, 111–14; Bronner, *William Penn's Holy Experiment*, 94–95, 106.

29. See Chapter Two, above.

30. Nash, *Quakers and Politics*, 103.

31. William Penn to Commissioners to State, 18/7mo/1688, in *PWP*, 3: 210; see also Markham to Penn, in *PWP*, 3 196.

32. *Sussex Courts*, 692.

33. *Sussex Courts*, 277–78, 287–88, 291–92.

34. William Markham to Penn, 22 August 1686, in *PWP*, 3: 103.

35. These disputes are recounted in Penn to Provincial Council, 11/9mo/1690, in *PWP*, 3: 286; Council of the Lower Counties to Penn, 6 April 1691, in *PWP*, 3: 297, 298; Provincial Council to Penn, 11/2mo/1691, in *PWP*, 3: 302; Robert Turner to Penn, 23/3mo/1691, in *PWP*, 3: 322; *MPCP*, 1: 321. These do not include Thomas Lloyd's fights with Blackwell over the Seal—see below.

36. The best narratives of Blackwell's tenure can be found in Bronner, *William Penn's Holy Experiment*, 109–33; Nash, *Quakers and Politics*, 114–26.

37. John Blackwell to Penn, 25 January 1689, in *PWP*, 3: 220.

38. *MPCP*, 1: 290–97.

39. Ibid., 250. See also Council of the Lower Counties to Penn, 6/2mo/1691, in *PWP*, 3: 297.

40. On the role of popular royal festive culture in Restoration England, see Tim Harris, *Restoration: Charles II and His Kingdoms, 1660–1685* (London: Penguin Global, 2006), 281–92. On the centrality of festive culture, royal and otherwise, in colonial politics, see Brendan McConville, *The King's Three Faces: The Rise and Fall of Royal America, 1688–1776* (Chapel Hill: University of North Carolina Press, 2006), 49–70; Simon P. Newman, *Parades and the Politics of the Street: Festive Culture in the Early American Republic* (Philadelphia: University of Pennsylvania Press, 1997), 11–22.

41. Blackwell to Penn, in *PWP*, 3: 231.

42. *MPCP*, 1: 244.

43. Cable, *Statutes*, 53, 103.

44. *MPCP*, 1: 278–83.

45. John Blackwell to Penn, 1 May 1689, in *PWP*, 3: 245.

46. Penn to Provincial Council, June 1686, in *PWP*, 3: 93–94.

47. Thomas Holme to Penn, 25 November 1686, in *PWP*, 3: 131.

48. Phineas Pemberton to Penn, April 1689, in *PWP*, 3: 248 ("one thus foreigne," "lett us have"); John Simcock et al. to Penn, 9 April 1689, in *PWP*, 3: 237 ("best of the People," "factious . . .").

49. Blackwell to Penn, in *PWP*, 3: 243; Sally Schwartz, *"A Mixed Multitude": The Struggle for Toleration in Colonial Pennsylvania* (New York: New York University Press, 1987), 41. On the persistence of this charge being levied against Friends, see William Penn to Jasper Batt, 5 February 1683, in *WPFP*, 199.

50. On the dangers of faction in seventeenth-century English thought, see Pocock, *Machiavellian Moment*, 362–64, 408.

51. On English and Scots citizenship during this period, see James H. Kettner, *The Development of American Citizenship, 1608–1870* (Chapel Hill: University of North Carolina Press, 1978), 3–61. On European traditions, see Peter N. Riesenberg, *Citizenship in the Western Tradition: Plato to Rousseau* (Chapel Hill: University of North Carolina Press, 1992), 203–34; and Tamar Herzog, *Defining Nations: Immigrants and Citizens in Early Modern Spain and Spanish America* (New Haven, Conn.: Yale University Press, 2003), 164–200. On German understandings of civic practice, see A. G. Roeber, *Palatines, Liberty, and Property: German Lutherans in Colonial British America* (Baltimore: Johns Hopkins University Press, 1993), 27–132. When I say ethnically German, I am referring to those German-speaking settlers born within one of the several principalities in central Europe; I am not presuming any unified "German" national identity existed at this time: see Philip Otterness, *Becoming German: The 1709 Palatine Migration to New York* (Ithaca, N.Y.: Cornell University Press, 2004), 3.

52. See, for example, Philadelphia County Court Minutes, 11 January 1683, in *WPFP*, 197–99; *MPCP*, 1: 134; *Sussex Courts*, 218. For this accusation, see Turner to Penn, in *PWP*, 3: 322.

53. On the role of citizenship laws defining the fundamental boundaries of a political or social community, see Rogers M. Smith, *Civic Ideals: Conflicting Visions of Citizenship in U.S. History* (New Haven, Conn.: Yale University Press, 1997), 30–31. On citizenship as a set of practices, see Karen Sykes, "Paying a School Fee Is a Father's Duty: Critical Citizenship in Central New Ireland," *American Ethnologist* 28, 1 (2001): 6.

54. Margaret R. Somers, "Rights, Relationality, and Membership: Rethinking the Making of Citizenship," *Law and Social Inquiry* 19, 1 (1994): 65, 79; Linda K. Kerber's emphasis on citizenship as a web of obligations rather than a nexus of rights has strongly influenced my thinking here; see Kerber, *No Constitutional Right to Be Ladies: Women and the Obligations of Citizenship* (New York: Hill and Wang, 1998), 8–11, 303–4 and passim; Somers, "Citizenship and the Place of the Public Sphere: Law, Community, and Political Culture in the Transition to Democracy," *American Sociological Review* 58, 5 (1993): 589.

55. Growden to Penn, 28/2mo/1691, in *PWP*, 3: 309; Kettner, *Development of American Citizenship*, 44–61; Riesenberg, *Citizenship in the Western Tradition*, 217.

56. Growden to Penn, in *PWP*, 3: 310.

57. See OED entry for "dative."

58. Provincial Council and Assembly to William Penn, 18/3mo/1691, in *PWP*, 3: 317.

59. Daniel J. Hulsebosch, "The Ancient Constitution and the Expanding Empire: Sir Edward Coke's British Jurisprudence," *Law and History Review* 21, 3 (2003): 439–82.

60. *MPCP*, 1: 300, 306; See also Schwartz, *"Mixed Multitude"*, 49; Nash, *Quakers and Politics*, 130–31; Robert L. D. Davidson, *War Comes to Quaker Pennsylvania, 1682–1756* (New York: Columbia University Press, 1957), 11.

61. *MPCP*, 1: 306–10.

62. See Riesenberg, *Citizenship in the Western Tradition*; Osvaldo Cavallar, "Regulating Arms in Late Medieval and Renaissance Italian City-States," in *Privileges and Rights of Citizenship: Law and the Juridical Construction of Civil Society*, ed. Julius Kirshner and Laurent Mayali (Berkeley, Calif.: Robbins Collection, 2002), 124–26; Pocock, *Machiavellian Moment*, 390, 392; Joyce Lee Malcolm, "The Creation of a True Antient and Indubitable Right: The English Bill of Rights and the Right to Be Armed," *Journal of British Studies* 32, 3 (1993): esp. 229–32.

63. *MPCP*, 1: 334; Nash, *Quakers and Politics*, 131; Davidson, *War Comes to Quaker Pennsylvania*, 11.

64. Lieutenant Governor Francis Nicholson to Lords of Trade and Plantation, 26 January 1691, in *CSPC*, 13: 381–82. On Pennsylvania as a liability for frontier defense, see also Nicholson to Lords of Trade and Plantations, 20 August 1690, in *CSPC*, 13: 308–10; Nicholson to Lords of Trade and Plantations, 12 October 1691, in *CSPC*, 13: 551–52.

65. Fletcher's commission and instructions are located in *MPCP*, 1: 345–64; Bronner, *William Penn's Holy Experiment*, 155–57; Nash, *Quakers and Politics*, 182–83.

66. *MPCP*, 1: 459.

67. *MPCP*, 1: 462–71; *Votes*, 133–34, 154–77; Davidson, *War Comes to Quaker Pennsylvania*, 12.

68. *MPCP*, 1:369.

69. Thomas Holme to Penn, 25 November 1686, in *PWP*, 3: 132; Nash, *Quakers and Politics*, 74–75, 82–83.

70. Council of the Lower Counties to Penn, in *PWP*, 3: 295–302; Provincial Council of Pennsylvania to Penn, 11 April 1691, 3: 302–6; Growden to Penn, in *PWP*, 3: 307.

71. Penn to Provincial Council, 11/7mo/1691, in *PWP*, 3: 328. See also Penn to Council, 11/7mo/1691, in *PWP (Micro)*, 6: 631. The editors of the *PWP*, print and microfilm, transcribe the phrase "in Civills" as "in Civilis," an ungrammatical Latin phrase that the former gloss as "as citizens." Looking at the manuscript microfilm, I think it more likely that Penn wrote "in Civills"—a phrase he used more than once in his writings on toleration—and have chosen to transcribe it as such here.

72. The extent of these treaties are detailed in *PWP*, 2: 491.

73. "Commission and Instructions to James Graham and William Haige," 2/6mo/1683, in *WPFP*, 293. For other details on Graham and Haige's negotiations with the Iroquois, see William Haige to Penn, 29/6mo/1683, in *PWP*, 2: 469–71; and "The Mohawks' Answer to William Haige and James Graham," 7/7mo/1683, in *PWP*, 2: 481–82.

74. The negotiations owed their failure to a Mohawk unwillingness to sell and efforts by New York governor Thomas Dongan to block Pennsylvania's expansion into the

Susquehanna Valley. On the Mohawks' reluctance and Dongan's fears of Pennsylvania's entrance into the Covenant Chain with the Iroquois, see Francis Jennings, *The Ambiguous Iroquois Empire: The Covenant Chain Confederation of Indian Tribes with English Colonies from Its Beginnings to the Lancaster Treaty of 1744* (New York: Norton, 1984), 226–30; Daniel K. Richter, *The Ordeal of the Longhouse: The Peoples of the Iroquois League in the Era of European Colonization* (Chapel Hill: University of North Carolina Press, 1992), 150; Eric Hinderaker, *Elusive Empires: Constructing Colonialism in the Ohio Valley, 1673–1800* (New York: Cambridge University Press, 1997), 103.

75. *MPCP*, 1: 105. See also Cable, *Statutes*, 115. Penn wrote after this treaty that the offer of English "justice gains and aws them" and that this treaty had secured comity and friendship between English and native peoples. Penn, *A Further Account of the Province of Pennsylvania and Its Improvements, for the Satisfaction of Those That Are Adventurers, and Enclined to Be So* (London, 1685), in *NEP*, 276.

76. "Commission and Instructions to Graham and Haige," 294.

77. Historians have disagreed on the Iroquois' tenuous claims of conquest. For an account that denies that the Iroquois conquered the Susquehannocks or the Susquehanna Valley region, see Jennings, *Ambiguous Iroquois Empire*, 229–30. Daniel Richter writes of the end of the Susquehannock-Iroquois war in 1675 that "The Susquehannocks' lands had not been exactly 'wonn with the sword' (as some Iroquois would claim a few years later), but they might as well have been" (*Ordeal of the Longhouse*, 136). See also Hinderaker's reference to the Iroquois' "supposed conquest": *Elusive Empires*, 103. After weighing these accounts—and Penn's own confusion on the matter—I deem the Iroquois claim "ambiguous."

78. On the "deed game," see Francis Jennings, *The Invasion of America: Indians, Colonialism, and the Cant of Conquest* (Chapel Hill: University of North Carolina Press, 1975).

79. For Penn's aboutface and firm displeasure with the rum trade, see *Votes*, 117. On the Quaker Meeting's efforts to end the trade, see PYMM Minutes, 15/7mo/1685, 8/7mo/1686, 7/7mo/1687.

80. Penn to Thomas Holme, 8/6mo/1685, in *PWP (Micro)*, 5: 254. This incident is discussed in greater depth in James O'Neil Spady, "Colonialism and the Discursive Antecedents of *Penn's Treaty with the Indians*," in *Friends and Enemies in Penn's Woods: Colonists, Indians, and the Racial Construction of Pennsylvania*, ed. William Pencak and Daniel K. Richter (University Park: Pennsylvania State University Press, 2004), 35–36, although Spady ignores the 1684 concession in which the Lenape agreed to be governed by English law, temporary as that concession may have been.

81. In this respect, the situation was similar to the phenomenon Richard White calls the "middle ground" in the *pays d'en haut*: White, *The Middle Ground: Indians, Empires, and Republics in the Great Lakes Region, 1650–1815* (New York: Cambridge University Press, 1990), 52 and passim.

82. *MPCP*, 1: 147, 148–49.

83. Markham to Penn, in *PWP*, 3: 106–7. For Nicholas Scull's relationship to Andrew Scull, Farmer's overseer, see *PWP*, 3: 113n77; also *MPCP*, 1: 187–88. The Scull incident is also discussed in Spady, "Colonialism and the Discursive Antecedents of *Penn's Treaty with the Indians*," 36.

84. Markham to Penn, in *PWP*, 3: 107.

85. Henry J. Cadbury and J. William Frost, "Caleb Pusey's Account of Pennsylvania," *Quaker History* 64, 1 (1975): 49–51; Robert Proud, *The History of Pennsylvania, in North America* (Philadelphia: Zachariah Poulson, 1797–98), 1: 337–38. For another early Indian claim that Penn or his agents had not fully paid for Indian lands, see Nicholas More to Penn, 1/8mo/1684, in *PWP*, 2: 608.

86. *MPCP*, 1: 299 (rumors), 334 (quotation).

87. *MPCP*, 1: 447–49.

88. Nancy Shoemaker, *A Strange Likeness: Becoming Red and White in Eighteenth-Century North America* (New York: Oxford University Press, 2004), 105–24.

89. *MPCP*, 1: 372–73. Although the Provincial Council minutes do not note the tribal affiliation of the Indians treating with Fletcher, Jennings argues that they were Minisink, part of the northern branch of the Lenape: see Jennings, *Ambiguous Iroquois Empire*, 202.

90. *MPCP*, 1: 373.

91. *MPCP*, 1: 447.

92. Record of the Philadelphia Courts, 1685–86, call #AM 3902, HSP, 24.

93. On the importance of Anglo-American courts in the daily lives of colonists vis-à-vis other governmental institutions, see Jack N. Rakove, *Original Meanings: Politics and Ideas in the Making of the Constitution* (New York: Knopf, 1996), 302.

94. *Chester Courts*, 305.

95. *Bucks Courts*, 80.

96. *Bucks Courts*, 80–81.

97. *Chester Courts*, 19–20.

98. Using a dramaturgical-anthropological approach, A. G. Roeber and Rhys Isaac have emphasized the importance of court-day rituals shaped by custom—and following a more careful script—in colonial Virginia; see Roeber, "Authority, Law, and Custom: The Rituals of Court Day in Tidewater Virginia, 1720 to 1750," *WMQ* 37, 1 (1980): 29–52; Isaac, *The Transformation of Virginia, 1740–1790* (Chapel Hill: University of North Carolina Press, 1999), 88–94. David T. Konig has emphasized the limitations of this approach, arguing that the realities of everyday life shaped behavior in the courtroom more than the rituals of power evident in other domains of colonial life: Konig, "A Summary View of the Law of British America," *WMQ* 50, 1 (1993): 44–45. My emphasis here is based on a dialogical cultural approach, locating colonial legal culture in the discursive interactions among colonists. See Mikhail M. Bakhtin, *The Dialogic Imagination: Four Essays*, ed. Michael Holquist, trans. Caryl Emerson and Holquist (Austin: University of Texas Press, 1981), esp. "Discourse in the Novel," 259–422; Bakhtin, "'The Problem of Speech Genres'

and 'Toward a Methodology for the Human Sciences,'" in Bakhtin, *Speech Genres and Other Late Essays*, trans. Holquist and Emerson (Austin: University of Texas Press, 1986), 60–102, 159–72; V. N. Vološinov, *Marxism and the Philosophy of Language*, trans. Ladislav Matejka and I. R. Titunik (Cambridge, Mass.: Harvard University Press, 1986).

99. The discussion in this and the following paragraphs is influenced heavily by William M. Offutt's extraordinarily detailed cataloging and analysis of legal choices in the colonial Delaware Valley: Offutt, *Of "Good Laws" and "Good Men": Law and Society in the Delaware Valley, 1680–1710* (Urbana: University of Illinois Press, 1995), 100–146.

100. These declarations followed the prescription in the colony's legal code that all deeds needed to be "declared & acknowledged in Open Court" as well as registered with the office of the public rolls. See Cable, *Statutes*, 46, 67.

101. *Chester Courts*, 29–30.

102. See, for example, *Chester Courts*, 36.

103. I am drawing on Richard L. Bushman's examination of the process through which "courts made farms from texts" in colonial North Carolina: Bushman, "Farmers in Court: Orange County, North Carolina, 1750–1776," in *The Many Legalities of Early America*, ed. Christopher L. Tomlins and Bruce H. Mann (Chapel Hill: University of North Carolina Press, 2001), 389.

104. See Offutt, *Of "Good Laws"*, 93–94. Alfred L. Brophy also makes this point regarding the typicality of Sussex courts during this period: Brophy, 'For the Preservation of the King's Peace and Justice': Community and English Law in Sussex County, Pennsylvania, 1682–1696," *American Journal of Legal History* 40, 2 (1996): 178. Both Bruce H. Mann and David Konig have found similar uses of civil courts in early Connecticut and Massachusetts; see Mann, *Neighbors and Strangers: Law and Community in Early Connecticut* (Chapel Hill: University of North Carolina Press, 1987); Konig, *Law and Society in Puritan Massachusetts: Essex County, 1629–1692* (Chapel Hill: University of North Carolina Press, 1979).

105. *Sussex Courts*, 700, 819, 997.

106. *Bucks Courts*, 346, 357.

107. My discussion of the frequency of speech infractions is drawn from the compilation here of offenses in three counties with continuous extant records for this period:

SPEECH INFRACTIONS (CHESTER, BUCKS, SUSSEX), 1680–95 (SLANDER AND DEFAMATION, SPEECH AGAINST AUTHORITY, AND MISCELLANEOUS SPEECH OFFENSES SUCH AS SWEARING, LYING, OR CURSING)

Year	Chester	Bucks	Sussex	Total
1680–85	11	6	27	44
1686–90	42	12	56	110
1691–95	23	4	13	40
Total	76	22	96	194

Sources: *Chester Courts*; *Bucks Courts*; *Sussex Courts*.

It is somewhat difficult to make comparisons between Pennsylvania and other colonies in this respect, largely due to the difficulty in estimating colonial population. Thus, I cannot make a direct comparison between the rate of speech offenses per 10,000 persons (the statistical measure preferred by legal historians) in Pennsylvania and other colonies; the best I can do is compare the annual rates of speech offenses in Pennsylvania and elsewhere. With respect to slander and defamation, I found 1.6 such accusations per county annually from 1681–95. Mary Beth Norton found 0.6 cases of slander and defamation per county per year in Maryland in 1636–82, a period in which that colony's population probably exceeded that of Pennsylvania. Cornelia Hughes Dayton found 2.9 instances of slander and defamation in New Haven colony before 1665. Kathleen Brown's examination of slander and defamation cases brought before the courts of Norfolk, Lancaster, and York Counties in the decades before Bacon's Rebellion found an average of 3.8, 1.2, and 1.1 per year respectively; this was a period in which Virginia's population far outstripped Pennsylvania's. See Norton, "Gender and Defamation in Seventeenth-Century Maryland," *WMQ* 44, 1 (1987): 3–4; Dayton, *Women Before the Bar: Gender, Law, and Society in Connecticut, 1639–1789* (Chapel Hill: University of North Carolina Press, 1995), 289–90; Brown, *Good Wives, Nasty Wenches, and Anxious Patriarchs: Gender, Race, and Power in Colonial Virginia* (Chapel Hill: University of North Carolina Press, 1996), 147.

Robert St. George, meanwhile, found higher annual rates of "detractive" speech (which includes slander and defamation as well as other speech infractions such as lying) in early Essex County, Massachusetts (7.6 per year in 1640–50). St. George, "'Heated' Speech and Literacy in Seventeenth-Century New England," *Publications of the Colonial Society of Massachusetts* 63 (1984): 289. Instances of "speech against authority" in Pennsylvania appeared to equal if not outstrip those in Essex, however; see n129 below.

108. Norton, "Gender and Defamation"; St. George, "'Heated' Speech."

109. *Bucks Courts*, 18, 21. Many women in early America used the courts to guard their reputation. See Ellen Hartigan-O'Connor, *The Ties That Buy: Women and Commerce in Revolutionary America* (Philadelphia: University of Pennsylvania Press, 2009), 87. Norton has argued that this was a greater concern for men. See the gender breakdown in her database of Maryland defamation cases, "Gender and Defamation," 9.

110. Edwin B. Bronner, ed., "Philadelphia County Court of Quarter Sessions and Common Pleas, 1695," *American Journal of Legal History* 1, 1–3 (1957): 79–85, 175–90, 236–50.

111. For accusations of theft, see *Sussex Courts*, 426; for writing fraudulent contracts, 395; for burning out other men's brands, 494.

112. Compare the breakdown of the content of defamation cases: Norton, "Gender and Defamation," 9; St. George, "'Heated' Speech," 297.

113. *Chester Courts*, 6.

114. On the origins and persistence of this prejudice, see Gunlög Maria Fur, *Colonialism in the Margins: Cultural Encounters in New Sweden and Lapland* (Boston: Brill, 2006), 243–44.

115. *Chester Courts*, 103; Herbert William Keith Fitzroy, "Richard Crosby Goes to Court, 1683–1697," *PMHB* 62, 1 (1938): 18. On the rumors of the Sculls' murder at Indian hands, see Markham to Penn, 22 August 1786, in *PWP*, 3: 106–8; and Chapter 5 below.

116. *Sussex Courts*, 481–82.

117. *Sussex Courts*, 942.

118. *Bucks Courts*, 87, 187–88. For Taylor's abuse of the jury, see 110, 208.

119. Speech against authority and other speech infractions (including cursing, swearing, and lying) accounted for 63 percent of speech infractions appearing in court. Criminal slander cases—in which a charge was presented by a grand jury—accounted for 22.5 percent of slander cases, meaning that 71.6 percent of all speech infraction cases that reached the courtroom were the result of criminal prosecution.

120. Offutt has noted that magistrates in the Delaware Valley region charged citizens with criminal contempt in numbers far outstripping the rest of colonial British America: see *Of "Good Laws"*, 196, 309–10n29.

121. Record of the Philadelphia Courts, 1685–86, 17.

122. Record of the Philadelphia Courts, 1685–86, 26.

123. *Chester Courts*, 264, 266.

124. *Chester Courts*, 405–6.

125. For the claim that colonists in Massachusetts were particularly sensitive to speech infractions, see Jane Kamensky, *Governing the Tongue: The Politics of Speech in Early New England* (New York: Oxford University Press, 1997), 6, 200–201.

126. For explanation of what counted as "speech against authority," see Kamensky, *Governing the Tongue*, 244n66. Kamensky found a total of 47 such presentments in the Essex County court between 1634 and 1640, 2.8 per year. I found a comparable rate in both Chester and Sussex counties (2 per year) between 1682 (the year Penn received his charter) and 1695—a period in which Essex's population likely exceeded Chester's and far exceeded Sussex's.

127. *Chester Courts*, 44.

128. On the role of ritual apology in colonial Massachusetts as a means of "unsaying" slander, as well as its increasing ineffectiveness, see Kamensky, *Governing the Tongue*, 146–48.

129. My claim regarding overrepresentation is grounded in Offutt's finding that women were over represented in criminal and civil slander cases in his four-county Delaware Valley region: Offutt, *Of "Good Laws"*, 201. My findings (see tables) also suggest that women were involved as litigants in slander and defamation cases in Pennsylvania at a comparable rate to women in other colonies; see Norton, "Gender and Defamation," 12; Dayton, *Women Before the Bar*, 289; Kamensky, *Governing the Tongue*, 196. Pennsylvania women were not, however, involved in such cases at the same rate as Brown has found for mid-seventeenth-century Virginia; see Brown, *Good Wives, Nasty Wenches, and Anxious Patriarchs*, 145–49.

DEFENDANTS IN SLANDER CASES IN PENNSYLVANIA COURTS, 1681–95

	N	Men	Women	Couples	Total w/female def.
Chester	26	21 (80.8%)	2 (7.7%)	3 (11.5%)	5 (19.2%)
Bucks	6	5 (8.3%)	0 (0.0%)	1 (16.7%)	1 (16.7%)
Sussex	39	28 (71.8%)	3 (7.7%)	8 (20.5%)	11 (28.2%)
Total	71	54 (76.1%)	5 (7.0%)	12 (16.9%)	17 (23.9%)

Source: *Chester Courts*; *Bucks Courts*; *Sussex Courts*.

BRINGING SUIT FOR SLANDER IN PENNSYLVAIA COURTS, 1681–95

	N	Men	Women	Couples	Total w/female plt.
Chester	26	25 (96.1%)	0 (0.0%)	1 (3.8%)	1 (3.8%)
Bucks	6	2 (33.3%)	1 (16.7%)	3 (50.0%)	4 (66.7%)
Sussex	39	34 (87.1%)	2 (5.1%)	3 (7.7%)	5 (12.8%)
Total	71	61 (85.9%)	3 (4.2 %)	7 (9.9%)	10 (14.1%)

Source: *Chester Courts*; *Bucks Courts*; *Sussex Courts*.

130. Of course, one major difference in sexual standards between men and women was that while femininity was defined through regulation of one's own sexuality, masculinity made claims to—and depended upon—the regulation of others' sexuality as well. See Brown, *Good Wives, Nasty Wenches, and Anxious Patriarchs*, 319–42.

131. This differs from Brown's findings regarding slander cases in Virginia, where men comprised little more than half of all defendants in such cases; see Brown, *Good Wives, Nasty Wenches, and Anxious Patriarchs*, 145.

132. Offutt, *Of "Good Laws"*, 69, 201, breaks down the legal population for the Delaware Valley by gender. He does not note, however, what percentage of women participated as defendants or plaintiffs in concert with a husband and what percentage participated alone.

133. For three cases with female "juries," see *Chester Courts*, 166; *Bucks Courts*, 75; *Sussex Courts*, 229. The appointment of married women to examine female bodies as evidence in cases dealing with sexuality was a common one in British America. I should note that the practice appears much less common in early Pennsylvania courts than in other colonies; see, for example, the importance Brown places on this practice in early Virginia (Brown, *Good Wives, Nasty Wenches, and Anxious Patriarchs*, 94–100). The discrepancy in the frequency of this practice in Virginia and Pennsylvania may result from two factors. First, much of the disciplining of female sexuality in early Pennsylvania appears to have been done through the Quaker Meeting and not through the courts, at least for Friends. Second, a large majority of the women presented in the three Pennsylvania courts for sexual offenses—including fornication and "bastardy"—pleaded guilty and submitted to the judgment of the court. It seems likely that these uncontested submissions

may have obviated the need to appoint matrons to investigate and prove the case against these women.

134. William Offutt, Jr., "The Limits of Authority: Courts, Ethnicity, and Gender in the Middle Colonies, 1670–1710," in *Many Legalities of Early America*, ed. Tomlins and Mann, 379, 383. Dayton (*Women Before the Bar*) has made a similar argument for Connecticut, detailing the power women had in certain spheres during the seventeenth century before their increasing marginalization in the eighteenth.

135. See Offutt's description of legal participation in the Delaware Valley, *Of "Good Laws"*, 30–42.

136. For native peoples selling land, see *Sussex Courts*, 286, 369, 894–95; Leon De Valinger, ed., *Court Records of Kent County, Delaware, 1680–1705* (Washington, D.C.: American Historical Association, 1959), 52, 54. On Captain Tom's civil claim, see *Sussex Courts*, 810. On African Americans, see, e.g., *Bucks Courts*, 33; *Sussex Courts*, 104, 141, 243, 286, 321, 637, 695, 810.

137. This emphasis on "whose words were law" is adapted from James H. Merrell, "'The Customes of Our Countrey': Indians and Colonists in Early America," in *Strangers Within the Realm: Cultural Margins of the First British Empire*, ed. Bernard Bailyn and Philip D. Morgan (Chapel Hill: University of North Carolina Press, 1991), 117–56. It should also be noted that the failure of Indians to participate in the colonial legal system may have been at least as much a conscious decision by native peoples as an exclusionary act on the part of Euro-American settlers. See Chapter 7 below.

138. See Offutt, *Of "Good Laws"*, 9–11, for the high legal participation in the Delaware Valley and its significance.

139. *Bucks Courts*, 218–20.

140. Jack D. Marietta and G. S. Rowe, *Troubled Experiment: Crime and Justice in Pennsylvania, 1682–1800* (Philadelphia: University of Pennsylvania Press, 2006), 10–11.

141. De Valinger, ed., *Court Records of Kent County*, 3.

142. *Chester Courts*, 115.

143. My phrasing here is adapted from Claude Lévi-Strauss's notion that animals become totems not because they are "good to eat" but because they are "good to think." Lévi-Strauss, *Totemism* (Boston: Beacon Press, 1963), 89. Kirsten Fischer describes a similar process in which diverging corporal punishments against whites and blacks hardened white colonials' belief in "race" as an immutable, embodied fact: Fischer, *Suspect Relations: Sex, Race, and Resistance in Colonial North Carolina* (Ithaca, N.Y.: Cornell University Press, 2002), 169–81, esp.180.

144. For a more detailed discussion of the significance of "sanctioning," in its various senses, to the ordering of colonial authority, see John Smolenski, "Introduction: The Ordering of Authority in the Colonial Americas," in *New World Orders: Violence, Sanction, and Authority in the Colonial Americas*, ed. Smolenski and Thomas J. Humphrey (Philadelphia: University of Pennsylvania Press, 2005), 3–4.

145. Pierre Bourdieu, "The Social Space and the Genesis of Groups," *Theory and Society* 14 (1985): 723–24.

146. On the use of peace bonds or recognizances in other British American colonies, see Konig, *Law and Society in Puritan Massachusetts*; Raphael Semmes, *Crime and Punishment in Early Maryland* (Baltimore: Johns Hopkins University Press, 1996); Douglas Greenberg, *Crime and Law Enforcement in the Colony of New York, 1691–1776* (Ithaca, N.Y.: Cornell University Press, 1976), 308; Kamensky, *Governing the Tongue*, 197–98. On their use in England, see Joel B. Samaha, "The Recognizance in Elizabethan Law Enforcement," *American Journal of Legal History* 25, 3 (1981): 189–204; Norma Landau, *The Justices of the Peace, 1679–1760* (Berkeley: University of California Press, 1984), 23–25, 180–208; Norma Landau, "Appearance at the Quarter Sessions of Eighteenth-Century Middlesex," *London Journal* 23, 2 (1998): 30–52.

147. Samaha, "Recognizance in Elizabethan Law Enforcement"; Landau, "Appearance at the Quarter Sessions of Eighteenth-Century Middlesex," 33–37.

148. Offutt has argued that the peace bond was the "ideal weapon to implement Quaker precepts of law reform": *Of "Good Laws"*, 197.

149. In linguistic terms, the peace bond can be considered what J. L. Austin has called a "commissive" performative, one that commits the speaking subject to perform a certain action in the future. This is in contrast to the public apologies and confessions that Jane Kamensky has argued were a central aspect of maintaining social and religious order in New England courts and congregations, which emphasized the speaker's past behavior and the relationship between the speaker's self and the speech community to which it was addressed. In this sense, the New England verbal performance can be considered (in an Austinian sense) behabitive or expositive performatives, an expression of present-time obeisance to the community without an explicit, open-ended commitment to self-discipline in the future. See Austin, *How to Do Things with Words*, 160–64; Kamensky, *Governing the Tongue*, 127–49.

150. The size of these bonds in Pennsylvania is in contrast to the £5 mean value peace bonds Joel Samaha has found common in Elizabethan England; see Samaha, "Recognizance in Elizabethan Law Enforcement," 196.

151. See also Offutt, *Of "Good Laws"*, 196–97.

152. *Bucks Courts*, 401, 402.

153. The first quote is taken from a sample peace bond recorded by Quaker jurist Francis Daniel Pastorius. See Alfred L. Brophy, "'Ingenium est Fateri per quos Profeceris': Francis Daniel Pastorius' *Young Country Clerk's Collection* and Anglo-American Legal Literature, 1682–1716," *University of Chicago Law School Roundtable: A Journal of Interdisciplinary Studies* 3 (1996): 729; the second is from a bond recorded in *Sussex Courts*, 800.

154. My discussion of the relative frequency of peace bonds and whippings is taken from the compilation here:

PEACE BONDS AND WHIPPINGS (CHESTER, BUCKS, SUSSEX), 1680–95

Year	Chester	Bucks	Sussex	Total
Peace bonds				
1680–85	4	3	2	9

1685–90	10	26	6	42
1691–95	16	4	2	22
Total	30	33	10	73
Whippings				
1680–85	2	2	5	9
1686–90	6	8	5	19
1691–95	1	1	2	4
Total	9	11	12	32

Sources: *Chester Courts*; *Bucks Courts*; *Sussex Courts*.

My assertion about the relative frequency of peace bonds in Pennsylvania relative to other colonies is based on Offutt's quantitative analysis of recognizances and their use in the criminal docket in Bucks and Chester Counties from 1681 to 1710. Offutt writes that Quaker-influenced justices raised "the use [of peace bonds] to new heights" during this period (*Of "Good Laws"*, 196).

155. My discussion of race, gender, and punishment is drawn from the following compilation of cases:

PEACE BONDS AND WHIPPINGS BY RACE AND GENDER (CHESTER, BUCKS, SUSSEX, KENT, PHILADELPHIA)

Year	N	White M	White W	Af Am M[a]
Peace bonds				
1680–85	9	8 (88.9%)	1 (11.1%)	0
1686–90	42	40 (95.2%)	2 (4.8%)	0
1691–95	26	24 (92.3%)	2 (7.7%)	0
Total	77	72 (95.3%)	5 (6.5%)0	0
Whippings				
1680–85	10	6 (60%)	4 (40%)	0
1686–90	19	12 (63.2%)	4 (21.5%)	3 (15.8%)
1691–95	6	3 (50%)	3 (50%)	0
Total	35	21 (60%)	11 (31.4%)	3 (8.6%)

Sources: *Chester Courts*; *Bucks Courts*; *Sussex Courts*; De Valinger, ed., *Court Records of Kent County*; Record of the Philadelphia Courts, 1685–86, HSP; Bronner, ed., "Philadelphia County Court of Quarter Sessions," 79–85, 175–90, 236–50.
[a] No African American women appeared in these records.

156. For Sarah Smith, see *Sussex Courts*, 610.
157. *Sussex Courts*, 401–42.
158. Bronner, "Philadelphia County Court of Quarter Sessions," 88.
159. *MPCP*, 1: 380–81.

160. For a broader definition and discussion of "economy of violence," see Smolenski, "Introduction," 14; Gene E. Ogle, "Natural Movements and Dangerous Spectacles: Beatings, Duels, and 'Play' in Saint Domingue," in *New World Orders*, ed. Smolenski and Humphrey, 226–48.

161. Fischer: "What could be done to a particular person was both a result and a symbol of their body's social status" (*Suspect Relations*, 180).

162. *MPCP*, 1: 92; Thompson, *Rum Punch*, 111.

163. Penn to Thomas Lloyd, 17/9mo/1686, in *PWP*, 3: 129.

CHAPTER 4. "BASTARD QUAKERS" IN AMERICA: THE KEITHIAN SCHISM AND THE CREATION OF CREOLE QUAKERISM IN EARLY PENNSYLVANIA, 1691–1693

1. The "Copy of the Publick Writing" has been reprinted in George Keith and Peter Boss, *The Tryals of Peter Boss, George Keith, Thomas Budd, and William Bradford, Quakers for Several Great Misdemeanors* . . . (London: Richard Baldwin, 1693), 7–8; Keith and Boss, *New England's Spirit of Persecution Transmitted to Pennsilvania, and the Pretended Quaker Found Persecuting the True Christian-Quaker* . . . ([New York]: William Bradford, 1693), 5–6; Samuel Jennings, *The State of the Case, Briefly but Impartially Given Betwixt the People Called Quakers, Pensilvania, &C. In America, Who Remain in Unity, and George Keith* . . . (London: T. Sowle, 1694), 47–51; Robert Proud, *The History of Pennsylvania, in North America* (Philadelphia: Printed by Zachariah Poulson junior . . . 1797–98), 1: 373–76. My references to the "Publick Writing" are from Keith and Boss, *Tryals*, 7–8.

2. Keith and Boss, *Tryals*, 7–8, 19.

3. Jane Kamensky has written of this same contradictory element in public apologies in seventeenth-century New England but argued that in New England this robbed the offending words of their power; see Kamensky, *Governing the Tongue: The Politics of Speech in Early New England* (New York: Oxford University Press, 1997), 140–41.

4. Orthodox Quakers' belief that print was capable of reaching larger audiences than speech was emphasized repeatedly during this schism; one of their chief complaints against Keith was that, through print, he had insulted his enemies to "the World." See Jennings, *State of the Case*, 289; and Caleb Pusey, *A Modest Account from Pensylvania of the Principal Differences in Point of Doctrine, between George Keith, and Those of the People Called Quakers, from Whom He Separated* . . . (London: T. Sowle, 1696), 11, 19, 41.

5. For a comparison to another European New World colony that has influenced my interpretation of this event, see Stephen Greenblatt's and Patricia Seed's discussions of Spanish ritual speech acts and the role of the Requerimiento in securing legitimacy for the Spanish Empire: Greenblatt, *Marvelous Possessions: The Wonder of the New World* (Chicago: University of Chicago Press, 1991), 54–65; Seed, *Ceremonies of Possession in Europe's Conquest of the New World, 1492–1640* (New York: Cambridge University Press, 1995), 69–99, esp. 97–98.

6. My distinction between these two forms of public communication is drawn from

Mikhail M. Bakhtin's and V. N. Vološinov's work on dialogue. For Bakhtin's discussion of the difference between what he terms "authoritative discourse" and "persuasive discourse," see Bakhtin, *The Dialogic Imagination: Four Essays*, ed. Michael Holquist, trans. Caryl Emerson and Holquist (Austin: University of Texas Press, 1981), esp. "Discourse in the Novel," 342–55. For Vološinov's discussion of the distinction between authoritarian and other modes of speech communication, see Vološinov, *Marxism and the Philosophy of Language*, trans. Ladislav Matejka and I. R. Titunik (Cambridge, Mass.: Harvard University Press, 1986), 123. For an application of Bakhtin's idea of "authoritative discourse" to the conquest of New Spain, see Seed, *Ceremonies of Possession*, 98.

7. Scholars have frequently opposed the "language of the marketplace" with the authoritative discourse employed by religious and political officials to communicate their power. See the classic formulation in Bakhtin, *Rabelais and His World*, trans. Hélène Iswolsky (Cambridge, Mass.: MIT Press, 1968), 145–95. Robert Blair St. George, however, has argued that while many scholars see "market places [as] critical sites for subversion, ... The 'open marketplace' so often imagined in ethnographic writing as a zone of inversive festivity was itself, in England and her North American colonies, an institution invented to guarantee the proper *surveillance* of exchanges." St. George, "Massacred Language: Courtroom Performance in Eighteenth-Century Boston," in *Possible Pasts: Becoming Colonial in Early America*, ed. St. George (Ithaca, N.Y.: Cornell University Press, 2000), 333. St. George's formulation, I think, comes closer to conveying the dynamic at play here.

8. A record of the Keithians' trials is in Keith and Boss, *Tryals*, 11–34.

9. For the fate of Keith's followers in Pennsylvania and New Jersey, see Jon Butler, "Into Pennsylvania's Spiritual Abyss: The Rise and Fall of the Later Keithians, 1693–1703," *PMHB* 101, 2 (1977): 152, 170.

10. Gary B. Nash, *Quakers and Politics: Pennsylvania, 1681–1726*, new ed. (Boston: Northeastern University Press, 1993), 144–60, esp. 156–58; Joel David Meyerson, "A Quaker Commonwealth: Society and the Public Order in Pennsylvania, 1681–1765" (Ph.D. dissertation, Harvard University, 1971), 39–73; Peter Thompson, *Rum Punch & Revolution: Taverngoing & Public Life in Eighteenth Century Philadelphia* (Philadelphia: University of Pennsylvania Press, 1999), 123–26; Jon Butler, "'Gospel Order Improved': The Keithian Schism and the Exercise of Quaker Ministerial Authority in Pennsylvania," *WMQ* 31, 3 (1974): 431–52.

11. Barry Levy, *Quakers and the American Family: British Settlement in the Delaware Valley* (New York: Oxford University Press, 1988), 157–72; Nancy F. Rosenberg, "The Sub-Textual Religion: Quakers, the Book, and Public Education in Philadelphia, 1682–1800" (Ph.D. dissertation, University of Michigan, 1991), 92–105; Ethyn Williams Kirby, *George Keith (1638–1716)* (New York: Appleton-Century, 1942), 62–94; J. William Frost, "Unlikely Controversialists: Caleb Pusey and George Keith," *Quaker History* 64, 1 (1975): 16–36; Edward Cody, "The Price of Perfection: The Irony of George Keith," *Pennsylvania History* 39, 1 (1972): 1–19.

12. Nash, *Quakers and Politics*, 145 (psychologically disturbed); Kirby, *George Keith*,

156–58 (not a true Quaker); Frost, "Unlikely Controversialists," 36 (failed Quaker founding father).

13. Extrapolating from a Chester Monthly Meeting census from 1688 and other information regarding Quaker congregations at that time, Richard T. Vann has estimated that there were approximately 3,300 Friends in Pennsylvania that year and 4,300–4,400 in 1700. (Vann, "Quakerism: Made in America?" in *World of William Penn*, 166, 169–70n21). These numbers suggest there were approximately 3,500–3,600 Friends in Pennsylvania at the height of the schism in 1691–92. I have found 290 known Keithians in Pennsylvania, a figure I have compiled from references in manuscript minutes from local Quaker Meetings and lists of Keithian followers published in Thomas Budd, *The Judgment Given Forth by Twenty-Eight Quakers Against George Keith and His Friends with Answers to the Said Judgment Declaring Those Twenty-Eight Quakers to Be No Christians* . . . (London: 1694), 9, 18, 22; "An Account of Such as have formerly frequented Friends Meetings and have Since followed George Keith or Others," in *The Keithian Controversy in Early Pennsylvania*, ed. J. William Frost (Norwood, Pa.: Norwood Editions, 1980), 371–76; and Jon Butler, "The Records of the First 'American' Denomination: The Keithians of Pennsylvania, 1694–1700," *PMHB* 120, 1 (1996): 89–105.

14. The initial confrontation between Keith and Stockdale is described in George Keith and Burlington Yearly Meeting, *An Appeal from the Twenty Eight Judges: To the Spirit of Truth & True Judgment in All Faithful Friends, Called Quakers, That Meet at This Yearly Meeting at Burlington, the 7 Month, 1692* (Philadelphia: William Bradford, 1692), 2–3; Keith and Thomas Budd, *The Plea of the Innocent against the False Judgment of the Guilty Being a Vindication of George Keith and His Friends* . . . ([Philadelphia]: William Bradford, [1692]), 2, 19; Keith and Boss, *New England's Spirit of Persecution*, 1. See also Butler, "'Gospel Order Improved'," 445; Kirby, *George Keith*, 62–63.

15. For Keith's allegations about Fitzwater, see "Some Propositions in Order to Heale the Breach that is Amongst us, Directed to Tho. Lloyd and Others Concerned with Him," 18/2mo./1692, in *Keithian Controversy*, ed. Frost, 155; Keith, *Some Reasons and Causes of the Late Seperation That Hath Come to Pass at Philadelphia Betwixt Us: Called by Some the Seperate Meeting, and Others That Meet Apart from Us* . . . (Philadelphia: William Bradford, 1692), 8; Gerardus Croese, *The General History of the Quakers* . . . (London, 1696), App., 3. This first appendix to Croese's *History* consisted of a letter from Keith responding to particular elements of or refuting particular charges in Croese's account of the controversy. See also Butler, "'Gospel Order Improved'," 445–46; Kirby, *George Keith*, 63.

16. See Chapter 1.

17. Kirby, *George Keith*, 19–46.

18. Kirby, *George Keith*, 49–53, summarizes this phase of Keith's itinerant career. On Keith's debating style, see Francis Makemie, *An Answer to George Keith's Libel* . . . (Boston: Benjamin Harris, 1694), 36. For Keith's response to Mather: Keith, *The Presbyterian and Independent Visible Churches in New-England and Else-Where, Brought to the Test* . . . (Philadelphia: William Bradford, 1689), 216. For Keith's insistence on the sufficiency of

the Light: Keith and John Cotton, *A Refutation of Three Opposers of Truth, by Plain Evidence of the Holy Scripture:* . . . (Philadelphia: William Bradford, 1690), 38–44, esp. 41. For Keith's claim of degeneracy: Keith, *The Pretended Antidote Proved Poyson* . . . (Philadelphia: William Bradford, 1690), 18; Keith, *A Serious Appeal to All the More Sober, Impartial & Judicious People in New-England to Whose Hands This May Come:* . . . (Philadelphia: William Bradford, 1692). Among the many responses to Keith's writings, see especially Cotton Mather, *Speedy Repentance Urged: a Sermon Preached at Boston, December 29, 1689* . . . (Boston: Samuel Green, 1690); Mather, *Little Flocks Guarded Against Grievous Wolves* . . . (Boston: Benjamin Harris & John Allen, 1691). See also Perry Miller, *The New England Mind, from Colony to Province* (Cambridge, Mass.: Belknap Press of Harvard University Press, 1983), 166, 218.

19. George Keith to George Whitehead and George Fox, 23/3mo./1688, in Whitehead, *The Power of Christ Vindicated Against the Magick of Apostacy* (London, 1708), 225–32, cited in Butler, " 'Gospel Order Improved'," 434.

20. See the discussion in Chapter 2, above.

21. This document has been reprinted as " 'Gospel Order and Discipline'," *Journal of the Friends' Historical Society* 10, 1 (1913): 70–76. Butler's assertion that the Keithian schism revolved around ministerial authority is based largely on his reading of this document; Butler, " 'Gospel Order Improved'," 435–39.

22. " 'Gospel Order and Discipline'," 70, 73–74. The implications of this change for Quaker notions of domesticity and child rearing are suggested in Levy, *Quakers and the American Family*, 162.

23. Butler, " 'Gospel Order Improved'," 438; and Richard T. Vann, *The Social Development of English Quakerism, 1655–1755* (Cambridge, Mass: Harvard University Press, 1969), 122–43.

24. Keith, " 'Gospel Order and Discipline'," 71.

25. " 'Gospel Order and Discipline'," 73.

26. " 'Gospel Order and Discipline'," 72.

27. " 'Gospel Order and Discipline'," 74–76.

28. Cotton Mather, *The Wonderful Works of God Commemorated Praises Bespoke for the God of Heaven in a Thanksgiving Sermon Delivered on Decemb. 19, 1689* . . . (Boston: S. Green, 1690), 34; John Canup, "Cotton Mather and Criolian Degeneracy," *Early American Literature* 24, 1 (1989): 20–34.

29. Philadelphia Meeting of Ministers Minutes, 1/1mo/1690; 9/4mo/1690; 6/7mo/1690 (minutes located at QCHC).

30. Franciscus Mercurius van Helmont, *Two Hundred Queries Moderately Propounded Concerning the Doctrine of the Revolution of Humane Souls and Its Conformity to the Truths of Christianity* (London: Rob. Kettlemell, 1684).

31. On van Helmont, see Allison Coudert, *The Impact of the Kabbalah in the Seventeenth Century* (Boston: Brill Academic, 1999), 1–20, 153–76; and on the Kabbalist doctrine of transmigration, see 119–24. On the notion that each soul went through twelve revolutions, see van Helmont, *Two Hundred Queries*, 7, 53, 64, 73, 83, 94.

32. George Keith, *Truth and Innocency Defended against Calumny and Defamation: In a Late Report Spread Abroad Concerning the Revolution of Humane Souls, with a Further Clearing of the Truth, by a Plain Explication of My Sence, &C* (Philadelphia: William Bradford, 1691).

33. Keith, *Some Reasons and Causes*, 8. The PMMM minutes, unfortunately, do not contain nearly as detailed a record of these events.

34. Keith, *Some Reasons and Causes*, 9. These details are corroborated, with a very different interpretation, in Jennings, *State of the Case*, 2-4.

35. Keith, *Some Reasons and Causes*, 9, 11.

36. Keith, *Some Reasons and Causes*, 10.

37. Jennings, *State of the Case*, 3-4.

38. Keith, *Some Reasons and Causes*, 12; Philadelphia Meeting of Ministers Minutes, 5/1mo./1692.

39. Philadelphia Meeting of Ministers Minutes, 7/1mo./1692.

40. Philadelphia Meeting of Ministers Minutes, 7/1mo./1692.

41. This quote was recorded in the Philadelphia Meeting of Ministers Minutes, 17/4mo/1692.

42. Keith, *Some Reasons and Causes*; "Some Propositions," in *Keithian Controversy*, ed. Frost, 155-64. Although the authorship of *Some Reasons* is unknown, it seems evident from the text of the document that Keith was its lead, if not its sole, author. Given that the exact publication date is unclear, some scholars have disagreed on whether *Some Reasons and Causes* was published before or after the Meeting of Ministers's condemnation of Keith at their June Meeting. I have placed the publication of this pamphlet sometime after the visitation committee's failed meeting with Keith in March and before the ministers' condemnation based on the fact that *Some Reasons* makes no mention of the ministers' condemnation. Here I am following Kirby's dating of *Some Reasons* and differing from Butler's (Kirby, *George Keith*, 69; Butler, " 'Gospel Order Improved'," 447).

43. Keith, *Some Reasons and Causes*, 2, 13.

44. Keith, *Some Reasons and Causes*, 20. For Keith's use of the term "bastard Quakers," see Jennings, *State of the Case*, 2. Given Keith's multiple assertions that many of Pennsylvania's Friends were not "true" Friends, along with Richard T. Vann's demographic evidence about the number of Quaker conversions in Pennsylvania (to be discussed below) and the fact that Keith never refuted Jennings's claim, I have taken Jennings's quotation of Keith to be accurate. Keith also complained of the "Scandalous conversation" of these nominal Friends.

45. Keith, *Some Reasons and Causes*, 3; "Some Propositions," 155.

46. Keith, *Some Reasons and Causes*, 22.

47. Keith, *Some Reasons and Causes*, 16-17, 23-26, 29-36. *Some Reasons and Causes* ended with extensive citations from Barclay's *Anarchy*.

48. Keith, *Some Reasons and Causes*, 23.

49. Philadelphia Meeting of Ministers Minutes, 17/4mo/1692.

50. Philadelphia Meeting of Ministers Minutes, 20/4mo/1692. This letter was also

reprinted several times: Keith and Burlington Yearly Meeting, *An Appeal from the Twenty Eight Judges*; Budd, *Judgment Given Forth by Twenty-Eight Quakers*.

51. Several scholars have suggested that "scolding" and "railing" (alternately "rayling") were specifically gendered crimes in early modern England and America, most frequently speech attacks by women on men. See Robert Blair St. George, "'Heated' Speech and Literacy in Seventeenth-Century New England," *Publications of the Colonial Society of Massachusetts* 63 (1984): 275–322; David Underdown, "The Taming of the Scold: The Enforcement of Patriarchal Authority in Early Modern England," in *Order and Disorder in Early Modern England*, ed. Anthony Fletcher and John Stevenson (New York: Cambridge University Press, 1985), 116–36; Mary Beth Norton, "Gender and Defamation in Seventeenth-Century Maryland," *WMQ* 44, 1 (1987): 3–39; Kamensky, *Governing the Tongue*, 140–41; Cornelia Hughes Dayton, *Women Before the Bar: Gender, Law, and Society in Connecticut, 1639–1789* (Chapel Hill: University of North Carolina Press, 1995), chap. 7; Anthony J. Fletcher, *Gender, Sex, and Subordination in England, 1500–1800* (New Haven, Conn.: Yale University Press, 1995), 12–29. The quotation is from Pusey, *Modest Account*, 19.

52. Robert Barclay, *The Anarchy of the Ranters and Other Libertines . . .* ([London]: 1676), in Barclay, *Truth Triumphant through the Spiritual Warfare, Christian Labours, and Writings of That Able and Faithful Servant of Jesus Christ, Robert Barclay, Who Deceased at His Own House at Urie in the Kingdom of Scotland, the 3 Day of the 8 Month 1690* (London: Thomas Northcott, 1692), 181–236; Barclay, *An Apology for the True Christian Divinity . . .* ([Aberdeen?]: 1678), in *Truth Triumphant*, 267–568; Barclay, *A Catechism and Confession of Faith . . .* ([London]: 1675), in *Truth Triumphant*, 109–80. Also see Chapter 1.

53. Keith, *An Appeal from the Twenty Eight Judges*, 4; Keith and Budd, *Plea of the Innocent*.

54. Keith, *An Appeal from the Twenty Eight Judges*, 7.

55. Jennings, *State of the Case*, 21

56. Keith and Boss, *Tryals*, 11; see Thompson, *Rum Punch*, 125, for McComb's role in the schism.

57. On the importance of taverns and public houses as channels of communication and information in seventeenth-century America, see Thompson, *Rum Punch*; David W. Conroy, *In Public Houses: Drink & the Revolution of Authority in Colonial Massachusetts* (Chapel Hill: University of North Carolina Press, 1995); and Richard D. Brown, *Knowledge Is Power: The Diffusion of Information in Early America, 1700–1865* (New York: Oxford University Press, 1989), 17–18.

58. Jennings, *State of the Case*, 44.

59. Jennings, *State of the Case*, 22.

60. The mittimus was reprinted in Budd, *Judgment Given Forth by Twenty-Eight Quakers*, 19, and Keith and Boss, *Tryals*, 5–6. The charge that Bradford's crime was printing books anonymously was not mentioned in the warrant, only in the trial; see below.

61. See the discussion on peace bonds in Chapter 3, above.

62. See discussion of trust in a Quaker's word and peace bonds in Chapters 1 and 3.

Bradford's and McComb's refusals to find sureties and their implication that Quaker magistrates were wrong to ask fellow Quakers to find them is mentioned in Jennings, *State of the Case*, [iii]. Frost, "Unlikely Controversialists," 31, suggests that it was against Quaker principles to offer bonds or sureties to appear in court. English Quakers' refusal to take oaths on the grounds that Friends should speak plainly and truthfully at all times is discussed in Richard Bauman, *Let Your Words Be Few: Symbolism of Speaking and Silence Among Seventeenth-Century Quakers* (New York: Cambridge University Press, 1983), 98–101.

63. The seizure of the press is noted in Keith and Boss, *Tryals*, 5. Sheriffs' seizure of artisans' tools during arrest was explicitly prohibited by Pennsylvania's Assembly; see Cable, *Statutes*, 45. On English Quakers' criticism of this practice, see Craig W. Horle, *The Quakers and the English Legal System, 1660–1688* (Philadelphia: University of Pennsylvania Press, 1988), 125–39.

64. Jürgen Habermas has described this type of public utterance as "representative publicity," a form of public communication intended to display authority rather than engage in a public debate: Jürgen Habermas, *The Structural Transformation of the Public Sphere: An Inquiry into a Category of Bourgeois Society* (Cambridge, Mass.: MIT Press, 1989), 5–14. See also Vološinov, *Marxism and the Philosophy of Language*, 123.

65. PYMM Minutes, 7/7mo/1692.

66. Although there are no extant court records for Philadelphia County Court of Quarter Sessions for 1692, a partial record of the trial was printed in Keith and Boss, *New England's Spirit of Persecution*, and reprinted in Keith and Boss, *Tryals*. While these Keithian pamphlets are biased—particularly in their commentary on the trial—I am taking their transcripts of the trial itself as relatively accurate. Given the Quaker tradition of reprinting trial transcripts in seventeenth-century England (most notably in the case of Penn's famous trial), I see no reasons to believe that Keith and Bradford (the most likely authors of these pamphlets) intentionally misrepresented their opponents' words. In fact, as my analysis of the trial will show, I believe they were consciously imitating this historical genre of Quaker writing in an attempt to show themselves more Quaker than their opponents.

67. Keith and Boss, *Tryals*, 13–14; William Sheppard, *The Faithful Councellor, or, the Marrow of the Law in English in Two Parts . . .* (London: R.W., 1654).

68. Keith and Boss, *Tryals*, 15. For the Philadelphia Yearly Meeting injunction to use gospel order rather than going to law, see PYMM Minutes, 2 May 1681.

69. Keith and Boss, *Tryals*, 18–19.

70. Keith and Boss, *Tryals*, 20.

71. Keith and Boss, *Tryals*, 21.

72. Keith and Boss, *Tryals*, 22.

73. Keith and Boss, *Tryals*, 22, 24–25.

74. Keith and Boss, *Tryals*, 28.

75. See Chapter 2.

76. Keith and Boss, *Tryals*, 29.

77. Keith and Boss, *Tryals*, 32.

78. I am borrowing Karl Marx's aphorism from Marx, *The Eighteenth Brumaire of Louis Bonaparte: With Explanatory Notes* (New York: International Publishers, 1981), 15.

79. The one key difference was that the sheriff in Penn's trial at the Old Bailey made no reference to denying the jurors tobacco in addition to meat, drink, or fire.

80. Monthly Meeting of Friends of Philadelphia, *A Testimony and Caution to Such as Do Make a Profession of Truth, Who Are in Scorn Called Quakers, and More Especially Such as Profess to Be Ministers of the Gospel of Peace, That They Should Not Be Concerned in Worldly Government* (Philadelphia: William Bradford, 1693).

81. Monthly Meeting of Friends of Philadelphia and George Keith, *An Exhortation & Caution to Friends Concerning Buying or Keeping of Negroes* (New York: William Bradford, 1693), 1.

82. Kirby, *George Keith*, 97.

83. Philadelphia Meeting of Ministers Minutes, 2/7mo/1693.

84. Robert Hannay and Benjamin Bealing, *A True Account of the Proceedings, Sence and Advice of the People Called Quakers at the Yearly Meeting of Faithful Friends and Brethren Begun in London . . .* (London: R. Levis, 1694), 4. Also see Kirby, *George Keith*, 100.

85. Kirby, *George Keith*, 102, 103.

86. George Whitehead to Thomas Lloyd, Arthur Cook, Samuel Jennings, Robert Ewer, Griffith Owen, and John Dellavall, 21/4mo/1694, cited in Butler, "'Gospel Order Improved'," 452.

87. For the Chesapeake, see Kathleen M. Brown, *Good Wives, Nasty Wenches, and Anxious Patriarchs: Gender, Race, and Power in Colonial Virginia* (Chapel Hill: University of North Carolina Press, 1996), 75–80; Karen Ordahl Kupperman, "Presentment of Civility: English Reading of American Self-Presentation in the Early Years of Colonization," *WMQ* 54, 1 (1997): 193–228; Joyce E. Chaplin, "Natural Philosophy and an Early Racial Idiom in North America: Comparing English and Indian Bodies," *WMQ* 54, 1 (1997): 229–52; Chaplin, *Subject Matter: Technology, the Body, and Science on the Anglo-American Frontier, 1500–1676* (Cambridge, Mass.: Harvard University Press, 2001). On a parallel process in colonial New England, see Robert Blair St. George, *Conversing by Signs: Poetics of Implication in Colonial New England Culture* (Chapel Hill: University of North Carolina Press, 1998), 115–205.

88. George Keith, *Truth's Defence . . .* (London: Benjamin Clark, 1682), 85.

89. Keith, *Truth and Innocency*, 48.

90. Croese, *General History*, Appendix, 12. This appendix consists of a letter from Keith responding to Croese's account of the schism in the *General History*, followed by a counter-response from Philadelphia Public Friends. On the notion that the revolution of souls was only logical: Keith, *Truth and Innocency*, 9. Keith denied he ever believed in this revolution, only that he entertained it as a "hypothesis." His previous support for von Helmont and his conflicting statements on the matter suggest his support of the doctrine.

91. Coudert, *Impact of the Kabbalah*, 119–24.

92. Keith, *Truth and Innocency*, 16.

93. This differs somewhat from the process Jorge Cañizares-Esguerra has observed for seventeenth-century Spanish America. Here, evangelists and scientists moved away from explaining the difference between Indians and creoles in terms of nurture—a difference that could be remedied through proper instruction—to explanations of difference that relied on immutable nature. Jorge Cañizares-Esguerra, "New World, New Stars: Patriotic Astrology and the Invention of Indian and Creole Bodies in Colonial Spanish America, 1600–1650," *AHR* 104, 1 (1999): 67.

94. Daniel Leeds, *An Almanack for the Year of Christian Account 1688* . . . ([Philadelphia]: [William Bradford], 1687); Leeds, Francis Bacon, and George Wither, *The Temple of Wisdom for the Little World: In Two Parts* . . . (Philadelphia: William Bradford, 1688); Jon Butler, *Awash in a Sea of Faith: Christianizing the American People* (Cambridge, Mass.: Harvard University Press, 1990), 82–83; Henry J. Cadbury, "Early Quakerism and Uncanonical Lore," *Harvard Theological Review* 40, 3 (1947): 204.

95. Marion Dexter Learned, *The Life of Francis Daniel Pastorius, the Founder of Germantown, Illustrated with Ninety Photographic Reproductions* (Philadelphia: W.J. Campbell, 1908), 256; James N. Green, "The Book Trade in the Middle Colonies, 1680–1720," in *The Colonial Book in the Atlantic World*, ed. Hugh Amory and David D. Hall (New York: Cambridge University Press, 2000), 220; Francis Daniel Pastorius, "A Few Onomastical Considerations enlarged From the Number of Sixty Six . . . ," 59–60. A photostat of this manuscript is appended to the edition of Pastorius, *A New Primmer or Methodical Directions to Attain the True Spelling, Reading & Writing of English. Whereunto Are Added, Some Things Necessary & Useful Both for the Youth of This Province, and Likewise for Those, Who from Foreign Countries and Nations Come to Settle Amongst Us* ([New York]: William Bradford, [1698]) located at QCHC. On Fox's similarities to Boehme, see Cadbury, "Early Quakerism and Uncanonical Lore," 183–87, 192–95; John L. Brooke, *The Refiner's Fire: The Making of Mormon Cosmology, 1644–1844* (New York: Cambridge University Press, 1994), 25–29.

96. Jon Butler, "Sir Walter Raleigh in Defense of Quaker Orthodoxy: A Phineas Pemberton Letter of 1694," *Quaker History* 66, 2 (1977): 109.

97. Pusey, *Modest Account*, 6, 14–15. On Barclay and the historical Christ: Barclay, *A Catechism and Confession of Faith*, 117–21. Hugh Barbour has argued that early Quakerism strongly deemphasized the historical Christ: Barbour, *The Quakers in Puritan England* (New Haven, Conn.: Yale University Press, 1964), 145–49. Both Butler and Frost have emphasized that there was little orthodoxy in seventeenth-century Quaker Christology: Butler, "'Gospel Order Improved'," 435; Frost, "Unlikely Controversialists," 26–28.

98. Pusey, *Modest Account*, 26.

99. Levy, *Quakers and the American Family*, 164–66.

100. Anthony Pagden, *The Fall of Natural Man: The American Indian and the Origins of Comparative Ethnology*, 1st pbk. ed. (New York: Cambridge University Press, 1986), 57–108.

101. Levy argues that the most salient issue here was Friends' "radical domesticity," implying that if Friends had not been so worried about their children's souls, then Keith's

theories would have been less threatening and the schism might not have occurred. While correct on its own terms, Levy fails to interrogate the other half of this equation and ask why debates about the place of Indians' souls in a spiritual hierarchy possessed such immediacy.

102. *Our Antient Testimony Renewed Concerning Our Lord and Saviour Jesus Christ, the Holy Scriptures, and the Resurrection Occasioned at This Time by Several Unjust Charges Published against Us, and Our Truly Christian Profession, by G. Keith* . . . (London: T. Sowle, 1695), 36. This follows the letter from Keith in the Appendix to Croese, *General History*. On George Fox's assertion that the saved were "babes of Christ," see *The Following PAPER Was Publish'd 1654* . . . (1654), in Fox, *Gospel-Truth*, 27; Phyllis Mack, *Visionary Women: Ecstatic Prophecy in Seventeenth-Century England* (Berkeley: University of California Press, 1992), 153–55; and Richard Bailey, *New Light on George Fox and Early Quakerism: The Making and Unmaking of a God* (San Francisco: Mellen Research University Press, 1992), 252–53.

103. Thomas Ellwood edited the first published edition of Fox's *Journal*: George Fox, *A Journal or Historical Account of the Life, Travels, Sufferings, Christian Experiences and Labour of Love in the Work of the Ministry, Of . . . George Fox, Who Departed This Life in Great Peace with the Lord, the 13th of the 11th Month, 1690, the First Volume,* London: Thomas Northcott, 1694. See also Bailey, *New Light,* 266.

104. On British Friends' move away from this doctrine, see Bailey, *New Light,* 137–290.

105. PYMM Minutes, 24/7mo/1686.

106. PYMM Minutes, 6/7mo/1682.

107. Falls Men's Monthly Meeting Minutes, 6/4mo/1683 and 1/6mo/1683, located at QCHC.

108. Kirby, *George Keith,* 51n17.

109. PMMM Minutes, 9/11mo/1682; Falls Men's Monthly Meeting Minutes, 1/6mo/1683.

110. Vann, "Quakerism: Made in America?" 159, 165. Vann's estimates are based on certificates of removal received by the Philadelphia Monthly Meeting contained in Albert Cook Myers and Philadelphia Monthly Meeting of Friends, *Quaker Arrivals at Philadelphia, 1682–1750; Being a List of Certificates of Removal Received at Philadelphia Monthly Meeting of Friends* (Baltimore: Southern Book Co., 1957). Vann suggests that the certificates received by the Philadelphia Monthly Meeting comprised between one-third and one-fourth of all certificates received by Pennsylvania Monthly Meetings. Myers lists 86 certificates received at Philadelphia in 1681–90 and 72 received in 1691–1700. Given Vann's estimates of the Quaker population in 1690 and 1700 (see n13 above), this would suggest that 8–10 percent of all Pennsylvania Friends had presented certificates of removal from British Meetings during the province's first decade and that 10–14 percent of all the province's Quakers had presented certificates of removal from British Meetings over the colony's first two decades.

111. Vann, "Quakerism: Made in America?" 167.

112. Of the 290 Keithians I have identified, 16 presented certificates of removal to the Philadelphia Monthly Meeting. Again, estimating that these certificates measured between one-quarter and one-third of the total received by Pennsylvania Meetings would suggest that 16.6–22.1 percent of all Keithians were Friends in good standing in Britain; 73 Quakers who cannot be identified as Keithians presented certificates of removal to the Philadelphia Meeting before the schism. Using the estimates above, I would suggest that 7.0–9.4 percent of non-Keithian Quakers were Friends in good standing before migration.

113. George Fox, *THE PEARL Found in ENGLAND. This is for the Poor Distressed, Scattered Ones in Foreign Nations. From the Royal Seed of God, and Heirs of Salvation, called QUAKERS, who are the Church of the Living* . . . (1658), in *Gospel-Truth*, 131–42. I am influenced here by Françoise Vergès's argument that "creolization = diversity *and* unity challenged by diversity, which in turn experiences a process of unification." See Vergès, "Indian-Oceanic Creolizations: Processes and Practices of Creolization on Réunion Island," in *Creolization: History, Ethnography, Theory*, ed. Charles Stewart (Walnut Creek, Calif.: Left Coast Press, 2007), 148–49.

CHAPTER 5. NARRATIVES OF EARLY PENNSYLVANIA, I: LIFE ON THE COLONIAL BORDERLANDS

1. Robert Suder to Governor, 20 November 1698, in William Stevens Perry, ed., *Historical Collections Relating to the American Colonial Church* (New York: AMS Press, 1969), 9–12.

2. Writing about Native Americans and the European contest for empire in North America, Jeremy Adelman and Stephen Aron use the term "borderlands" to denote "the contested boundaries between colonial domains." Adelman and Aron, "From Borderlands to Borders: Empires, Nation-States, and the Peoples in Between in North American History," *AHR* 104, 3 (1999): 816. I use "borderlands" here in a slightly unorthodox way, to describe the porous boundary lines between different cultural, political, and administrative institutions that made the empire work. Here I am following and extending Lauren A. Benton's persuasive argument about European colonialism that the "indeterminacy of power" along the boundary lines between European and non-Europeans "was simply a more visible example of the many 'orders' separating groups with different legal and cultural status within the empire." Benton, *Law and Colonial Cultures: Legal Regimes in World History, 1400–1900* (New York: Cambridge University Press, 2002), 101. See also Michael J. Braddick, *State Formation in Early Modern England, c. 1550–1700* (New York: Cambridge University Press, 2000), 405.

3. On the role similar conflicts played in shaping early modern European and colonial American society more generally, see Michael Zuckerman, "The Fabrication of Identity in Early America," in Zuckerman, *Almost Chosen People: Oblique Biographies in the American Grain* (Berkeley: University of California Press, 1993), 26.

4. Lieutenant Governor Francis Nicholson to the Council of Trade and Plantations,

20 August 1698, in *CSPC*, 16: 387. On Nicholson's career, see Stephen Saunders Webb, "The Strange Career of Francis Nicholson," *WMQ* 23, 4 (1966): 514–48.

5. *MPCP*, 1: 551.

6. John M. Murrin, "Political Development," in *Colonial British America: Essays in the New History of the Early Modern Era*, ed. Jack P. Greene and J. R. Pole (Baltimore: Johns Hopkins University Press, 1984), 417–32; Richard S. Dunn, "The Glorious Revolution and America," in *The Oxford History of the British Empire*, vol. 1, *The Origins of Empire: British Overseas Enterprise to the Close of the Seventeenth Century*, ed. Nicholas P. Canny and Alaine M. Low (New York: Oxford University Press, 1998), 445–48; Brendan McConville, *The King's Three Faces: The Rise and Fall of Royal America, 1688–1776* (Chapel Hill: University of North Carolina Press, 2006), 29–31; J. H. Elliott, *Empires of the Atlantic World: Britain and Spain in America, 1492–1830* (New Haven, Conn.: Yale University Press, 2006), 147–52; Jenny Hale Pulsipher, *Subjects unto the Same King: Indians, English, and the Contest for Authority in Colonial New England* (Philadelphia: University of Pennsylvania Press, 2005), 37–100; Wesley Frank Craven, *The Colonies in Transition, 1660–1713* (New York: Harper and Row, 1967), 32–44; Edmund S. Morgan, *American Slavery, American Freedom: The Ordeal of Colonial Virginia* (New York: Norton, 1975), 202–3, 277.

7. W. A. Speck, "The International and Imperial Context," in *Colonial British America*, ed. Greene and Pole, 393–97; Michael J. Braddick, "The English Government: War, Trade, and Settlement, 1625–1688," in *Oxford History of the British Empire*, vol. 1, ed. Canny and Low, 297–301.

8. Governor Benjamin Fletcher to Sir John Trenchard, 19 November 1694, in *CSPC*, 14: 403; Governor Markham to Governor Fletcher, 26 May 1696, in *CSPC*, 15: 17; Fletcher to Lords of Trade and Plantations, 10 June 1696, in *CSPC*, 15: 11–12; Penn to the Board of Trade, 12 September 1699, in *PWP*, 3: 577; "A Collection of Papers Relating to pirates and other Matters in Pennsylvania," 29 November 1697, in *CSPC*, 16: 43–44; "Petition of inhabitants of Newcastle to Governor Markham," August 1699, in *CSPC*, 17: 469–70; Council of Trade to the Lords Justice of England, 30 September 1696, in *CSPC*, 15: 165; "The Humble Remonstrance of his Majesties most Loyall Subjects of His Majesties Province of Pennsylvania," Ellesmere Collection #9596, HL.

9. Lieutenant Governor Francis Nicholson to the Duke of Shrewsbury, 14 June 1695, in *CSPC*, 14: 510–13; "Memorial of Sir Thomas Laurence," 26 June 1695, in *CSPC*, 14: 518–20; Gary B. Nash, *Quakers and Politics: Pennsylvania, 1681–1726*, new ed. (Boston: Northeastern University Press, 1993), 190–91.

10. Robert Quary to the Council of Trade and Plantations, [22 September 1697], in *CSPC*, 15: 617; Nicholson to Shrewsbury, in *CSPC*, 14: 511.

11. Henry Bouton, "Proclamation Regarding Piracy," 1697, Ellesmere Collection #9560, HL; Jeremiah Basse to Penn, 26 July 1697, in *CSPC*, 15: 563–65; Journal of the Council of Trade and Plantations, 20 September 1697, in *CSPC*, 15: 615–16; Robert Snead to Francis Nicholson, 8 September 1697, Ellesmere Collection #9589, HL; Minutes of the Council of Maryland, 14 December 1696, in *CSPC*, 15: 253–54; Edward Randolph to William Popple, 25 April 1698, in *CSPC*, 16: 180–81; "A Collection of Papers Relating to pirates and other matters in Pennsylvania," in *CSPC*, 16: 43–44.

12. Robert Snead, "A Narrative of Capt. Robert Snead One of the Justices of the Peace in the Province of Pennsylvania in America Relating the Discourse between W. Markham Ye Governor & Himself About Pyrates . . . ," 7 April 1698, Ellesmere Collection #9597, HL; Snead to Sir John Houblon, [20 September 1697], in *CSPC*, 15: 613.

13. Snead, "Narrative"; Thomas Robinson, "Information of Thomas Robinson," 13 July 1697, Ellesmere Collection #9591, HL.

14. Robert Quary to Lieutenant Governor Francis Nicholson, 9 July 1698, in *CSPC*, 16: 395; Roy N. Lokken, *David Lloyd, Colonial Lawmaker* (Seattle: University of Washington Press, 1959), 77.

15. Nicholson to the Council of Trade and Plantations, in *CSPC*, 16:387.

16. Edward Randolph to Commissioners of Customs, 10 November 1696, in *CSPC*, 15: 212–15.

17. Robert Quary to the Council of Trade and Plantations, 25 August 1698, in *CSPC*, 16: 404.

18. Lokken, *David Lloyd*, 78.

19. Cable, *Statutes*, 246–54; Winfred Trexler Root, *The Relations of Pennsylvania with the British Government, 1696–1765* (New York: B. Franklin, 1970), 93, 97; Lokken, *David Lloyd*, 80–82.

20. My account is drawn from *MPCP*, 1: 602–4; Robert Quary to the Council of Trade and Plantations, 18 May 1699, in *CSPC*, 17: 235–37; and Suder to Governor, 11. See also Lokken, *David Lloyd*, 83–85.

21. John Egerton, Ph. Meadows, John Pollexsen, John Locke, and Abr. Hill to The Excellent Lords Justice, 7 September 1697, Ellesmere Collection #9832, HL; Lokken, *David Lloyd*, 76–77.

22. McConville, *King's Three Faces*, 128.

23. *MPCP*, 1: 604; Council of Trade and Plantations to the Lords Justices of England, 4 August 1699, in *CSPC*, 17: 383.

24. Board of Trade to Penn, 12 September 1699, in *PWP*, 3: 577.

25. Cable, *Statutes*, 347–58.

26. On the 1701 conference, see below.

27. Cable, *Statutes*, 359–65.

28. William Penn to Charlwood Lawton, 21/10mo/1700, in *PWP*, 3: 630.

29. Penn to Lawton, in *PWP*, 3: 630.

30. Sydney E. Ahlstrom, *A Religious History of the American People* (New Haven, Conn.: Yale University Press, 1972), 214–29; Jon Butler, *Awash in a Sea of Faith: Christianizing the American People* (Cambridge, Mass.: Harvard University Press, 1990), 99–105; Boyd Stanley Schlenther, "Religious Faith and Commercial Empire," in *The Oxford History of the British Empire*, vol. 2, *The Eighteenth Century*, ed. P. J. Marshall and Alaine M. Low (New York: Oxford University Press, 1998), 130–33.

31. Minister and Vestry of Christ Church in Philadelphia to the Council of Trade and Plantations, [31 March 1702], in *CSPC*, 20: 183–84; "Dispute with Robert Quary before the Board of Trade," 16 April 1702–28 April 1702, in *PWP*, 4: 161.

32. For Anglican accusations of a Quaker conspiracy to promote Friends above Anglicans, see "A Brief Narrative of the Proceedings of William Penn," in Perry, ed., *Historical Collections Relating to the American Colonial Church*, 4; Minister and Vestry of Christ Church in Philadelphia to the Council of Trade and Plantations, in *CSPC*, 20: 183–84.

33. Vestrymen of Christchurch in Philadelphia to the Council of Trade and Plantations, 28 January 1701, in *CSPC*, 19: 57–58; Robert Quary to the Council of Trade and Plantations, 7 April 1701, in *CSPC*, 20: 198.

34. William Penn to Baron Somers, 8 October 1700, in *PWP*, 3: 621.

35. Any estimate of Pennsylvania's total population or its religious composition is necessarily a rough one at best. For my purposes here, I am assuming that the relative Quaker population of the colony lay somewhere between Penn's guess of 75% and James Logan's of slightly more than 50%. See Penn to the Council of Trade and Plantations, 17 February 1700, in *CSPC*, 18: 86, and Logan to Penn, 11 May 1702, in *PLC*, 1: 102.

36. Penn to Somers, in *PWP*, 3: 621.

37. Penn to Lawton, in *PWP*, 3: 633.

38. William Penn to William Penn, Jr., 2 January 1701, in *PWP*, 4: 27.

39. Penn to Lawton, in *PWP*, 6: 333; Penn to the Earl of Romney, 6/7mo/1701, in *PWP*, 4: 80; see also Penn to Charlwood Lawton, 18/6mo/1701, in *PWP*, 4: 68.

40. Patricia Seed, *Ceremonies of Possession in Europe's Conquest of the New World, 1492–1640* (New York: Cambridge University Press, 1995), 16–40; Francis Jennings, *The Invasion of America: Indians, Colonialism, and the Cant of Conquest* (Chapel Hill: University of North Carolina Press), 82–84.

41. "Remonstrance of Diverse . . . " 12 March 1697, in *PWP*, 3: 499.

42. For Penn's earliest discussions of this theme, see Chapter 3. He later returned to this theme in his negotiations with the Board of Trade over the governance of the colony: "Proposal for the Advancement of Trade in America," 3 April 1697, in *PWP*, 3: 493.

43. I am influenced here by the distinction that scholars have made between "societies with slaves" and "slave societies." See Philip D. Morgan, "British Encounters with Africans and African-Americans, circa 1600–1780," in *Strangers Within the Realm: Cultural Margins of the First British Empire*, ed. Bernard Bailyn and Morgan (Chapel Hill: University of North Carolina Press, 1991), 163.

44. Penn to Romney, in *PWP*, 4: 80.

45. "Dispute with Robert Quary before the Board of Trade," in *PWP*, 4: 161.

46. See below.

47. Pennsylvania et al., *The Governour's Speech to the Assembly, at Philadelphia the 15 September 1701* (Philadelphia: Reynier Jansen, 1701); *MPCP*, 2: 40.

48. Penn to James Logan, 28/5mo/1702, in *PWP*, 4: 179.

49. Bruce P. Lenman, "Colonial Wars and Imperial Instability, 1688–1703," in *Oxford History of the British Empire*, vol. 2, ed. Marshall and Low, 154–55.

50. James Logan to Penn, 9 July 1702, in *PLC*, 1: 123; Lenman, "Colonial Wars and Imperial Instability," 153. On Logan's assessment that the province was "destitute of Indians," see Logan to Penn, 2 May 1702, in *PLC*, 1: 89.

51. *MPCP*, 2: 70, 79; Logan to Penn, in *PLC*, 1: 88; Logan to Penn, 29/5mo/1702, JLLB, I, p. 34; Alan Tully, *Forming American Politics: Ideals, Interests, and Institutions in Colonial New York and Pennsylvania* (Baltimore: Johns Hopkins University Press, 1994), 108.

52. Penn to James Logan, 28/5mo/1702, in *PWP*, 179; Logan to Penn, in *PLC*, 1: 123.

53. James Logan to Penn, 1/10mo/1702, in JLLB, I, pp. 65–68.

54. Hamilton died in February 1703; the Provincial Council governed the colony until Evans's arrival in February 1704.

55. Penn to Provincial Council, 31/10mo/1703, in *PWP*, 4: 253; James Logan to Penn, 14/5mo/1704, in *PWP*, 4: 289.

56. *MPCP*, 2: 162, 207.

57. *MPCP*, 2: 161, 205.

58. *MPCP*, 2: 243.

59. My account of this militia scare is taken from James Logan to Penn, 28/3mo/1706, in *PWP*, 4: 534; Logan to Penn, 12/4mo/1706, in *PLC*, 2: 133–35; *MPCP*, 2: 241, 243, 250.

60. 300 men represented a fairly sizable number. For context, Philadelphia's population at the time was approximately 2,300: Gary B. Nash and Billy G. Smith, "The Population of Eighteenth-Century Philadelphia," *PMHB* 99, 3 (1975): 366.

61. James Logan to Penn, 12 June 1706, in *PLC*, 2: 130.

62. James Logan to Edward Hackett, 13 August 1706, in *PLC*, 2: 165.

63. *MPCP*, 2: 243.

64. James Logan to Penn, 10 August 1710, in *PLC*, 2: 145; Logan to Penn, 24 February 1709, in *PLC*, 2: 318.

65. James Logan to Penn, 11/3mo/1709, in JLLB, I, pp. 334–35.

66. Isaac Norris to Thomas Lloyd, 13/3mo/1709, in Isaac Norris INLB, I, p. 11; Norris to Benjamin Poole, 24/3mo/1709, in INLB I, p. 16; Norris to Henry Goldney, 3/4mo/1709, in INLB, I, 1709–16, p. 26.

67. *MPCP*, 2: 62–63, 68–69.

68. Mitchell, *Statutes*, 307, 308.

69. Root, *Relations of Pennsylvania with the British Government*, 129.

70. Journal of the Council of Trade and Plantations, 31 August 1699, in *CSPC*, 17: 420.

71. Edward Randolph to the Council of Trade and Plantations, 26 April 1698, in *CSPC*, 16: 182.

72. James Logan to Penn, 11 September 1702, in *PLC*, 1: 138.

73. James Logan to Penn, 3 March 1703, in *PLC*, 1: 175–76.

74. James Logan to Penn, 24 June 1703, in *PLC*, 1: 193–98.

75. "Order of Queen in Council," 21 January 1703, in *CSPC*, 21: 146–47; *MPCP*, 2: 89.

76. Provincial Council to Penn, 26 August 1703, in *PWP*, 4: 235, 236; James Logan to Penn, 2 September 1703, in *PLC*, 1: 229–30; Nash, *Quaker and Politics*, 249–50; Tully, *Forming American Politics*, 77.

77. Council to Penn, in *PWP*, 4: 234; James Logan to Penn, 2 September 1703, in *PLC*, 1: 229–30; Logan to Penn, 29 September 1703, in *PLC*, 1: 245; Logan to Penn, 7 September 1703, in *PLC*, 1: 237.

78. David Lloyd to G[eorge] W[hitehead] & others, 3 October 1704, in *PLC*, 1: 327; *MPCP*, 2: 180; Isaac Norris to Jonathan Dickinson, 27 September 1704, in *PLC*, 1: 315 ("shut [Friends] out . . . ").

79. "William Penn's Reply to Col. Quary's answer to his Memorial," in *CSPC*, 20: 515.

80. *MPCP*, 2: 280, 301.

81. For the negotiations behind this process, see Attorney General to the Council of Trade and Plantations, 13 October 1704, in *CSPC*, 22: 276–81; and Mitchell, *Statutes*, 2: 446–98.

82. The following table charts the changes in the administration of peace bonds and corporal punishment after 1695:

PEACE BONDS AND WHIPPINGS (CHESTER, BUCKS, SUSSEX), 1696–1710

Year	Chester	Bucks	Sussex	Total
Peace bonds				
1696–1700	10	10	2	22
1701–5	8	4	0	12
1706–10	9	3	0	12
Total	27	17	2	46
Whippings				
1696–1700	6	0	0	6
1701–5	8	2	0	10
1706–10	11	2	5	18
Total	25	4	5	34

Source: *Chester Courts*; Bucks County Combined Common Pleas and Quarter Sessions Docket, 1684–1731, HSP; *Sussex Courts*.

83. For 1680–95, see table in Chapter 3, note 107.

84. Whippings accounted for 7 percent of all criminal sentences between 1680 and 1699; (17/241); between 1700 and 1710 they accounted for 25% (17/68); See Jack D. Marietta and G. S. Rowe, *Troubled Experiment: Crime and Justice in Pennsylvania, 1682–1800* (Philadelphia: University of Pennsylvania Press, 2006), 79.

85. William M. Offutt, *Of "Good Laws" and "Good Men": Law and Society in the Delaware Valley, 1680–1710* (Urbana: University of Illinois Press, 1995), 92.

86. Offutt notes that while women comprised 7.4% of all plaintiffs in his analysis of Delaware Valley courts, they accounted for only 4.2% of "megaplaintiffs," those who brought suit six or more times. He found no women "megadefendants" in his sample

(69). He found that megaplaintiffs and megadefendants were significantly more likely to experience favorable outcomes than others (Offutt, *Of "Good Laws"*, 131–32). On women's declining status in another legal reform colony, see Cornelia Hughes Dayton, *Women Before the Bar: Gender, Law, and Society in Connecticut, 1639–1789* (Chapel Hill: University of North Carolina Press, 1995).

87. The following table charts the changes in administration of peace bonds and corporal punishment by race and gender:

WHIPPINGS BY RACE AND GENDER (CHESTER, BUCKS, SUSSEX, KENT, PHILADELPHIA)

Year	N	White M	White W	Af Am M	Af Am W
1696–1700	10	4 (40%)	6 (60%)	0	0
1701–5	28	8 (28.6%)	18 (64.3%)	2 (7.1%)	0
1706–10	17	7 (41.1%)	8 (47.1%)	0	2 (11.8%)
Total	55	19 (34.5%)	32 (58.1%)	2 (3.6%)	2 (3.6%)

Sources: *Chester Courts*; Bucks County Combined Common Pleas and Quarter Sessions Docket, 1684–1731, HSP; *Sussex Courts*; Leon De Valinger, ed., *Court Records of Kent County, Delaware, 1680–1705* (Washington, D.C.: American Historical Association, 1959).

88. My account of this incident is taken from *Votes*, 488, 493–94, 495–96; *MPCP*, 2: 202; James Logan to Penn, 4/5mo/1705, in *PWP*, 4: 362; Logan to Penn, 6/5mo/1705, in JLLB II, pp. 57–58; and Logan to Penn, 28 May 1706, in *PLC*, 2: 129.

89. Logan Papers, 11: 2, HSP. See also *PWP*, 3: 599–602.

90. "Treaty with the Susquehannah Indians, 12 September 1700," George Vaux Collection of Correspondence and Documents #1167, QCHC.

91. On William Penn's early attempts to force outsiders to carry physical tokens of their good character such as passes or seals, see John Justin Smolenski, "Friends and Strangers: Religion, Diversity, and the Ordering of Public Life in Colonial Pennsylvania, 1681–1764" (Ph.D. Dissertation, University of Pennsylvania, 2001), 101–6.

92. Daniel K. Richter, *The Ordeal of the Longhouse: The Peoples of the Iroquois League in the Era of European Colonization* (Chapel Hill: University of North Carolina Press, 1992), 150; Francis Jennings, *The Ambiguous Iroquois Empire: The Covenant Chain Confederation of Indian Tribes with English Colonies from Its Beginnings to the Lancaster Treaty of 1744* (New York: Norton, 1984), 228.

93. For the deed, see *MPCP*, 1: 122–23; on the tenuousness of the Dongan's claim, see Jennings, *Ambiguous Iroquois Empire*, 235.

94. *MPCP*, 1: 133–34.

95. On the Shawnee as "strange" Indians new to the territory, see Amy C. Schutt, *Peoples of the River Valleys: The Odyssey of the Delaware Indians* (Philadelphia: University of Pennsylvania Press, 2007), 70. On the Susquehannocks' defeat and scattering, see Richter, *Ordeal of the Longhouse*, 145; Barry C. Kent, *Susquehanna's Indians* (Harrisburg: Penn-

sylvania Historical and Museum Commission, 1984), 46–56; Peter C. Mancall, *Valley of Opportunity: Economic Culture Along the Upper Susquehanna, 1700–1800* (Ithaca, N.Y.: Cornell University Press, 1991), 31–32. Francis Jennings has argued that the Iroquois conquest of the Susquehannocks was a myth perpetuated by the Confederacy, but his account is less persuasive that the orthodox view espoused by those cited above. On the importance of collective possession of land to eastern native peoples, see Nancy Shoemaker, *A Strange Likeness: Becoming Red and White in Eighteenth-Century North America* (New York: Oxford University Press, 2004), 13–34. On a second settlement on the Susquehanna: William Penn, *Some Proposals for a Second Settlement in the Province of Pennsylvania* ([London]: A. Sowle, 1690).

96. Conestoga Indians: Kent, *Susquehanna's Indians*, 58–61; Schutt, *Peoples of the River Valleys*, 65–70. Shawnee Indians: Kent, *Susquehanna's Indians*, 80–85; Mancall, *Valley of Opportunity*, 31; Jane T. Merritt, *At the Crossroads: Indians and Empires on a Mid-Atlantic Frontier, 1700–1763* (Chapel Hill: University of North Carolina Press, 2003), 23.

97. Schutt, *Peoples of the River Valleys*, 70; *MPCP*, 2: 448; Kent, *Susquehanna's Indians*, 58–59.

98. On the often paradoxical relationship between indigenous agency and authority and the limits of colonial law more generally, see Lauren Benton, "Colonial Law and Cultural Difference: Jurisdictional Politics and the Formation of the Colonial State," *Comparative Studies in Society and History* 41, 3 (1999): 563–88.

99. "Articles of Agreement Between William Penn and Susquehannah Indians," 23 April 1701, in *MPCP*, 144–47 (quote 144). See also *MPCP*, 2: 15.

100. *MPCP*, 2: 15, 16 (quotation).

101. I am borrowing the phrase "whose rules were law" from James H. Merrell, "'The Customes of Our Countrey': Indians and Colonists in Early America," in *Strangers Within the Realm*, ed. Bailyn and Morgan, 145.

102. On territorial and personal jurisdiction in Indian-colonial relations, see Katherine A. Hermes, "Jurisdiction in the Colonial Northeast: Algonquian, English and French Governance," *American Journal of Legal History* 43, 1 (1999): 52–73.

103. For wampum in establishing authority at the outset of conferences, see James H. Merrell, *Into the American Woods: Negotiators on the Pennsylvania Frontier* (New York: Norton, 1999), 32, 189.

104. *MPCP*, 2: 245; see also *PLC*, 2: 83.

105. *MPCP*, 2: 386–87.

106. *MPCP*, 2: 472. See, e.g., the paucity of gifts Evans gave in return for pipes, tobacco, and skins in 1707, as well as his pointed reminder in 1706 that he had, at an earlier conference, given out three times as many gifts as he received—a true breach of etiquette; 2: 246, 386.

107. My discussion of the communicative role of wampum relies partly on Merrell's discussion of its meaning (*Into the American Woods*, 187–93 and passim) and Gordon M. Sayre's analysis of the relationship between wampum and writing: Sayre, *Les Sauvages Américains: Representations of Native Americans in French and English Colonial Literature*

(Chapel Hill: University of North Carolina Press, 1997), 144–218, esp. 162–63, 186–88, 213. As I hope my discussion shows, I think the functional differences between wampum and alphabetic script in colonial political, legal, and diplomatic relations were smaller than Sayre suggests.

108. *MPCP*, 1: 372.

109. *MPCP*, 2: 447.

110. *MPCP*, 2: 403.

111. *MPCP*, 2: 387.

112. *MPCP*, 2: 471.

113. *MPCP*, 2: 511–12.

114. *MPCP*, 2: 200, 204.

115. *MPCP*, 2: 510.

116. *MPCP*, 2:247.

117. *MPCP*, 2: 403–5.

118. *MPCP*, 2: 512.

119. *MPCP*, 2: 454–46.

120. "Articles of Agreement," in *MPCP*, 1: 144.

121. *MPCP*, 2: 247.

122. Penn Manuscripts, Indian Affairs, 1: 34, HSP.

123. *MPCP*, 2: 244–48, 469–72.

124. Here I disagree with Jane T. Merritt's assertion that whites used treaty councils for a fundamentally different purpose than Indians. Merritt writes, "Instead of seeking consensus or the fluidity of an ongoing dialogue about mutual problems, however, the goal of a treaty conference generally was to negotiate for, and to claim, absolute legal control over land, resources, labor, or groups of people." Merritt, "Metaphor, Meaning, and Misunderstanding: Language and Power on the Pennsylvania Frontier," in *Contact Points: American Frontiers from the Mohawk Valley to the Mississippi, 1750–1830*, ed. Andrew R. L. Cayton and Fredrika J. Teute (Chapel Hill: University of North Carolina Press, 1998), 62.

125. On Indian negotiations discussing rumors of war, see *MPCP*, 2: 138, 244–45, 471–74, 511–12, 516. On provincial fears of French efforts to "debauch all" Indian allies, see James Logan to Penn, 3 March 1703, in *PLC*, 1: 179. On fears about French efforts more generally, see Logan to Penn, 5 February 1702, in *PLC*, 1: 89; Logan to Penn, 18 June 1702, in *PLC*, 1: 107; Logan to Penn, in *PLC*, 1: 123. On Indian fears of French invasion, see *MPCP*, 2: 474–76.

126. See Merrell, *Into the American Woods*, 32, 111, on the process and product of diplomacy and rituals of friendship during this period.

127. On the use of "chain of friendship language," see *MPCP*, 244, 470, 474. On the "brightening" metaphor applied to a different diplomatic "chain," the Covenant Chain between the Iroquois and English, see Richter, *Ordeal of the Longhouse*, 141.

128. *MPCP*, 2: 244, 470. Colonial negotiators had first invoked William Penn to justify their authority in 1696; see William Markham to Penn, 25 June 1696, in *PWP*, 3: 453.

129. *MPCP*, 1: 447, 2: 15, 244.

130. *PLC*, 1: 89.

131. Nancy Shoemaker has likewise argued that Europeans frequently saw alliances with Indians as a means to further the imperial contest for North America rather than a compact between equals (*Strange Likeness*, 89).

132. On this point see Benton, *Law and Colonial Cultures*, 263.

133. McConville, *King's Three Faces*, 29–40.

CHAPTER 6. NARRATIVES OF EARLY PENNSYLVANIA, II: THE FOUNDING OF PENNSYLVANIA

1. Penn to James Logan, 18/3mo/1708, in *PWP*, 4: 602; Logan to Penn, 14/4mo/1709, in *PWP*, 4: 648; Penn to Logan, 17/8mo/1709, in *PWP*, 4: 661.

2. On the role similar conflicts played in shaping early modern European and colonial American society more generally, see Michael Zuckerman, "The Fabrication of Identity in Early America," in Zuckerman, *Almost Chosen People: Oblique Biographies in the American Grain* (Berkeley: University of California Press, 1993), 26–27.

3. *MPCP*, 2: 126.

4. *MPCP*, 2: 144–45. For this provision in the 1701 Charter, see Cable, *Statutes*, 362.

5. Cable, *Statutes*, 361. The 1701 Charter gave the representatives of the freemen the power to "sitt upon their own adjournments."

6. *MPCP*, 2: 174.

7. The Assembly did repass a handful of laws that the Privy Council outlawed in 1705. Mitchell, *Statutes*, 2: 171–294, covers the 1705 laws, with the laws for 1709 in 2: 294–301.

8. *MPCP*, 2: 195, 2: 92.

9. *MPCP*, 2: 241–42.

10. *MPCP*, 2: 286, 2: 305.

11. *MPCP*, 2: 285.

12. James Logan to Penn, 22/9mo/1704, in *PWP*, 4: 309; *MPCP*, 2: 293–94, 334.

13. *MPCP*, 2: 281–82.

14. *MPCP*, 2: 292.

15. *MPCP*, 2: 310–11.

16. *MPCP*, 2: 358.

17. *MPCP*, 2: 282.

18. Michael Zuckerman, "Identity in British America: Unease in Eden," in *Colonial Identity in the Atlantic World, 1500–1800*, ed. Nicholas P. Canny and Anthony Pagden (Princeton, N.J.: Princeton University Press, 1987), 159–212.

19. *MPCP*, 2: 283–84.

20. Impeachment: James Logan to Penn, 5 May 1707, in *PLC*, 2: 217; Gary B. Nash, *Quakers and Politics: Pennsylvania, 1681–1726*, new ed. (Boston: Northeastern University Press, 1993), 267; Libel: *MPCP*, 2: 507–8.

21. *MPCP*, 2: 313–14.

22. Isaac Norris to Penn, 2/10mo/1709, in INLB, I, p. 112.

23. David Lloyd to Penn, 19/5mo/1705, in *PWP*, 4: 381.

24. Richard S. Dunn, "Penny Wise and Pound Foolish: Penn as a Businessman," in *WWP*, 49; Edwin B. Bronner, *William Penn's Holy Experiment: The Founding of Pennsylvania, 1681–1701* (New York: Temple University Publications, 1962), 231; Nash, *Quakers and Politics*, 199, 215; Penn to James Logan, 4/11mo/1701–2, in *PWP*, 3: 142.

25. Nash, *Quakers and Politics*, 252–55.

26. *Votes*, 404–6; Roy N. Lokken, *David Lloyd, Colonial Lawmaker* (Seattle: University of Washington Press, 1959), 133–34.

27. Lokken, *David Lloyd*, 137–39.

28. Assembly to Penn, 25 August 1704, in *PWP*, 4: 295–96.

29. Assembly to Penn, in *PWP*, 4: 295–97, 303.

30. David Lloyd to George Whitehead, William Mead, and Thomas Lower, 3/8mo/1704, in *PWP*, 4: 305. On the petition to Fletcher, see Chapter 3 above.

31. James Logan to Penn, *PWP*, 4: 309; Logan to Penn, 27 October 1704, in *PLC*, 1: 338.

32. Penn to James Logan, 16/11mo/1704–5, in *PWP*, 4: 324, 326; Penn to Logan, 30/2mo/1705, in *PWP*, 4: 349; Penn to Roger Mompesson [17 February 1705], in *PWP*, 4: 336.

33. Griffith Owen to Penn, 9/9mo/1705, in *PWP*, 4: 513.

34. Lloyd to Penn, in *PWP*, 4: 373, 374.

35. James Logan to Penn, 7 May 1702, in *PLC*, 1: 99; Logan to Penn, 9 July 1702, in *PLC*, 1: 121; Logan to Penn, 29 September 1703, in *PLC*, 1: 245.

36. Penn to William Popple, 14 August 1707, in *CSPC*, 23: 535 See also Penn to the Earl of Romney, 6/7mo/1701, in *PWP*, 4: 80; Penn to the Board of Trade, 30 November 1702, in *PWP*, 4: 196–97; Penn to John Evans, 9 August 1703, in *PWP*, 4: 231; Penn to Robert Harley, 9/12mo/1703–4, in *PWP*, 4: 259; and "The Memorial of William Penn, Proprietor and Governor of Pennsylvania, in relation to his Government," in *CSPC*, 25: 150–51.

37. Penn to Mompesson, in *PWP*, 4: 335; Penn to the Board of Trade, 11 January 1705, in *PWP*, 4: 319, 421; William Popple and the Board of Trade to Penn, 11 January 1705, in *PWP*, 4: 320; Penn to the Board of Trade, 11 January 1705, in *PWP*, 4: 321; Penn to Harley, in *PWP*, 4: 259.

38. Penn to James Logan, 11/5mo/1704, in *PWP*, 4: 283; Penn to Provincial Council, 10/11mo/1701–2, *PWP*, 4: 151.

39. James Logan to Penn, 4/5mo/1705, 4: 361–62; Owen to Penn, in *PWP*, 4: 513.

40. Nash argues that Penn's demands for this kind of "semifeudal" authority was the essential cause of political conflict in Pennsylvania during this period: *Quakers and Politics*, 237.

41. Samuel Jennings, *The State of the Case, Briefly but Impartially Given Betwixt the*

People Called Quakers, Pensilvania, &C. In America, Who Remain in Unity, and George Keith . . . (London: T. Sowle, 1694), 28, 54, 56, 66; PYMM Minutes, Epistle to the Quarterly and Monthly Meetings, 7/7mo/1692. J. William Frost argues that "The informal Quaker network of traveling ministers and consultation between meetings worked extraordinarily well in procuring condemnations from Maryland and Barbados against Keith and limited the spread of the self-named Christian Quakers." Frost, "Unlikely Controversialists: Caleb Pusey and George Keith," *Quaker History* 64, 1 (1975): 30–31.

42. Ethyn Williams Kirby's bibliography of Keith's published works lists over three dozen publications by Keith dealing with the schism from his disownment through 1707. Kirby, *George Keith (1638–1716)* (New York: Appleton-Century, 1942), 62–94.

43. See, among others, Daniel Leeds, *The Innocent Vindicated from the Falshoods & Slanders of Certain Certificates Sent from America on Behalf of Samuell Jenings, and Made Publick by J.P. In Old England by Daniel Leeds* ([New York]: 1695); Leeds, *News of a Trumpet Sounding in the Wilderness,* . . . ([New York]: William Bradford, 1697); Leeds, *A Trumpet Sounded out of the Wilderness of America Which May Serve as a Warning to the Government and People of England to Beware of Quakerisme* . . . (New York: William Bradford, 1699); Leeds, *The Case Put & Decided by George Fox, George Whitehead, Stephen Crisp, and Other the Most Antient & Eminent Quakers between Edward Billing on the One Part, and Some West-Jersians, Headed by Samuell Jenings on the Other Part* . . . (New York: William Bradford, 1699); Leeds, *News of a Strumpet Co-Habiting in the Wilderness or, a Brief Abstract of the Spiritual & Carnal Whoredoms & Adulteries of the Quakers in America* . . . (New York: [William Bradford], 1701); Leeds, *A Challenge to Caleb Pusey, and a Check to His Lyes & Forgeries, &C* (New York: William Bradford, 1701); Leeds, *The Rebuker, Rebuked in a Brief Answer to Caleb Pusey His Scurrilous Pamphlet, Entituled a Rebuke to Daniel Leeds, & C: Wherein William Penn His Sandy Foundation Is Fairly Quoted, Shewing That He Calls Christ, the Finite Impotent Creature* (New York: William Bradford, 1703); Leeds, *The Great Mistery of Fox-Craft Discovered and the Quaker Plainness & Sincerity Demonstrated* . . . (New York: William Bradford, 1705); Leeds, *The Second Part of the Mystry of Fox-Craft Introduced with About Thirty Quotations Truly Taken from the Quaker Books* . . . (New York: William Bradford, 1705).

44. George Keith, *The Standard of the Quakers Examined or an Answer to the Apology of Robert Barclay* (London: Aylmer, 1702); Leeds, *The Great Mistery of Fox-Craft Discovered*; Leeds, *News of a Strumpet.*

45. Jennings, *State of the Case*; Caleb Pusey, *A Modest Account from Pensylvania of the Principal Differences in Point of Doctrine, between George Keith, and Those of the People Called Quakers, from Whom He Separated* . . . (London: T. Sowle, 1696). Each of these pamphlets appears in Alfred L. Brophy's catalog of Francis Daniel Pastorious's library of Quaker-related texts: Brophy, "The Quaker Bibliographic World of Francis Daniel Pastorius's Bee Hive," *PMHB* 122, 3 (1998): 241–91.

46. The PYMM argued for years about the desirability of replacing Jansen with someone more competent. Assurances that "the current printer is getting better" kept Jansen in his job until his death in 1706, when the Meeting began to make formal plans

for his replacement. PYMM Minutes, 15–18/7mo/1700; 24/7mo/1701; 26–28/7mo/1704; 18/7mo/1706.

47. Caleb Pusey, *Satan's Harbinger Encountered, His False News of a Trumpet Detected, His Crooked Ways in the Wildrnesse Laid Open to the View of the Imperial and Iudicious: . . .* (Philadelphia: Reynier Jansen, 1700); Pusey, *Daniel Leeds, Justly Rebuked for Abusing William Penn and His Foly and Falls-Hoods . . .* (Philadelphia: Reynier Jansen, 1702); Pusey, *Proteus Ecclesiasticus or George Keith Varied in Fundamentalls; Acknowledged by Himself to Be Such, and Prov'd an Apostat, from His Own Definition, Arguments, and Reasons . . .* (Philadelphia: Reynier Jansen, 1703); Pusey, *George Keith Once More Brought to the Test, and Proved a Prevaricator: . . .* (Philadelphia: Reynier Jansen, 1703); Pusey, *Some Remarks Upon a Late Pamphlet Signed Part by John Talbot, and Part by Daniel Leeds, Called the Great Mystery of Fox-Craft* (Philadelphia: Reynier Jansen, 1705); Pusey, *The Bomb Search'd and Found Stuff'd with False Ingredients: Being a Just Confutation of an Abusive Printed Half-Sheet, Call'd a Bomb, Originally Published against the Quakers, by Francis Bugg . . .* (Philadelphia: Raynier Jansen, 1705); Pusey, *Some Brief Observations Made on Daniel Leeds His Book, Entituled the Second Part of the Mystery of Fox-Craft: Published for the Clearing the Truth against the False Aspersions, Calumnies and Perversions of That Often-Refuted Author* (Philadelphia: Reynier Jenson, 1706); Pusey and John Talbot, *False News from Gath Rejected: Containing Some Reasons of the People Called Quakers for Their Declining to Answer John Talbot's Proposall (at the Foot of F. Bugg's Bomb) to Their Last Yearly Meeting at Burlington* (Philadelphia: Reynier Jansen, 1704).

48. Jon Butler, "Into Pennsylvania's Spiritual Abyss: The Rise and Fall of the Later Keithians, 1693–1703," *PMHB* 101, 2 (1977): 157, 165, notes that nearly all the Keithian congregations had either disbanded or been incorporated into Baptist or Anglican congregations by 1703.

49. See Kirby, *George Keith*, 62–94.

50. Kirby, *George Keith*, 102–24.

51. Boyd Stanley Schlenther, "Religious Faith and Commercial Empire," in *The Oxford History of the British Empire*, vol. 2, *The Eighteenth Century*, ed. P. J. Marshall and Alaine M. Low (New York: Oxford University Press, 1998), 130–32; Jon Butler, *Awash in a Sea of Faith: Christianizing the American People* (Cambridge, Mass.: Harvard University Press, 1990), 34, 104; Sydney E. Ahlstrom, *A Religious History of the American People* (New Haven, Conn.: Yale University Press, 1972), 219–21.

52. James Logan to Penn, 21 February 1703, in JLLB, I, p. 83; Kirby, *George Keith*, 137–47; Ahlstrom, *Religious History*, 221; George Keith, *A Journal of Travels from New-Hampshire to Caratuck, on the Continent of North-America. By George Keith* (London: Joseph Downing, 1706).

53. George Keith, *Some of the Many False, Scandalous, Blasphemous & Self-Contradictory Assertions of William Davis, Faithfully Collected out of His Book, Printed Anno 1700. Entituled, Jesus the Crucified Man, the Eternal Son of God, &C. In Exact Quotations Word for Word, without Adding or Diminishing* (New York: William Bradford, 1703); Keith, *Some Brief Remarks Upon a Late Book, Entituled, George Keith Once More Brought to the*

Test, &C. Having the Name Caleb Pusey at the End of the Preface, and C.P. At the End of the Book (New York: William Bradford, 1704).

54. Jon Butler, "'Gospel Order Improved': The Keithian Schism and the Exercise of Quaker Ministerial Authority in Pennsylvania," *WMQ* 31, 3 (1974): 432; William Sewel, *The History of the Rise, Increase, and Progress of the Christian People Called Quakers, Intermixed with Several Remarkable Occurrences. Written Originally in Low-Dutch by William Sewel, and by Himself Translated into English. Now Revis'd and Publish'd, with Some Amendments* (London: J. Sowle, 1722), 2: 345–46.

55. Pusey, *Satan's Harbinger*, 3–4; Pusey, *Proteus Ecclesiasticus*, 8–9, 25. For Keith's earlier interest in Native Americans and salvations, see George Keith, *Truth's Defence . . .* (London: Benjamin Clark, 1682), Chapter 4 above.

56. Pusey, *Modest Account*, 38.

57. Pusey, *Satan's Harbinger*, 54, 78.

58. Pusey, *Satan's Harbinger*, 61.

59. Pusey, *Satan's Harbinger*, 55, 56.

60. Pusey, *Daniel Leeds*, 26.

61. PYMM Minutes, 15/7mo/1695; 23/7mo/1696; 22/7mo/1697; 28/7mo/1698; 16–20/7mo/1699; 15–18/7mo/1701; PYWM, Epistle to the Meeting of Women's Friends in London, 18/7mo/1695.

62. PYMM Minutes, 28/7mo/1698; 24/7mo/1701, 26/7mo/1707; Chichester Monthly Meeting, Acknowledgements and Disownments, 27/2mo/1702, located at QCHC.

63. PWMM Minutes, 27/8mo/1706.

64. William Davis, *Jesus the Crucifyed Man, the Eternal Son of God, or, an Answer to an Anathema or Paper of Excommunication, of John Wats Entituled, Points of Doctrine Preached & Asserted by William Davis: Wherein the Mystry of Christs Descention, Incarnation and Crucifixion Is Unfolded* (Philadelphia: Reynier Jansen, 1700). For the twists and turns of Davis's spiritual biography, see Butler, "Into Pennsylvania's Spiritual Abyss," 153.

65. PYMM Minutes, 15/7mo/1716. They had allowed Andrew Bradford to use the press since his arrival in 1713.

66. George Whitehead, *A Seasonable Account of the Christian and Dying-Words, of Some Young-Men: Fit for the Consideration of All: But Especialy of the Youth of This Generation . . .* (Philadelphia: Reynier Jansen, 1700), 3, 4.

67. Fox, *Instructions for Right-spelling, and Plain Directions for Reading and Writing True English . . .* (Philadelphia: Reynier Jansen, 1702); Fox, *Gospel Family-order, Being a Short Discurse* [sic] *Concerning the Ordering of Families, both of Whites, Blacks and Indians* (Philadelphia: Reynier Jansen, 1701).

68. PYMM Minutes, 15–18/7mo/1695 (appointment of overseers); 28/7mo/1698 (establishment of preparative meetings); Jon Butler, *Power, Authority, and the Origins of American Denominational Order: The English Churches in the Delaware Valley, 1680–1730* (Philadelphia: American Philosophical Society, 1978), 39–43.

69. "Rules of Discipline of Phila. Yearly Meeting 1704," manuscript copy, call

#976, QCHC. See also Rayner W. Kelsey, "Early Disciplines of the Philadelphia Yearly Meeting," *Bulletin of the Friends Historical Association* 24 (Spring 1935): 20–30.

70. "Rules of Discipline of Phila. Yearly Meeting 1704," 1, 3.

71. "Rules of Discipline of Phila. Yearly Meeting 1704," 10, 15.

72. PYMM "Book of Discipline," 1719, manuscript (Thomas Lewis copy), call #976, QCHC; on English codification, see Peter Collins, "Discipline: The Codification of Quakerism as Orthopraxy, 1650–1738," *History and Anthropology* 13, 2 (2002): 17–32.

73. Francis Daniel Pastorius, *A New Primmer or Methodical Directions to Attain the True Spelling, Reading & Writing of English. Whereunto Are Added, Some Things Necessary & Useful Both for the Youth of This Province, and Likewise for Those, Who from Foreign Countries and Nations Come to Settle Amongst Us* ([New York]: William Bradford, [1698]), title, 31–35.

74. Pastorius, *New Primmer*, 27.

75. See Chapter 4 above.

76. Cited in Stephanie Grauman Wolf, *Urban Village: Population, Community, and Family Structure in Germantown, Pennsylvania, 1683–1800* (Princeton, N.J.: Princeton University Press, 1976), 140.

77. Pastorius, *New Primmer*, 47.

78. Alfred L. Brophy, "'Ingenium est Fateri per quos Profeceris': Francis' Daniel Pastorius' *Young Country Clerk's Collection* and Anglo-American Legal Literature, 1682–1716," *University of Chicago Law School Roundtable: A Journal of Interdisciplinary Studies* 3 (1996): 637. On legal literacy, see Chapters 2 and 3, above.

79. For the text of the writ, see Brophy, "'Ingenium est Fateri per quos Profeceris'," 730.

80. Most telling in this respect is the listing of CD's occupation as "Taylor." The writ presented against Bradford and McComb listed the latter's occupation as "Taylor" as well; all other surviving documentation on McComb, however, lists his occupation as tavern keeper.

81. Textual clues suggest that the writs in this section of the "Collection" were written in 1709. See Brophy, "'Ingenium est Fateri per quos Profeceris'."

82. Dunn, "Penny Wise and Pound Foolish," 51.

83. Isaac Norris to Joseph Wyeth, 26/6mo/1709, in INLB, I, p. 62.

84. Norris to Penn, in INLB, I, p. 112

85. Penn to Friends in Pennsylvania, 29/4mo/1710, in *PWP*, 4: 675–80.

86. Isaac Norris to Joseph Pike, 18/12mo/1709–10, in INLB, I, p. 134. See also Penn to Baron Somers, 8 October 1700, in *PWP*, 3: 622; James Logan to Penn, 10 August 1706, in *PLC*, 2: 147; Logan to Penn, 20 December 1706, in *PLC*, 2: 187, 90.

87. Norris to Pike, in INLB, I, p. 134.

88. PYMM 27/7mo/1701; James Logan to Penn, in *PWP*, 4: 309.

89. PYMM, 19/7mo/1710.

90. [Isaac Norris], *Friendly Advice to the Inhabitants of Pensilvania* (Philadelphia: 1710). On the Meeting's support for the publication, see Norris to James Logan, 25/7mo/1710, in INLB, I, 213–14; Nash, *Quakers and Politics*, 307–8.

91. [Norris], *Friendly Advice*, 1.

92. [Norris], *Friendly Advice*, 2.

93. [Norris], *Friendly Advice*, 2–3.

94. [Norris], *Friendly Advice*, 3.

95. My thinking on speech genres, public opinion, and claims to similitude is heavily influenced by Tzvetan Todorov, *Introduction to Poetics* (Minneapolis: University of Minnesota Press, 1981), 18–20.

96. For similar claims to a special "nation within a nation" status for another region of English America, see Robert Blair St. George, *Conversing by Signs: Poetics of Implication in Colonial New England Culture* (Chapel Hill: University of North Carolina Press, 1998), 12. For evidence of Pennsylvanians' claims that their "Pennsylvania liberties" exceeded "English liberties," see Alan Tully, *Forming American Politics: Ideals, Interests, and Institutions in Colonial New York and Pennsylvania* (Baltimore: Johns Hopkins University Press, 1994), 69, 288, 300.

97. My understanding of the role of implication and indirection in colonial public discourse is influenced by St. George, *Conversing by Signs*, 4–5.

98. Isaac Norris to Penn, 23 November 1710, in *PLC*, 2: 429.

99. Nash, *Quakers and Politics*, 308; *MPCP* 2: 516; "Sessions List: The General Assembly of Pennsylvania, 1710–1756," in *LLP*, 2: 81–82.

100. *LLP*, 1: 111, 2: 29, 30.

101. "Richard Hill," "Isaac Norris," in *LLP*, 2: 483, 760.

102. William Penn, *A Serious Expostulation with the Inhabitants of Pensilvania: In a Letter from the Proprietary & Governour* (Philadelphia: 1710). Norris to Penn, in *PLC*, 2: 429.

103. Penn to Friends in Pennsylvania, [10 February 1711], in *PWP*, 4: 687–88.

104. John Canup, *Out of the Wilderness: The Emergence of an American Identity in Colonial New England* (Middletown, Conn.: Wesleyan University Press, 1990); Jack P. Greene, "Changing Identity in the British West Indies in the Early Modern Era: Barbados as a Case Study" and "Travails of an Infant Colony: The Search for Viability, Coherence, and Identity in Colonial Georgia," in Greene, *Imperatives, Behaviors, and Identities: Essays in Early American Cultural History* (Charlottesville: University Press of Virginia, 1992), 42–65; 114, 137–41; Susan Scott Parrish, "William Byrd II and the Cross Languages of Science, Satire, and Empire in British America," in *Creole Subjects in the Colonial Americas: Empires, Texts, Identities*, ed. Ralph Bauer and José Antonio Mazzotti (Chapel Hill: University of North Carolina Press, 2009).

105. Greene, "Changing Identity," 39–40.

106. Antonio de la Calancha, *Chrónica moralizada del orden de San Augustin en el Perú* (1638), cited in D. A. Brading, *The First America: The Spanish Monarchy, Creole Patriots, and the Liberal State, 1492–1867* (New York: Cambridge University Press, 1991), 330. See more generally Brading, *First America*, 253–464; Anthony Pagden, "Identity Formation in Spanish America," in *Colonial Identity in the Atlantic World, 1500–1800*, ed. Canny and Pagden; and Jorge Cañizares-Esguerra, *How to Write the History of the New*

World: Histories, Epistemologies, and Identities in the Eighteenth-Century Atlantic World (Stanford, Calif.: Stanford University Press, 2001).

107. Perry Miller, *The New England Mind, from Colony to Province* (Cambridge, Mass.: Belknap Press of Harvard University Press, 1983), 31. On this rhetorical form more generally see Miller, *New England Mind, from Colony to Province*, 27–39; Stephen Foster, *The Long Argument: English Puritanism and the Shaping of New England Culture, 1570–1700* (Chapel Hill: University of North Carolina Press, 1991), 205–37; Robert Middlekauff, *The Mathers: Three Generations of Puritan Intellectuals, 1596–1728* (Berkeley: University of California Press, 1999), 113–16; Harry S. Stout, *The New England Soul: Preaching and Religious Culture in Colonial New England* (New York: Oxford University Press, 1986), 62–63, 75–76.

108. Foster, *Long Argument*, 286–87; Miller, *New England Mind*, 189–90.

109. Keith, *The Anti-Christs and Sadduces Detected among a Sort of Quakers, or, Caleb Pusie of Pensilvania and John Pennington . . .* (London, 1696), 15.

110. On political parables as a form of history making, see Greg Dening, "A Poetic for Histories," in Dening, *Performances* (Chicago: University of Chicago Press, 1996), 52. J. H. Elliot's discussion of colonial identity formation suggests that while literary efforts and strategic political claims each played a role in the development of creole consciousness in the Atlantic world, the former usually played a large role than the latter. Elliott, *Empires of the Atlantic World: Britain and Spain in America, 1492–1830* (New Haven, Conn.: Yale University Press, 2006), 238–45.

111. José Antonio Mazzotti, "The Lightning Bolt Yields to the Rainbow: Indigenous History and Colonial Semiosis in the *Royal Commentaries* of El Inca Garcilaso de la Vega," *Modern Language Quarterly* 57, 2 (1996): 211.

112. Here I disagree with Alan Tully's analysis of the evolution of what he calls "civil Quakerism." Tully argues that Friends had already largely succeeded in establishing a powerful religious identity prior to their immigration. Thus, "What preoccupied them far more on their arrival in Pennsylvania was their need for supplementary, and very extensive, self-definition as participants in, and governors of, a new worldly experiment" (*Forming American Politics*, 287). As I hope I have shown here, I believe Tully assumes too great a degree of cultural coherence among early Quakers and pays insufficient attention to the relationship between political conflict in Pennsylvania's early years and other forms of cultural conflict.

113. Dunn, "Pennywise and Pound Foolish," 51; Joseph E. Illick, *William Penn, the Politician: His Relations with the English Government* (Ithaca, N.Y., Cornell University Press, 1965), 243.

CHAPTER 7. THE PARABLES OF PENNSYLVANIA POLITICS: THE POWER OF QUAKER MYTHOLOGY

1. Patrick Gordon to John Penn, 18 October 1726, PPOC, 1: 243; Joan de Lourdes Leonard, "Elections in Colonial Pennsylvania," *WMQ* 11, 3 (1954): 390; Thomas Wendel,

"The Keith-Lloyd Alliance: Factional and Coalition Politics in Colonial Pennsylvania," *PMHB* 92, 3 (1968): 301–2; Gary B. Nash, *The Urban Crucible: Social Change, Political Consciousness, and the Origins of the American Revolution* (Cambridge, Mass.: Harvard University Press, 1979), 153.

2. In labeling Keithian modes of political display "popular," I mean to suggest forms and behaviors that were commonly understood and acceptable, not that this style represented "popular" culture in opposition to elite or "high" culture. As Brendan McConville has argued, political rituals in eighteenth-century British America often crossed lines of class or status, rendering attempts to separate "popular" and "high" culture difficult. See McConville, "Pope's Day Revisited, Popular Culture Reconsidered," *Explorations in Early American Culture* 4 (2000): 258–80. See also Simon P. Newman, *Parades and the Politics of the Street: Festive Culture in the Early American Republic* (Philadelphia: University of Pennsylvania Press, 1997), 4–7; William Pencak, Matthew Dennis, and Simon P. Newman, eds., *Riot and Revelry in Early America* (University Park: Pennsylvania State University Press, 2002).

3. Francis Jennings, *The Ambiguous Iroquois Empire: The Covenant Chain Confederation of Indian Tribes with English Colonies from Its Beginnings to the Lancaster Treaty of 1744* (New York: Norton, 1984), 223–308; Jennings, " 'Pennsylvania Indians' and the Iroquois," in *Beyond the Covenant Chain: The Iroquois and Their Neighbors in Indian North America, 1600–1800*, ed. Daniel K. Richter and James H. Merrell (University Park: Pennsylvania State University Press, 2003), 82–87.

4. Greg Dening, "A Poetic for Histories," in Dening, *Performances* (Chicago: University of Chicago Press, 1996), 44.

5. On the predominance of Quakers in the Assembly for this period, see *LLP*, 2: 133.

6. Gary B. Nash, *Quakers and Politics: Pennsylvania, 1681–1726*, new ed. (Boston: Northeastern University Press, 1993), 320–21; Nash, "The Early Merchants of Philadelphia: The Formation and Disintegration of a Founding Elite," in *World of William Penn*, 347. John J. McCusker and Russell R. Menard argue that grain exports increased only slightly from 1690 to 1720, though this estimate (which lumps the difficult years 1690–1710 and stronger years 1710–20), understates the successes of the latter period. McCusker and Menard, *The Economy of British America, 1607–1789* (Chapel Hill: University of North Carolina Press, 1985), 204.

7. Mitchell, *Statutes*, 2: 3–140, 464–67; Winfred Trexler Root, *The Relations of Pennsylvania with the British Government, 1696–1765* (New York: B. Franklin, 1970), 131.

8. The Board of Trade disallowed five of the fifty laws it considered in 1709. Root, *Relations*, 131.

9. J. William Frost, *A Perfect Freedom: Religious Liberty in Pennsylvania* (University Park: Pennsylvania State University Press, 1993), 24–25.

10. Alan Tully, *Forming American Politics: Ideals, Interests, and Institutions in Colonial New York and Pennsylvania* (Baltimore: Johns Hopkins University Press, 1994), 261.

11. See Chapter 2 above.

12. Lawrence Henry Gipson, "The Criminal Codes of Pennsylvania: The Laws of

the Duke of York; the Laws of Chester (1682); the Code of 1701; the Law of 1718," *Journal of the American Institute of Criminal Law and Criminology* 6, 3 (1915): 329.

13. Mitchell, *Statutes*, 3: 199–221; Herbert William Keith Fitzroy, "The Punishment of Crime in Provincial Pennsylvania," *PMHB* 60, 3 (1936): 242–69; Gipson, "Criminal Codes of Pennsylvania"; Jack D. Marietta and G. S. Rowe, *Troubled Experiment: Crime and Justice in Pennsylvania, 1682–1800* (Philadelphia: University of Pennsylvania Press, 2006), 18, 22.

14. Pusey wrote nine different tracts from 1700 to 1706; a total of eight were printed between 1707 and 1712.

15. James N. Green, "The Book Trade in the Middle Colonies, 1680–1720," in *The Colonial Book in the Atlantic World*, ed. Hugh Amory and David D. Hall (New York: Cambridge University Press, 2000), 216.

16. See, for instance, *Gospel-Times, or Oaths Forbidden under the Gospel . . .* (Philadelphia: 1712); William Chandler, Alexander Pyot, and Joseph Hodges, *A Brief Apology in Behalf of the People in Derision Call'd Quakers . . .* (Philadelphia: Andrew Bradford, 1719); Hannah Hill, *A Legacy for Children, Being Some of the Last Expressions and Dying Sayings of Hannah Hill, Junior . . .* (Philadelphia: Andrew Bradford, 1717).

17. Notably, one of the few controversialist works published after the schism, Thomas Chalkley, *Forcing a Maintenance Not Warrantable from the Holy Scripture, for a Minister of the Gospel . . .* (Philadelphia: Andrew Bradford, 1714), had been written as a rejoinder to a New England minister, not a Pennsylvanian.

18. The compilation *An Abstract or Abridgment of the Laws Made and Past by William Penn Absolute Proprietary, and Governour in Chief of the Province of Pensilvania and Territories . . .* (Philadelphia: Reynier Jansen, 1701) was the only such publication until Pennsylvania, *The Laws of the Province of Pennsilvania Collected into One Volumn* [sic]*: By Order of the Governour and Assembly of the Said Province* (Philadelphia: Andrew Bradford, 1714).

19. William Keith, *A Letter to His Majesty's Justices of the Peace for the County of Chester: With the Governour's Spceeh [Sic] from the Bench, at a Court of Oyer and Terminer . . .* (Philadelphia: Andrew Bradford, 1718); *AWM*, 12 January 1719; Keith, *By William Keith, Esq; Governour of the Province of Pennsylvania . . . A Proclamation: Whereas It Has Been Certified to Me, That Robert Moore, Late of Philadelphia Gent. Hath Made His Escape out of the Goal of the City of New-York . . .* (Philadelphia: Andrew Bradford, 1720).

20. See Chapter 3 above.

21. *AWM*, 3 January 1721; Nash, *Urban Crucible*, 119; Sharon V. Salinger, *"To Serve Well and Faithfully": Labor and Indentured Servants in Pennsylvania, 1682–1800* (New York: Cambridge University Press, 1987), 35, 49.

22. Benjamin Franklin, *The Autobiography of Benjamin Franklin*, ed. Leonard W. Labaree et al., new Foreword by Edmund S. Morgan (New Haven, Conn.: Yale University Press, 2003), 124.

23. Patrick Griffin, *The People with No Name: Ireland's Ulster Scots, America's Scots Irish, and the Creation of a British Atlantic World, 1689–1764* (Princeton, N.J.: Princeton University Press, 2001), 65–98.

24. John J. McCusker, *Money and Exchange in Europe and America, 1600–1775: A Handbook* (Chapel Hill: University of North Carolina Press, 1978), 176.

25. Francis Rawle, *Some Remedies Proposed, for the Restoring the Sunk Credit of the Province of Pennsylvania: With Some Remarks on Its Trade: Humbly Offer'd to the Consideration of the Worthy Representatives in the General Assembly of This Province* (Philadelphia: Andrew Bradford, 1721); Nash, *Quakers and Politics*, 332; James Logan to Henry Goldney, 9/2mo/1723, in John B. Linn and Dr. William Henry Engle, eds., *Pennsylvania Archives*, 2nd Ser., 19 vols., (Harrisburg: Lane S. Hart, 1874–1900), 7: 70.

26. On the paper money fights, see Nash, *Quakers and Politics*, 332–34; Frederick B. Tolles, *Meeting House and Counting House: The Quaker Merchants of Colonial Philadelphia, 1682–1763* (Chapel Hill: University of North Carolina Press, 1948), 100–104.

27. Isaac Norris to James Logan, 16/10mo./1723, INLB II, pp. 364–65.

28. Nash, *Urban Crucible*, 149.

29. Isaac Norris to Joseph Pike, 7 May 1723, INLB, II, 329.

30. *Votes*, 1459–60.

31. McCusker, *Money and Exchange in Europe and America*, 176; Nash, *Urban Crucible*, 149–50.

32. Roy N. Lokken, *David Lloyd, Colonial Lawmaker* (Seattle: University of Washington Press, 1959), 209.

33. See Chapter 3, above.

34. James Logan to John Penn, Thomas Penn, and Richard Penn, 29/5mo/1729, Logan Papers 10: 45, HSP; Root, *Relations of Pennsylvania with the British Government*, 252–53.

35. See the Philadelphia Men's Monthly Meeting's request for Keith's aid in a conflict surrounding seating Friends on the chancery court and Keith's response pledging his support: PMMM Minutes, 28/3mo/1725. See also Nash, *Quakers and Politics*, 117–26, 132, 146, 160, 186, 264–67, 312–19.

36. The exact religious and ethnic proportion of Pennsylvania's population is difficult to gauge, but scholars generally agree that Friends were a minority by 1720 and possibly earlier. See Frost, *Perfect Freedom*, 19; Nash, *Urban Crucible*, 103; David Hackett Fischer, *Albion's Seed: Four British Folkways in America* (New York: Oxford University Press, 1989), 421–22, 424; William M. Offutt, *Of "Good Laws" and "Good Men": Law and Society in the Delaware Valley, 1680–1710* (Urbana: University of Illinois Press, 1995), 8; Barry Levy, *Quakers and the American Family: British Settlement in the Delaware Valley* (New York: Oxford University Press, 1988), 155. Marianne S. Wokeck has argued that well over 55,000 German-speaking passengers disembarked in Philadelphia between 1720 and 1755, though not all stayed in Pennsylvania after their arrival. Wokeck, *Trade in Strangers: The Beginnings of Mass Migration to North America* (University Park: Pennsylvania State University Press, 1999), 44–45. The number of immigrants (primarily of Scottish descent) who arrived from northern Ireland between 1715 and 1755 is harder to quantify but was certainly in the tens of thousands (166–73).

37. Nash, *Urban Crucible*, 151.

38. James Logan, *The Charge Delivered from the Bench to the Grand-Jury, at the Court of Quarter Sessions, Held for the County of Philadelphia, the Second Day of September 1723: Published at the Desire of the Said Grand-Jury: Together with Their Address* (Philadelphia: Andrew Bradford, 1723).

39. Logan, *Charge*, 13, 14.

40. Logan, *Charge*, 3–5. Lokken has analyzed the role that Enlightenment theories about "the passions" played in Logan's thought, placing a greater emphasis on this strain of thought in Logan's political philosophy than I do. See Roy N. Lokken, "The Social Thought of James Logan," *WMQ* 27, 1 (1970): 69–89.

41. Logan, *Charge*, 6.

42. Logan, *Charge*, 7, 8, 12.

43. A search of Charles Evans's list of Early American imprints yields no such publications before Logan's. A search of the Early English Books Online and Eighteenth-Century Collections Online databases yields only sixteen grand jury charges before 1723.

44. Logan, *Charge*, 7, 8.

45. Wendel, "Keith-Lloyd Alliance," 301.

46. Frederick B. Tolles, *James Logan and the Culture of Provincial America* (Boston: Little, Brown, 1957), 128.

47. Hannah Callowhill Penn, *London, 26th of the 3d Month, 1724: Sir William Keith, in My Last of the 25th of February, by the Bearer, Inclosing an Agreement Made with the Lord Baltemore* (Philadelphia: Samuel Keimer, 1724), 1–2.

48. Sir William Keith, *The Speech of Sir William Keith, Bart. Governour of the Province of Pennsylvania . . . To the Representatives of the Freemen of the Said Province of Pennsylvania, in General Assembly Met, January 5, 1724–5* (Philadelphia: Andrew Bradford, 1725), reprinted in *AWM*, 12 January 1725. For the publication of Penn's instructions, see Penn, *London, 26th of the 3d Month, 1724*; *AWM*, 25 January 1725; Wendel, "Keith-Lloyd Alliance," 298; Tolles, *James Logan*, 133. Keith claimed Logan had first printed the instructions as a means of discrediting Keith; Logan denied these charges, *AWM*, 19 January 1725; James Logan to John Wright, in Linn et al., eds., *Pennsylvania Archives*, 2nd Ser., 7: 86.

49. *AWM*, 19 January, 26 January, 2 February 1725.

50. "A Memorial from James Logan, in Behalf of the Proprietary's Family, and of himself, Servant to the said Family," in *Votes*, 1639.

51. *Votes*, 1655; *AWM*, 9 February 1725. On the posting of Assembly minutes in the coffeehouse, see *AWM*, 2 February 1725.

52. David Lloyd, *A Vindication of the Legislative Power: Submitted to the Representatives of All the Free-Men of the Province of Pennsylvania, Now Sitting in Assembly* (Philadelphia: Andrew Bradford, 1725), 2, 4.

53. Lloyd, *Vindication*, 3.

54. See above.

55. James Logan, *The Antidote: In Some Remarks on a Paper of David Lloyd's, Called a Vindication of the Legislative Power. Submitted to the Representatives of All the Freemen of Pennsylvania . . .* (Philadelphia: Andrew Bradford, 1725).

56. Logan, *Antidote*, 4, 7.

57. Logan, *Antidote*, 5, 8.

58. Logan, *Antidote*, 8.

59. This process, I would argue, can best be accounted for by Pierre Bourdieu's explanation of the practical relationship between orthodox, heterodox, and doxic. Bourdieu argues that orthodoxy and heterodoxy function as opposite poles in the "universe of argument" in any cultural milieu. The "doxa," however, exists in the "universe of the undiscussed [or] (undisputed)," consisting of the "aggregates of 'choices'" made unconsciously within a given cultural community: "The truth of the doxa is only ever fully revealed when negatively constituted" in moments of cultural conflict. The assumptions "tacitly posited" in the realm of the doxic, he argues, only emerge "retrospectively," after they have been acted on. Bourdieu, *Outline of a Theory of Practice* (New York: Cambridge University Press, 1977), 168, 59–71. Lloyd and Logan, I would argue, debated the terms of political orthodoxy, leaving the doxa of Quaker cultural power untouched.

60. Gary B. Nash, "The Transformation of Urban Politics 1700–1765," *Journal of American History* 60, 3 (1973): 617. Nash and I disagree about the exact numbers but we chart the same trend.

61. Pennsylvania, *The Charter of Privileges Granted by the Honourable William Penn, Esq; to the Freeholders and Inhabitants of Pennsylvania. October 28, 1701* (Philadelphia: Samuel Keimer, 1725).

62. William Keith, *A Letter from Sir William Keith, Bart. Governour of Pennsylvania, to Mr. James Logan . . .* (Philadelphia: Andrew Bradford, 1725).

63. James Logan, *A Dialogue Shewing, What's Therein to Be Found . . .* (Philadelphia: Samuel Keimer, 1725), 35–36.

64. *A Dialogue between Mr. Robert Rich, and Roger Plowman* (Philadelphia: Samuel Keimer, 1725); *The Triumvirate of Pennsylvania: In a Letter to a Friend in the Country* (Philadelphia: Andrew Bradford, 1725); T. T., *A Letter to a Friend* (Philadelphia: Andrew Bradford, 1725).

65. *AWM*, 13 February 1722; John Trenchard and Thomas Gordon, *The Independent Whig* (Philadelphia: S. Keimer, 1724). On the influence of Trenchard and Gordon's writings in Pennsylvania, see Tolles, *Meeting House and Counting House*, 178–79; on their influence in America more generally, Bernard Bailyn, *The Ideological Origins of the American Revolution*, enl. ed. (Cambridge, Mass.: Belknap Press of Harvard University Press, 1992), 35–37; Chad Reid, "'Widely Read by American Patriots': The *New York Weekly Journal* and the Influence of *Cato's Letters* on Colonial America," in *Periodical Literature in Eighteenth-Century America*, ed. Mark Kamrath and Sharon M. Harris (Knoxville: University of Tennessee Press, 2005), 143–78. I am extremely grateful to Chad Reid for sharing his research on the spread of *Cato's Letters* in American publications during the colonial period.

66. Philadelphia Yearly Meeting of the Religious Society of Friends, *An Epistle from Our Yearly-Meeting in Burlington, for the Jerseys and Pennsylvania, &C: Held by Adjournments from the 15th to the 19th Day of the Seventh Month, 1722 . . .* (Philadelphia: Andrew

Bradford, 1722); *An Epistle from Our Yearly Meeting Held in Philadelphia: For Pennsylvania and the Jerseys, &C. From the Fourteenth to the Eighteenth Day of the Seventh Month, 1723* . . . (Philadelphia: Andrew Bradford, 1723); *An Epistle from Our Yearly Meeting at Burlington, for the Jerseys and Pennsylvania, &C: Held by Adjournment, from the Nineteenth to the Twenty Third Day of the Seventh Month, 1724* . . . (Philadelphia: Andrew Bradford, 1724); *An Epistle from the Yearly Meeting of Friends, Held at Burlington: The Seventeenth, to the Twenty First of the Seventh Month, 1726* . . . (Philadelphia: Andrew Bradford, 1727); *An Epistle from Our Yearly Meeting Held in Philadelphia: For Pennsylvania and the Jersey's, from the 20th, to the 24th of the 7th Month, 1729* . . . (Philadelphia: Andrew Bradford, 1729).

67. Robert Barclay, *The Antient Testimony of the People Called Quakers, Reviv'd: By the Order and Approbation of the Yearly Meeting Held for the Province of Pennsylvania and Jerseys. 1722* (Philadelphia: Andrew Bradford, 1723); Barclay, *A Catechism and Confession of Faith: Approved of and Agreed unto by the General Assembly of the Patriarchs, Prophets, and Apostles, Christ Himself Chief Speaker in and Among Them* . . . (Philadelphia: Samuel Keimer, 1726).

68. The one exception was Bradford's 1725 reprint of William Sewel's eighteenth-century history of the rise of the Society of Friends, done at the Philadelphia Yearly Meeting's request. Bradford was left with so many unsold copies of the book that he threatened to take legal action if the Meeting did not purchase the remaining copies. PYMM Minutes, 18–22/7mo./1725. No copy of Bradford's 1725 edition of Sewel's text exists, though a 1728 edition printed by Samuel Keimer, in conjunction with Benjamin Franklin and Hugh Meredith, does: William Sewel, *The History of the Rise, Increase, and Progress, of the Christian People Called Quakers: Intermixed with Several Remarkable Occurrences*, 3rd ed., corrected (Philadelphia: Samuel Keimer, 1728); Franklin, *Autobiography*, 118–19.

69. London Yearly Meeting of the Society of Friends and Meeting for Sufferings, *An Epistle of Caution to Friends in General Relating to the Solemn Affirmation: From a Meeting Held in London the Second of the First Month 1721–22* (Philadelphia: Andrew Bradford, 1722); *A Conference between a Parish-Priest, and a Quaker: Published for the Preventing (If Possible) the Vile Deceits of Priestcraft in America* (Philadelphia: Samuel Keimer, 1725); Stephen Crisp, *A Short History of a Long Travel, from Babylon to Bethel* (Philadelphia: Samuel Keimer, 1724); Thomas Lurting, *The Fighting Sailor Turn'd Peaceable Christian* . . . (Philadelphia: Samuel Keimer, 1725); Elizabeth Stirredge and John Whiting, *Strength in Weakness Manifest in the Life, Trials and Christian Testimony of That Faithful Servant and Handmaid of the Lord, Elizabeth Stirredge, Who Departed This Life, at Her House at Hempsted in Hertford-Shire, in the 72d Year of Her Age* (Philadelphia: Samuel Keimer, 1726).

70. James Logan to Joshua Gee, 4/4mo/1725, JLLB II, p. 278; James Logan to Simon Clement, 17/3mo/1725, JLLB II, p. 270.

71. James Logan to Springett Penn, 24/9mo/1725, JLLB II, p. 285.

72. *The Case of the Heir at Law and Executrix of the Late Proprietor of Pennsilvania, & C. In Relation to the Removal of Sir William Keith, and the Appointing Major Patrick*

Gordon to Succeed Him as Deputy-Governor There (Philadelphia: Andrew Bradford, 1726), 5; "Order of the King in Council," 11 March 1726, in *CSPC*, 35: 33–34; *MPCP*, 3: 250.

73. [Sir William Keith], *The Observator's Trip to America, in a Dialogue between the Observator and His Country-Man Roger* (Philadelphia: Andrew Bradford, 1726), 7, 9; Keith, *A Just and Plain Vindication of Sir William Kieth, Bart. Late Governour of Pensilvania: From the Untruths and Aspersions Contain'd in a Paper Printed at London, under the Title of the Case of the Heir at Law, and Executrix of the Late Proprietor of Pensilvania, &C* (Philadelphia: Samuel Keimer, 1726), 2.

74. *Votes*, 1755–56; *AWM*, 2 June 1726.

75. *Votes*, 1760, 1765; *AWM*, 9 June 1726.

76. James Logan to H Taylor, in Linn and Engle, eds., *Pennsylvania Archives*, 2nd Ser., 7: 91.

77. Isaac Norris to James Scarth, 21/8mo/1726, INLB, II, p. 475; Gordon to John Penn, Oct 18 1726, PPOC, 1: 237, 243; Isaac Norris to Joseph Pike, 26/8mo/1726, INLB, II, p. 516.

78. Gordon to John Penn, Oct 18 1726, in PPOC, 1: 237.

79. James Logan to John Penn, 17/10mo/1726, in PPOC, 1: 237.

80. Norris to Scarth, in INLB, II,, 475.

81. *Votes*, 1791; *AWM*, 24 November 1726.

82. *Advice and Information to the Freeholders and Freemen of the Province of Pensilvania: And Particularly to Those of the County and City of Philadelphia* (Philadelphia: Andrew Bradford, 1727), 1.

83. Wendel, "Keith-Lloyd Alliance," 303.

84. Samson Davis et al., *The Two Following Depositions Were Laid before the House the Ninth Day of August, 1728* (Philadelphia: Andrew Bradford, 1728).

85. Pennsylvania et al., *To the Honourable Patrick Gordon Esq; Lieutenant Governour of the Province of Pennsylvania: The Representation of the Assembly of the Said Province Humbly Sheweth* (Philadelphia: Andrew Bradford, 1728), 10. On Keith's Jacobite sympathies, see "Sir William Keith," in *LLP*, 2: 561.

86. David Lloyd and John Swift, *A Defence of the Legislative Constitution of the Province of Pennsylvania, as It Now Stands Confirmed and Established, by Law and Charter . . .* (Philadelphia: Andrew Bradford, 1728).

87. Alan Tully notes this ideological flexibility as part of what he calls "civil Quakerism." He does not, however, trace the processes of selective memory behind this discursive tradition nor connect it to the colony's religious and cultural evolution in other dimensions. Tully, *Forming American Politics*, 300, 302.

88. *LLP*, 2: 113; Tully, *Forming American Politics*, 147.

89. See note 36, esp. Wokeck, *Trade in Strangers*.

90. Constant Truman, *Advice to the Free-Holders and Electors of Pennsylvania, &C* (Philadelphia: Andrew Bradford, 1735).

91. Tully, *Forming American Politics*, 146–49.

92. The evidence for Sawantaeny's death is found in *MPCP*, 3: 148–56; and "An

Indian Council held at Philadelphia, 21 March 1721/2," Society Miscellaneous Collections, Indians, 1682–1900, box 11C, folder 2, HSP. Pp. 10–12 of the latter manuscript, labeled "Depositions of Jonathan Swindel and William Wilkins," provide the fullest account of the incident. In the manuscript of the March 1722 council, Logan indicated that he thought the crime had been committed on 9 January. According to the date written at the top of p. 10, Swindel's and Wilkins's depositions were taken before Governor Sir William Keith on 22 March 1722. Less useful depositions given by witnesses George Rescarrick and Richard Satler Jr. can be found in Indian Treaties, Du Simitière Collection, folder no. 2, LCP. Satler's deposition, given on 10 March 1722, dates Sawantaeny's death in the last week of February, which contradicts Logan's account and the depositions of Swindel and Wilkins. Sawantaeny's death has also been discussed in Jennings, *Ambiguous Iroquois Empire*, 290–91; Daniel K. Richter, *The Ordeal of the Longhouse: The Peoples of the Iroquois League in the Era of European Colonization* (Chapel Hill: University of North Carolina Press, 1992), 241–42; Eric Hinderaker, *Elusive Empires: Constructing Colonialism in the Ohio Valley, 1673–1800* (New York: Cambridge University Press, 1997), 123–24; James H. Merrell, *Into the American Woods: Negotiators on the Pennsylvania Frontier* (New York: Norton, 1999), 115–21.

93. Although the recorded council minutes for these meetings describe Tanachaha as a representative of the "Five Nations" of the Iroquois, the appellation may be incorrect. Given that the Tuscarosas became the sixth member of the Iroquois League at some point during 1721 or 1722, it is difficult to fit the change from the Five to the Six Nations into the chronology of Sawantaeny's death and its aftermath told here. To avoid confusion, I have used the terms "Iroquois nations" or "Iroquois Confederacy" instead of either the Five or Six Nations.

94. The term is Robert Cover's: Cover et al., "The Folktales of Justice: Tales of Jurisdiction," in *Narrative, Violence, and the Law: The Essays of Robert Cover*, ed. Martha Minow, Michael Ryan, and Austin Sarat (Ann Arbor: University of Michigan Press, 1992). James H. Merrell discusses the struggle between colonizers and Indians to determine "whose words were law" in Merrell, "'The Customes of Our Countrey': Indians and Colonists in Early America," in *Strangers Within the Realm: Cultural Margins of the First British Empire*, ed. Bernard Bailyn and Philip D. Morgan (Chapel Hill: University of North Carolina Press, 1991), 117–56.

95. I am not suggesting that the Pennsylvanians' position was monolithic or that there was a single "Indian" stance toward Sawantaeny's death. The distinctions among Pennsylvanians and Indians and between various Pennsylvanians and Indians will be treated below. For an account of early provincial-Indian relations that emphasizes Penn's role in constructing the myth of his own benevolence toward the Indians, see James O'Neil Spady, "Colonialism and the Discursive Antecedents of *Penn's Treaty with the Indians*," in *Friends and Enemies in Penn's Woods: Colonists, Indians, and the Racial Construction of Pennsylvania*, ed. William Pencak and Daniel K. Richter (University Park: Pennsylvania State University Press, 2004), 18–40.

96. *MPCP*, 3: 148–49.

97. MPCP, 3: 149. As Jennings has pointed out, Logan failed to include the depositions of Swindel and Wilkins in his official report. Jennings's speculation that Logan suppressed these testimonies because they showed Cartlidge's culpability is more dubious, however. The manuscript account that Logan "suppressed" notes that Keith was present at the depositions; this raises the question of from whom, exactly, Logan was trying to hide the depositions. See "An Indian Council held at Philadelphia, 21 January 1721/2," Society Miscellaneous Collections, Indians, 1682–1900, Box 11C, Folder 2, pp. 10–12, HSP; and Jennings, *Ambiguous Iroquois Empire*, 291n2.

98. This fact was in some dispute, as one witness claimed not to have seen Sawantaeny with his gun, while four claimed that he did have it. Since one of these witnesses, Sawantaeny's wife, claimed she was in the cabin when he left with his gun, I believe he actually did retrieve it.

99. *MPCP*, 3: 150–52.

100. *MPCP*, 3: 155.

101. *MPCP*, 3: 155.

102. See Chapter 2, above.

103. The most recent interracial death was that of Francis LeTore, at the hands of a group of Indians (probably Shawnee warriors). LeTore, a servant, had run away from his master, who hired local Indians to capture or kill him. They killed him. *MPCP*, 2: 533–34.

104. The only indirect evidence that Logan, at least, may have been aware of this statute is his long association with William Penn as the proprietor's agent. Logan arrived in 1699—when the mixed-jury statute was still on the books, though not enforced—and was in all likelihood aware of Penn's unusual and progressive ideas on diplomatic and legal relations with Indians.

105. Weynepeeweyta was, as noted above, a Shawnee with close ties to the Seneca on the Pennsylvania frontier. It is difficult to know whether Sawantaeny's place of residence and status were defined by his or his wife's tribal background and lineage, though the Shawnee were at this time both patrilineal and patrilocal. Charles Callender, "Shawnee," in *Northeast*, ed. Bruce G. Trigger (Washington, D.C.: Smithsonian Institution, 1978), 6: 622–23, 626–27. The Seneca Indians were matrilocal and matrilineal, as were the Delaware and Conestoga in the region. This confluence of political lineage systems in one community makes determining Sawantaeny's political affiliation in death even more problematic.

106. *MPCP*, 2: 608.

107. *MPCP*, 3: 24.

108. Jennings has traced this trend elsewhere in colonial Anglo-American: *Ambiguous Iroquois Empire*, 45, 49, 77–81, 132.

109. Indian Treaties, Du Simitière Collection. This Indian Council was not recorded in the official minutes of the Provincial Council. See *MPCP*, 3: 160–61.

110. The Cartlidges, in their petition for bail to the Provincial Council on 22 March, had implied that Sawantaeny might still be alive, noting that they were "heartily sorry for the Death of the Indian (if He be really dead)" (*MPCP*, 3: 156).

111. Aquila Rose, Elias Bockett, and Joseph Rose, *Poems on Several Occasions* (Philadelphia: Printed by Benjamin Franklin at the new printing-office, near the market), 25–26; David S. Shields, "The Wits and Poets of Pennsylvania: New Light on the Rise of Belles Lettres in Provincial Pennsylvania, 1720–1740," *PMHB* 109, 2 (1985): 105–6.

112. Indian Treaties, Du Simitière Collection. Although this manuscript does not say which treaty Civility was referring to when he held "a Parchment in his Hand," it was most likely a 1700 treaty between Logan (on Penn's behalf) and the Susquehanna Indians in southeastern Pennsylvania. The text promised "That no person whatsoever Shall at any time live amongst or trade with the Said Indians, or bring any Liquors or Goods to Sell or dispose of amongst them" except with special dispensation from Penn. See Treaty with the Susquehannah Indians, 12 September 1700, George Vaux Collection, QCHC. This treaty became an issue in 1735, see below.

113. *MPCP*, 3: 163–65.

114. *MPCP*, 3: 168.

115. See Keith's message to the Iroquois nations, *MPCP*, 3: 194, and his reiteration of the same theme at a September meeting in Philadelphia, *MPCP*, 3: 197.

116. *MPCP*, 3: 198.

117. *MPCP*, 3: 200.

118. Jennings sees this as the true beginning of Pennsylvania's participation in the Covenant Chain, arguing that Penn had largely ignored the Iroquois in his dealings, making treaties primarily with the Delaware and the Susquehanna (Conestoga) Indians. Jennings, *Ambiguous Iroquois Empire*, 290–94.

119. This point is also made by Jennings, *Ambiguous Iroquois Empire*, 293–94. In one critical respect, however, Keith did reject the Iroquois claim to sovereignty over the region. While he gladly took control of the lands the Iroquois ceded around Conestoga, he told those assembled at Albany, "You know very well that the Lands about Conestogoe, upon the River Susquehannah, belong to your old friend and kind Brother William Penn." Keith had managed to accept their gift without recognizing their authority to give it (*MPCP*, 3: 202).

120. On narrative contextualization and fact making, see Clifford Geertz, "Local Knowledge: Fact and Law in Comparative Perspective," in Geertz, *Local Knowledge: Further Essays in Interpretive Anthropology* (New York: Basic Books, 1983), 167–234.

121. Jane T. Merritt and Nancy Shoemaker have recently argued for the significance of familial and body language respectively as structuring metaphors in Indian-colonial diplomacy in Pennsylvania. See Merritt, "Metaphor, Meaning, and Misunderstanding: Language and Power on the Pennsylvania Frontier," in *Contact Points: American Frontiers from the Mohawk Valley to the Mississippi, 1750–1830*, ed. Andrew R. L. Cayton and Fredrika J. Teute (Chapel Hill: University of North Carolina Press, 1998), 60–87; Shoemaker, "Body Language," in *A Centre of Wonders: The Body in Early America*, ed. Janet Moore Lindman and Michele Lise Tarter (Ithaca, N.Y.: Cornell University Press, 2001), 211–22. I do not intend to suggest that familial or body language is insignificant to Civility's speech or to any other Indian-colonial interactions. I am suggesting, that, while Civility

employs these metaphors in describing the relationship between his people and the provincial government, his normative statements regarding how the provincials should act are grounded in a history of alliance, friendship, and reciprocity. In this case, normative folktales of justice are used in combination with descriptive metaphors of connection.

122. *MPCP*, 3:46.

123. *MPCP*, 2:599–600, 607–8. For other examples of Pennsylvania's Indians invoking Penn's example, see *MPCP*, 3: 46, 123; "Acount of Indian Council held at Philadelphia 15 Sept. 1718," Logan Papers, IX: 7; "James Logan's Report on Meeting with Indians," in *Memoirs of the Historical Society of Pennsylvania* (Philadelphia: HSP, 1858). James Spady has discussed Keith's (and later Patrick Gordon's) references to Penn's history with the Indians as a continuation of a myth propagated by the proprietor himself about his own benevolence. See Spady, "Colonialism and the Discursive Antecedents." I would argue from the evidence presented here that Civility and other negotiators for the Conestoga and Delaware Indians were more instrumental in making the mythic relationship between Penn and provincial Indians central to colonial-Indian treaty discourse in the 1720s than was Penn's earlier propaganda. It seems likely that Keith's and Gordon's mentions of the myth were more directly related to Indians' repeated invocation of the Penn-Indian relationship in the 1710s and 1720s than to anything Penn said or wrote about his relations with local natives.

124. "Miquon" and "Onas" are puns meaning "quill" or "pen," thus working as cognates for Penn.

125. My discussion is influenced by Robert A. Williams, *Linking Arms Together: American Indian Treaty Visions of Law and Peace, 1600–1800* (New York: Oxford University Press, 1997).

126. *MPCP*, 3: 221.

127. Merrell suggests that Civility conspired with the Cartlidges to bury Sawantaeny immediately both to keep the peace and to keep the Iroquois out of Pennsylvania, although he does not develop the question of whether any Indians in Pennsylvania would have desired that the Cartlidges be tried under English law for murder (*Into the American Woods*, 117).

128. I do not intend to further the "myth" of the Iroquois empire or to suggest that the attempt to bring the Indians on the Susquehanna under their influence was the equivalent of the colonial expansion of Pennsylvania's government and authority. As Jennings, Richter, and Matthew Dennis have argued, the notion that the Iroquois nations functioned as an imperial or colonial power in any way comparable to European colonialism is inaccurate. See Jennings, *Ambiguous Iroquois Empire*, 10–24; Jennings, "'Pennsylvania Indians' and the Iroquois"; Richter, *Ordeal of the Longhouse*; Dennis, *Cultivating a Landscape of Peace: Iroquois-European Encounters in Seventeenth-Century America* (Ithaca, N.Y.: Cornell University Press, 1993), 6, 67, 229, 256, 257–68. Hinderaker may go too far in this direction; his discussion of the settlement of Sawantaeny's death ignores the fact that non-Iroquois Indians were affected by the agreements between the Iroquois and Keith. He thus misses the fact that many Indians on Pennsylvania's borders did consider the Iroquois

unwanted intruders, if not "imperial" in the sense above (Hinderaker, *Elusive Empires*, 125–28).

129. *MPCP*, 3: 302–4; Samuel Hazard, ed., *Pennsylvania Archives*, 1st ser., 19 vols. (Harrisburg: 1852–56), 1: 215–21; "James Logan's Report on Meeting with Indians," 258–63; Merrell, *Into the American Woods*, 158–64; Jennings, *Ambiguous Iroquois Empire*, 247; Hinderaker, *Elusive Empires*, 123–24.

130. "James Logan's Report on Meeting with Indians," 258–63.

131. *AWM*, 4 July 1728.

132. *MPCP*, 3: 313.

133. *MPCP*, 3: 329–31.

134. *MPCP*, 3: 337.

135. *Pennsylvania Archives*, 1st Ser. 1: 303–4; *MPCP*, 3: 605.

136. *MPCP*, 3: 500–505.

137. *MPCP*, 3: 448–49. See also *MPCP*, 3:331.

138. *MPCP*, 3: 606.

139. Steven Craig Harper, *Promised Land: Penn's Holy Experiment, the Walking Purchase, and the Dispossession of Delawares, 1600–1763* (Bethlehem, Pa.: Lehigh University Press, 2006), 46–53.

140. Account of the Walking Purchase by Moses Tetamie, Friendly Association Papers, 1: 407, QCHC, cited in Harper, *Promised Land*, 56.

141. James Logan to Conrad Weiser, Logan Papers 2: 58, HSP.

142. *MPCP*, 3: 448–49. Critically, however, while Gordon described this agreement on harboring fugitive slaves as implying that *all* Pennsylvania laws would be upheld on the frontier—including punishing those guilty of intercultural assault or homicide—his Iroquois counterparts were silent on that issue. *MPCP*, 4: 90–95.

143. Harper, *Promised Land*, 46–53 is the most recent account of the Walking Purchase. See also Jennings, *Ambiguous Iroquois Empire*, 329–47, for a classic account.

CONCLUSION: CALEB PUSEY, MILLER PHILOSOPHER AND MAN OF LETTERS

1. Henry J. Cadbury and J. William Frost, "Caleb Pusey's Account of Pennsylvania," *Quaker History* 64, 1 (1975): 41.

2. Cadbury and Frost, "Caleb Pusey's Account," 42, 43.

3. Cadbury and Frost, "Caleb Pusey's Account," 47–49.

4. Cadbury and Frost, "Caleb Pusey's Account," 49, 52.

5. PYMM Minutes, 16–20/7mo/1727, 14–18/7mo/1728, 14–18/7mo/1734, 23–24/7mo/1735; Kyle P. Farley, "A Holy Experiment: History and Memory in Pennsylvania, 1682–1800" (Ph.D. dissertation, University of Pennsylvania, 2006), 155n6; Robert Proud, *The History of Pennsylvania, in North America* (Philadelphia: Printed by Zachariah Poulson junior . . . , 1797–98).

6. J. G. A. Pocock, *Barbarism and Religion*, vol. 4, *Barbarians, Savages, and Empires* (New York: Cambridge University Press, 2005), 319. This theme is also discussed in Jack

D. Marietta and G. S. Rowe, *Troubled Experiment: Crime and Justice in Pennsylvania, 1682–1800* (Philadelphia: University of Pennsylvania Press, 2006), Introduction.

7. In this sense, Pusey's selective memory may reflect the more general process of remembering and forgetting that Benedict Anderson sees at the heart of all nationalism, especially the creole nationalisms of the Americas: Benedict R. O'G. Anderson, *Imagined Communities: Reflections on the Origin and Spread of Nationalism*, rev. ed. (New York: Verso, 1991), 6, 47–66, 187–206.

8. See John Smolenski, "From Men of Property to Just Men: Deference, Masculinity, and the Evolution of Political Discourse in Early America," *EAS* 3, 2 (2005): 253–85; and Smolenski, "'Incorporated . . . into a Body Politic': Clubs, Print, and the Gendering of the Civic Subject in Eighteenth-Century Pennsylvania," in *Periodical Literature in Eighteenth-Century America*, ed. Mark Kamrath and Sharon M. Harris (Knoxville: University of Tennessee Press, 2005), 47–73.

9. Alan Tully has persuasively shown that the ideology of what he terms "civil Quakerism" exercised a powerful hold on non-Quaker voters and politicians. He also notes that its influence extended even after Friends became a minority in the Assembly. Tully, *Forming American Politics: Ideals, Interests, and Institutions in Colonial New York and Pennsylvania* (Baltimore: Johns Hopkins University Press, 1994), 289–309.

10. On the need to historicize creolization, see Michel-Rolph Trouillot, "Culture on the Edges: Caribbean Creolization in Historical Context," in *From the Margins: Historical Anthropology and Its Futures*, ed. Brian Keith Axel (Durham, N.C.: Duke University Press, 2002), 189–210. On the double meaning of history as "both 'what happened' and 'that which is said to have happened'," see Trouillot, *Silencing the Past: Power and the Production of History* (Boston.: Beacon Press, 1995), 2. Stephan Palmié and Richard Price have similarly argued for a more historicized understanding of creolization that locates "creole" social formations in the structural position in which they were created: Palmié, "Creolization and Its Discontents," *Annual Review of Anthropology* 35 (2006): 440; Price, "The Miracle of Creolization: A Retrospective," *New West Indian Guide/Nieuwe West-Indische Gids* 75, 1 (2001): 35–64; Trouillot, *Silencing the Past*, 2.

11. D. A. Brading, *The First America: The Spanish Monarchy, Creole Patriots, and the Liberal State, 1492–1867* (New York: Cambridge University Press, 1991), 199, 224–27, 243, 293–313 (quote 293); Anthony Pagden, "From Noble Savages to Savage Nobles: The *Criollo* Uses of the Amerindian Past," in Pagden, *Spanish Imperialism and the Political Imagination: Studies in European and Spanish-American Social and Political Theory, 1513–1830* (New Haven, Conn.: Yale University Press, 1990); Jorge Cañizares-Esguerra, *How to Write the History of the New World: Histories, Epistemologies, and Identities in the Eighteenth-Century Atlantic World* (Stanford, Calif.: Stanford University Press, 2001); Cañizares-Esguerra, "New World, New Stars: Patriotic Astrology and the Invention of Indian and Creole Bodies in Colonial Spanish America, 1600–1650," *AHR* 104, 1 (1999): 33–68; Cañizares-Esguerra, *Puritan Conquistadors: Iberianizing the Atlantic, 1550–1700* (Stanford, Calif.: Stanford University Press, 2006); J. H. Elliott, *Empires of the Atlantic World: Britain and Spain in America, 1492–1830* (New Haven, Conn.: Yale University Press, 2006),

239–42; Ralph Bauer and José Antonio Mazzotti, "Introduction," in *Creole Subjects in the Colonial Americas: Empires, Texts, Identities*, ed. Bauer and Mazzotti (Chapel Hill: University of North Carolina Press, 2009), 22–25 .

12. Perry Miller, *The New England Mind, from Colony to Province* (Cambridge, Mass.: Belknap Press of Harvard University Press, 1983), 27–39, 149–90; Stephen Foster, *The Long Argument: English Puritanism and the Shaping of New England Culture, 1570–1700* (Chapel Hill: University of North Carolina Press, 1991), 205–37, 286–87; Robert Middlekauff, *The Mathers: Three Generations of Puritan Intellectuals, 1596–1728* (Berkeley: University of California Press, 1999), 113–16. On the 1680s as the collapse of the "cultural dominance" New England's ministers had enjoyed, see Darren Staloff, *The Making of an American Thinking Class: Intellectuals and Intelligentsia in Puritan Massachusetts* (New York: Oxford University Press, 1998). On the symbolic and social influence of the generation of the "Great Migration," see Virginia DeJohn Anderson, *New England's Generation: The Great Migration and the Formation of Society and Culture in the Seventeenth Century* (New York: Cambridge University Press, 1991).

13. Here I am following Greg Dening's definition of history as "making a present out of the past." Dening, *Performances* (Chicago: University of Chicago Press, 1996), 34.

14. Ira Berlin, "From Creole to African: Atlantic Creoles and the Origins of African-American Society in Mainland North America," *WMQ* 53, 2 (1996): 251–88. On the evolution of "Atlantic creole" culture inland, see Linda M. Heywood and John K. Thornton, *Central Africans, Atlantic Creoles, and the Foundation of the Americas, 1585–1660* (New York: Cambridge University Press, 2007), 49–235. On Anthony Johnson, see T. H. Breen and Stephen Innes, *"Myne Owne Ground": Race and Freedom on Virginia's Eastern Shore, 1640–1676* (New York: Oxford University Press, 1980), 17.

15. Berlin, "From Creole to African," 274–76; Ira Berlin, "Time, Space, and the Evolution of Afro-American Society on British Mainland North America," *AHR* 85, 1 (1980): 44–78; Kamau Brathwaite, *The Development of Creole Society in Jamaica, 1770–1820*, rev. ed. (Kingston: Ian Randle, 2005). Gwendolyn Midlo Hall argues that maroon communities exerted a disproportionate influence even as a large growth in the slave trade "Africanized" Louisiana during Spanish rule. Hall, *Africans in Colonial Louisiana: The Development of Afro-Creole Culture in the Eighteenth Century* (Baton Rouge: Louisiana State University Press, 1992), 156–236, 275–315. Hall has elsewhere made a much stronger argument in favor of the continuing significance of "charter groups," though her evidence suggests they were more important in the Caribbean and Latin America than in mainland British America. Hall, *Slavery and African Ethnicities in the Americas: Restoring the Links* (Chapel Hill: University of North Carolina Press, 2007), 15. Joseph C. Miller has argued that the "opportunistic, *bricoleur*-like" capacity of constructing "new identities under the constraints of slavery in the Americas" reflected common experiences of the enslaved in Africa, rather than the influence of any particular founding generation; see Joseph C. Miller, "Retention, Reinvention, and Remembering: Restoring Identities Through Enslavement in Africa and Under Slavery in Brazil," in *Enslaving Connections: Changing Cultures of Africa and Brazil During the Era of Slavery*, ed. José C. Curto and Paul E.

Lovejoy (Amherst, N.Y.: Humanity Books, 2004), 93. See also Price, "The Miracle of Creolization: A Retrospective"; and Stephan Palmié, "Is There a Model in the Muddle? 'Creolization' In African Americanist History and Anthropology," in *Creolization: History, Ethnography, Theory*, ed. Charles Stewart (Walnut Creek, Calif.: Left Coast Press, 2007), 178–200.

16. Bernard Bailyn, "Politics and Social Structure in Virginia," in *Seventeenth-Century America: Essays in Colonial History*, ed. James Morton Smith (Chapel Hill: University of North Carolina Press, 1959), 106 (quote); Edmund S. Morgan, *American Slavery, American Freedom: The Ordeal of Colonial Virginia* (New York: Norton, 1975); Carole Shammas, "English-Born and Creole Elites in Turn-of-the-Century Virginia," in *The Chesapeake in the Seventeenth Century: Essays on Anglo-American Society*, ed. Thad W. Tate and David Ammerman (Chapel Hill: University of North Carolina Press, 1979), 284 (quote); Anthony S. Parent, *Foul Means: The Formation of a Slave Society in Virginia, 1660–1740* (Chapel Hill: University of North Carolina Press, 2003), 105–34; Kathleen M. Brown, *Good Wives, Nasty Wenches, and Anxious Patriarchs: Gender, Race, and Power in Colonial Virginia* (Chapel Hill: University of North Carolina Press, 1996), 107–34, 212–43. On Maryland, see Trevor G. Burnard, *Creole Gentlemen: The Maryland Elite, 1691–1776* (New York: Routledge, 2002); and Michal Rozbicki, *Transformation of the English Cultural Ethos in Colonial America: Maryland, 1634–1720* (Lanham, Md.: University Press of America, 1988).

17. David Hackett Fischer makes a strong argument that the Virginian notion of "hegemonic liberty" persisted through the nineteenth and even twentieth centuries. Fischer, *Albion's Seed: Four British Folkways in America* (New York: Oxford University Press, 1989), 410–18.

18. Berlin, "From Creole to African," 263. See also Palmié's reminder that the cultural creativity creolization entailed was fundamentally a response to exploitation: "Is There a Model in the Muddle?" 194.

19. See Kenneth A. Lockridge, *The Diary and Life of William Byrd II of Virginia, 1674–1744* (Chapel Hill: University of North Carolina Press, 1987); Bernard Bailyn, *The Peopling of British North America: An Introduction* (New York: Vintage, 1988), esp. 102, 120, 131; Michael Zuckerman, "The Fabrication of Identity in Early America," in Zuckerman, *Almost Chosen People: Oblique Biographies in the American Grain* (Berkeley: University of California Press, 1993), 43; Parent, *Foul Means*, 197–235. My emphasis here differs from Mechal Sobel's argument about the nature of black and white cultures in colonial Virginia: Sobel, *The World They Made Together: Black and White Values in Eighteenth-Century Virginia* (Princeton, N.J.: Princeton University Press, 1987). Though I agree with Sobel's characterization of Virginian culture as "symbiotic" (11), I am more cautious about characterizing this symbiosis as mixture. I would contend that the cultural habits Virginian leaders developed represented an *adaptation* to their interactions with racial and cultural others much more than an *adoption* of African or Native American values.

INDEX

Page numbers in *italics* refer to illustrations in the text.

ACKNOWLEDGMENTS

I WANTED MY acknowledgments to be witty and self-effacing. But upon reflection, I am not all that witty. And as Benjamin Franklin said in his *Autobiography*, "I scarce ever heard or saw the introductory Words, *Without Vanity I may say*, &c. but some vain thing immediately follow'd." So let me eschew modesty, note that I worked hard on this book, and simply thank those who provided steadfast support along the way.

First, I would like to express my gratitude to those institutions that provided financial assistance. At the University of Pennsylvania, I received a Benjamin Franklin Graduate Fellowship and an Andrew W. Mellon Fellowship. A Gest Fellowship from the Quaker Collection at Haverford College helped fund forays into Quaker history. Fellowships from the Pew Program in Religion and American History at Yale University and the Spencer Foundation helped fund my writing at crucial moments. Since my arrival at UC Davis, I have been fortunate enough to receive internal and external sources of support. Grants from the faculty Committee on Research and the Institute for Governmental Affairs helped fund research trips to Philadelphia and the purchase of much needed microfilm. A Barbara Thom Postdoctoral Fellowship from the Huntington Library gave me the time and space to reconstruct the manuscript along much different lines than I had originally. A University of California President's Fellowship in the Humanities allowed me to finish revisions on the project. Without the generous support of these institutions, I could never have completed this project.

I would also like to thank those undergraduate teachers who shaped my intellectual development at a young age. Barbara Oberg and Doron Ben-Atar convinced me to be an undergraduate history major, and Doron was the first person to suggest that I might be good at the Ph.D. thing. As a teacher and thesis advisor, David Brion Davis helped me understand the moral dimensions of historical scholarship. Special thanks go to Jon Butler. Jon was a model mentor during my time at Yale and has continued in that capacity since I graduated. He was kind (and patient) enough to treat me as a colleague even when I was a very junior (and very callow) scholar. For that especially, he has my gratitude.

At Penn, I was fortunate to work with a number of brilliant, and demanding, early Americanists. Richard Dunn encouraged me when I needed it and offered an appropriately skeptical eye when my work went off track. Kathy Brown was patient with my early struggles to understand gender history. She was a tough, but fair, critic and offered me crucial guidance on this project at several critical points along the way. Dan Richter showed me that Indian history was colonial history. He also offered a heavy editorial hand on one section of this book that greatly improved its prose. Last, but most certainly not least, I must thank my teacher, mentor, and friend Mike Zuckerman. The personal and professional debts I owe Mike are too great to list here, but suffice it to say that I would not be the scholar I am today without his guidance. His voluminous and incisive commentary on this project at every stage forced me to refine my ideas and my prose at every turn. He always encouraged me to find my own voice. That this book deals squarely with many issues central to his own work represents a meeting of the minds, not any attempt on his part to train a junior version of himself. If I disagree with Mike about a vast number of the particulars of early American history, I can safely say that we agree on one big thing: the continued relevance of studying early American history in a multicultural United States. I am deeply grateful for Mike's example.

I would also like to thank two research institutions whose help was invaluable. I cannot imagine a place more ideal for studying colonial America than the McNeil Center for Early American Studies. The Center's founding and current directors, Richard Dunn and Dan Richter, each provided me office space during my multiple stays in Philadelphia, and each invited me to present portions of this work at the Center's Friday seminar. I am grateful to those members of the Center community for their camaraderie and their willingness to listen to me talk about my work, particularly Niki Eustace, Brooke Hunter, Tom Humphrey, Kirsten Wood, Karim Tiro, John Fea, Roderick McDonald, George Boudreau, Bill Pencak, and Liam Riordan. I must give special praise to two individuals. Randolph Scully was brave enough to share an office with me, which surely qualifies him for hazard pay. Brendan McConville has been a consistent supporter of my work from the beginning of my career, writing letters, reading drafts, and offering much constructive criticism. The year I spent at the Huntington Library was an amazing experience. I am grateful to the Library's Director of Research Roy Ritchie for his hospitality and to Peter Mancall and fellow cat-person Alison Games for being outstanding lunchtime companions.

I am grateful to several other scholars for their support as well. Roger Abrahams, William Offutt, Jack Marietta, Stephen Foster, Michael John Goode, and Ken Lockridge for their willingness to answer multiple (and often lengthy) emails about various research questions. Ken was also kind enough to write letters on my behalf, for which I thank him. The fine folks at Historiann.com have provided invaluable intellectual and social camaraderie, especially Historiann herself, Ann Little.

I count myself lucky to be a member of the History Department at UC Davis, where I have been surrounded with a number of helpful and support-ive coworkers. Alan Taylor has been the most generous colleague a young scholar could have. His feedback on various chapters in this book played a critical role in shaping its overall development. He is also an exemplary host and a fair pool shark. Ellen Hartigan-O'Connor also read part of the manu-script and offered much needed advice as well. Eric Rauchway read a draft of the entire thing and gave valuable tips for its revision. Norma Landau tutored me in the finer points of English legal history, while Joan Cadden and Daniel Stolzenberg patiently fielded questions about medieval and early modern her-metic thought. Sally McKee has been and continues to be a wonderful men-tor. Lisa Materson and Phil Kaminsky provided much needed distractions from writing, commiserating over academia, life, and cats. Of my esteemed hallmate Clarence Walker, I can say that I have learned a lot from him. I could not have asked for more supportive departmental chairs than Susan Mann and Ted Margadant. I worked out some of the ideas in this book in various classes at UCD, and I am grateful to those students who helped me do so. My research assistant Sara Main has done yeoman work in the final stages of this book. I should also give special thanks to the members of my seminars on creolization, especially Nate McKean, Miran Park, Ari Von Gemeren, Mandy Bell, James Estes, Jessica DeSalvo, Andy Prull, Sonia Pare-cadan, and Sarah Thibault.

Portions of this book appeared in an earlier form in " 'As The Discharge of My Conscience to God': Narrative, Personhood, and the Construction of Legal Order in Seventeenth-Century Quaker Culture," *Prospects: An Annual of American Cultural Studies* 24 (1999): 117–75, and "The Death of Sawantaeny and the Problem of Justice on the Frontier," in *Friends and Enemies in Penn's Woods: Indians, Colonists, and the Racial Construction of Pennsylvania*, ed. Daniel K. Richter and William Pencak (University Park: Pennsylvania State University Press, 2004), 104–28. I thank Cambridge University Press and Pennsylvania State University Press respectively for permission to reprint revised versions of these essays. I have also presented portions of this work at various venues, including annual meetings of the Pennsylvania Historical Association, the McNeil Center for Early American Studies, the Bay Area Seminar in Early American Studies, the British Group in Early American History, the Harvard Seminar in the History of the Atlantic World, and the Omohundro Institute for Early American History. My thanks to all the commentators and participants at these sessions, especially Simon Middleton, Carla Pestana, Carol Karlsen, and Ron Hoffman.

My experience at the University of Pennsylvania Press has been wonderful. It is safe to say that my editor, Bob Lockhart, has had more faith in this project over the years than I have. He also gave thoughtful insightful readings of the book, put up with missed deadlines, and fielded requests for quick turnaround times without ever once suggesting that I am a high-maintenance author. (Hint: I am.) Alison Anderson has shown amazing patience shepherding this book to publication. John Brooke wrote an extremely detailed and generous reader's report that helped me clarify and refine some particular unruly passages in the text. My special thanks go to David Waldstreicher, who worked with me as series editor in the Early American Studies line. I have known David as long as I have known anyone in academia; he TA'd the first American history class I ever took in college, and I was fortunate enough to take the first seminar he ever taught. He has been a supporter of my work and my career ever since. David's comments and suggestions on the book improved it immensely.

Finally, I would like to thank my family. I could not have written this book without the continued support of my parents, Ben and Ann Smolenski (as my father has so often reminded me). They managed to hit the right balance of knowing when to ask about my progress and when not to during the many years it has taken for this to see print. I am also deeply grateful to the rest of my family for their love and support: Meg, Rob, Emma, Grace, Ben, and Annie Ramsdell; Beth and Nick Warren; Tom and Nisha Smolenski; and Kate, Evan, Maggie, and Clare Benanti. The Dyers—Bill, Margaret, Paul, Leigh, Erin, and Taylor—welcomed me into their family while I was first writing this book and have been so kind and generous to me since. Most of all, I would like to thank my wife, Stephanie Dyer. My self-described "number one fan," she requested that I forego a series of long and flowery compliments, and so I shall. I will simply say that I am her number one fan, and thank her from the bottom of my heart.